Biographi
William Hogarth
With a Catalogue of His Works

John Nichols

Alpha Editions

This edition published in 2021

ISBN : 9789354941351

Design and Setting By
Alpha Editions
www.alphaedis.com
Email - info@alphaedis.com

As per information held with us this book is in Public Domain. This book is a reproduction of an important historical work. Alpha Editions uses the best technology to reproduce historical work in the same manner it was first published to preserve its original nature. Any marks or number seen are left intentionally to preserve its true form.

Contents

MEMORANDUM.	- 1 -
ADVERTISEMENT TO THE SECOND EDITION.	- 2 -
ADVERTISEMENT TO THE FIRST EDITION.	- 3 -
PREFACE.	- 4 -
HOGARTH.	- 6 -
CATALOGUE OF HOGARTH'S PRINTS.[1]	- 80 -
POSTSCRIPT.	- 300 -
ADDITION.	- 303 -
APPENDIX.	- 303 -

MEMORANDUM.

Respect and gratitude having engaged me to compile a memoir of my deceased Master and Patron Mr. BOWYER, in the same performance I included anecdotes of all the eminent persons any way connected with him. A note of about a page's length was allotted to HOGARTH. While it was printing, Mr. WALPOLE'S Fourth Volume on the subject of English Painters came out, and was followed by an immediate rage for collecting every scrap of our Artist's designs. Persevering in my enquiries among my friends, I had now amassed so much intelligence relative to these engravings, that it could no longer be crowded into the situation originally meant for it. I was therefore advised to publish it in the form of a sixpenny pamphlet. This intended publication, however, grew up by degrees into a three-shilling book, and, within a year and a half afterwards, was swelled into almost its present bulk, at the price of six shillings. Such was the origin and progress of the following sheets, which, with many corrections, &c. have now reached a Third Edition.

J. N.

Nov. 10, 1785.

ADVERTISEMENT
TO THE SECOND EDITION.

The author of these imperfect sheets cannot present them a second time to the world, before he has expressed his gratitude for the extreme candour with which they have been treated by the *Monthly Reviewers*. If *J. N.* has not availed himself of all the corrections designed for his service, it is because the able critic who proposes them has been deluded by intelligence manifestly erroneous. *J. N.* received each particular he has mentioned, in respect to the assistance bestowed on *Hogarth* while his *Analysis* was preparing, from Dr. *Morell*, a gentleman who on that subject could not easily mistake. Implicit confidence ought rather to be reposed in a literary coadjutor to the deceased, than in any consistory of females that ever "mumbled their wisdom over a gossip's bowl." Authors rarely acquaint domestic women with the progress of their writings, or the proportion of aid they solicit from their friends. If it were needful that Dr. *Morell* should translate a *Greek* passage[1] for *Hogarth*, how chanced it that our artist should want to apply what he did not previously understand? I must add, that the sentiments, published by the *Reviewer* concerning these *Anecdotes*, bear no resemblance to the opinion circulated by the cavillers with whom he appears to have had a remote connection. The parties who furnished every circumstance on which he founds his reiterated charges of error and misinformation, are not unknown. Ever since this little work was edited, the people about Mrs. *Hogarth* have paid their court to her by decrying it as "low, stupid, or false," without the slightest acknowledgement for the sums of money it has conducted to *The Golden Head* in *Leicester Fields*. While the talents of the writer alone were questioned by such inadequate judges of literary merit, a defence on his part was quite unnecessary. He has waited, however, with impatience for an opportunity of making some reply to their groundless reflections on his veracity. This purpose he flatters himself will have been completely executed after he has observed that all credentials relative to his disputed assertion shall be ready (as they are at this moment) for the Reviewer's inspection. *J. N.* cannot indeed dismiss his present advertisement without observing, that though the amiable partialities of a wife may apologize for any contradiction suggested by Mrs. *Hogarth* herself, the *English* language is not strong enough to express the contempt he feels in regard to the accumulated censure both of her male and her female Parasites.

J. N.

Nov. 1, 1782.

[1] Whereabouts is this translation of a *Greek* passage to be found in the Analysis? It may have escaped my hasty researches.

ADVERTISEMENT TO THE FIRST EDITION.

When this pamphlet was undertaken, the Author had no thought of swelling it to it's present bulk; but communicating his design to his friends, they favoured him with various particulars of information. Some of these accommodated themselves to his original plan, if he can be supposed to have had any, but others were more intractable. Still aware of the value even of disjointed materials, which his profession would not afford him leisure to compact into a regular narrative, and conscious that these sheets, rude and imperfect as they are, may serve to promote a publication less unworthy of its subject, he dismisses his present work without any laboured apology for the errors that may be detected in it; claiming, indeed, some merit on account of intelligence, but not the least on the score of arrangement or composition. He takes the same opportunity to observe, that many curious anecdotes of extraordinary persons have been unfortunately lost, because the possessors of those fugitive particulars had not the power of communicating them in proper form, or polished language, and were unwilling to expose them in such a state as these are offered to the world.

May 9, 1781.

PREFACE.

To the GERMAN READER.

Collectors of the Fine Arts were already possessed of *Catalogues* and *Memoires Raisonnées* of the engravings of many great masters, for which their acknowledgements are due to the industry of a *Gersaint*, a *Jombert*, a *Hecquet*, a *Vertue*, a *de Winter*, &c. &c.

But a similar illustration of HOGARTH'S copper-plates was still wanting; though it may be asked what works have a juster claim to a distinguished place in a compleat collection, than those of this instructive moral painter, this creative genius?

On this account, it is presumed that the *German* Lover of the Arts will deem himself indebted to the Translator, for giving him, in his own tongue, a concise and faithful version of a book that has lately made its appearance in *London*, under the title of "Biographical Anecdotes of *W. Hogarth*, and a Catalogue of his Works chronologically arranged."

The Compiler as well as Editor of this work is Mr. JOHN NICHOLS, a *Printer* and *Bookseller* in *London*, who, by much reading, and an intimate acquaintance with the Arts and Literature of his Country, has honourably distinguished himself among his professional brethren. How modestly he himself judges of this his useful performance, appears from his preface to the work.

It is true, Mr. HORACE WALPOLE, who possesses perhaps the compleatest collection of the prints of this Master, some years ago published a Catalogue of them; but this is only to be found in his work, intituled, "*Anecdotes of Painting in England collected by G. Vertue, and published by H. Walpole*," a performance consisting of four volumes in 4to, too costly for many collectors, and inconvenient for others. Moreover all that is to be found there relative to *Hogarth*, is not only included in Mr. *Nichols's* publication, but is also improved by considerable additions, so that the curious reader has *Walpole's* Catalogue incorporated with the present work.

The liberty of abridgement, as mentioned in the title, is ventured only in regard to such diffuse illustrations, repetitions, anecdotes, and local stories, as would be alone interesting to an *Englishman*; in a word, in such parts as do not immediately contribute to the illustration of *Hogarth's* plates, and would have tired the patience of the *German* reader. Of the verses affixed to each copper-plate the first and last words only are given, as those afford sufficient indication for a collector who wishes to become acquainted with any particular print. How far some remarks of the Translator are useful, or otherwise, is left to the indulgent decision of Judges in the Arts.

He must not however forget it is his duty to acknowledge the goodness of old Mr. HANSEN of *Leipsig*. This gentleman's readiness in permitting him to examine his excellent collection of the engravings of *British* artists, for the purpose of comparing and illustrating several passages in the original of this work, claims his warmest thanks, and a public acknowledgement.

Leipsig, February 1783.

THE TRANSLATOR.

HOGARTH.

This great and original Genius is said by Dr. *Burn* to have been the descendant of a family originally from *Kirkby Thore*,[1] in *Westmoreland*: and I am assured that his grandfather was a plain yeoman, who possessed a small tenement in the vale of *Bampton*, a village about 15 miles North of *Kendal*, in that county. He had three sons. The eldest assisted his father in farming, and succeeded to his little freehold. The second settled in *Troutbeck*, a village eight miles North West of *Kendal*, and was remarkable for his talent at provincial poetry.[2] The third, educated at *St. Bee's*, who had kept a school in the same county, and appears to have a man of some learning, went early to *London*, where he resumed his original occupation of a school-master in *Ship Court* in *The Old Bailey*, and was occasionally employed as a corrector of the press. A *Latin* letter, from Mr. *Richard Hogarth*, in 1697 (preserved among the MSS. in *The British Museum*, N° 4277. 50.) relates to a book which had been printed with great expedition. But the letter shall speak for itself.[3]

A Dictionary in *Latin* and *English*, which he composed for the use of schools,[4] still exists in MS. He married in *London*; and our Hero, and his sisters *Mary* and *Anne*, are believed to have been the only product of the marriage.

WILLIAM HOGARTH[5] it said (under the article THORNHILL in the *Biographia Britannica*) to have been born in 1698, in the parish of *St. Bartholomew*,[6] *London*, to which parish, it is added, he was afterwards a benefactor. The outset of his life, however, was unpromising. "He was bound," says Mr. *Walpole*, "to a mean engraver of arms on plate." *Hogarth* probably chose this occupation, as it required some skill in drawing, to which his genius was particularly turned, and which he contrived assiduously to cultivate. His master, it since appears, was Mr. *Ellis Gamble*, a silversmith of eminence, who resided in *Cranbourn-street, Leicester-fields*. In this profession it is not unusual to bind apprentices to the single branch of engraving arms and cyphers on every species of metal; and in that particular department of the business young *Hogarth* was placed;[7] "but, before his time was expired, he felt the impulse of genius, and that it directed him to painting."

During his apprenticeship, he set out one *Sunday*, with two or three companions, on an excursion to *Highgate*. The weather being hot, they went into a public-house, where they had not been long, before a quarrel arose between some persons in the same room. One of the disputants struck the other on the head with a quart pot, and cut him very much. The blood running down the man's face, together with the agony of the wound, which had distorted his features into a most hideous grin, presented *Hogarth*, who shewed himself thus early "apprised of the mode Nature had intended he should pursue," with too laughable a subject to be overlooked. He drew out his pencil, and produced on the spot one of the most ludicrous figures that ever was seen. What rendered this piece the more valuable was, that it exhibited an exact likeness of the man, with the portrait of his antagonist, and the figures in caricature of the principal persons gathered round him. This anecdote was furnished by one of his fellow apprentices then present, a person of indisputable character, and who continued his intimacy with *Hogarth* long after they both grew up into manhood.

"His apprenticeship was no sooner expired," says Mr. *Walpole*, "than he entered into the academy in *St. Martin's Lane*, and studied drawing from the life, in which he never attained to great excellence. It was character, the passions, the soul, that his genius was given him to copy. In colouring he proved no greater a master: his force lay in expression, not in tints and chiaro scuro."

To a man who by indefatigable industry and uncommon strength of genius has been the artificer of his own fame and fortune, it can be no reproach to have it said that at one period he was not rich. It has been asserted, and we believe with good foundation, that the skill and assiduity of *Hogarth* were, even in his servitude, a singular assistance to his own family, and to that of his master. It happened, however, that when he was first out of his time, he certainly was poor. The ambition of indigence is ever productive of distress. So it fared with *Hogarth*, who, while he was furnishing himself with materials for subsequent perfection, felt all the contempt which penury could produce. Being one day distressed to raise so trifling a sum as twenty shillings, in order to be revenged of his landlady, who strove to compel him to payment, he drew her as ugly as possible, and in that single portrait gave marks of the dawn of superior genius.[8] This story I had once supposed to be founded on certainty; but since, on other authority, have been assured, that had such an accident ever happened to him, he would not have failed to talk of it afterwards, as he was always fond of contrasting the necessities of his youth with the affluence of his maturer age. He has been heard to say of himself, "I remember the time when I have gone moping into the city with scarce a shilling in my pocket; but as soon as I had received ten guineas there for a plate, I have returned home, put on my sword, and sallied out again, with all the confidence of a man who had ten thousand pounds in his pocket." Let me add, that my first authority may be to the full as good as my second.

How long he continued in obscurity we cannot exactly learn; but the first piece in which he distinguished himself as a painter, is supposed to have been a representation of *Wanstead Assembly*.[9] In this are introduced portraits of the first earl *Tylney*, his lady, their children, tenants, &c. The faces were said to be extremely like, and the colouring is rather better than in some of his late and more highly finished performances.

From the date of the earliest plate that can be ascertained to be the work of *Hogarth*, it may be presumed that he began business, on his own account, at least as early as the year 1720.

His first employment seems to have been the engraving of arms and shop-bills. The next step was to design and furnish plates for booksellers; and here we are fortunately supplied with dates.[10] Thirteen folio prints, with his name to each, appeared in "*Aubry de la Motraye's* Travels," in 1723; seven smaller prints for "*Apuleius'* Golden Ass" in 1724; fifteen head-pieces to "*Beaver's* Military Punishments of the Ancients," and five frontispieces for the translation of *Cassandra*, in five volumes, 12°, 1725; seventeen cuts for a duodecimo edition of *Hudibras* (with *Butler's* head) in 1726; two for "*Perseus* and *Andromeda*," in 1730; two for *Milton* [the date uncertain]; and a variety of others between 1726 and 1733.

"No symptom of genius," says Mr. *Walpole*, "dawned in those plates. His *Hudibras* was the first of his works that marked him as a man above the common; yet, what made him then noticed, now surprises us, to find so little humour in an undertaking so congenial to his talents."—It is certain that he often lamented to his friends the having parted with his property in the prints of the large *Hudibras*, without ever having had an opportunity to improve them. They were purchased by Mr. *Philip Overton*,[11] at the *Golden Buck*, near *St. Dunstan's Church* in *Fleet-Street*; and still remain in the possession of his successor Mr. *Sayer*.

Mr. *Bowles* at the *Black Horse* in *Cornhill* was one of his earliest patrons. I had been told that he bought many a plate from *Hogarth* by the weight of the copper; but am only certain that this occurrence happened in a single instance, when the elder Mr. *Bowles* of *St. Paul's Church-yard* offered, over a bottle, half a crown a pound for a plate just then completed. This circumstance was within the knowledge of Dr. *Ducarel*.—Our artist's next friend in that line was Mr. *Philip Overton*, who paid him a somewhat better price for his labour and ingenuity.

When Mr. *Walpole* speaks of *Hogarth's* early performances, he observes, that they rose not above the labours of the people who are generally employed by booksellers. Lest any reader should inadvertently suppose this candid writer designed the minutest reflection on those artists to whom the decoration of modern volumes is confided, it is necessary to observe, that his account of *Hogarth*, &c. was printed off above ten years ago, before the names of *Cipriani*, *Angelica*, *Bartolozzi*, *Sherwin*, and *Mortimer* were found at the bottom of any plates designed for the ornament of poems, or dramatic pieces.

"On the success, however, of those plates," Mr. *Walpole* says, "he commenced painter, a painter of portraits; the most ill-suited employment imaginable to a man whose turn certainly was not flattery, nor his talent adapted to look on vanity without a sneer. Yet his facility in catching a likeness, and the method he chose of painting families and conversations in small, then a novelty, drew him prodigious business for some time. It did not last, either from his applying to the real bent of his disposition, or from his customers apprehending that a satirist was too formidable a confessor for the devotees of self-love." There are still many family pictures by Mr. *Hogarth* existing, in the style of serious conversation-pieces. He was not however lucky in all his resemblances, and has sometimes failed where a crowd of other artists have succeeded. The whole-length of Mr. *Garrick* sitting at a table, with his wife behind him taking the pen out of his hand,[12] confers no honour on the painter or the persons represented.[13] He has certainly missed the character of our late *Roscius's* countenance while undisturbed by passion; but was more lucky in seizing his features when aggravated by terror, as in the tent scene of King *Richard* III. It is by no means astonishing, that the elegant symmetry of Mrs. *Garrick's* form should have evaded the efforts of one to whose ideas *la basse nature* was more familiar than the grace inseparable from those who have been educated in higher life. His talents, therefore, could do little justice to a pupil of Lady *Burlington*.

What the prices of his portraits were, I have strove in vain to discover; but suspect they were originally very low, as the people who are best acquainted with them chuse to be silent on that subject.

In the Bee, vol. V. p. 552. and also in the Gentleman's Magazine, vol. IV. p. 269. are the following verses to Mr. *Hogarth*, on Miss *F.'s* picture, 1734.

"To *Chloe's* picture you such likeness give,
The animated canvas seems to live;
The tender breasts with wanton heavings move,
And the soft sparkling eyes inspire with love:
While I survey each feature o'er and o'er,
I turn *Idolater*, and paint adore:
Fondly I here can gaze without a fear,
That, *Chloe*, to my love you'd grow severe;
That in your *Picture*, as in *Life*, you'd turn
Your eyes away, and kill me with your scorn:
No, here at least with transport I can see
Your eyes with softness languishing on me.
While, *Chloe*, this I boast, with scornful heart
Nor rashly censure *Hogarth*, or his *art*,
Who all your *Charms* in strongest *Light* has laid,
And kindly thrown your *Pride* and *Scorn* in *Shade*."

At *Rivenhall*, in *Essex*, the seat of Mr. *Western*, is a family picture, by *Hogarth* of Mr. *Western* and his mother (who was a daughter of Sir *Anthony Shirley*), Chancellor *Hoadly*, Archdeacon *Charles Plumptre*, the Rev. Mr. *Cole* of *Milton* near *Cambridge*, and Mr. *Henry Taylor* the Curate there,[14] 1736.

In the gallery of the late Mr. *Cole* of *Milton*, was also a small whole-length picture of Mr. *Western*,[15] by *Hogarth*, a striking resemblance. He is drawn sitting in his Fellow-Commoner's habit, and square cap with a gold tassel, in his chamber at *Clare Hall*, over the arch towards the river; and our artist, as the chimney could not be expressed, has drawn a cat sitting near it, agreeable to his humour, to shew the situation.

"When I sat to him," says Mr. *Cole*, "near fifty years ago, the custom of giving vails to servants was not discontinued. On my taking leave of our painter at the door, and his servant's opening it or the coach door, I cannot tell which, I offered him a small gratuity; but the man very politely refused it, telling me it would be as much as the loss of his place, if his master knew it. This was so uncommon, and so liberal in a man of Mr. *Hogarth's* profession at that time of day, that it much struck me, as nothing of the sort had happened to me before."

It was likewise Mr. *Hogarth's* custom to sketch out on the spot any remarkable face which particularly struck him, and of which he wished to preserve the remembrance. A gentleman still living informs me, that being once with our painter at the *Bedford Coffee-house*, he observed him to draw something with a pencil on his nail. Enquiring what had been his employment, he was shewn the countenance (a whimsical one) of a person who was then at a small distance.

It happened in the early part of *Hogarth's* life, that a nobleman, who was uncommonly ugly and deformed, came to sit to him for his picture. It was executed with a skill that did honour to the artist's abilities; but the likeness was rigidly observed, without even the necessary attention to compliment or flattery. The peer, disgusted at this counterpart of his dear self, never once thought of paying for a reflector that would only insult him with his deformities. Some time was suffered to elapse before the artist applied for his money; but afterwards many applications were made by him (who had then no need of a banker) for payment, without success. The painter, however, at last hit upon an expedient, which he knew must alarm the nobleman's pride, and by that means answer his purpose. It was couched in the following card:

"Mr. *Hogarth's* dutiful respects to Lord ———; finding that he does not mean to have the picture which was drawn for him, is informed again of Mr. *H.'s* necessity for the money; if, therefore, his lordship does not send for it in three days, it will be disposed of, with the addition of a tail, and some other little appendages, to Mr. *Hare*, the famous wild-beast man; Mr. *H.* having given that gentleman a conditional promise of it for an exhibition-picture, on his lordship's refusal."

This intimation had the desired effect. The picture was sent home, and committed to the flames.

To the other anecdotes of this comic Painter may be added the following. Its authenticity must apologize for its want of other merit.

A certain old Nobleman, not remarkably generous, having sent for *Hogarth*, desired he would represent, in one of the compartments on a staircase, *Pharaoh* and his Host drowned in the *Red Sea*; but at the same time gave our artist to understand, that no great price would be given for his performance. *Hogarth* agreed. Soon after, he waited on his employer for payment, who seeing that the space allotted for the picture had only been daubed over with red, declared he had no idea of paying a painter when he had proceeded no further than to lay his *ground*. "*Ground!*" said *Hogarth*, "there is no *ground* in the case, my lord. The red you perceive, is the *Red Sea*. *Pharaoh* and his Host are drowned as you desired, and cannot be made objects of sight, for the ocean covers them all."

Mr. *Walpole* has remarked, that if our artist "indulged his spirit of ridicule in personalities, it never proceeded beyond sketches and drawings," and wonders "that he never, without intention, delivered the very features of any identical person." But this elegant writer, who may be said to have received his education in a Court, perhaps had few opportunities of acquaintance among the low popular characters with which *Hogarth* occasionally peopled his scenes.[16] The Friend to whom I owe this remark was assured by an ancient gentleman of unquestionable veracity and acuteness of observation, that almost all the personages who attend the levee of the Rake were undoubted portraits; and that, in *Southwark Fair* and the *Modern Midnight Conversation*, as many more were discoverable. In the former plate he pointed out *Essex* the dancing-master; and in the latter, as well as in the second plate to the *Rake's Progress*, *Figg* the prize-fighter.[17] He mentioned several others by name, from his immediate knowledge both of the painter's design and the characters represented; but the rest of the particulars, by which he supported his assertions, have escaped the memory of my informant. I am also assured, that while *Hogarth* was painting the *Rake's Progress*, he had a summer residence at *Isleworth*; and never failed to question the company who came to see these pictures, if they knew for whom one or another figure was designed. When they guessed wrong, he set them right.

Mr. *Walpole* has a sketch in oil, given to him by *Hogarth*, who intended to engrave it. It was done at the time when the House of Commons appointed a committee to inquire into the cruelties exercised on prisoners in the *The Fleet*, to extort money from them. "The scene," he says, "is the committee; on the table are the instruments of torture. A prisoner in rags, half-starved, appears before them; the poor man has a good countenance, that adds to the interest. On the other hand is the inhuman gaoler. It is the very figure that *Salvator Rosa* would have drawn for *Iago* in the moment of detection. Villainy, fear, and conscience, are mixed in yellow and livid on his countenance; his lips are contracted by tremor, his face advances as eager to lie, his legs step back as thinking to make his escape; one hand is thrust precipitately into his bosom, the fingers of the other are catching uncertainly at his button-holes. If this was a portrait, it is the most striking that ever was drawn; if it was not, it is still finer." The portrait was that of *Bambridge*[18] the warden of *The Fleet*; and the sketch was taken in the beginning of the year 1729, when *Bambridge* and *Huggins* (his predecessor)[19] were under examination. Both were declared "notoriously guilty of great breaches of trust, extortions, cruelties, and other high crimes and misdemeanors;" both were sent to *Newgate*; and *Bambridge* was disqualified by act of parliament.[20] The son[21] of *Huggins* was possessed of a valuable painting from this sketch, and also of a scene in the *Beggar's Opera*; both of them full of real portraits. On the dispersion of his effects, the latter was purchased by the Rev. Dr. *Monkhouse* of *Queen's College, Oxford*. It is in a gilt frame, with a bust of *Gay* at the top. It's companion, whose present possessor I have not been able to trace out, had, in like manner, that of Sir *Francis Page*, one of the judges, remarkable for his severity;[22] with a halter round his neck.

The Duke of *Leeds* has also an original scene in the *Beggar's Opera*, painted by *Hogarth*. It is that in which *Lucy* and *Polly* are on their knees, before their respective fathers, to intercede for the life of the hero of the piece. All the figures are either known or supposed to be portraits. If I am not misinformed, the late Sir *Thomas Robinson* (as well known by the name of *Long Sir Thomas*) is standing in one of the side-boxes. *Macheath*, unlike his spruce representative on our present stage, is a slouching bully; and *Polly* appears happily disencumbered of such a hoop as the daughter of *Peachum* within our younger memories has worn. His Grace gave 35 *l.* for this picture at Mr. *Rich's* auction. Another copy of the same scene was bought by the late Sir *William Saunderson*; and is now in the possession of Sir *Henry Gough*. Mr. *Walpole* has a painting of a scene in the same piece, where *Macheath* is going to execution. In this also the likenesses of *Walker*, and Miss *Fenton* afterwards Dutchess of *Bolton* (the original *Macheath* and *Polly*), are preserved.

In the year 1726, when the affair of *Mary Tofts*, the rabbit-breeder of *Godalming*, engaged the public attention, a few of our principal surgeons subscribed their guinea a-piece to *Hogarth*, for an engraving from a ludicrous sketch he had made on that very popular subject. This plate, amongst other portraits, contains that of the notorious *St. André*, the anatomist to the royal household, and in high credit as a surgeon. The additional celebrity of this man arose either from fraud or ignorance, perhaps from a due mixture of both. It was supported, however, afterwards, by the reputation of a dreadful crime. His imaginary wealth, in spite of these disadvantages, to the last insured him a circle of flatterers, even though, at the age of fourscore, his conversation was offensive to modest ears, and his grey hairs were rendered still more irreverend by repeated acts of untimely lewdness.[23] A particular description of this plate will be given in the future catalogue of *Hogarth's* works.

In 1727, *Hogarth* agreed with *Morris*, an upholsterer, to furnish him with a design on canvas, representing the element of Earth, as a pattern for tapestry. The work not being performed to the satisfaction of *Morris*, he refused to pay for it; and our artist sued him for the money. This suit (which was tried before Lord Chief Justice *Eyre* at *Westminster*, May 28, 1728) was determined in favour of *Hogarth*. The brief for the defendant in the cause, is preserved below.[24]

In 1730, Mr. *Hogarth* married the only daughter of Sir *James Thornhill*,[25] by whom he had no child. This union, indeed, was a stolen one, and consequently without the approbation of Sir *James*, who, considering the youth of his daughter, then barely eighteen, and the slender finances of her husband, as yet an obscure artist,[26] was not easily reconciled to the match. Soon after this period, however, he began his *Harlot's Progress* (the coffin in the last plate is inscribed *September* 2, 1731); and was advised by Lady *Thornhill* to have some of the scenes in it placed in the way of his father-in-law. Accordingly, one morning early, Mrs. *Hogarth* undertook to convey several of them into his dining-room. When he arose, he enquired from whence they came; and being told by whom they were introduced, he cried out, "Very well; the man who can furnish representations like these, can also maintain a wife without a portion." He designed this remark as an excuse for keeping his purse-strings close; but, soon after, became both reconciled and generous to the young couple.

Our artist's reputation was so far established in 1731, that it drew forth a poetical compliment from Mr. *Mitchell*, in the epistle already quoted.

An allegorical cieling by Sir *James Thornhill* is at the house of the late Mr. *Huggins*, at *Headley Park, Hants*. The subject of it is the story of *Zephyrus* and *Flora*; and the figure of a Satyr and some others were painted by *Hogarth*.

In 1732 (the year in which he was one of the party who made *A Tour by land and Water*, which will be duly noticed in the Catalogue) he ventured to attack Mr. *Pope*, in a plate called "The Man of Taste;" containing a view of the Gate of *Burlington-house*, with *Pope* whitewashing it, and bespattering the Duke of *Chandos's* coach.[27] This plate was intended as a satire on the translator of *Homer*, Mr. *Kent* the architect, and the Earl of *Burlington*. It was fortunate for *Hogarth* that he escaped the lash of the former. Either *Hogarth's* obscurity at that time was his protection, or the bard was too prudent to exasperate a painter who had already given such proof of his abilities for satire. What must *he* have felt who could complain of the "pictured shape" prefixed to *Gulliveriana, Pope Alexander's Supremacy and Infallibility examined*, &c. by *Ducket*, and other pieces, had our artist undertaken to express in colours a certain transaction recorded by *Cibber*?

Soon after his marriage, *Hogarth* had summer-lodgings at *South-Lambeth*; and being intimate with Mr. *Tyers*, contributed to the improvement of *The Spring Gardens* at *Vauxhall*, by the hint of embellishing them with paintings, some of which were the suggestions of his own truly comic pencil. Among these were the "Four parts of the Day," copied by *Hayman* from the designs of our artist. The scenes of "Evening" and "Night" are still there; and portraits of *Henry* VIII. and *Anne Bullen* once adorned the old great room on the right hand of the entry into the gardens. For his assistance, Mr. *Tyers* gratefully presented him with a gold ticket of admission for himself and his friends, inscribed

   in perpetuam beneficii memoriam.

This ticket, now in the possession of his widow, is still occasionally made use of.

In 1733 his genius became conspicuously known. The third scene of his "Harlot's Progress" introduced him to the notice of the great. At a board of Treasury which was held a day or two after the appearance of that print, a copy of it was shewn by one of the lords, as containing, among other excellencies, a striking likeness of Sir *John Gonson*.[28] It gave universal satisfaction; from the Treasury each lord repaired to the print-shop for a copy of it, and *Hogarth* rose completely into fame. This anecdote was related to Mr. *Huggins* by *Christopher Tilson*, esq. one of the four chief clerks in the Treasury, and at that period under-secretary of state. He died *August* 25, 1742, after having enjoyed the former of these offices fifty-eight years. I should add, however, that Sir *John Gonson* is not here introduced to be made ridiculous, but is only to be considered as the image of an active magistrate identified.

The familiarity of the subject, and the propriety of it's execution, made the "Harlot's Progress" tasted by all ranks of people. Above twelve hundred names were entered in our artist's subscription-book. It was made into a pantomime by *Theophilus Cibber*, and again represented on the stage, under the title of *The Jew decoyed, or a Harlot's Progress*, in a Ballad Opera. Fan-mounts were likewise engraved, containing miniature representations of all the six plates. These were usually printed off with red ink, three compartments on one side, and three on the other.[29]

The ingenious Abbé *Du Bos* has often complained, that no history-painter of his time went through a series of actions, and thus, like an historian, painted the successive fortune of an hero, from the cradle to the grave. What *Du Bos* wished to see done, *Hogarth* performed. He launches out his young adventurer a simple girl upon the town, and conducts her through all the vicissitudes of wretchedness to a premature death. This was painting to the understanding and to the heart; none had ever before made the pencil subservient to the purposes of morality and instruction; a book like this is fitted to every soil and every observer, and he that runs may read. Nor was the success of *Hogarth* confined to his persons. One of his excellencies consisted in what may be termed the furniture[30] of his pieces; for as in sublime and historical representations the fewer trivial circumstances are permitted to divide the spectator's attention from the principal figures, the greater is their force; so in scenes copied from familiar life, a proper variety of little domestic images contributes to throw a degree of verisimilitude on the whole. "The Rake's levee-room," says Mr. *Walpole*, "the nobleman's dining-room, the apartments of the husband and wife in Marriage Alamode, the Alderman's parlour, the bed-chamber, and many others, are the history of the manners of the age."

It may also be observed, that *Hogarth*, both in the third and last plate of the *Harlot's Progress*, has appropriated a name to his heroine which belonged to a well-known wanton then upon the town. The *Grub-street Journal* for *August* 6, 1730, giving an account of several prostitutes who were taken up, informs us that "the fourth was *Kate Hackabout* (whose brother was lately hanged at *Tyburn*), a woman noted in and about the hundreds of *Drury*, *&c.*"

In 1735 our artist lost his mother, as appears by the following extract from an old Magazine: "*June* 11, 1735. Died Mrs. *Hogarth*, mother to the celebrated painter, of a fright from the fire which happened on the 9th, in *Cecil Court, St. Martin's Lane,* and burnt thirteen houses;[31] amongst others, one belonging to *John Huggins*, esq. late Warden of *The Fleet*, was greatly damaged."

The "Rake's Progress" (published in the same year, and sold at *Hogarth's* house, the *Golden Head* in *Leicester Fields*), though "perhaps superior, had not," as Mr. *Walpole* observes, "so much success, from want of novelty; nor is the print of the arrest equal in merit to the others.[32]

"The curtain, however," says he, "was now drawn aside, and his genius stood displayed in its full lustre. From time to time our artist continued to give those works that would be immortal, if the nature of his art will allow it. Even the receipts for his subscriptions had wit in them. Many of his plates he engraved himself, and often expunged faces etched by his assistants, when they had not done justice to his ideas. Not content with shining in a path untrodden before, he was ambitious of distinguishing himself as a painter of history; and in 1736 presented to the hospital of *St. Bartholomew*, of which he had been appointed a governor,[33] a painting of the *Pool of Bethesda*, and another of the *Good Samaritan*. But the genius that had entered so feelingly into the calamities and crimes of familiar life, deserted him in a walk that called for dignity and grace. The burlesque turn of his mind mixed itself with the most serious subjects. In the *Pool of Bethesda*, a servant of a rich ulcerated lady beats back a poor man that sought the same celestial remedy; and in his *Danae* [for which the Duke of *Ancaster* paid 60 guineas] the old nurse tries a coin of the golden shower with her teeth, to see if it is true gold. Both circumstances are justly thought, but rather too ludicrous. It is a much more capital fault that *Danae* herself is a mere nymph of *Drury*. He seems to have conceived no higher degree of beauty." Dr. *Parsons* also, in his Lectures on Physiognomy, 410. p. 58, says, "Thus yielded *Danae* to the Golden Shower, and thus was her passion painted by the ingenious Mr. *Hogarth*."

The novelty and excellence of *Hogarth's* performances soon tempted the needy artist and print-dealer to avail themselves of his designs,[34] and rob him of the advantages which he was entitled to derive from them. This was particularly the case with the "Midnight Conversation," the "Harlot's" and "Rake's" Progresses,[35] and the rest of his early works. To put a stop to depredations like these on the property of himself and others, and to secure the emoluments resulting from his own labours, as Mr. *Walpole* observes, he applied to the legislature, and obtained an act of parliament, 8 *George* II. chap. 3°, to vest an exclusive right in designers and engravers, and to restrain the multiplying of copies of their works without the consent of the artist.[36]

This statute was drawn by his friend Mr. *Huggins*,[37] who took for his model the eighth of Queen *Anne*, in favour of literary property; but it was not so accurately executed as entirely to remedy the evil; for, in a cause founded on it, which came before Lord *Hardwicke* in Chancery, that excellent Lawyer determined that no assignee, claiming under an assignment from the original inventor, could take any benefit by it. *Hogarth*, immediately after the passing the act, published a small print, with emblematical devices, and the following inscription expressing his gratitude to the three branches of the legislature:

"In humble and grateful acknowledgment
Of the grace and goodness of the LEGISLATURE,
Manifested
In the ACT of PARLIAMENT for the Encouragement
Of the Arts of Designing, Engraving, &c.
Obtained
By the Endeavours, and almost at the sole Expence,
Of the Designer of this Print in the Year 1735;
By which
Not only the Professors of those Arts were rescued
From the Tyranny, Frauds, and Piracies
Of Monopolizing Dealers,
And legally entitled to the Fruits of their own Labours;
But Genius and Industry were also prompted
By the most noble and generous Inducements to exert themselves;
Emulation was excited,
Ornamental Compositions were better understood;
And every Manufacture, where Fancy has any concern,
Was gradually raised to a Pitch of Perfection before unknown;
Insomuch, that those of GREAT-BRITAIN
Are at present the most Elegant
And the most in Esteem of any in EUROPE."

This plate he afterwards made to serve for a receipt for subscriptions, first to a print of an "Election Entertainment;" and afterwards for three prints more, representing the "polling for members for parliament, canvassing for votes, and chairing the members." The royal crown at the top of this receipt is darting its rays on mitres, coronets, the Chancellor's great seal, the Speaker's hat, &c. &c. and on a scroll is written, "An Act for the Encouragement of the Arts of Designing, Engraving, and Etching, by vesting the Properties thereof in the Inventors and Engravers, during the Time therein mentioned." It was "Designed, etched, and published as the Act directs, by *W. Hogarth, March* 20, 1754." After *Hogarth's* death, the legislature, by Stat. 7 *Geo.* III. chap. 38. granted to his widow a further exclusive term of twenty years in the property of her husband's works.

In 1736 he had the honour of being distinguished in a masterly poem of a congenial Humourist. The Dean of *St. Patrick's*, in his "Description of the Legion Club," after pourtraying many characters with all the severity of the most pointed satire, exclaims,

"How I want thee, humorous *Hogarth!*
Thou, I hear, a pleasant rogue art!
Were but you and I acquainted,
Every monster should be painted:
You should try your graving tools
On this odious group of fools;
Draw the beasts as I describe them;
Form their features, while I gibe them;
Draw them like, for I assure ye,
You will need no *caricatura*.
Draw them so, that we may trace
All the soul in every face."

An elegant compliment was soon after paid to *Hogarth* by *Somervile*, the author of *The Chace*, who dedicates his *Hobbinol* to him as to "the greatest master in the burlesque way." Yet *Fielding*, in the Preface to *Joseph Andrews*, says, "He who should call the ingenious *Hogarth* a burlesque painter, would, in my opinion, do him very little honour, for sure it is much easier, much less the subject of admiration, to paint a man with a nose, or any other feature of a preposterous size, or to expose him in some absurd or monstrous attitude, than to express the affections of men on canvas. It hath been thought a vast commendation of a painter, to say his figures seem to breathe; but surely it is a much greater and nobler applause, that they appear to think."[38]

Vincent Bourne, that classical ornament of *Westminster School*, addressed the following copy of hendecasyllables

"Ad GULIELMUM HOGARTH, Παρουνετικόν [Greek: Parounetikon]

"Qui mores hominum improbos, ineptos,
Incidis, nec ineleganter, æri,
Derisor lepidus, sed & severus,
Corrector gravis, at nec invenustus;
Seu pingis meretricios amores,
Et scenas miseræ vicesque vitæ;
Ut tentat pretio rudem puellam
Corruptrix anus, impudens, obesa;
Ut se vix reprimit libidinosus
Scortator, veneri paratus omni:
Seu describere vis, facete censor,
Bacchanalia sera protrahentes
Ad confinia crastinæ diei,

> Fractos cum cyathis tubos, matellam
> Non plenam modò sed superfluentem,
> Et fortem validumque combibonem
> Lætantem super amphorâ repletâ;
> Jucundissimus omnium ferêris,
> Nullique artificum secundus, ætas
> Quos præsens dedit, aut dabit futura.
> Macte ô, eja age, macte sis amicus
> Virtuti: vitiique quod notâris,
> Pergas pingere, & exhibere coràm,
> Censura utilior tua æquiorque
> Omni vel satirarum acerbitate,
> Omni vel rigidissimo cachinno."

By printed proposals, dated *Jan.* 25, 1744-5, *Hogarth* offered to the highest bidder "the six pictures called *The Harlot's Progress*, the eight pictures called *The Rake's Progress*, the four pictures representing *Morning, Noon, Evening,* and *Night,* and that of *A Company of Strolling Actresses dressing in a Barn*; all of them his own original paintings, from which no other copies than the prints have ever been taken." The biddings were to remain open from the first to the last day of *February,* on these conditions: "1. That every bidder shall have an entire leaf numbered in the book of sale, on the top of which will be entered the name and place of abode, the sum paid by him, the time when, and for which picture.—That, on the last day of sale, a clock (striking every five minutes) shall be placed in the room; and when it hath struck five minutes after twelve, the first picture mentioned in the sale-book will be deemed as sold; the second picture when the clock hath struck the next five minutes after twelve; and so on successively till the whole nineteen pictures are sold. 3. That none advance less than gold at each bidding. 4. No person to bid on the last day, except those whose names were before entered in the book.—As Mr. *Hogarth's* room is but small, he begs the favour that no persons, except those whose names are entered in the book, will come to view his paintings on the last day of sale."

The pictures were sold for the following prices:

Six Harlot's Progress, at 14 guineas each	£.88	4	0
Eight Rake's Progress, at 22 guineas each	184	16	0
Morning, 20 guineas	21	0	0

Noon, 37 guineas	38	17	0
Evening, 38 guineas	39	18	0
Night, 26 guineas	27	6	0
Strolling Players, 26 guineas	27	6	0
	427	7	0

At the same time the six pictures of *Marriage à-la-mode* were announced as intended for sale as soon as the plates then taking from them should be completed. This set of Prints may be regarded as the ground-work of a novel called "The Marriage Act," by Dr. *Shebbeare,* and of "The Clandestine Marriage." In the prologue to that excellent comedy, Mr. *Garrick* thus handsomely expressed his regard for the memory of his friend:

> "Poets and painters, who from nature draw
> Their best and richest stores, have made this law:
> That each should neighbourly assist his brother,
> And steal with decency from one another.
> To-night, your matchless *Hogarth* gives the thought,
> Which from his canvas to the stage is brought.
> And who so fit to warm the poet's mind,
> As he who pictur'd morals and mankind?
> But not the same their characters and scenes;
> Both labour for one end, by different means:
> Each, as it suits him, takes a separate road,
> Their one great object, *Marriage à la Mode!*
> Where titles deign with cits to have and hold,
> And change rich blood for more substantial gold!
> And honour'd trade from interest turns aside,
> To hazard happiness for titled pride.
> The painter dead, yet still he charms the eye;
> While *England* lives, his fame can never die:
> But he, 'who struts his hour upon the stage,'
> Can scarce extend his fame for half an age;
> Nor pen nor pencil can the actor save,
> The art, and artist, share one common grave."[39]

Hogarth had projected a *Happy Marriage,* by way of counterpart to his *Marriage à la Mode.* A design for the first of his intended six plates he had sketched out in colours; and the following is as accurate an account of it as could be furnished by a gentleman who, long ago enjoyed only a few minutes' sight of so imperfect a curiosity.

The time supposed was immediately after the return of the parties from church. The scene lay in the hall of an antiquated country mansion. On one side, the married couple were represented sitting. Behind them was a group of their young friends of both sexes, in the act of breaking bride-cake over their heads. In front appeared the father of the young lady, grasping a bumper, and drinking, with a seeming roar of exultation, to the future happiness of her and her husband. By his side was a table covered with refreshments. Jollity rather than politeness was the designation of his character. Under the screen of the hall, several rustic musicians in grotesque attitudes, together with servants, tenants, &c. were arranged. Through the arch by which the room was entered, the eye was led along a passage into the kitchen, which afforded a glimpse of sacerdotal luxury. Before the dripping-pan stood a well-fed divine, in his gown and cassock, with his watch in his hand, giving directions to a cook, drest all in white, who was employed in basting a haunch of venison.

Among the faces of the principal figures, none but that of the young lady was completely finished. *Hogarth* had been often reproached for his inability to impart grace and dignity to his heroines. The bride was therefore meant to vindicate his pencil from so degrading an imputation. The effort, however, was unsuccessful. The girl was certainly pretty; but her features, if I may use the term, were uneducated. She might have attracted notice as a chambermaid, but would have failed to extort applause as a woman of fashion. The parson, and his culinary associate, were more laboured than any other parts of the picture. It is natural for us to dwell longest on that division of a subject which is most congenial to our private feelings. The painter sat down with a resolution to delineate beauty improved by art; but seems, as usual, to have deviated into meanness; or could not help neglecting his original purpose, to luxuriate in such ideas as his situation in early life had fitted him to express. He found himself, in short, out of his element in the parlour, and therefore hastened, in quest of ease and amusement, to the kitchen fire. *Churchill*, with more force than delicacy, once observed of him, that he only painted the *backside* of nature. It must be allowed, that such an artist, however excellent in his walk, was better qualified to represent the low-born parent, than the royal preserver of a foundling.

The sketch already described (which I believe is in Mrs. *Garrick's* possession) was made after the appearance of *Marriage à la Mode*, and many years before the artist's death. Why he did not persevere in his plan, during such an interval of time, we can only guess. It is probable that his undertaking required a longer succession of images relative to domestic happiness, than had fallen within his notice, or courted his participation. *Hogarth* had no children; and though the nuptial union may be happy without them, yet such happiness will have nothing picturesque in it; and we may observe of this truly natural and faithful painter, that he rarely ventured to exhibit scenes with which he was not perfectly well acquainted.

Let us, however, more completely obviate an objection that may be raised against the propriety of the foregoing criticism. Some reader may urge, that perhaps, all circumstances considered, a wedding celebrated at an old mansion-house did not require the appearance of consummate beauty, refined by the powers of education. The remark has seeming justice on its side; but *Hogarth* had previously avowed his intent to exhibit a perfect face, divested of vulgarity; and succeeded so well, at least in his own opinion, that he carried the canvas, of which we are now speaking, in triumph to Mr. *Garrick*, whose private strictures on it coincided with those of the person who furnishes this additional confirmation of our painter's notorious ignorance in what is styled—THE GRACEFUL. From the account I have received concerning a design for a previous compartment belonging to the same story, there is little reason to lament the loss of it. It contained no appeal either to the fancy or to the heart. An artist, who, representing the marriage ceremony in a chapel, renders the clerk, who lays the hassocks, the principal figure in it, may at least be taxed with want of judgement.

Soon after the peace of *Aix la Chapelle*, he went over to *France*, and was taken into custody at *Calais*, while he was drawing the gate of that town, a circumstance which he has recorded in his picture, intituled, "O the Roast Beef of *Old England*!" published *March* 26, 1749. He was actually carried before the governor as a spy, and, after a very strict examination, committed a prisoner to *Grandsire*, his landlord, on his promising that *Hogarth* should not go out of his house till it was to embark for *England*. This account, I have good authority for saying, he himself gave to his friend Mr. *Gostling* at *Canterbury*, at whose house he lay the night after his arrival.

The same accident, however, has been more circumstantially related by an eminent *English* engraver, who was abroad when it happened. *Hayman*, and *Cheere* the statuary, were of the same party.

While *Hogarth* was in *France*, wherever he went, he was sure to be dissatisfied with all he saw. If an elegant circumstance either in furniture, or the ornaments of a room, was pointed out as deserving approbation, his narrow and constant reply was, "What then? but it is *French*! Their houses are all gilt and b—t." In the streets he was often clamourously rude. A tatter'd bag, or a pair of silk stockings with holes in them, drew a torrent of imprudent language from him. In vain did my informant (who knew that many *Scotch* and *Irish* were often within hearing of these reproaches, and would rejoice at least in an opportunity of getting our painter mobbed) advise him to be more cautious in his public remarks. He laughed at all such admonition, and treated the offerer of it as a pusillanimous wretch, unworthy of a residence in a free country, making him the butt of his ridicule for several evenings afterwards. This unreasonable pleasantry was at length completely extinguished by what happened while he was drawing the Gate at *Calais*; for though the innocence of his design was rendered perfectly apparent on the testimony of other sketches he had about him, which were by no means such as could serve the purpose of an engineer, he was told by the Commandant, that, had not the peace been actually signed, he should have been obliged to have hung him up immediately on the ramparts. Two guards were then provided to convey him on shipboard; nor did they quit him till he was three miles from the shore. They then spun him round like a top, on the deck; and told him he was at liberty to proceed on his voyage without farther attendance or molestation. With the slightest allusion to the ludicrous particulars of this affair, poor *Hogarth* was by no means pleased. The leading circumstance in it his own pencil has recorded.

Soon after this period he purchased a little house at *Chiswick*; where he usually passed the greatest part of the summer season, yet not without occasional visits to his dwelling in *Leicester Fields*.

In 1753, he appeared to the world in the character of art author, and published a quarto volume, intituled, "The Analysis of Beauty, written with a view of fixing the fluctuating Ideas of Taste." In this performance he shews, by a variety of examples, that a curve is the line of beauty, and that round swelling figures are most pleasing to the eye; and the truth of his opinion has been countenanced by subsequent writers on the subject.

Among the letters of Dr. *Birch* is the following short one, sent with the "Analysis of Beauty," and dated *Nov.* 25, 1753; "Sir, I beg the favour of you to present to the Royal Society the enclosed work, which will receive great honour by their acceptance of it. I am, Sir, your most obedient humble servant, WM. HOGARTH."

In this book, the leading idea of which was hieroglyphically thrown out in a frontispiece to his works in 1745, he acknowledges himself indebted to his friends for assistance, and particularly to one gentleman for his corrections and amendments of at least a third part of the *wording*. This friend, I am assured, was Dr. *Benjamin Hoadly* the physician, who carried on the work to about a *third* part, Chap. IX. and then, through indisposition, declined the friendly office with regret. Mr. *Hogarth* applied to his neighbour, Mr. *Ralph*; but it was impossible for two such persons to agree, both alike vain and positive. He proceeded no farther than about a sheet, and they then parted friends, and seem to have continued such. In the *Estimate of the Manners and*

Principles of the Times, vol. I. p. 47, published in 1757 by Dr. *Brown*, that author pays a compliment to Mr. *Hogarth's* genius. Mr. *Ralph*, animadverting on the work, amongst other things, says, "It is happy for Mr. *Hogarth*, in my humble opinion, that he is brought upon the stage in such company, rather for the sake of fastening some additional abuse upon the public, than of bestowing any special grace upon him. 'Neither the comic pencil, nor the serious pen of our ingenious countrymen (so the Estimator or Appraiser's Patent of Allowance runs) have been able to keep alive the taste of Nature or of Beauty.' For where he has chosen to be a niggard of his acknowledgements, every other man would chuse to be a prodigal: Nature had played the *Proteus* with us, had invited us to pursue her in every shape, but had never suffered us to overtake her: Beauty all had been smitten with, but nobody had been able to assign us a rule by which it might be defined: This was Mr. *Hogarth's* task; this is what he has succeeded in; composition is at last become a science; the student knows what he is in search of; the connoisseur what to praise; and fancy or fashion, or prescription, will usurp the hacknied name of taste no more. So that, whatever may be said in disparagement of the age on other accounts, it has more merit and honour to claim on this, than any which preceded it. And I will venture for once to prophesy, from the improvements already manifested, that we shall have the arts of designing to value ourselves upon, when all our ancient virtues are worn out."

The office of finishing the work, and superintending the publication, was lastly taken up by Dr. *Morell*, who went through the remainder of the book.[40] The preface was in like manner corrected by the Rev. Mr. *Townley*. The family of *Hogarth* rejoiced when the last sheet of the *Analysis* was printed off; as the frequent disputes he had with his coadjutors, in the progress of the work, did not much harmonize his disposition.

This work was translated into *German* by Mr. *Mylins*, when in *England*, under the author's inspection; and the translation, containing twenty-two sheets in quarto, and two large plates, was printed in *London*, price five dollars.

Of the same performance a new and correct edition was (*July* 1, 1754) proposed for publication at *Berlin*, by *Ch. Fr. Vok*, with an explanation of Mr. *Hogarth's* satirical prints, translated from the *French*; the whole to subscribers for one dollar, but after six weeks to be raised to two dollars.

An *Italian* translation was also published at *Leghorn* in 1761, 8vo, dedicated "All' illustrissime Signora Diana *Molineux*, Dama *Inglese*."

"This book," Mr. *Walpole* observes, "had many sensible hints and observations; but it did not carry the conviction, nor meet the universal acquiescence he expected. As he treated his contemporaries with scorn, they triumphed over this publication,[41] and irritated him to expose him. Many wretched burlesque prints came out to ridicule his system. There was a better answer to it in one of the two prints that he gave to illustrate his hypothesis. In the ball, had he confined himself to such outlines as compose awkwardness and deformity, he would have proved half his assertion; but he has added two samples of grace in a young lord and lady, that are strikingly stiff and affected. They are a *Bath* beau and a county Beauty."

Hogarth had one failing in common with most people who attain wealth and eminence without the aid of liberal education. He affected to despise every kind of knowledge which he did not possess. Having established his fame with little or no obligation to literature, he either conceived it to be needless, or decried it because it lay out of his reach. His sentiments, in short, resembled those of *Jack Cade*, who pronounced sentence on the clerk of *Chatham*, because he could write and read. Till, in evil hour, this celebrated artist commenced an author, and was obliged to employ the friends already mentioned to correct his *Analysis of Beauty*,[42] he did not seem to have discovered that even spelling was a necessary qualification; and yet he had ventured to ridicule[43] the late Mr. *Rich's* deficiency as to this particular, in a note which lies before the Rake whose play is refused while he remains in confinement for debt. Previous to the time of which we are now speaking, one of our artist's common topicks of declamation was the uselessness of books to a man of his profession. In *Beer-street*, among other volumes consigned by him to the pastry cook, we find *Turnbull on ancient Painting*, a treatise which *Hogarth* should have been able to understand, before he ventured to condemn. *Garrick* himself, however, was not more ductile to flattery. A word in favour of *Sigismunda*, might have commanded a proof print, or forced an original sketch out of our artist's hands. The furnisher of this remark owes one of his scarcest performances to the success of a compliment, which might have stuck even in Sir *Godfrey Kneller's* throat.

The following authenticated story of our artist will also serve to shew how much more easy it is to detect ill-placed or hyperbolical adulation respecting others, than when applied to ourselves. *Hogarth* being at dinner with the great *Cheselden*, and some other company, was told that Mr. *John Freke*, surgeon of *St. Bartholomew's Hospital*, a few evenings before at *Dick's Coffee-house*, had asserted, that *Greene* was as eminent in composition as *Handel*. "That fellow *Freke*," replied *Hogarth*, "is always shooting his bolt absurdly one way or another! *Handel* is a giant in music; *Greene* only a light *Florimel* kind of a composer."—"Ay," says our artist's informant, "but at the same time Mr. *Freke* declared you were as good a portrait-painter as *Vandyck*."—"*There* he was in the right," adds *Hogarth*; "and so by G— I am, give me my time, and let me choose my subject!"

With Dr. *Hoadly*, the late Chancellor of *Winchester*, Mr. *Hogarth* was always on terms of the strictest friendship, and frequently visited him at *Winchester, St. Cross,* and *Alresford*. It is well known, that Dr. *Hoadly's* fondness for theatrical exhibitions was so great, that few visitors were ever long in his house before they were solicited to accept a part in some interlude or other. He himself, with *Garrick* and *Hogarth*, once performed a laughable parody on the scene in *Julius Cæsar*, where the *Ghost* appears to *Brutus*. *Hogarth* personated the spectre; but so unretentive was his memory, that, although his speech consisted only of two lines, he was unable to get them by heart. At last they hit on the following expedient in his favour. The verses he was to deliver were written in such large letters, on the outside of an illuminated paper-lanthorn, that he could read them when he entered with it in his hand on the stage. *Hogarth* painted a scene on this occasion, representing a sutling booth, with the *Duck of Cumberland's* head by way of sign. He also prepared the play-bill, with characteristic ornaments. The original drawing is still preserved, and we could wish it were engraved; as the slightest sketch from the design of so grotesque a painter would be welcome to the numerous collectors of his works.

Hogarth was also the most absent of men. At table he would sometimes turn round his chair as if he had finished eating, and as suddenly would return it, and fall to his meal again. I may add, that he once directed a letter to Dr. *Hoadly*, thus,—"To the Doctor at *Chelsea*." This epistle, however, by good luck, did not miscarry; and was preserved by the late Chancellor of *Winchester*, as a pleasant memorial of his friend's extraordinary inattention.

Another remarkable instance of *Hogarth's* absence was told me, after the first edition of this work, by one of his intimate friends. Soon after he set up his carriage, he had occasion to pay a visit to the lord-mayor (I believe it was Mr. *Beckford*). When he went, the weather was fine; but business detained him till a violent shower of rain came on. He was let out of the Mansion-house by a different door from that at which he entered; and, seeing the rain, began immediately to call for a hackney-coach. Not one was to be met with on any of the neighbouring stands; and our artist sallied forth to brave the storm, and actually reached *Leicester-fields* without bestowing a thought on his own carriage, till Mrs. *Hogarth* (surprized to see him so wet and splashed) asked where he had left it.

Mr. *Walpole*, in the following note, p. 69, is willing to expose the indelicacy of the *Flemish* painters, by comparing it with the purity of *Hogarth*. "When they attempt humour," says our author, "it is by making a drunkard vomit; they take evacuations for jokes; and when they make us sick, think they make us laugh. A boor hugging a frightful frow is a frequent incident, even in the works of *Teniers*." Shall we proceed to examine whether the scenes painted by our countryman are wholly free from the same indelicacies? In one plate of *Hudibras*, where he encounters a *Skimmington*, a man is making water against the end of a house, while a taylor's wife is most significantly attending to the dirty process. In another plate to the same work, a boy is pissing into the shoe of *Ralpho*, while the widow is standing by. Another boy in the *Enraged Musician* is easing nature by the same mode; and a little miss is looking earnestly on the operation. In the *March to Finchley*, a diseased soldier has no better employment; and a woman is likewise staring at him out of a window. This circumstance did not escape the observation of *Rouquet* the enameller, whose remarks[44] on the plates of our artist I shall have more than once occasion to introduce. "Il y a," says he, "dans quelques endroits de cet excellent tableau, des objets peut être plus propres à peindre qu'à décrire. D'ou vient que les oreilles sont plus chaste que les yeux? Ne seroit ce pas parce qu'on peut regarder certains objets dans un tableau, et feindre de ne pas les voir; et qu'il n'est pas si aisé d'entendre une obscénité, et de feindre de ne l'entendre pas! L'objet, dont je veux parler, est toutefois peu considérable; il s'agit seulement d'un soldat à qui le voyage de *Montpelier* conviendroit mieux que celui d'*Ecosse*. L'amour lui a fait une blessure, &c." Was this occurrence delicate or precious enough to deserve such frequency of repetition? In the burlesque *Paul before Felix*, when the High Priest applies his fingers to his nose, we have reason to imagine that his manœuvre was in consequence of some offensive escape during the terrors of the pro-consul of *Judea*, who, as he is here represented, conveys no imperfect image of a late Lord Mayor, at the time of the riots in *London*. In this last instance, indeed, I ought to have observed that *Hogarth* meant to satirize, not to imitate, the painters of *Holland* and *Flanders*. But I forbear to dwell any longer on such disgusting circumstances; begging leave only to ask, whether the canvas of *Teniers* exhibits nastier objects than those of the woman cracking a louse between her nails in the fourth plate of the *Harlot's Progress*; a *Scotch* bag-piper catching another in his neck while he is performing at the Election feast; *Aurora* doing the same kind office for a *Syren* or *Nereid*, in the *Strollers*, &c.; the old toothless *French* beldams, slobbering (*Venus* forbid we should call it kissing) each other in the comic print entitled *Noon*; the chamber-pot emptied on the Free Mason's head, in the *Rejoicing Night*; or the *Lilliputians* giving a clyster to *Gulliver*? In some of these instances, however, the humour may compensate for the indelicacy, which is rarely the case with such *Dutch* pictures as have justly incurred the censure of Mr. *Walpole*. Let us now try how far some of the compositions of *Hogarth* have befriended the cause of modesty. In the *Harlot's Progress*, Plate VI. we meet with a hand by no means busied in manner suitable to the purity of its owner's function. *Hogarth* indeed, in three different works, has delineated three clergymen; the one as a drunkard; the second as a glutton; and the third as a whoremaster, who (I borrow *Rouquet's* words) "est plus occupé de sa voisine que de son vin, qu'il repand par une distraction qu'elle lui cause." He who, in the eyes of the vulgar, would degrade our professors of religion, deserves few thanks from society. In the *Rake's Progress*, Plate the last, how is the hand of the ideal potentate employed, while he is gazing with no very modest aspect on a couple of young women who pass before his cell numbered 55? and to what particular object are the eyes of the said females supposed to be directed?[45] Nay, in what pursuit is the grenadier engaged who stands with his face toward the wall in Plate 9. of *Industry and Idleness*? May we address another question to the reader? Is the "*smile* of *Socrates*," or the "*benevolence* of the designer," very distinguishable in the half dozen last instances? It has been observed indeed by physiognomists, that the *smile* of the real *Socrates* resembled the *grin* of a *satyr*; and perhaps a few of the particulars here alluded to, as well as the prints entitled BEFORE and AFTER, ought to be considered as a *benevolence* to speculative old maids, or misses not yet enfranchised from a boarding school. Had this truly sensible critic, and elegant writer, been content to observe, that such gross circumstances as form the chief subject of *Flemish* pictures, are only incidental and subordinate in those of our artist, the remark might have escaped reprehension. But perhaps he who has told us that "*St. Paul's* hand was once *improperly* placed before the wife of *Felix*" should not have suffered more glaring insults on decency to pass without a censure. On this occasion, though I may be found to differ from Mr. *Walpole*, I am ready to confess how much regard is due to the opinions of a gentleman whose mind has been long exercised on a subject which is almost new to me; especially when I recollect that my present researches would have had no guide, but for the lights held out in the last volume of the Anecdotes of Painting in *England*.

Hogarth boasted that he could draw a Serjeant with his pike, going into an alehouse, and his Dog following him, with only three strokes;—which he executed thus:

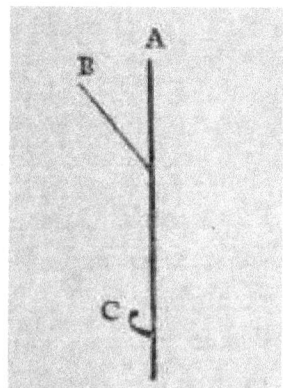

A. The perspective line of the door.
B. The end of the Serjeant's pike, who is gone in.

C. The end of the Dog's tail, who is following him.
There are similar whims of the *Caracci*.

A specimen of *Hogarth's* propensity to merriment, on the most trivial occasions, is observable in one of his cards requesting the company of Dr. *Arnold King* to dine with him at the *Mitre*.[46] Within a circle, to which a knife and fork are the supporters, the written part is contained. In the center is drawn a pye, with a *mitre* on the top of it; and the invitation of our artist concludes with the following sport on three of the *Greek* letters—to *Eta Beta Pi*.[47] The rest of the inscription is not very accurately spelt. A quibble by *Hogarth* is surely as respectable as a conundrum by *Swift*.

"Some nicer virtuosi have remarked, that in the serious pieces, into which *Hogarth* has deviated from the natural biass of his genius, there are some strokes of the ridiculous discernible, which suit not with the dignity of his subject. In his PREACHING OF ST. PAUL, a dog snarling at a cat;[48] and in his PHARAOH'S DAUGHTER, the figure of the infant *Moses*, who expresses rather archness than timidity; are alledged as instances, that this artist, unrivalled in his own walk, could not resist the impulse of his imagination towards drollery. His picture, however, of *Richard* III. is pure and unmixed, without any ridiculous circumstances, and strongly impresses terror and amazement." As these observations are extracted from the *first* edition of Dr. *Warton's* "Essay on the Genius and Writings of *Pope*," it would be uncandid if we did not accompany them with the following note from a subsequent edition of that valuable performance: "The author gladly lays hold of the opportunity of this third edition of his work to confess a mistake he had committed with respect to two admirable paintings of Mr. *Hogarth*, his PAUL PREACHING, and his INFANT MOSES; which, on a closer examination, are not chargeable with the blemishes imputed to them. Justice obliges him to declare the high opinion he entertains of the abilities of this inimitable artist, who shines in so many different lights, and on such very dissimilar subjects; and whose works have more of what the ancients called the HθOΣ [Greek: Ethos] in them, than the compositions of any other Modern. For the rest, the author begs leave to add, that he is so far from being ashamed of retracting his error, that he had rather appear a MAN OF CANDOUR, than the best CRITIC that ever lived."[49]

In one of the early exhibitions at *Spring Gardens*, a very pleasing small picture by *Hogarth* made its first appearance. It was painted for the earl of *Charlemont*, in whose collection it remains.[50] It was intituled, *Picquet, or Virtue in Danger*, and shews us a young lady, who, during a *tête-à-tête*, had just lost all her money to a handsome officer of her own age. He is represented in the act of returning her a handful of bank bills, with the hope of exchanging them for a softer acquisition, and more delicate plunder. On the chimney piece is a watch-case and a figure of Time over it, with this motto—NUNC. *Hogarth* has caught his heroine during this moment of hesitation, this struggle with herself, and has marked her feelings with uncommon success. Wavering chastity, as in this instance, he was qualified to display; but the graceful reserve of steady and exalted virtue he would certainly have failed to express. He might have conveyed a perfect idea of such an *Iphigenia* as is described by Mr. *Hayley*, in one of the cantoes of his beautiful poem on the *Triumphs of Temper*; but the dignity of the same female at the *Tauric* altar would have baffled the most vigorous efforts of his pencil.

Hogarth's Picquet, or *Virtue in Danger*, when exhibited at *Spring Gardens*, in *May*, 1761, produced the following explanation:

>Ye fair, be warn'd, and shun those arts,
>That faithless men do use for hearts:
>Weigh o'er and o'er the destin'd man,
>And oft this little lesson scan;
>If he his character don't fear,
>For yours he'll very little care:
>With scorn repulse the wretch so bold,
>Nor pawn your virtue for his gold!
>Of gaming (cards or not) beware,
>'Tis very often found a snare;
>But, lest my precept still should fail,
>Indulge me—whilst I tell a tale:
>
>*Dorinda*, chearful, young, and gay,
>Oft shone at Balls, at Park, and Play;
>Blest with a free, engaging air,
>In short, throughout quite debonnair;
>(Excuse me—shall I tell the truth?)
>That bane of misled, heedless youth,
>Gaming—had quite possess'd her mind,
>To this (no other vice) inclin'd:
>She oft would melancholy sit,
>No partner near for dear Picquet!
>"At last a cruel spoiler came,"
>And deeply learn'd in all the game;
>A son of *Mars*, with iron face,
>Adorn'd with impudence and lace!
>Acquaintance with her soon he gains,
>He thinks her virtue worth his pains:

    Cards (after nonsense) came in course,
By sap advances, not by force.
The table set, the cards are laid,
Dorinda dreams not she's betray'd;
The cards run cross, she fumes and frets,
Her brilliant necklace soon she betts,
She fears her watch, but can't resist,
A miniature can scarce be mist!
At last both watch and trinkets go,
A prey to the devouring foe:
Nay more (if fame but tells us true),
She lost her di'mond buckles too!
Her bracelets next became his prize,
And in his hat the treasure lies.
Upon her Virtue next he treats,
And Honour's sacred name repeats:
Tenders the trinkets, swears and lies,
And vows her person is a prize!
Then swears (with hand upon his breast)
That he without her can't be blest!
Then plies her with redoubled pains,
T' exchange her virtue for his gains:
Shame's purple wings o'ershade her face,
He triumphs over her disgrace;
Soon turns to jest her scruples nice,
In short, she falls!—a sacrifice!
Spoil'd of her virtue in her prime,
And, knowing Heaven detests the crime,
Is urg'd, perhaps, to dare his rod,
"And rush unsummon'd to her God!"

    Ye fair, if happiness ye prize,
Regard this rule, Be timely wise.

In the "Miser's Feast," Mr. *Hogarth* thought proper to pillory Sir *Isaac Shard*, a gentleman proverbially avaricious. Hearing this, the son of Sir *Isaac*, the late *Isaac Pacatus Shard*,[51] esq. a young man of spirit, just returned from his travels, called at the painter's to see the picture; and, among the rest, asking the *Cicerone* "whether that odd figure was intended for any particular person;" on his replying, "that it was thought to be very like one Sir *Isaac Shard*;" he immediately drew his sword, and slashed the canvas. *Hogarth* appeared instantly in great wrath; to whom Mr. *Shard* calmly justified what he had done, saying, "that this was a very unwarrantable licence; that he was the injured party's son, and that he was ready to defend any suit at law;" which, however, was never instituted.

About 1757, his brother-in-law, Mr. *Thornhill*, resigned the place of king's serjeant-painter in favour of Mr. *Hogarth*; who soon after made an experiment in painting, which involved him in some disgrace. The celebrated collection of pictures belonging to Sir *Luke Schaub* was in 1758 sold by public auction;[52] and the admired picture of *Sigismunda* (purchased by Sir *Thomas Sebright* for 404. *l.* 5 *s.*) excited Mr. *Hogarth's* emulation.

"From a contempt of the ignorant virtuosi of the age," says Mr. *Walpole*, "and from indignation at the impudent tricks of picture-dealers, whom he saw continually recommending and vending vile copies to bubble collectors, and from having never studied, indeed having seen, few good pictures of the great *Italian* masters, he persuaded himself that the praises bestowed on those glorious works were nothing but the effects of prejudice. He talked this language till he believed it; and having heard it often asserted, as is true, that time gives a mellowness to colours and improves them, he not only denied the proposition, but maintained that pictures only grew black and worse by age, not distinguishing between the degrees in which the proportion might be true or false. He went farther: he determined to rival the ancients—and unfortunately chose one of the finest pictures in *England* as the object of his competition. This was the celebrated *Sigismunda* of Sir *Luke Schaub*, now in the possession of the Duke of *Newcastle*, said to be painted by *Correggio*, probably by *Furino*, but no matter by whom. It is impossible to see the picture, or read *Dryden's* inimitable tale, and not feel that the same soul animated both. After many essays, *Hogarth* at last produced HIS *Sigismunda*—but no more like *Sigismunda*, than I to *Hercules*. Not to mention the wretchedness of the colouring, it was the representation of a maudlin strumpet just turned out of keeping, and, with eyes red with rage and usquebaugh, tearing off the ornaments her keeper had given her. To add to the disgust raised by such vulgar expression, her fingers were bloodied by her lover's heart,[53] that lay before her, like that of a sheep, for her dinner.[54] None of the sober grief, no dignity of suppressed anguish, no involuntary tear, no settled meditation on the fate she meant to meet, no amorous warmth turned holy by despair; in short, all was wanting that should have been there, all was there that such a story would have banished from a mind capable of conceiving such complicated woe; woe so sternly felt, and yet so tenderly. *Hogarth's* performance was more ridiculous than any thing he had ever ridiculed. He set the price of 400 *l.* on it, and had it returned on his hands by the person for whom it was painted. He took subscriptions for a plate of it; but had the sense, at last, to suppress it. I make no more apology for this account than for the encomiums I have bestowed on him. Both are dictated by truth, and are the history of a great man's excellencies and errors. *Milton*, it is said, preferred his *Paradise Regained* to his immortal poem."[55]

Hogarth, however, gave directions before his death that the *Sigismunda* should not be sold under 500 *l.* and, greatly as he might have been mortified by *Churchill's* invective, and the coldness with which the picture was received by the rest of the world,[56] he never wholly abandoned his design of having a plate prepared from it. Finding abundant consolation in the flattery of self-love, he appealed from the public judgement to his own, and had actually talked with the celebrated Mr. *Hall* about the price of the engraving, which was to have been executed from a smaller painting,[57] copied by himself from the large one. Death alone secured him from the contempt such obstinacy would have riveted on his name. To express a sorrow like that of *Tancred's* daughter, few modern artists are fully qualified. We must except indeed Sir *Joshua Reynolds*, with whose pencil Beauty in all her forms, and the passions in all their varieties, are equally familiar.

Since the preceding paragraph was written, the compiler of this volume has seen an unfinished plate of *Sigismunda*, attempted after the manner of *Edelinck*, etched by Mr. *Basire*, but not bit-in, and from which consequently no proof can have been taken. The size of the plate is 18 inches by 16½. The outlines in general, and particularly of the face, were completed under the immediate direction of Mr. *Hogarth*.[58] It was intended to be published by subscription.[59] The plate itself is still in the hands of Mr. *Basire*.

This unfortunate picture, which was the source of so much vexation to Mr. *Hogarth*, at least made a versifier of him, and furnished vent to his anger in the following lines; which, as I know of no other specimen of his poetry,[60] may serve to gratify the curiosity of the reader. The old adage *facit indignatio versum*, seems scarcely to have been realised in this splenetic effusion, which is intituled "An Epistle to a Friend," occasioned by Sir *Richard Grosvenor* (now lord) returning the picture of *Sigismunda* on our artist's hands:

"To your charge, the other day
About my picture and my pay,
In metre I've a mind to try,
One word by way of a reply.

"To risque, you'll own, 'twas most absurd,
Such labour on a rich man's word;
To lose at least an hundred days
Of certain gain, for doubtful praise;
Since living artists ne'er were paid;
But then, you know, it was agreed,

I should be deem'd an artist dead.
Like *Raphael, Rubens, Guido Rene,*
This promise fairly drew me in;
And having laid my pencil by,[61]
What painter was more dead than I?
But dead as *Guido* let me be,
Then judge, my friend, 'twixt him and me
If merit crowns alike the piece,
What treason to be like in price;
Because no copied line you trace,
The picture can't be right, you're sure;
But say, my critic connoisseur,
Moves it the heart as much or more
Than picture ever did before?
This is the painter's truest test,
And this Sir *Richard's* self confess'd.
Nay, 'tis so moving, that the knight
Can't even bear it in his sight;
Then who would tears so dearly buy,
As give four hundred pounds to cry?
I own, he chose the prudent part,
Rather to break his word than heart;
And yet, methinks, 'tis ticklish dealing,
With one so delicate—in feeling.

"However, let the picture rust,
Perhaps time's price-enhancing dust,
As statues moulder into earth,
When I'm no more, may mark its worth;
And future connoisseurs may rise,
Honest as ours, and full as wise,
To puff the piece and painter too,
And make me then what *Guido's* now."

"The last memorable event in our artist's life," as Mr. *Walpole* observes, "was his quarrel with Mr. *Wilkes*, in which, if Mr. *Hogarth* did not commence direct hostilities on the latter, he at least obliquely gave the first offence, by an attack on the friends and party of that gentleman. This conduct was the more surprizing, as he had all his life avoided dipping his pencil in political contests, and had early refused a very lucrative offer that was made to engage him in a set of prints against the head of a court-party. Without entering into the merits of the cause, I shall only state the fact. In *September* 1762, Mr. *Hogarth* published his print of *The Times*. It was answered by Mr. *Wilkes* in a severe *North Briton*.[62] On this the painter exhibited the caricatura of the writer. Mr. *Churchill*, the poet, then engaged in the war, and wrote his epistle to *Hogarth*, not the brightest of his works,[63] in which the severest strokes fell on a defect that the painter had neither caused nor could amend—his age;[64] and which, however, was neither remarkable nor decrepit; much less had it impaired his talents, as appeared by his having composed but six months before one of his most capital works, the satire on the Methodists. In revenge for this epistle, *Hogarth* caricatured *Churchill*, under the form of a canonical bear, with a club and a pot of porter—*et vitulá tu dignus & hic*—never did two angry men of their abilities throw mud with less dexterity."

The concluding observation of Mr. *Walpole* is mortifyingly true. It may be amusing to compare the account given of this squabble, which long engrossed the attention of the town, with the narrative of it printed by Mr. *Wilkes*; who states the circumstances of it in the following manner:

"Mr. *Hogarth* was one of the first who, in the paper war begun by lord *Bute* on his accession to the Treasury, sacrificed private friendship at the altar of party madness. In 1762, the *Scotch* minister took a variety of hirelings into his pay, some of whom were gratified with pensions, others with places and pensions. Mr. *Hogarth* was only made *serjeant-painter* to his majesty, as if it was meant to insinuate to him, that he was not allowed to paint any thing but the wainscot of the royal apartments. The term means no more than *house-painter*, and the nature of the post confined him to that business. He was not employed in any other way. A circumstance can scarcely be imagined more humiliating to a man of spirit and genius, who really thought that he more particularly excelled in *portrait-painting*.

"The new minister had been attacked in a variety of political papers. *The North Briton* in particular, which commenced the week after *The Briton*, waged open war with him. Some of the numbers had been ascribed to Mr. *Wilkes*, others to Mr. *Churchill*, and Mr. *Lloyd*. Mr. *Hogarth* had for several years lived on terms of friendship and intimacy with Mr. *Churchill* and Mr. *Wilkes*. As the *Buckinghamshire* militia, which this gentleman had the honour of commanding, had been for some months at *Winchester* guarding the *French* prisoners, the Colonel was there on that duty. A friend wrote to him, that Mr. *Hogarth* intended soon to publish a political print of *The Times*, in which Mr. *Pitt*, Lord *Temple*, Mr. *Churchill*, and himself, were held out to the public as objects of ridicule. Mr. *Wilkes*, on this notice, remonstrated by two of their common friends to Mr. *Hogarth*, that such a proceeding would not only be unfriendly in the highest degree, but extremely injudicious; for such a pencil ought to be universal and moral, to speak to all ages, and to all nations, not to be dipt in the dirt of the faction of a day, of an insignificant part of the country, when it might command the admiration of the whole. An answer was sent, that neither Mr. *Wilkes* nor Mr. *Churchill* were attacked in *The Times*, though Lord *Temple* and Mr. *Pitt* were, and that the print should soon appear.

A second message soon after told Mr. *Hogarth*, that Mr. *Wilkes* should never believe it worth his while to take notice of any reflections on himself; but if his friends were attacked, he should then think he was wounded in the most sensible part, and would, as well as he was able, revenge their cause; adding, that if he thought the *North Briton* would insert what he sent, he would make an appeal to the public on the very *Saturday* following the publication of the print. *The Times* soon after appeared, and on the *Saturday* following [*Sept.* 25, 1762,] N° 17, of the *North Briton*, which is a direct attack on the king's *serjeant-painter*.[65] If Mr. *Wilkes* did write that paper, he kept his word better with Mr. *Hogarth*, than the painter had done with him.

"It is perhaps worth remarking, that the painter proposed to give a series of political prints, and that *The Times* were marked Plate I. No farther progress was however made in that design. The public beheld the first feeble efforts with execrations, and it is said that the caricaturist was too much hurt by the general opinion of mankind, to possess himself afterwards sufficiently for the execution of such a work.

"When Mr. *Wilkes* was the second time brought from the *Tower* to *Westminster-hall*, Mr. *Hogarth* skulked behind in a corner of the gallery of the Court of *Common Pleas*; and while the Chief Justice *Pratt*,[66] with the eloquence and courage of old *Rome*, was enforcing the great principles of *Magna Charta*, and the *English* constitution, while every breast from him caught the holy flame of liberty, the painter was wholly employed in caricaturing the *person* of the man; while all the rest of his fellow citizens were animated in his *cause*, for they knew it to be their own cause, that of their country, and of its laws. It was declared to be so a few hours after by the unanimous sentence of the judges of that court, and they were all present.

"The print of Mr. *Wilkes* was soon after published, *drawn from the life by William Hogarth*. It must be allowed to be an excellent *compound caricatura*, or a *caricatura* of what nature had already *caricatured*. I know but one short apology can be made for this gentleman, or, to speak more properly, for the *person* of Mr. *Wilkes*. It is, that he did not make himself, and that he never was solicitous about the *case* of his soul, as *Shakspeare* calls it, only so far as to keep it clean and in health. I never heard that he once hung over the glassy stream, like another *Narcissus*, admiring the image in it, nor that he ever stole an amorous look at his counterfeit in a side mirrour. His form, such as it is, ought to give him no pain, because it is capable of giving pleasure to others. I fancy he finds himself tolerably happy in the *clay-cottage*, to which he is *tenant for life*, because he has learnt to keep it in good order. While the share of health and animal spirits, which heaven has given him, shall hold out, I can scarcely imagine he will be one moment peevish about the *outside* of so precarious, so temporary a habitation, or will even be brought to own, *ingenium Galbæ male habitat. Monsieur est mal logé.*

"Mr. *Churchill* was exasperated at this *personal* attack on his friend. He soon after published the Epistle to *William Hogarth*,[67] and took for the motto, *ut pictura poesis*. Mr. *Hogarth's* revenge against the poet terminated in vamping up an old print of a pug-dog and a bear, which he published under the title of The Bruiser *C. Churchill* (once the Revd.!) in the character of a *Russian Hercules*, &c."

The Editor of the *Monthly Review* for *November*, 1769, in an account of Mr. *Wilkes's* correspondence, remarks, "The writer of this article had in substance the same relation from the mouth of Mr. *Hogarth* himself, but a very little while before his death;[68] and the leading facts appeared, from his candid representation, in nearly the same light as in this account which our readers have been just perusing."

I have been assured by the friend[69] who first carried and read the invective of *Churchill* to *Hogarth*, that he seemed quite insensible to the most sarcastical parts of it. He was so thoroughly wounded before by the *North Briton*, especially with regard to what related to domestic happiness, that he lay no where open to a fresh stroke. Some readers, however, may entertain a doubt on this subject. A man feels most exquisitely when the merit of which he is proudest is denied him; and it might be urged, that *Hogarth* was more solicitous to maintain the character of a good painter, than of a tender husband.

One quotation, however, from *Churchill's* Epistle the warmest admirers of our matchless artist must be pleased with:

> "In walks of humour, in that cast of style,
> Which, probing to the quick, yet makes us smile;
> In Comedy, his natural road to fame,
> Nor let me call it by a meaner name,
> Where a beginning, middle, and an end,
> Are aptly join'd; where parts on parts depend,
> Each made for each, as bodies for their soul,
> So as to form one true and perfect whole,
> Where a plain story to the eye is told,
> Which we conceive the moment we behold;[70]
> *Hogarth* unrival'd stands, and shall engage
> Unrival'd praise to the most distant age."

Hogarth having been said to be in his dotage when, he produced his print of the Bear, it should seem as if he had been provoked to make the following additions to this print, in order to give a further specimen of his still existing genius.

In the form of a framed picture on the painter's palette, he has represented an *Egyptian* pyramid, on the side of which is a *Cheshire* cheese,[71] and round it 3000 *l. per annum*; and at the foot a *Roman* Veteran in a reclining posture, designed as an allusion to Mr. *Pitt's* resignation. The cheese is meant to allude to a former speech of his, wherein he said that he would rather subsist a week on a *Cheshire* cheese and a shoulder of mutton, than submit to the implacable enemies of his country.

But to ridicule this character still more, he is, as he lies down, firing a piece of ordnance at the standard of *Britain*, on which is a dove with an olive-branch, the emblem of peace. On one side of the pyramid is the City of *London*, represented by the figure of one of the *Guildhall* giants, going to crown the reclining hero. On the other side is the king of *Prussia*, in the character of one of the *Cæsars*, but smoking his pipe. In the center stands *Hogarth* himself, whipping a Dancing Bear (*Churchill*) which he holds in a string. At the side of the Bear is a Monkey, designed for Mr. *Wilkes*. Between the legs of the little animal is a mop-stick, on which he seems to ride, as children do on a hobby-horse: at the top of the mop-stick is the cap of liberty. The Monkey is undergoing the same discipline as the Bear. Behind the Monkey is the figure of a man, but with no lineaments of face, and playing on a fiddle. This was designed for Earl *Temple*.

At the time these hostilities were carrying on in a manner so virulent and disgraceful to all the parties, *Hogarth* was visibly declining in his health. In 1762, he complained of an inward pain, which, continuing, brought on a general decay that proved incurable.[72] This last year of his life he employed in retouching his plates with the assistance of several engravers whom he took with him to *Chiswick*. On the 25th of *October*, 1764, he was conveyed from thence to *Leicester-fields*, in a very weak condition, yet remarkably chearful; and, receiving an agreeable letter from the *American* Dr. *Franklin*, drew up a rough draught of an answer to it; but going to bed, he was seized with a vomiting, upon which he rung his bell with such violence that he broke it, and expired about two hours afterwards in the arms of Mrs. *Mary Lewis*, who was called up on his being taken suddenly ill. To this lady, for her faithful services, he bequeathed 100 *l*. After the death of *Hogarth's* sister, Mrs. *Lewis* succeeded to the care of his prints; and, without violation of truth, it may be observed, that her good nature and affability recommend these performances which she continues to dispose of at Mrs. *Hogarth's* house in *Leicester-square*. Before our artist went to bed, he boasted of having eaten a pound of beef-steaks for his dinner,[73] and was to all appearance heartier than he had been for a long time before. His disorder was an aneurism; and his corpse was interred in the church-yard at *Chiswick*, where a monument is erected to his memory, with this inscription, under his family arms:

> "Here lieth the body
> Of *William Hogarth*, Esq.
> Who died *October* the 26th, 1764;
> Aged 67 years."

On another side, which is ornamented with a masque, a laurel wreath, a palette, pencils, and a book, inscribed "Analysis of Beauty," are the following verses by his friend Mr. *Garrick*:

> "Farewell, great painter of mankind,
> Who reach'd the noblest point of art;
> Whose pictur'd morals charm the mind,
> And through the eye correct the heart.
> If *genius* fire thee, reader, stay,
> If *nature* touch thee, drop a tear;
> If neither move thee, turn away,
> For *Hogarth's* honoured dust lies here."

On a third side is this inscription:

> "Here lieth the body
> Of Dame *Judith Thornhill*,
> Relict of Sir *James Thornhill*, knight,
> Of *Thornhill* in the county of *Dorset*.
> She died *November* the 12th, 1757,
> Aged 84 years."

And on the fourth side:

> "Here lieth the body
> Of Mrs. *Anne Hogarth*, sister
> to *William Hogarth*, Esq.
> She died *August* the 13th, 1771,
> Aged 70 years."

Mr. *Hayley*, in his justly admired *Epistle to an Eminent Painter* (Mr. *Romney*), has since expressed himself concerning our artist in terms that confer yet higher honours on his comic excellence:

> "Nor, if her favour'd hand may hope to shed
> The flowers of glory o'er the skilful dead,

> Thy talents, *Hogarth!* will she leave unsung;
> Charm of all eyes, and Theme of every tongue!
> A separate province 'twas thy praise to rule;
> Self-form'd thy Pencil! yet thy works a School,
> Where strongly painted, in gradations nice,
> The Pomp of Folly, and the Shame of Vice,
> Reach'd thro' the laughing Eye the mended Mind,
> And moral Humour sportive Art refin'd.
> While fleeting Manners, as minutely shown
> As the clear prospect on the mirror thrown;
> While Truth of Character, exactly hit,
> And drest in all the dyes of comic wit;
> While these, in *Fielding's* page, delights supply,
> So long thy Pencil with his Pen shall vie.
> Science with grief beheld thy drooping age
> Fall the sad victim of a Poet's rage:
> But Wit's vindictive spleen, that mocks controul,
> Nature's high tax on luxury of soul!
> This, both in Bards and Painters, Fame forgives
> Their Frailty's buried, but their Genius lives."

Thus far the encomiast, who seeks only for opportunities of bestowing praise. A more impartial narrative will be expected from the biographer.

It may be truly observed of *Hogarth*, that all his powers of delighting were restrained to his pencil.[74] Having rarely been admitted into polite circles, none of his sharp corners had been rubbed off, so that he continued to the last a gross uncultivated man. The slightest contradiction transported him into rage. To be member of a Club consisting of mechanics, or those not many removes above them, seems to have been the utmost of his social ambition; but even in these assemblies he was oftener sent to *Coventry* for misbehaviour, than any other person who frequented them. To some confidence in himself he was certainly entitled; for, as a comic painter, he could have claimed no honour that would not most readily have been allowed him;[75] but he was at once unprincipled and variable in his political conduct and attachments. He is also said to have beheld the rising eminence and popularity of Sir *Joshua Reynolds* with a degree of envy; and, if I am not misinformed, frequently spoke with asperity both of him and his performances. Justice, however, obliges me to add, that our artist was liberal, hospitable, and the most punctual of pay-masters; so that, in spite of the emoluments his works had procured to him, he left but an inconsiderable fortune to his widow. His plates indeed are such resources as may not speedily be exhausted. Some of his domestics had lived many years in his service, a circumstance that always reflects credit on a master. Of most of these he painted strong likenesses on a canvas still in Mrs. *Hogarth's* possession.

His widow has also a portrait of her husband, and an excellent bust of him by *Roubilliac*, a strong resemblance; and one of his brother-in-law Mr. *Thornhill*, much resembling the countenance of Mrs. *Hogarth*. Several of his portraits also remain in her possession: *viz.* a finished portrait of Mrs. *Mary Lewis*; *Thomas Coombes* of *Dorsetshire*, aged 108; Lady *Thornhill*; Mrs. *Hogarth* herself, &c. &c.

A portrait of *Hogarth* with his hat on, painted for the late Rev. Mr. *Townley* by *Weltdon*, and said to be finished by himself, is in the possession of Mr. *James Townley*, proctor in *Doctors Commons*. A mezzotinto print from it will be mentioned under the year 1781 in the Catalogue.

Mr. *Edwards*, of *Beaufort Buildings*, has the portrait of Sir *George Hay*, *The Savoyard Girl*, *The Bench*, and *Mary Queen of Scots*,[76] by *Hogarth*.

A conversation-piece by him is likewise at *Wanstead* in *Essex*, the seat of Earl *Tylney*.[77] And Mrs. *Hoadly* has a scene of *Ranger* and *Clarinda* in *The Suspicious Husband*; and the late Chancellor *Hoadly* repeating a song to Dr. *Greene*, for him to compose; both by *Hogarth*. The first of these is an indifferent picture, and contains very inadequate likenesses of the persons represented.

One of the best portraits *Hogarth* ever painted, is at *Lichfield*. It is of a gentleman with whom he was very intimate, and at whose houses at *Mortlake* and in *Ironmongers-Lane* he spent much of his time—Mr. *Joseph Porter*, of *London*, merchant, who died *April* 7, 1749. Mrs. *Porter* the sister of this gentleman (who was daughter of Dr. *Johnson's* wife by a former husband) is in possession of the picture.—*John Steers*, esq. (of *The Paper Buildings* in *The Temple*) has an auction by *Hogarth*, in which Dr. *Chauncey*, Dr. *Snagg*, and others, are introduced; and the Earl of *Exeter* has a butcher's shop, with *Slack* fighting, &c.

Of *Hogarth's* lesser plates many were destroyed. When he wanted a piece of copper on a sudden, he would take any from which he had already worked off such a number of impressions as he supposed he should sell. He then sent it to be effaced, beat out, or otherwise altered to his present purpose.

The plates which remained in his possession were secured to Mrs. *Hogarth* by his will, dated *August* 12, 1764, chargeable with an annuity of 80 *l.* to his sister *Anne*,[78] who survived him. When, on the death of his other sister, she left off the business in which she was engaged (see, in the Catalogue, the first article among the "Prints of uncertain date,") he kindly took her home, and generously supported her, making her, at the same time, useful in the disposal of his prints. Want of tenderness and liberality to his relations was not among the failings of *Hogarth*.

Of *Hogarth's* drawings and contributions towards the works of others, perhaps a number, on enquiry, might be found. An acquaintance of his, the late worthy Mr. *John Sanderson*, architect, who repaired *Woburn Abbey*, as well as *Bedford House* in *Bloomsbury-square*, possessed several of his curiosities. One was a sketch in black-lead of a celebrated young engraver (long since dead) in a salivation. The best that can be said of it is, that it was most disgustingly natural. Even the coarse ornaments on the corners of the blankets which enwrapped him, were characteristically expressed. Our artist seems to have repeated the same idea, though with less force, and fewer adjuncts, in the third of his Election prints, where a figure swaddled up in flannel is conveyed to the hustings. Two other works, viz. a drawing in *Indian* ink, and a painting in oil colours, exhibited *Bedford House* in different points of view; the figures only by *Hogarth*. Another represented the corner of a street, with a man drinking under the spout of a pump, and heartily angry with the water, which, by issuing out too fast, and in too great quantities, had deluged his face. Our great painter had obliged Mr. *Sanderson* with several other comic sketches, &c. but most of them had been either begged or stolen, before the communicator of these particulars became acquainted with him.

In the year 1745, *Launcelot Burton* was appointed naval officer at *Deal*. *Hogarth* had seen him by accident; and on a piece of paper, previously impressed by a plain copper-plate, drew his figure with a pen, in imitation of a coarse etching. He was represented on a lean *Canterbury* hack, with a bottle sticking out of his pocket; and underneath was an inscription, intimating that he was going down to take possession of his place. This was inclosed to him in a letter; and some of his friends, who were in the secret, protested the drawing to be a print which they had seen exposed to sale at the shops in *London*; a circumstance that put him in a violent passion, during which he wrote an abusive letter to *Hogarth*, whose name was subscribed to the work. But, after poor *Burton's* tormentors had kept him in suspence throughout an uneasy three weeks, they proved to him that it was no engraving, but a sketch with a pen and ink. He then became so perfectly reconciled to his resemblance, that he shewed it with exultation to Admiral *Vernon*, and all the rest of his friends.

In 1753, *Hogarth* returning with Dr. *Morell* from a visit to Mr. *Rich* at *Cowley*, stopped his chariot, and got out, being struck by a large drawing (with a coal) on the wall of an alehouse. He immediately made a sketch of it with triumph; it was a St. *George and the Dragon*, all in strait lines.

Hogarth made one essay in sculpture. He wanted a sign to distinguish his house in *Leicester-fields*; and thinking none more proper than the *Golden Head*, he, out of a mass of cork made up of several thicknesses compacted together, carved a bust of *Vandyck*, which he gilt and placed over his door. It is long since decayed, and was succeeded by a head in plaster, which has also perished; and is supplied by a head of Sir *Isaac Newton*. *Hogarth* modelled another resemblance of *Vandyck* in clay; which is likewise destroyed.

It is very properly observed by Mr. *Walpole*, that "If ever an author wanted a commentary, that none of his beauties might be lost, it is *Hogarth*; not from being obscure (for he never was that but in two or three of his first prints, where transient national follies, as Lotteries, Free-masonry, and the *South Sea*, were his topics) but for the use of foreigners, and from a multiplicity of little incidents, not essential to, but always heightening the principal action. Such is the spider's web extended over the poor's box in a parish church; the blunders in architecture in the nobleman's seat, seen through the window, in the first print of *Marriage à la Mode*; and a thousand in the Strollers dressing in a barn, which, for wit and imagination, without any other aid, is perhaps the best of all his works; as, for useful and deep satire, that on the Methodists is the most sublime. *Rouquet*, the enameller, published a *French* explanation, though a superficial one, of many of his prints, which, it was said, he had drawn up for the use of Marshal *Belleisle*, then a prisoner in *England*."

However great the deficiencies in this work may be, it was certainly suggested by *Hogarth*, and drawn up at his immediate request. I receive this information from undoubted authority. Some of the circumstances explanatory of the plates, he communicated; the rest he left to be supplied by *Rouquet* his near neighbour, who lived in the house at which *Gardelle* the enameller afterwards lodged, and murdered his landlady Mrs. *King*. *Rouquet*, who (as I learn from Mr. *Walpole*) was a *Swiss* of *French* extraction, had formerly published a small tract on the state of the Arts in *England*, and another, intituled "L'Art de peinture en fromage ou en ramequin, 1755;" 12mo. (V. "La *France* litteraire, ou Dictionaire des Auteurs *François* vivans, par *M. Formey*, 1757.") On the present occasion he was liberally paid by *Hogarth*, for having cloathed his sentiments and illustrations in a foreign dress. This pamphlet was designed, and continues to be employed, as a constant companion to all such sets of his prints as go abroad. Only the letter descriptive of the *March to Finchley* was particularly meant for the instruction of Marshal *Belleisle*.[79]

It was added after the three former epistles had been printed off, and before the plate was published. The entire performance, however, in my opinion, exhibits very strong marks of the vivacious compiler's taste, country, and prejudices. Indeed many passages must have been inserted without the privity of his employer, who had no skill in the *French* language. That our *clergy* always *affect to ride on white horses*, and other remarks of a similar turn, &c. &c. could never have fallen from the pen of *Hogarth*, or any other *Englishman*.

This epistle bears also internal evidence to the suggestions *Rouquet* received from *Hogarth*. Are not the self-congratulations and prejudices of our artist sufficiently visible in the following passage?

"Ce Tableau dis-je a le defaut d'etre encore tout brillant de cette ignoble fraîcheur qu'on decouvre dans la nature, et *qu'on ne voit jamais dans les cabinets bien célèbres. Le tems ne l'a point encore obscurci de cette decte fumée, de ce usage sacré, qui le cachera quelque jour aux yeux profanes du vulgaire, pour ne laisser voir ses beautés qu'aux initiés.*"

The title of this performance, is, "Lettres de Monsieur * * à un de ses Amis à *Paris*, pour lui expliquer les Estampes de Monsieur *Hogarth*.—Imprimé à *Londres*: et se vend chez R. *Dodsley*, dans *Pall Mall*; et chez M. *Cooper*, dans *Paternoster Row*, 1746." (Le prix est de douze sols.)

I should here observe, that this pamphlet affords only descriptions of the *Harlot's* and *Rake's Progress, Marriage à la Mode*, and the *March to Finchley*. Nine other plates, viz. the *Modern Midnight Conversation*, the *Distressed Poet*, the *Enraged Musician*, the *Fair, Strolling Actresses dressing in a Barn*, and the *Four Times of the Day*, are enumerated without particular explanation.

I am authorized to add, that *Hogarth*, not long before his death, had determined, in compliance with the repeated solicitations of his customers, to have this work enlarged and rendered into *English*, with the addition of ample comments on all his performances undescribed by *Rouquet*.

"*Hogarth* Moralised"[80] will however in some small degree (a very small one) contribute to preserve the memory of those temporary circumstances which Mr. *Walpole* is so justly apprehensive will be lost to posterity. Such an undertaking indeed, requires a more intimate acquaintance with fleeting customs, and past occurrences, than the compiler of this work can pretend to. Yet enough has been done by him to awaken a spirit of enquiry, and point out the means by which it may be farther gratified.

The works of *Hogarth*, as his elegant biographer has well observed, are his history;[81] and the curious are highly indebted to Mr. *Walpole* for a catalogue of prints, drawn up from his own valuable collection, in 1771. But as neither that catalogue, nor his appendix to it in 1780, have given the whole of Mr. *Hogarth's* labours, I hope that I shall not be blamed if, by including Mr. *Walpole's* catalogue, I have endeavoured from later discoveries of our artist's prints in other collections, to arrange them in chronological order. It may not be unamusing to trace the rise and progress of a Genius so strikingly original.

Hogarth gave first impressions of all his plates to his late friends the Rev. Mr. *Townley* and Dr. *Isaac Schomberg*.[82] Both sets were sold since the death of these gentlemen. That which was Dr. *Schomberg's* became the property of the late Sir *John Chapman*, baronet; and passed after his death into the hands of his brother, the late Sir *William Chapman*. I should add, indeed, that our artist never sorted his impressions, selecting the slight from the strong ones: so that they who wish to possess any equal series of his prints, must pick it out of different sets.

A portrait of *Samuel Martin*, esq. the antagonist of Mr. *Wilkes*, which Mr. *Hogarth* had painted for his own use, he gave as a legacy to Mr. *Martin*.

Mrs. *Baynes*, of *Kneeton-Hall*, near *Richmond, Yorkshire*, has an original picture by *Hogarth*, four feet two inches long, by two feet four inches wide. It is a landscape, with several figures; a man driving sheep; a boat upon a piece of water, and a distant view of a town. This picture was bought in *London*, by her father, many years ago.

At Lord *Essex's* sale, in *January* 1777, Mr. *Garrick* bought a picture by *Hogarth*, being the examination of the recruits before the justices *Shallow* and *Silence*. For this, it was said in the news-papers, he gave 350 guineas. I have since been told, that remove the figure 3, and the true price paid by the purchaser remains. In private he allowed that he never gave the former of these sums, though in the public prints he did not think such a confession necessary. It was in reality an indifferent performance, as those of *Hogarth* commonly were, when he strove to paint up to the ideas of others.

Mr. *Browning*, of *King's College, Cambridge*, has a small picture by *Hogarth*, representing *Clare-Market*. It seems to have been one of our artist's early performances.

There are three large pictures by *Hogarth*, over the altar in the church of *St. Mary Redcliff* at *Bristol*; the sealing of the sacred Sepulchre, the Ascension, and the three *Maries*, &c. A sum of money was left to defray the expence of these ornaments, and it found its way into *Hogarth's* pocket. The original sketches in oil for these performances, are now at Mrs. *Hogarth's* house in *Leicester-fields*.

In Lord *Grosvenor's* house, at *Milbank, Westminster*, is a small painting by our artist on the following subject. A boy's paper-kite in falling become entangled with furze: the boy arrives just as a crow is tearing it in pieces. The expression in his face is worthy of *Hogarth*.

Hogarth was also supposed to have had some hand in the exhibition of signs,[83] projected above 20 years ago by *Bonnel Thornton*, of festive memory; but I am informed, that he contributed no otherwise towards this display, than by a few touches of chalk. Among the heads of distinguished personages, finding those of the King of *Prussia* and the Empress of *Hungary*, he changed the cast of their eyes so as to make them leer significantly at each other. This is related on the authority of Mr. *Colman*.

Mr. *Richardson* ("now," as Dr. *Johnson* says, "better known by his books than his pictures," though his colouring is allowed to be masterly) having accounted for some classical quotations in his notes on *Milton*, unlearned as he was, by his son's assisting him as a telescope does the eye in astronomy; *Hogarth* shewed him with a telescope looking through his son (in no very decent attitude) at a *Virgil* aloft on a shelf; but afterwards destroyed the plate, and recalled the prints. Qu. if any remain, and what date?—I much question whether this subject was ever thrown upon copper, or meant for the public eye.

In the "Nouveau Dictionnaire Historique, *Caen*, 1783," our artist is thus characterized: "Ses compositions sont mal dessinées & foiblement colories; mais ce sont des tableaux parlans de diverses scènes comiques ou morales de la vie. Il avoit négligé le méchanisme de son art, c'est à-dire, les traits du pinceau, le rapport des parties entr'elles, l'effèt du clare obscure, l'harmonie du coloris, &c. pour s'élever jusqu'à la perfection de ce méchanisme, c'est à-dire, au poétique & au moral de la peinture. 'Je reconnois,' disoit-il, 'tout le monde pour juge compétent de mes tableaux, excepté les connoisseurs de profession.' Un seul exemple prouvera combien réussit. Il avoit fait graver une estampe, dans laquelle il avoit exprimé avec énergie les différens tourmens qu'on fait éprouver aux animaux. Un charrier fouettoit un jour ses chevaux avec beaucoup de dureté; un bon homme, touché de pitié, lui dit, 'Miserable! tu n'as donc pas vu l'estampe d'*Hogarth*?' Il n'étoit pas seulement peintre, il fut écrivain. Il publia en 1750 un traité en *Anglois*, intitulé, '*Analyse de la Beauté*.' L'auteur pretend que les formes arrondies constituent la beauté du corps: principe vrai à certains égards, faux a plusieurs autres. *Voy*. sur cet artiste, la sécond volume du 'Mercure de France,' Janvier, 1770."

Mr. *Peter Dupont*, a merchant, had the drawing of *Paul before Felix*, which he purchased for 20 guineas, and bound up with a set of *Hogarth's* prints. The whole set was afterwards sold by auction, at *Baker's*, for 17 *l.* to Mr. *Ballard* of *Little Britain*, in whose catalogue it stood some time marked at 25 *l.* and was parted with for less than that sum.

The following original drawings, by *Hogarth*, are now in the collection of the Rev. Dr. *Lort*:

A coloured sketch of a Family Picture, with ten whole-length figures, most insipidly employed. A Head of a Sleeping Child, in colours, as large as life, &c. &c. &c.

When *Hogarth* designed the print intituled *Morning*, his idea of an *Old Maid* appears to have been adopted from one of that forlorn sisterhood, when emaciated by corroding appetites, or, to borrow *Dryden's* more forcible language, by "agony of unaccomplished love." But there is in being, and perhaps in *Leicester-fields*, a second portrait by our artist, exhibiting the influence of the same misfortune on a more fleshy carcase. The ancient virgin[84] now treated of, is corpulent even to shapelessness. Her neck resembles a collar of brawn; and had her arms been admitted on the canvas, they must have rivalled in magnitude the thighs of the *Farnesian* god. Her bosom, luckily for the spectator, is covered; as a display of it would have served only to provoke abhorrence. But what words can paint the excess of malice and vulgarity predominant in her visage!—an inflated hide that seems bursting with venom—a brow wrinkled by a *Sardonic* grin that threatens all the vengeance an affronted Fury would rejoice to execute. Such ideas also of warmth does this mountain of quaggy flesh communicate, that, without hyperbole, one might swear she would parch the earth she trod on, thaw a frozen post-boy, or over-heat a glasshouse. "How dreadful," said a bystander, "would be this creature's hatred!" "How much more formidable," replied his companion, "would be her love!"—Such, however, was the skill of *Hogarth*, that he could impress similar indications of stale virginity on features directly contrasted, and force us to acknowledge one identical character in the brim-full and exhausted representative of involuntary female celibacy.

Mr. *S. Ireland* has likewise a sketch in chalk, on blue paper, of *Falstaff* and his companions; two sketches intended for the "Happy Marriage;" a sketch for a picture to shew the pernicious effects of masquerading; sketch of King *George* II. and the royal family; sketch of his present Majesty, taken hastily on seeing the new coinage of 1764; portrait of *Hogarth* by himself, with a palette; of Justice *Welsh*;[85] of Sir *James Thornhill*; of Sir *Edward Walpole*;[86] of his friend *George Lambert*, the landscape-painter; of a boy; of a girl's head, in the character of *Diana*, finished according to *Hogarth's* idea of beauty; of a black girl; and of Governor *Rogers* and his family, a conversation-piece; eleven Sketches from Nature, designed for Mr. *Lambert*; four drawings of conversations at *Button's Coffee-house*; *Cymon* and *Iphigenia*; two black chalk drawings (landscapes) given to Mr. *Kirby* in 1762; three heads, slightly drawn with a pen by *Hogarth*, to exemplify his distinction between *Character* and *Caricature*, done at the desire of Mr. *Townley*, whose son gave them to Dr. *Schomberg*; a landscape in oil: with several other sketches in oil.

The late Mr. *Forrest*, of *York Buildings*, was in possession of a sketch in oil of our Saviour (designed as a pattern for painted glass), together with the original portrait of *Tibson* the Laceman,[87] and several drawings descriptive of the incidents that happened during a five days tour by land and water. The parties were Messieurs *Hogarth, Thornhill* (son of the late Sir *James*), *Scott* (the ingenious landscape-painter of that name), *Tothall*,[88] and *Forrest*. They set out at midnight, at a moment's warning, from the *Bedford Arms* Tavern, with each a shirt in his pocket. They had particular departments to attend to; *Hogarth* and *Scott* made the drawings; *Thornhill* the map; *Tothall* faithfully discharged the joint office of treasurer and caterer; and *Forrest* wrote the journal. They were out five days only; and on the second night after their return, the book was produced, bound, gilt, and lettered, and read at the same tavern to the members of the club then present. Mr. *Forrest* had also drawings of two of the members (*Gabriel Hunt* and *Ben Read*), remarkable fat men, in ludicrous situations. Etchings from all these having been made in 1782, accompanied by the original journal in letter-press, an account of them will appear in the Catalogue under that year.

A transcript of the journal was left in the hands of Mr. *Gostling*,[89] who wrote an imitation of it in *Hudibrastic* verse; TWENTY COPIES only of which having been printed in 1781, as a literary curiosity,[90] I was requested by some of my friends to reprint it at the end of the second edition of this work. It had originally been kept back, in compliment to the writer of the prose journey; but, as that in the mean time had been given to the public by authority, to preserve the Tour in a more agreeable dress cannot, it is presumed, be deemed an impropriety. See the Appendix, N° III.

[1] History of *Westmoreland*, Vol. I. p. 479.

[2] "I must leave you to the annals of Fame," says Mr. *Walker*, the ingenious Lecturer on Natural Philosophy, who favoured me with these particulars, "for the rest of the anecdotes of this great Genius; and shall endeavour to shew you, that his family possessed similar talents, but they were destined, like the wild rose,

"'To waste their sweetness in the desart air.'

"Happy should I be to rescue from oblivion the name of *Ald Hogart*, whose songs and quibbles have so often delighted my childhood! These simple strains of this mountain *Theocritus* were fabricated while he held the plough, or was leading his fewel from the hills. He was as critical an observer of nature as his nephew, for the narrow field he had to view her in: not an incident or an absurdity in the neighbourhood escaped him. If any one was hardy enough to break through any decorum of old and established repute; if any one attempted to over-reach his neighbour, or cast a leering eye at his wife; he was sure to hear himself sung over the whole parish, nay, to the very boundaries of the *Westmoreland* dialect: so that his songs were said to have a greater effect on the manners of his neighbourhood, than even the sermons of the parson himself.

"But his poetical talents were not confined to the incidents of his village. I myself have had the honour to bear a part in one of his plays (I say *one*, for there are several of them extant in MS. in the mountains of *Westmoreland* at this hour). This play was called 'The Destruction of *Troy*.' It was written in metre, much in the manner of *Lopez de Vega*, or the ancient *French* drama; the unities were not too strictly observed, for the siege of ten years was all represented; every hero was in the piece; so that the Dramatis Personæ consisted of every lad of genius in the whole parish. The wooden horse—*Hector* dragged by the heels—the fury of *Diomed*—the flight of *Æneas*—and the burning of the city, were all represented. I remember not what Fairies had to do in all this; but as I happened to be about three feet high at the time of this still-talked-of exhibition, I personated one of these tiny beings. The stage was a fabrication of boards placed about six feet high, on strong posts; the green-room was partitioned off with the same materials; it's cieling was the azure canopy of heaven; and the boxes, pit, and galleries, were laid into one by the Great Author of Nature, for they were the green slope of a fine hill. Despise not, reader, this humble state of the provincial drama; let me tell you, there were more spectators, for three days together, than your three theatres in *London* would hold; and let me add, still more to your confusion, that you never saw an audience half so well pleased.

"The exhibition was begun with a grand procession, from the village to a great stone (dropt by the Devil about a quarter of a mile off, when he tried in vain to erect a bridge across *Windermere*; so the people, unlike the rest of the world, have remained a very good sort of people ever since). I say the procession was begun by the minstrels of five parishes, and were followed by a yeoman on bull-back—you stare!—stop then till I inform you that this adept had so far civilised his bull, that he would suffer the yeoman to mount his back, and even to play upon his fiddle there. The managers besought him to join the procession; but the bull, not being accustomed to much company, and particularly so much applause; whether he was intoxicated with praise; thought himself affronted, and made game of; or whether a favourite cow came across his imagination; certain it was, that he broke out of the procession; erected his tail, and, like another *Europa*, carried off the affrighted yeoman and his fiddle, over hedge and ditch, till he arrived at his own field. This accident rather inflamed than depressed the good humour arising from the procession; and the clown, or jack-pudding of the piece, availed himself so well of the incident, that the lungs and ribs of the spectators were in manifest danger. This character was the most important personage in the whole play: for his office was to turn the most serious parts of the drama into burlesque and ridicule: he was a compound of Harlequin and the Merry

Andrew, or rather the Arch-fool of our ancient kings. His dress was a white jacket, covered with bulls, bears, birds, fish, &c. cut in various coloured cloth. His trowsers were decorated in like manner, and hung round with small bells; and his cap was that of Folly, decorated with bells, and an otter's brush impending. The lath sword must be of great antiquity in this island, for it has been the appendage of a jack-pudding in the mountains of *Westmoreland* time out of mind.

"The play was opened by this character with a song, which answered the double purpose of a play-bill and a a prologue, for his ditty gave the audience a foretaste of the rueful incidents they were about to behold; and it called out the actors, one by one, to make the spectators acquainted with their names and characters, walking round and round till the whole Dramatis Personæ made one great circle on the stage. The audience being thus become acquainted with the actors, the play opened with *Paris* running away with *Helen*, and *Menelaus* scampering after them; then followed the death of *Patroclus*, the rage of *Achilles*, the persuasions of *Ulysses*,&c. &c. and the whole interlarded with apt songs, both serious and comic, all the production of *Ald Hogart*. The bard, however, at this time had been dead some years, and I believe this Fete was a Jubilee to his memory; but let it not detract from the invention of Mr. *Garrick*, to say that his at *Stratford* was but a copy of one forty years ago on the banks of *Windermere*. Was it any improvement, think you, to introduce several *bulls* into the procession instead of one? But I love not comparisons, and so conclude. Yours, &c. ADAM WALKER."

However *Ald Hogart* might have succeeded in the dramatic line, and before a rustic audience, his poems of a different form are every way contemptible. Want of grammar, metre, sense, and decency, are their invariable characteristics. This opinion is founded on a thorough examination of a whole bundle of them, transmitted by a friend since the first publication of this work.

[3] Vir Clarissime, Excusso *Malpighio* intra sex vel plurimum septem septimanas te tamen per totum inconsulto, culpa est in Bibliopolam conferenda, qui adeo festinanter urgebat opus ut moras nectere nequivimus. Utut sit, tamen mihimet adulor me satis recte authoris & verba & mentem cepisse (diligenter enim noctes atque dies opere incubui ne tibi vel ulli regiorum tuorum sodalium molestus forem). Rudiora tamen quorum specimen infra exhibere placuit, & *Italico-Latina*, juxta præceptum tuum, *similia feci* aliter si fecissem, totus fere liber mutationem sul iisset. Authorem tam pueriliter & barbare loquentem nunquam antehac evolvi quod meminerim; faciat ergo lector, ut solent nautæ, qui dum fœtet aqua, nares pilissando comprimunt, spretis enim verbis sensum, si quis est, attendat. Multa (infinita pœnè dixerim) authoris errata emendavi, quædam tamen non animadversa vereor; *Augeæ* enim stabulum non nisi *Hercules* repurgavit.

Partem *Italico* sermone conscriptam præetermitto, istam enim provinciam adornare suscepit Doctor *Pragestee Italus*; quam bene rem gessit, ipse viderit. Menda Typographica, spero, aut nulla, aut levia apparebunt. Tuam tamen & Regiæ Societatis censuram exoptat facilem, Tibi omni studio addictissimus,

"RICHARDUS HOGARTH, ...Preli Curator."

[4] He published "Grammar Disputations; or, an Examination of the eight parts of speech by way of question and answer, *English* and *Latin*, whereby children in a very little time will learn, not only the knowledge of grammar, but likewise to speak and write *Latin*; as I have found by good experience. At the end is added a short Chronological index of men and things of the greatest note, alphabetically digested, chiefly relating to the Sacred and *Roman* History, from the beginning of the World to the Year of Christ 1640, and downwards. Written for the use of schools of *Great-Britain*, by *Richard Hogarth* Schoolmaster, 1712." This little book has also a *Latin* title-page to the same purpose, "Disputationes Grammaticales, &c." and is dedicated, "Scholarchis, Ludimagistris, *et Hypodidascalis Magnæ Britanniæ*."

[5] *Hogart* was the family name, probably a corruption of *Hogherd*, for the latter is more like the local pronunciation than the first. This name disgusted Mrs. *Hogart*; and before the birth of her son, she prevailed upon her husband to liquify it into *Hogarth*. This circumstance was told to me by Mr. *Walker*, who is a native of *Westmoreland*. By Dr. *Morell*, I was informed that his real name was *Hoggard*, or *Hogard*, which, himself altered, by changing *d* into ð, the Saxon *th*.

[6] On what authority this is said, I am yet to learn. The registers of *St. Bartholomew the Great*, and of *St. Bartholomew the Less*, have both been searched for the same information, with fruitless solicitude. The school of *Hogarth's* father, in 1712, was in the parish of *St. Martin's Ludgate*. In the register of that parish, therefore, the births of his children, and his own death, may probably be found.[A]

[A] The register of *St. Martin's Ludgate*, has also been searched to no purpose.

[7] This circumstance has, since it was first written, been verified by a gentleman who has often heard a similar account from one of the *last Head Assay-Masters* at *Goldsmiths-Hall*, who was apprentice to a silversmith in the same street with *Hogarth*, and intimate with him during the greatest part of his life.

[8] Universal Museum, 1764. p. 549. The same kind of revenge, however, was taken by *Verrio*, who, on the cieling of *St. George's Hall* at *Windsor*, borrowed the face of Mrs. *Marriot*, the housekeeper, for one of the Furies.

[9] This picture is noticed in the article *Thornhill*, in the *Biographia Britannica*, where, instead of *Wanstead*, it is called the *Wandsworth* assembly. There seems to be a reference to it in "A Poetical Epistle to Mr. *Hogarth*, an eminent History and Conversation Painter," written *June* 1730, and published by the author (Mr. *Mitchell*), with two other epistles, in 1731, 4to.

> "Large families obey your hand;
> *Assemblies* rise at your command."

Mr. *Hogarth* designed that year the frontispiece to Mr. *Mitchell's* Opera, *The Highland Clans*.

[10] Of all these a more particular account will be given in the Catalogue annexed.

[11] Brother to *Henry Overton*, the well-known publisher of ordinary prints, who lived over against *St. Sepulchre's Church*, and sold many of *Hogarth's* early pieces coarsely copied, as has since been done by *Dicey* in *Bow Church-yard*.

[12] This conceit is borrowed from *Vanloo's* picture of *Colley Cibber*, whose daughter has the same employment.

[13] It appears that Mr. *G.* was dissatisfied with his likeness, or that some dispute arose between him and the painter, who then struck his pencil across the face, and damaged it. The picture was unpaid for at the time of his death. His widow then sent it home to Mr *Garrick*, without any demand.

[14] Afterwards rector of *Crawley* in *Hampshire*; author of "*Ben Mordecai's* Letters," "Confusion worse confounded," and many other celebrated works.

[15] He died of the small-pox, Aug. 12, 1729, and is said, in the "Political State," to have possessed 5000 l. a year. He married a sister of lord *Bateman*, by whom he left a son and two daughters.

[16] I have heard that he continually took sketches from nature as he met with them, and put them into his works; and it is natural to suppose he did so.

[17] See the Catalogue at the end of these Anecdotes. A very considerable number of personalities are there pointed out under the account of each plate in which they are found.

[18] The late Mr *Cole*, of *Milton*, in his copy of these Memoirs, had written against the name of *Bambridge*, "Father to the late attorney of that name, a worthy son of such a father. He lived at *Cambridge*." And in a copy of the first edition on occasion of a note (afterwards withdrawn) which mentioned "Mr. *Baker's* having quarrelled with *Hearne*;" Mr. *Cole* wrote, "Mr. *Baker* quarrelled with no man: he might coolly debate with Mr. *Hearne* on a disputable point.

It is, therefore, a misrepresentation of Mr. *Baker's* private character, agreeable to the petulance of this age."

[19] The wardenship of *The Fleet*, a patent office, was purchased of the earl of *Clarendon*, for 5000 *l.* by *John Huggins*, esq. who was in high favour with *Sunderland* and *Craggs*, and consequently obnoxious to their successors. *Huggins's* term in the patent was for his own life and his son's. But, in *August* 1728, being far advanced in years, and his son not caring to take upon him so troublesome an office, he sold their term in the patent for the same sum it had cost him, to *Thomas Bambridge* and *Dougal Cuthbert*. *Huggins* lived to the age of 90.

[20] Mr. *Rayner*, in his reading on Stat. 2 *Geo.* II. chap. 32. whereby *Bambridge* was incapacitated to enjoy the office of warden of *The Fleet*, has given the reader a very circumstantial account, with remarks, on the notorious breaches of trust, &c. committed by *Bambridge* and other keepers of *The Fleet-Prison*. For this publication, see *Worral's* Bibliotheca Legum by *Brooke*, 1777, p. 16.

"A report from the Committee appointed to enquire into the State of the Gaols of this Kingdom, relating to the *Marshalsea* prison; with the Resolutions of the House of Commons thereupon," was published in 4to. 1729; and reprinted in 8vo, at *Dublin* the same year. It appears by a MS. note of *Oldys*, cited in *British Topography*, vol. I. p. 636, that *Bambridge* cut his throat 20 years after.

[21] *William Huggins*, esq. of *Headly Park, Hants*, well-known by his translation of the *Orlando Furioso* of *Ariosto*. Being intended for holy orders, he was sent to *Magdalen College, Oxford*, where he took the degree of M. A. *April* 30, 1761; but, on the death of his elder brother in 1756, declined all thoughts of entering into the church. He died *July* 2, 1761; and left in MS. a tragedy, a farce, and a translation of *Dante*, of which a specimen was published in the *British Magazine*, 1760. Some flattering verses were addressed to him in 1757, on his version of *Ariosto*; which are preserved in the *Gentleman's Magazine*, vol. XXVII. p. 180; but are not worth copying. The last Mr. *Huggins* left an estate of 2000 *l.* a year to his two sons-in-law *Thomas Gatehouse*, Esq; and Dr. *Musgrave* of *Chinnor*.

[22] Sir *Francis Page's*, "Character," by *Savage*, thus gibbets him to public detestation:

> "Fair Truth, in courts where Justice should preside,
> Alike the Judge and Advocate would guide;
> And these would vie each dubious point to clear,
> To stop the widow's and the orphan's tear;
> Were all, like *Yorke*,[A] of delicate address,

Strength to discern, and sweetness to express,
Learn'd, just, polite, born every heart to gain,
Like *Comyns*[B] mild; like *Fortescue*[C] humane,
All-eloquent of truth, divinely known,
So deep, so clear, all Science is his own.

"Of heart impure, and impotent of head,
In history, rhetoric, ethics, law, unread;
How far unlike such worthies, once a drudge,
From floundering in low cases, rose a Judge.
Form'd to make pleaders laugh, his nonsense thunders,
And on low juries breathes contagious blunders.
His brothers blush, because no blush he knows,
Nor e'er 'one uncorrupted finger shows.'[D]
See, drunk with power, the circuit-lord exprest!
Full, in his eye, his betters stand confest;
Whose wealth, birth, virtue, from a tongue so loose,
'Scape not provincial, vile, buffoon abuse.
Still to what circuit is assigned his name,
There, swift before him, flies the warner—Fame.
Contest stops short, Consent yields every cause
To Cost; Delay endures them, and withdraws.
But how 'scape prisoners? To their trial chain'd,
All, all shall stand condemn'd, who stand arraign'd,
Dire guilt, which else would detestation cause,
Prejudg'd with insult, wondrous pity draws.
But 'scapes e'en Innocence his harsh harangue?
Alas!—e'en Innocence itself must hang;
Must hang to please him, when of spleen possest,
Must hang to bring forth an abortive jest.

"Why liv'd he not ere Star-chambers had fail'd,
When fine, tax, censure, all but law prevail'd;
Or law, subservient to some murderous will,
Became a precedent to murder still?
Yet e'en when portraits did for traitors bleed,
Was e'er the jobb to such a slave decreed,
Whose savage mind wants sophist-art to draw,
O'er murder'd virtue, specious veils of law?

"Why, Student, when the bench your youth admits,
Where, though the worst, with the best rank'd he sits;
Where sound opinions you attentive write,

As once a *Raymond*, now a *Lee* to cite,
Why pause you scornful when he dins the court?
Note well his cruel quirks, and well report.
Let his own words against himself point clear,
Satire more sharp than verse when most severe."

Nor was *Savage* less severe in his prose. On the trial of this unfortunate poet, for the murder of *James Sinclair* in 1727, Judge *Page*, who was then on the bench, treated him with his usual insolence and severity; and, when he had summed up the evidence, endeavoured to exasperate the jury, as Mr. *Savage* used to relate it, with this eloquent harangue: "Gentlemen of the Jury, you are to consider that Mr. *Savage* is a very great man, a much greater man than you or I, gentlemen of the jury; that he wears very fine cloaths, much finer cloaths than you or I, gentlemen of the jury; that he has abundance of money in his pocket, much more money than you or I, gentlemen of the jury: but, gentlemen of the jury, is it not a very hard case, gentlemen of the jury, that Mr. *Savage* should therefore kill you or me, gentlemen of the jury?"

Pope also, *Horace*, B. II. Sat. r, has the following line:

"Hard words or hanging, if your judge be *Page*."

And *Fielding*, in *Tom Jones*, makes *Partridge* say, with great *naiveté*, after premising that judge *Page* was a very brave man, and a man of great wit, "It is indeed charming sport to hear trials on life and death!"

[A] Sir *Philip Yorke*, chief justice of the King's Bench, afterwards lord-chancellor and earl *Hardwicke*.

[B] Sir *John Comyns*, chief baron of the Exchequer.

[C] Hon. *William Fortescue*, then one of the justices of the court of Common Pleas, afterwards master of the Rolls.

[D] "When *Page* one uncorrupted finger shows." D. of WHARTON.

[23] The truth and propriety of these strictures having been disputed by an ingenious correspondent in the *Public Advertiser*, his letter, with remarks on it, is subjoined by way of appendix to the present work. In this place performances of such a length would have interrupted the narrative respecting *Hogarth* and his productions. See Appendix I.

[24] In co'i Banco.

WILLIAM HOGARTH, Plaintiff. JOSHUA MORRIS, Defendant.

Middlesex.

The Plaintiff declares, that on the 20th of *December*, 1727, at *Westminster* aforesaid, Defendant was indebted to him 30 *l.* for painter's work, and for divers materials laid out for the said work; which Defendant faithfully promised to pay when demanded.

Plaintiff also declares, that Defendant promised to pay for the said work and other materials, as much as the same was worth; and Plaintiff in fact says the same was worth other 30 *l.*

Plaintiff also declares for another sum of 30 *l* for money laid out and expended for Defendant's use, which he promised to pay.

The said Defendant not performing his several promises, the Plaintiff hath brought this action to his damage 30 *l.* for which this action is brought.

To which the Defendant hath pleaded *non assumpsit* and thereupon issue is joined.

CASE.

The Defendant is an upholsterer and tapestry-worker, and was recommended to Plaintiff as a person skilful in painting patterns for that purpose; the Plaintiff accordingly came to Defendant, who informing him that he had occasion for a tapestry design of the Element of Earth, to be painted on canvas, Plaintiff told Defendant he was well skilled in painting that way, and promised to perform it in a workmanlike manner; which if he did, Defendant undertook to pay him for it twenty guineas.

Defendant, soon after, hearing that Plaintiff was an engraver, and no painter, was very uneasy about the work, and ordered his servant to go and acquaint Plaintiff what he had heard; and Plaintiff then told the said servant, 'that it was a bold undertaking, for that he never did any thing of that kind before; and that, if his master did not like it, he should not pay for it.'

That several times sending after Plaintiff to bring the same to Defendant's house, he did not think fit so to do; but carried the same to a private place where Defendant keeps some people at work, and there left it. As soon as Defendant was informed of it, he sent for it home, and consulted with his workmen whether the design was so painted as they could work tapestry by it, and they were all unanimous that it was not finished in a workmanlike manner, and that it was impossible for them to work tapestry by it.

Upon this, Defendant sent the painting back to Plaintiff by his servant, who acquainted him, 'that the same did not answer the Defendant's purpose, and that it was of no use to him; but if he would finish it in a proper manner, Defendant would take it, and pay for it.'

Defendant employs some of the finest hands in *Europe* in working tapestry, who are most of them foreigners, and have worked abroad as well as here, and are perfect judges of performances of this kind.

The Plaintiff undertook to finish said piece in a month, but it was near three months before he sent to the Defendant to view it; who, when he saw it, told him that he could not make any use of it, and was so disappointed for want of it, that he was forced to put his workmen upon working other tapestry that was not bespoke, to the value of 200 *l.* which now lies by him, and another painter is now painting another proper pattern for the said piece of tapestry.

To prove the case as above set forth, call Mr. *William Bradshaw*.

To prove the painting not to be performed in a workmanlike manner, and that it was impossible to make tapestry by it, and that it was of no use to Plaintiff, call Mr. *Bernard Dorrider*, Mr. *Phillips*, Mr. *De Friend*, Mr. *Danten*, and Mr. *Pajon*.

By the counsel's memoranda on this brief it appears, that the witnesses examined for the Plaintiff were *Thomas King, Vanderbank, Le Gard, Thornhill,* and *Cullumpton*.

[25] *James Thornhill*, esq. serjeant-painter and history-painter to King *George* I. In *June* 1715, he agreed to paint the cupola of *St. Paul's* church for 4000 *l.* and was knighted in *April* 1720. In a flattering account given of him immediately after his death, which happened *May* 13, 1734, in his 57th year, he is said to have been "the greatest history-painter this kingdom ever produced, witness his elaborate works in *Greenwich-Hospital*, the cupola of *St. Paul's*, the altar-pieces of *All-Souls College* in *Oxford*, and in the church of *Weymouth*, where he was born; a cieling in the palace of *Hampton-Court*, by order of the late Earl of *Halifax:* his other works shine in divers noblemens' and gentlemens' houses. His later years were employed in copying the rich cartoons of *Raphael* in the gallery of *Hampton-Court*, which, though in decay, will be revived by his curious pencil, not only in their full proportions, but in many other sizes and shapes, he in a course of years had drawn them. He was chosen representative in the two last parliaments for *Weymouth*, and having, by his own industry, acquired a considerable estate, re-purchased the seat of his ancestors, which he re-edified and embellished. He was not only by patents appointed history-painter to their late and present majesties, but serjeant-painter, by which he was to paint all the royal palaces, coaches, barges, and the royal navy. This late patent he surrendered in favour of his only son *John Thornhill*, Esq. He left no other issue but one daughter, now the wife of Mr *Wm. Hogarth*, admired for his curious miniature conversation paintings. Sir *James* has left a most valuable Collection of pictures and other curiosities."

[26] He was called on this occasion, in the Craftsman, "Mr. *Hogarth*, an ingenious designer and engraver."

[27] "*Pope* published in 1731 a poem called *False Taste*, in which he very particularly and severely criticises the house, the furniture, the gardens, and the entertainments of *Timon*, a man of great wealth and little taste. By *Timon* he was universally supposed, and by the Earl of *Burlington*, to whom the poem is addressed, was privately said to mean the Duke of *Chandos*; a man perhaps too much delighted with pomp and shew, but of a temper kind and beneficent, and who had consequently the voice of the publick in his favour. A violent outcry was therefore raised against the ingratitude and treachery of *Pope*, who was said to have been indebted to the patronage of *Chandos* for a present of a thousand pounds, and who gained the opportunity of insulting him by the kindness of his invitation. The receipt of the thousand pounds *Pope* publickly denied; but from the reproach which the attack on a character so amiable brought upon him, he tried all means of escaping. The name of *Cleland* was employed in an apology, by which no man was satisfied; and he was at last reduced to shelter his temerity behind dissimulation, and endeavour to make that disbelieved which he never had confidence openly to deny. He wrote an exculpatory letter to the Duke, which was answered with great magnanimity, as by a man who accepted his excuse without believing his professions. He said, that to have ridiculed his taste, or his buildings, had been an indifferent action in another man; but that in *Pope*, after the reciprocal kindness that had been exchanged between them, it had been less easily excused." *Dr. Johnson, in his Life of Pope.*

[28] That Sir *John Gonson* took a very active part against the Ladies of Pleasure, is recorded by more than one of their votaries: In "A View of the Town, 1735," by Mr. *T. Gilbert*, a fellow of *Peter House Cambridge*, and an intimate companion of *Loveling*,[A] I meet with these lines:

> "Though laws severe to punish guilt were made,
> What honest man is of these laws afraid?
> All felons against judges will exclaim,
> As harlots startle at a *Gonson's* name."

The magistrate entering with his myrmidons was designed as the representative of this gentleman, whose vigilance on like occasions is recorded in the following elegant Sapphic Ode, by Mr. *Loveling*. This gentleman was educated at *Winchester-school*, became a commoner of *Trinity College, Oxford*, was ordained deacon, lived gaily, and died young. His style, however, appears to have been formed on a general acquaintance with the language of *Roman* poetry; nor do any of his effusions betray that poverty of expression so conspicuous in the poems of *Nicholas Hardinge*, esq. who writes as if *Horace* was the only classic author he had ever read.

Ad *Johannem Gonsonum*, Equitem.

Pellicum, *Gonsone*, animosus hostis,
Per minus castas *Druriæ* tabernas
Lenis incedens, abeas *Diones*
Æquus alumnis!
Nuper (ah dictu miserum!) *Olivera*
Flevit ereptas viduata mœchas,
Quas tuum vidit genibus minores
Ante tribunal.
Dure, cur tantâ in *Veneris* ministras
Æstuas irâ? posito furore
Huc ades, multà & prece te vocantem
Gratior audi!
Nonne sat mœchas malè feriatas
Urget infestis fera sors procellis?
Adderis quid tu ulterior puellis
Causa doloris?
Incolunt, eheu! thalamos supernos,
Nota quæ sedes fuerat Poetis;
Nec domum argento gravis, ut solebat,
Dextra revertit.
Nympha quæ nuper nituit theatro,
Nunc stat obscuro misera angiportu,
Supplici vellens tunicam rogatque
Voce *Lyæum*.
Te voco rebus *Druriæ* mentis;
Voci communi *Britonum* Juventus
Te vocat, nunc ô! dare te benignum
Incipe votis.
Singulum tunc dona feret lupanar:
Liberum mittet *Rosa* Lusitanum,
Gallici *Haywarda* et generosa mittet
Munera *Bacchi*.
Sive te forsan moveat libido,
Aridis pellex requiescet ulnis,
Callida effœtas renovare lento
Verbere vires.

The same poet, speaking of the exhilarating effects of Gin, which had just been an object of Parliamentary notice, has the following stanza:

Utilis mœchae fuit & Poetæ;
Sprevit hinc Vates Dolopum catervas,
Mœcha *Gonsonum* tetricâ minantem
Fronte laborem.

Thus, between the poet and the painter, the fame of our harlot-hunting Justice is preserved. But as a slave anciently rode in the same chariot with the conqueror, the memory of a celebrated street-robber and highwayman will descend with that of the magistrate to posterity, *James Dalton's* wig-box being placed on the tester of the Harlot's bed. I learn from the *Grubstreet Journal*, that he was executed on the 12th of *May*, 1730. Sir *John Gonson* died *January* 9, 1765. He was remarkable for the charges which he used to deliver to the grand juries, which are said to have been written by Orator *Henley*. The following puffs, or sneers, concerning them, are found in the first number of the *Grubstreet Journal*, dated *January* 8, 1730. "Yesterday began the General Quarter Sessions, &c. when Sir *John Gonson*, being in the chair, gave a most *incomparable, learned,* and *fine* charge to the Grand Jury." *Daily Post.*

"The *Morning Post* calls Sir *John's* charge *excellent, learned* and *loyal*. The *Evening Post* calls it an *excellent lecture* and *useful charge.*"

Three of these performances had been published in 1728.[B] Sir *John's* name is also preserved in Mr *Pope's* works:

> "Talkers I've learn'd to bear: *Motteux* I knew;
> *Henley* himself I've heard, and *Budgell* too.
> The Doctor's wormwood style, the hash of tongues
> A pedant makes, the storm of *Gonson's* lungs."
> Fourth Sat. of Dr. *Donne* versified.

[A] In the collection of *Loveling's* Poems, 1741, are two by *Gilbert. Loveling* also addressed a poem, not printed in his works, "*Gilberto suo,*" and in *Gilbert's* Poems, published 1747, is "A familiar Epistle to my friend *Ben Loveling.*"

[B] One charge by Sir *John Gonson* is in the Political State, vol. XXXV. p. 50; and two others in vol. XXXVI. pp 314. 333.

[29] It was customary in *Hogarth's* family to give these fans to the maids.

[30] Among the small articles of furniture in the scenes of *Hogarth*, a few objects may speedily become unintelligible, because their archetypes, being out of use, and of perishable natures, can no longer be found. Such is the *Dare for Larks* (a circular board with pieces of looking-glass inserted in it), hung up over the chimney-piece of the *Distress'd Poet*; and the *Jews Cake* (a dry tasteless biscuit perforated with many holes, and formerly given away in great quantities at the Feast of Passover), generally used only as a fly-trap, and hung up as such against the wall in the sixth plate of the *Harlot's Progress.* I have frequently met with both these articles in mean houses.

[31] The fire began at the house of Mrs. *Calloway*, who kept a brandy-shop. This woman was committed to *Newgate*, it appearing among other circumstances, that she had threatened "to be even with the landlord for

having given her warning, and that she would have a bonfire on the 20th of *June*, that should warm all her rascally neighbours."

[32] *Hogarth* attempted to improve it, but without much success. The additional figures are quite episodical. See the Catalogue.

[33] In *Seymour's* history of *London*, vol. II. p. 883. is the following notice of our artist:

"Among the Governors of *St. Bartholomew's Hospital*, was lately chosen Mr. *William Hogarth* the celebrated printer, who, we are told, designs to paint the stair-case of the said hospital, and thereby become a benefactor to it, by giving his labour gratis."

[34] He bought up great quantities of the copies of his works; and they still remain in possession of his widow. The "Harlot's" and the "Rake's" Progress, in a smaller size than the original, were published, with his permission, by *Thomas Bakewell*, a printseller, near the *Horn Tavern, Fleet-street.*

[35] Of the *Harlot's Progress* I have seen no less than eight piratical imitations.

[36] *Lord Gardenston*, one of the lords of session in *Scotland*, on delivering his opinion in the court of session upon the question of literary property, in the cause of *Hinton* and *Donaldson* and others, all booksellers, in *July* 1773 thus introduced the works of *Hogarth*: "There is nothing can be more similar than the work of engraving is to literary composition. I will illustrate this proposition by the works of Mr *Hogarth*, who, in my humble opinion, is the only true original artist which this age has produced in *England*. There is hardly any character of an excellent author, which is not justly applicable to his works. What composition, what variety, what sentiment, what fancy, invention, and humour, we discover in all his performances! In every one of them an entertaining history, a natural description of characters, and an excellent moral. I can read his works over and over, *Horace's* characteristic of excellency in writing, *decies repetita placebit*; and every time I peruse them, I discover new beauties, and feel fresh entertainment: can I say more in commendation of the literary compositions of a *Butler* or a *Swift?* There is great authority for this parallel; the legislature has considered the works of authors and engravers in the same light; they have granted the same protection to both; and it is remarkable, that the act of parliament for the protection of those who invent new engravings, or prints, is almost in the same words with the act for the protection and encouragement of literary compositions." This is taken from a 4to pamphlet, published in 1774 by *James Boswell*, esq. advocate, one of the counsel in the cause.

[37] "That *Huggins* penned the statute, I was told by Mr. *Hogarth* himself. The determination of Lord *Hardwicke* was thus occasioned. *Jefferys*, the printseller at the corner of *St. Martin's Lane*, had employed an artist to draw and engrave

a print representing the *British* Herring Fishery; and, having paid him for it, took an assignment of the right to the property in it accruing to the artist by the act of parliament. The proprietors of one of the magazines pirated it in a similar size, and *Jefferys* brought his bill for an injunction, to which the defendants demurred: and, upon argument of the demurrer, the same was allowed, for the reason abovementioned, and the bill dismissed. *Hogarth* attended the hearing; and lamented to me that he had employed *Huggins* to draw the act, adding, that, when he first projected it, he hoped it would be such an encouragement to engraving and printselling, that printsellers would soon become as numerous as bakers' shops; which hope, notwithstanding the above check, does at this time seem to be pretty nearly gratified." *For this note my readers are indebted to Sir* John Hawkins.

[38] "What Caricatura is in painting," says *Fielding*, "Burlesque is in writing; and in the same manner the comic writer and painter correlate to each other. And here I shall observe, that as in the former the painter seems to have the advantage; so it is in the latter infinitely on the side of the writer: for the Monstrous is much easier to paint than describe, and the Ridiculous to describe than paint. And though perhaps this latter species doth not in either science so strongly affect and agitate the muscles as the other; yet it will be owned, I believe, that a more rational and useful pleasure arises to us from it."

[39] This idea originally occurred in *Colley Cibber's Apology*. From thence it was transplanted by *Lloyd* into his celebrated poem intituled *The Actor*. Lying thus in the way of *Garrick*, he took it up for the use of the *prologue* already quoted. Lastly, Mr. *Sheridan*, in his beautiful *Monody*, condescended to borrow it, only because it spared him the labour of unlocking the richer storehouse of his own imagination.

I may however remark that *Cibber*, when he suggested this mortifying reflection, had more reason on his side than some of his successors who have indulged themselves in the same dolorous strain of complaint. To whatever oblivion the celebrated actors of the last age have been resigned, the pencil of *Hogarth, Dance, Zoffani,* and *Reynolds*, had left Mr. *Garrick* not the slightest reason to be apprehensive that, in his own particular case, the art and the artist would alike be forgotten. Meanwhile, let our heroes of the stage be taught to moderate their anxiety for posthumous renown, by a recollection that their peculiar modes of excellence will, at least, be as well preserved to futurity as those of the lords *Chatham* and *Mansfield*, whose talents, perhaps, might support an equal claim to perpetuation.

[40] Dr. *M.* once observed to *J. N.* in a letter on this subject, "In the 13th chapter I was somewhat puzzled with the *flat* and *round*, or the *concave* and *convex*, appearing the reverse; till the sun happily shining in upon the cornice,

I had a fair example of what he intended to express. The next chapter, with regard to *colouring*, did not go on quite so smooth; for, if I satisfied *him*, I was not satisfied *myself* with his peculiar principles; nor could I relish his laying the blame on the *colourmen*, &c."

[41] One exception to this remark occurs in the *Gentleman's Magazine* for 1754, p. 14; where the reviewer of the Analysis observes, that it is "a book written with that precision and perspicuity which can only result from a perfect knowledge of his subject in all its extent. His rules are illustrated by near two hundred figures, engraved by himself; the knowledge which it contains is universally useful, and as all terms of art are avoided, the language will be universally understood. The player and the dancing-master, whom others consider as patterns of just action and genteel deportment, are not less instructed than the statuary and the painter; nor is there any species of beauty or elegance that is not here investigated and analysed.

"A book, by which the author has discovered such superiority, could scarce fail of creating many enemies; those who admit his Analysis to be just, are disposed to deny that it is new. Though in the year 1745, having drawn a serpentine line on a painter's pallet, with these words under it, 'the line of beauty,' as a frontispiece to his prints, no *Egyptian* hieroglyphic ever produced greater variety of speculation; both painters and sculptors then came to enquire the meaning of a symbol, which they soon pretended to have been their old acquaintance; though the account they could give of its properties were scarce so satisfactory as that of a day-labourer, who constantly uses the *lever*, could give of that instrument, as a mechanical power. The work, however, will live when these cavils are forgotten; and except the originals, of which it is pretended to be a copy, are produced, there is no question but that the name of the author will descend to posterity with that honour which competitors only can wish to withhold."

It should be observed, however, that the general decision on *Hogarth's* performance may be just. Certain we are, that it has not been reversed by the opinion of the First of our Modern Painters.

[42] The *Analysis* itself however affords sufficient specimens of inaccuracy in spelling. Thus we have (pref. p. xix.) *Syclamen* instead of *Cyclamen*; (p. 44.) calc*i*donian for C*h*alcedonian; (p. 65.) nuckles for *k*nuckles; (p. 97.) Iris*h*-stitch for Iris-stitch, &c. &c. In the sheets that contain these errors, it is easy to conceive that *Hogarth* must have been his own corrector of the press.

[43] It is so extraordinary for an illiterate person to ridicule inaccuracy of spelling, that this might probably be a real blunder.

[44] Some account of this work will be given in a future page.

[45] See a note on *Marriage-a-la-Mode* (under the year 1745); from whence it sufficiently appears, that *indelicacies*, &c. had been imputed to *Hogarth's* performances, and that, therefore, when he advertised the six plates of *Marriage-a-la-Mode*, he thought it necessary to assure the public that no *indelicacy, indecency,* or *personality,* would be found in any of these representations.

[46] The exigence of this card having been doubted, it is engraved in our title-page, from the original now in *Charles Street, Grosvenor Square*, in the possession of Dr. *Wright*.

[47] This pun reminds us of a similar one from *Garth* to *Rowe*, who making repeated use of his snuff-box, the *Doctor* at last sent it to him with the two *Greek* letters written on the lid, Φ, ϱ, (*Phi, Ro*). At this the sour *Dennis* was so provoked, as to declare, that "a man who could make such a vile pun, would not scruple to pick a pocket."

[48] The cat spitting at the dog is a circumstance in the fourth plate of *Industry and Idleness*, where it is naturally introduced. The dog attends on a porter who is bringing in goods; and the warehouse cat, who considers this animal as an invader, is preparing to defend her person and premises.

[49] When this ample, nay, redundant, apology by Dr. *Joseph Warton* first made its appearance, *Hogarth* was highly delighted with as much of it as he understood. But, not knowing the import of the word ΗθΟΣ [Greek: Ethos], he hastened to his friends for information. All, in their turn, sported with his want of skill in the learned languages; first telling him it was Greek for one strange thing, and then for another, so that his mind remained in a state of suspence; as, for aught he knew to the contrary, some such meaning might lie under these crooked letters, as would overset the compliments paid him in the former parts of the paragraph. No short time, therefore, had passed before he could determine whether he ought to retract or continue his charge against his adversary: but it was at last obliterated. For several months afterwards, however, poor *Hogarth* never praised his provision or his wine, without being asked what proportion of the ΗθΟΣ [Greek: Ethos] he supposed to be in either.

[50] An engraving from this picture may be expected from Mr. *Livesay*.

[51] A polite gentleman, of great learning, and much esteemed. He had some good pictures, and a very fine library, in the great house at *Peckham* (formerly inhabited by Lord *Trevor*), which, together with a considerable estate there, was bequeathed to him by his aunt Mrs. *Hill*.

[52] See the names of the purchasers, and prices of this collection, in the *Gentleman's Magazine*, 1758, p. 225.

[53] He painted the heart from an injected one provided for him by *Cæsar Hawkins* the surgeon; and, on the authority of repeated inspection, I venture to affirm, that the fingers of *Sigismunda* are unstained with blood, and that neither of her hands is employed in rending ornaments from her head, or any other part of her person. In this instance Mr. *Walpole's* memory must have failed him, as I am confident that his misrepresentation was undesigned. It is whispered (we know not with how much truth) that Mrs. *H.* was hurt by this description of the picture, and that she returned no thanks for the volume that contains it, when it was sent to her as a present by its author. It should seem that she still designs to dispose of this ill-fated performance, and thinks that its reputation required no additional blast.

I have reprinted this note, without correction, that I might thereby obtain the fairer opportunity of doing justice to Mr. *Walpole*, concerning the faithfulness of whose memory I had ventured to express a doubt. Genuine information is not always to be had; nor shall I hesitate a moment to apologize for the fallaciousness of mine. The fingers of *Sigismunda* were *originally* stained with blood. This indelicate and offensive circumstance was pointed out by some intelligent friend to *Hogarth*, who reluctantly effaced it.

A correspondent, however, on reading this work, has furnished an additional reason why the lady already mentioned may be offended by the severity of Mr. *Walpole's* strictures on *Sigismunda*. "It has been whispered that Count *Guiscard's* widow was a copy from the *daughter of Sir James Thornhill*. If this circumstance be true, the very accomplished Critick of *Strawberry Hill* will own at least that her wrath and *Juno's* had the same provocation, '*Judiciam Paridis, spretæque injuria formæ.*' Impartiality, however, obliges us to add, that Mrs. *Hogarth*, though in years, is still a very fine woman; and that Mr. *Walpole's* idea of what a picture of *Sigismunda* ought to express, is poetically conceived, and delivered with uncommon elegance and force of language. The *sober grief*, the *dignity of suppressed anguish*, the *involuntary tear*, the *settled meditation on the fate she meant to meet*, and the *amorous warmth turned holy by despair*, are words that fill the place of colours, supply all the imperfections of *Hogarth's* design, and succeed even where a *Furino* or a *Correggio* may have failed."

[54] This circumstance was ridiculed in a grotesque print, called *A Harlot blubbering over a bullock's heart. By William Hogart.*

[55] "Many causes may vitiate a writer's judgement of his own works. On that which has cost him much labour he sets a high value, because he is unwilling to think that he has been diligent in vain; what has been produced without toilsome efforts is considered with delight, as a proof of vigorous faculties and fertile invention; and the last work, whatever it be, has necessarily most of the grace of novelty. *Milton*, however it happened, had this prejudice, and had it to himself." Dr. JOHNSON.

[56] *Sigismunda*, however, though she missed of judicious admirers, had, at least, the good fortune to meet with a flatterer in the late Mr. *Robert Lloyd*, whose poem intituled *Genius, Envy*, and *Time*, addressed to *William Hogarth*, esq. has the following lines. *Time* is the speaker.

> "While *Sigismunda's* deep distress
> Which looks the soul of wretchedness,
> When I, with slow and softening pen,
> Have gone o'er all the tints agen,
> Shall urge a bold and proper claim,
> To level half the ancient fame;
> While future ages, yet unknown,
> With critic air shall proudly own
> Thy *Hogarth* first of every clime
> For humour keen, or strong sublime, &c."

It is but justice, on one hand, to add, that when *Lloyd* wrote this eulogium, he was not yet enlisted under the banners of fashion; but impartiality, on the other hand, requires we should observe that, having, like *Hogarth*, seen few pictures by the best masters, he was treating of an art he did not understand.

The authors of the *Monthly Review* are of opinion, that *Mr. Walpole* speaks too contemptuously of *Sigismunda*, and that there is no ground for the insinuation that the person for whom it was painted thought meanly of it. "We have in our possession (say they) a letter to *Hogarth* from the noble person referred to, in which he expresses himself in the following terms;—*I really think the performance so striking and inimitable, that the constantly having it before one's eyes, would be often occasioning melancholy ideas to arise in one's mind, which, a curtain being drawn before it, would not diminish in the least.*" Surely this epistle, if genuine, was ironical. Or shall we suppose that, afterwards, his lordship only saw the picture through the disgusting medium of the price? Mr. *Wilkes's* opinion of the piece will be best conveyed in his own words, which are therefore copied in note 65, below.

Dr. *Morell*, an intimate friend of Mr. *Hogarth*, who was applied to for information, returned for answer: "His excellencies, as well as his foibles, are so universally known, that I cannot add to the former, and would not, if I could, to the latter. I should think we lived in a very ill-natured world, if the whims and follies in a man's life were to be exposed, and his oddities and mistakes, *ubi plura nitent*, seriously condemned. But the unhappy affair of *Sigismunda* requires animadversion. And I will venture to say that even this *Sigismunda* would not have deserved so many hard things as have been said of it, if Mr. *Hogarth* had timely and properly observed the caution—*Manum de Tabula*. But it was so altered, upon the criticism of one Connoisseur or another; and especially when, relying no longer upon strength of genius, he had recourse to the *feigned* tears and *fictitious* woe of a female friend; that, when it appeared at the exhibition, I scarce knew it again myself, and from a passable picture it became little better than the wretched figure here represented. In my opinion, I never saw a finer resemblance of flesh and blood, while the canvas was warm, I mean *wet*; but, like that of real flesh, as soon as it was chilled, the beauty wore off. And this, he said, could not be helped, as no colours, but those of pure nature, as *ultramarine*, &c. would keep their natural brightness. But it is granted that colouring was not Mr. *Hogarth's* forte; and the subject we are upon is a disagreeable one."

[57] The first sketch in oil for *Sigismunda*, and a drawing from the finished picture, are in the possession of Mr. *Samuel Ireland*.

[58] At the Club of Artists, it was not unusual to reproach *Hogarth* with want of due attention to the Ancients, whom he always affected to despise. It accidentally happened that Mr. *Basire*, whilst this plate was in hand, was employed likewise in engraving, for the Society of Antiquaries, two plates of an antique bronze from the collection of Mr. *Hollis*, so remarkably grotesque, that Mr. *Hogarth* very readily consented that his plate should be postponed, and declared, "he could not have imagined that the Ancients had possessed so much humour."

[59] Some subscriptions were actually received, and the money returned. The munificient Mr. *Hollis*, who was one of the subscribers, refused to take back what he had paid; and it was given by Mr. *Basire* to a public charity.

[60] Two other little pieces are ascribed to him; the distich under the subscription-ticket for his *Sigismunda*, 1761,

> 'To Nature and yourself appeal;
> Nor learn of others how to feel.'

And the following well-known Epigram:

> "Your servant, Sir," says surly *Quin*,
> "Sir, I am yours," replies *Macklin*,
> "Why, you're the very *Jew* you play,
> Your face performs the task well."
> "And you are *Sir John Brute*, they say,
> And an accomplished *Maskwell*."
> Says *Rich*, who heard the sneering elves,
> And knew their horrid hearts;
> "Acting too much your very selves,
> You overdo your parts."[A]

[A] The censure contained in these poor lines is eminently unjust. *Macklin* is known to have been an anxious and affectionate parent, and *Quin* a benevolent and liberal friend.

[61] On what account I know not, but he had then forborn painting for more than a year.

[62] See hereafter, note 65.

[63] In the Beauties of all the Magazines, 1773, p. 440, is a droll "Epistle from *Jacob Henriques*, born anno Domini, &c. to Messieurs *Hogarth* and *Churchill* greeting."

[64] For this the Satirist unmercifully apologizes in the conclusion of his poem, which may be seen in the Catalogue, under the year 1763, in a note on N° 2.

[65] As much of this paper as relates to our artist is here subjoined:

"The humourous Mr. *Hogarth*, the *supposed* author of the *Analysis of Beauty*, has at last entered the list of politicians, and given us a print of *The Times*. *Words are man's province*, says *Pope*; but they are not Mr. *Hogarth's* province. He somewhere mentions his being indebted to a friend for a third part of the *wording*: that is his phrase. We all titter the instant he takes up a *pen*, but we tremble when we see the *pencil* in his hand. I will do him the justice to say, that he possesses the rare talent of gibbetting in colours, and that in most of his works he has been a very good moral satirist. His forte is there, and he should have kept it. When he has at any time deviated from *his own peculiar walk*, he has never failed to make himself perfectly ridiculous. I need only make my appeal to any one of his *historical* or *portrait* pieces, which are now considered as almost beneath all criticism. The favourite *Sigismunda*, the labour of so many years, the boasted effort of his art, was not *human*. If the figure had a resemblance of any thing ever on earth, or had the least pretence to meaning or expression, it was what he had seen, or perhaps made, in real life, his own wife in an agony of passion; but of what passion no connoisseur could guess. All his friends remember what tiresome discourses were held by him day after day about the transcendent merit of it, and how the great names of *Raphael*, *Vandyke*, and others, were made to yield the palm of beauty, grace, expression, &c. to him, for this long laboured, yet still, *uninteresting*, single figure. The value he himself set on this, as well as on some other of his works, almost exceeds belief; yet from politeness or fear, or some other motives, he has actually been paid the most astonishing sums, as the price, not of his merit, but of his unbounded vanity.

"The darling passion of Mr. *Hogarth* is to shew the *faulty* and *dark* side of every object. He never gives us in perfection the *fair face of nature*, but admirably well holds out her deformities to ridicule. The reason is plain. All objects are painted on his *retina* in a grotesque manner, and he has never felt the force of what the *French* call *la belle nature*. He never caught a single idea of beauty, grace, or elegance; but, on the other hand, he never missed the least flaw in almost any production of nature or of art. This is his true character. He has succeeded very happily in the way of humour, and has miscarried in every other attempt. This has arisen in some measure from his head, but much more from his heart. After *Marriage à la Mode*, the public wished for a series of prints of a *happy* marriage. *Hogarth* made the attempt, but the rancour and malevolence of his mind made him very soon turn with envy and disgust from objects of so pleasing contemplation, to dwell and feast a bad heart on others of a hateful cast, which he pursued, for he found them congenial, with the most unabating zeal, and unrelenting gall.

"I have observed some time his *setting sun*. He has long been very *dim*, and almost *shorn of his beams*. He seems so conscious of this, that he now glimmers with *borrowed light*. *John Bull's house in flames* has been hackney'd in fifty different prints; and if there is any merit in the figure on stilts, and the mob prancing around, it is not to be ascribed to *Hogarth*, but to *Callot*. That spirited *Italian*, whom the *English* painter has so carefully studied, has given us in the *Balli di Sfessania di Jacomo Callot*, the very same ideas, but infinitely more ludicrous in the execution. The piece is *Smaraolo cornuto. Ratsa di Boio. The Times* must be confessed destitute of every kind of original merit. The print at first view appears too much crouded with figures; and is in every part confused, perplexed, and embarrassed. The *story is not well told to the eye*; nor can we any where discover the faintest ray of that genius, which with a few strokes of the pencil enabled us to penetrate into the deepest recesses of thought, and even caprice, in a *rake*, a *harlot*, and a *profligate young man of quality*.

"I own too that I am grieved to see the genius of *Hogarth*, which should take in all ages and countries, sunk to a level with the miserable tribe of party-etchers, and now, in his rapid decline, entering into the poor politics of the faction of the day, and descending into low personal abuse, instead of instructing the world, as he could once, by manly moral satire. Whence can proceed so surprizing a change? Is it the frowardness of old age? Or is it that envy and impatience of resplendent merit in every way, at which he has always sickened? How often has he been remarked to droop at the fair and honest applause given even to a friend, though he had particular obligations to the very same gentleman! What wonder then that some of the most respectable characters of the age become the objects of his ridicule? It is sufficient that the rest of mankind applaud; from that moment he begins the attack, and you never can be well with him, till he hears an universal outcry against you, and till all your friends have given you up. There is besides a silly affectation of singularity, joined to a strong desire of leading the rest of the world: when that is once found impracticable, the spleen engendered on such an occasion is discharged at a particular object, or ends in a general misanthropy. The public never had the least share of *Hogarth's* regard, or even good-will. *Gain* and *vanity* have steered his little bark quite through life. He has never been consistent but with respect to those two principles. What a despicable part has he acted with regard to the society of *Arts and Sciences*! How shuffling has his conduct been to the whole body of *Artists*! Both these useful societies have experienced the most ungenteel and offensive behaviour from him. There is at this hour scarcely a single man of any degree of merit in his own profession, with whom he does not hold a professed enmity. It is impossible the least degree of friendship could ever subsist in this intercourse of the arts with him; for his insufferable vanity will never allow the least merit in another, and no man of a liberal turn of mind will ever condescend to feed his pride with the gross and fulsome praise he expects, or to burn the incense he claims, and indeed snuffs like a most gracious god. To this he joins no small share of jealousy; in consequence of which, he has all his life endeavoured to suppress rising merit, and has been very expert in every mean underhand endeavour, to extinguish the least spark of genuine fire. Rut all *genius* was not born, nor will die, with Mr. *Hogarth*: and notwithstanding all his ungenerous efforts to damp or chill it in another, I will trust to a discerning and liberal spirit in the *English* nation, to patronize and reward all real merit. It will in the end rise superior to the idle laugh of the hour, which these triflers think it the highest praise to be able to raise. For my part, I scarcely know a more profligate principle, than the indiscriminately sacrificing every thing, however great or good, to the dangerous talent of ridicule; and a man, whose sole object is *dummodo risum excutiat*, ought to be avoided as the worst pest of society, as the *enemy* most to be feared, I mean a treacherous *friend*. Such a man will go all lengths to raise a laugh at your expence, and your whole life will be made miserable from his ambition of diverting the company for half an hour.

"I love to trace the ideas of a Genius, and to mark the progress of every art. Mr. *Hogarth* has heard much of the *cobwebs* of the law, and the *spinning fine spider-webs*, &c. This is thrown on paper, and the idea carefully treasured. Lord *Hardwicke* being at the head of the law, and deservedly in as high esteem with his countrymen as any man who ever held the seals, unspotted in life, and equally revered by prince and people, becomes an excellent subject for the satirical pencil of a malevolent painter. He is accordingly emblematically represented by Mr. *Hogarth* as a great spider in a large, thick web, with myriads of the carcases of *flies, clients* I suppose, sucked to death by the gloomy tyrant. Mr. *Hogarth* had heard of Mr. *Pitt's* being *above* all his fellow-citizens, and of his superior virtue having *raised* him to an envied and dangerous *height* of grandeur. Now this he has taken literally, and, with the kind aid of *Callot*, has put Mr. *Pitt* on stilts, and made the people *look up* to him; which, after all this insipid ridicule, they will continue to do, as a kind of tutelar deity, from whom they expect that security and those blessings they despair of from others. As to the conceit of the *bellows*, to signify, I suppose, Mr. *Pitt's* endeavours to blow up the flames of war and discord, it is at once very poor and very false. His whole conduct the last session in parliament, and out of the house ever since, has demonstrated the contrary: *neque vero hoc* oratione *solum, sed multo magis* vitâ *et* moribus *comprobavit*. Cic. de Fin.

"Lord *Temple* is a nobleman of fine parts and unsullied honour, who has shewn a thorough disinterestedness, a great love of liberty, and a steady attachment to the public, in every part of his conduct through life. It was impossible such a character could be missed by the poisonous shafts of envy, which we see pointed at all superior virtue.... Mr. *Hogarth's* wit on this noble lord is confined to the wretched conceits of the *Temple Coffee-house*, and a *squirt* to signify the *playing on* the ministry. I really believe this wit is all Mr. *Hogarth's* own.

"When a man of parts dedicates his talents to the service of his country, he deserves the highest rewards: when he makes them subservient to base purposes, he merits execration and punishment. Among the *Spartans*, music and poetry were made to serve the noblest purposes of the *Lacedemonian* state. A manly courage and great contempt of death were inspired by them; and the poet, musician, soldier, and patriot, were often the same good citizen, who despised the low *mechanic lucre* of the profession, and was zealous only for the glory of his country. In the year 1746, when the *Guards* were ordered to march to *Finchley*, on the most important service they could be employed in, the extinguishing a *Scottish* rebellion, which threatened the intire ruin of the illustrious family on the throne, and, in consequence, of our liberties, Mr. *Hogarth* came out with a print to make them ridiculous to their countrymen and to all *Europe*; or perhaps it rather was to tell the *Scots* in his way how little the Guards were to be feared, and that they might safely advance. That the ridicule might not stop here, and that it might be as offensive as possible to his own *sovereign*, he dedicated the print to the king of *Pru[s]ia*[A] *as an encourager of arts*. Is this patriotism! In old *Rome*, or in any of the *Grecian* states, he would have been punished as a profligate citizen, totally devoid of all principle. In *England* he is rewarded, and made *serjeant* painter to that very king's grandson. I think the term means the same as what is vulgarly called *house*-painter; and indeed he has not been suffered to *caricature* the royal family. The post of portrait-painter is given to a *Scotsman*, one *Ramsay*. Mr. *Hogarth* is only to paint the wainscot of the rooms, or, in the phrase of the art, may be called their *pannel-painter*. But how have the *Guards* offended Mr. *Hogarth*, for he is again attacking them in *The Times?* Lord *Harrington's* second troop of grenadier guards is allowed to be very perfect in every part of military discipline; and *Hogarth's* friend, the king of *Prussia*, could have shewn him the real importance of it. He had heard them much applauded, and therefore must abuse them. The ridicule ends however in airs composed by *Harrington*, and in a piece of *clock-work*; but he ought to have known, that though *l'homme machine* is not sound philosophy, it is the true doctrine of tactics.

"The *Militia* has received so many just testimonies of applause, both from their king and country, that the attack of envy and malevolence was long expected. But I dare say this poor jester will have Mr. *George Townshend's* free consent to vent his spleen upon him and the gentlemen of *Norfolk*. I believe he may ever go on in this way almost unnoticed; at one time ridiculing the *Guards* for a *disorderly*, and at another the *Militia* for an exact and *orderly* march. Mr. *Townshend* will still have the warm applause of his country, and the truest satisfaction, that of an honest heart, for his patriot labours in establishing this great plan of internal defence, a *Militia*, which has delivered us from the ignominy of *foreign hirelings*, and the ridiculous fears of invasion, by a brave and well-disciplined body of *Englishmen*, at all times ready and zealous for the defence of their country, and of its laws and constitution."

[A] This is the orthography of Mr. *Hogarth*. See the print.

[66] The present Lord *Camden*.

[67] This gave rise to a catchpenny, intituled, "*Pug's* Reply to Parson *Bruin*; or, a Political Conference, occasioned by an Epistle to *William Hogarth*, Esq;" 4to.

[68] "Which was probably accelerated by this unlucky (we had almost said unnatural) event; for *Wilkes*, *Churchill*, and *Hogarth*, had been intimate friends, and might have continued such as long as they lived, had not the dæmon of politics and party sown discord among them, and dissolved their union."

[69]—the friend——Dr. *Morell*. The conduct of this gentleman cannot fail to put the reader in mind of *Sir Fretful Plagiary's* complaint in Mr. Sheridan's *Critic*. "—if it is abuse, why one is always sure to hear of it from one damn'd good-natured *friend* or another."

[70]

"While thinking figures from the canvas start,
And *Hogarth* is the *Garrick* of his art,"

is a couplet in *Smart's Hilliad*.

The compliment from the *Hilliad* to Mr. *Hogarth*, Mr. *Smart* observes, "is reciprocal, and reflects a lustre on Mr. *Garrick*, both of them having similar talents, equally capable of the highest elevation, and of representing the ordinary scenes of life with the most exquisite humour."

[71] The pyramid, &c. This stroke of satire was retorted on *Hogarth*, and employed to express his advanced age and declining abilities; while the *Cheshire* cheese, with 3000 *l.* on it, seemed to imply that he himself merited an annual pension.

I received this explanation from an ingenious friend.—The late Mr. *Rogers* explained it thus: "Mr. *Pitt* is represented in it sitting at his ease [in the position of the great Sir *Isaac Newton* in *Westminster-Abbey*], with a mill-stone hanging over his head, on which is written 3000 *l.* in allusion to his saying, that *Hanover* was a mill-stone round the neck of *England*, on account of the expences attending it; and his afterwards adding himself to the public expences by accepting a pension of 3000 *l.* a year. He is firing a mortar-piece levelled at a Dove bearing an olive-branch (the symbol of peace) perched on the standard of *England*; and is supported by the City of *London*, denoted by the two Giants in *Guildhall*. *Hogarth* is flogging *Wilkes* and *Churchill*, and making them dance to the scrapings of a fidler; designed to represent a Nobleman [Earl *Temple*], who patronized them in 1763, and who, for his unmeaning face, has ever been described without a feature. See *Trusler's* Preface, p. vii."

[72] It may be worth observing, that in "Independence," a poem which was not published by *Churchill* till the last week of *September*, 1764, he considers his antagonist as a departed Genius:

"*Hogarth* would draw him (Envy must allow)
E'en to the life, WAS HOGARTH LIVING NOW."

How little did the sportive Satirist imagine that the power of pleasing was so soon to cease in both! *Hogarth* died in four weeks after the publication of this poem; and *Churchill* survived him but nine days. In some lines which were printed in *November* 1764, the compiler of these Anecdotes took occasion to lament that

"———Scarce had the friendly tear,
For *Hogarth* shed, escap'd the generous eye
Of feeling Pity, when again it flow'd
For *Churchill's* fate. Ill can we bear the loss
Of Fancy's twin-born offspring, close ally'd
In energy of thought, though different paths
They sought for fame! Though jarring passions sway'd
The living artists, let the funeral wreath
Unite their memory!"

[73] The *Monthly Reviewer* unintentionally reads *supper*, instead of *dinner*. As to this article of minute intelligence, whether it be true or false, it was communicated by Mrs. *Lewis*.

[74] Mr. *Walpole* once invited *Gray* the Poet and *Hogarth* to dine with him; but what with the reserve of the one, and a want of colloquial talents in the other, he never passed a duller time than between these representatives of *Tragedy* and *Comedy*, being obliged to rely entirely on his own efforts to support conversation.

[75] The most solid praise, perhaps, that ever was given to our artist, was a legacy of 100 *l.* "for the great pleasure the testator had received from his works."

[76] Originally begun for a portrait of Mrs. *Cholmondeley*, but altered, after one or two sittings, to the Queen.

[77] See p. 9.

[78] To whom, in case of Mrs. *Hogarth's* marrying again, he gave the plates of Marriage à la Mode, and of the Harlot's and Rake's Progress.

[79] Whilst the Marshal was a prisoner in *England*, Monsieur *Coetlagon* opened a subscription at two guineas, one to be paid on subscribing, the other on the delivery of "A Dictionary of Arts and Sciences," in two large folio volumes. Many of the nobility, as well as gentry subscribed; but very few of them made good their second payments, or had the work; and the author dedicated it (in gratitude, it is supposed, for the generous patronage he received from the *English*) to Marshal *Belleisle*; whose place of confinement was in *The Round Tower* at *Windsor Castle*; where the large dining-room is still ornamented with a variety of humourous *French* engravings; and a small library of *French* books.

[80] In the year 1768 was published a work, intituled, "*Hogarth* Moralised. Being a complete Edition of *Hogarth's* Works. Containing near Fourscore Copper-Plates, most elegantly engraved. With an Explanation, pointing out the many Beauties that may have hitherto escaped Notice, and a Comment on their Moral Tendency, &c. With the Approbation of *Jane Hogarth*, Widow of the late Mr. *Hogarth*."

The history of the work is as follows: The Rev. *John Trusler* engaged with some engravers in this design, after *Hogarth's* death, when they could carry it into execution with impunity. Mrs. *Hogarth*, finding her property would be much affected by it, was glad to accept an offer they made her, of entering into partnership with them; and they were very glad to receive her, knowing her name would give credit to the publication, and that she would certainly supply many anecdotes to explain the plates. Such as are found in the work are probably all hers. The other stuff was introduced by the editor to eke out the book. We are informed, that, when the undertaking was completed, in order to get rid of her partners, she was glad to buy out their shares, so that the whole expence which fell on her amounted to at least 700 *l.*

[81] "They abound," says an excellent judge, "in true humour; and satire, which is generally well-directed: they are admirable moral lessons, and afford a fund of entertainment suited to every taste: a circumstance, which shews them to be just copies of nature." We may consider them too as valuable repositories of the manners, customs, and dresses of the present age. What amusement would a collection of this kind afford, drawn from every period of the history of *Britain!*—How far the works of *Hogarth* will bear a critical examination, may be the subject of a little more enquiry. In design *Hogarth* was seldom at a loss. His invention was fertile, and his judgement accurate. An improper incident is rarely introduced; a proper one rarely omitted. No one could tell a story better; or make it, in all its circumstances, more intelligible. His genius, however, it must be owned, was suited only to low, or familiar subjects. It never soared above common life: to subjects naturally sublime, or which from antiquity, or other accidents, borrowed dignity, he could not rise. In composition we see little in him to admire. In many of his prints, the deficiency is so great, as plainly to imply a want of all principle; which makes us ready to believe, that when we do meet with a beautiful group, it is the effect of chance. In one of his minor works, the Idle Prentice, we seldom see a crowd more beautifully managed, than in the last print. If the sheriff's officers had not been placed in a line, and had been brought a little lower in the picture, so as to have formed a pyramid with the cart, the composition had been unexceptionable: and yet the first print of this work is so striking an instance of disagreeable composition, that it is amazing, how an artist, who had any idea of beautiful forms, could suffer so unmasterly a performance to leave his hands. Of the distribution of light *Hogarth* had as little knowledge as of composition. In some of his pieces we see a good effect; as in the execution just mentioned; in which, if the figures at the right and left corners had been kept down a little, the light would have been beautifully distributed on the fore-ground, and a little fine secondary light spread over part of the crowd: but at the same time there is so obvious a deficiency in point of effect, in most of his prints, that it is very evident he had no principles. Neither was *Hogarth* a master in drawing. Of the muscles and anatomy of the head and hands he had perfect knowledge; but his trunks are often badly moulded, and his limbs ill set on. I tax him with plain bad drawing; I speak not of the niceties of anatomy, and elegance of outline: of these indeed he knew nothing; nor were they of use in that mode of design which he cultivated: and yet his figures, upon the whole, are inspired with so much life and meaning, that the eye is kept in good humour, in spite of its inclination to find fault. The author of the Analysis of Beauty, it might be supposed, would have given us more instances of grace, than we find in the works of *Hogarth*; which shews strongly that theory and practice are not always united. Many opportunities his subjects naturally afford of introducing graceful attitudes; and yet we have very few examples of them.

With instances of picturesque grace his works abound. Of his expression, in which the force of his genius lay, we cannot speak in terms too high. In every mode of it he was truly excellent. The passions he thoroughly understood, and all the effects which they produce in every part of the human frame: he had the happy art also of conveying his ideas with the same precision with which he conceived them.—He was excellent too in expressing any humorous oddity, which we often see stamped upon the human face. All his heads are cast in the very mould of nature. Hence that endless variety, which is displayed through his works: and hence it is, that the difference arises between his heads, and the affected caricaturas of those masters, who have sometimes amused themselves with patching together an assemblage of features from their own ideas. Such are *Spagniolet's*; which, though admirably executed, appear plainly to have no archetypes in nature. *Hogarth's*, on the other hand, are collections of natural curiosities. The *Oxford-heads*, the physicians-arms, and some of his other pieces, are expressly of this humorous kind. They are truly comic; though ill-natured effusions of mirth: more entertaining than *Spagniolet's*, as they are pure nature; but less innocent, as they contain ill-directed ridicule.—But the species of expression, in which this master perhaps most excels, is that happy art of catching those peculiarities of air, and gesture, which the ridiculous part of every profession contract; and which, for that reason, become characteristics of the whole. His counsellors, his undertakers, his lawyers, his usurers, are all conspicuous at sight. In a word, almost every profession may see, in his works, that particular species of affectation which they should most endeavour to avoid. The execution of this master is well-suited to his subjects, and manner of treating them. He etches with great spirit; and never gives one unnecessary stroke. For myself, I greatly more value the works of his own needle, than those high-finished prints on which he employed other engravers. For as the production of an effect is not his talent; and as this is the chief excellence of high finishing; his own rough manner is certainly preferable; in which we have most of the force and spirit of his expression. The manner in none of his works pleases me so well as in a small print of a corner of a play-house. There is more spirit in a work of this kind, struck off at once, warm from the imagination, than in all the cold correctness of an elaborate engraving. If all his works had been executed in this style, with a few improvements in the compositions, and the management of light, they would certainly have been a much more valuable collection of prints than they are. The Rake's Progress, and some of his other works, are both etched and engraved by himself: they are well done; but it is plain he meant them as furniture. As works designed for a critick's eye, they would certainly have been better without the engraving, except a few touches in a very few places. The want of effect too would have been less conspicuous, which in his highest-finished prints is disagreeably striking." *Gilpin, Essay on Prints,* p. 165.

[82] To whom *Hogarth* bequeathed ten guineas for a ring.

[83] It having been requested in the Catalogue of this exhibition (which was in *Bow-Street, Covent-Garden*) that all remarks on the artists, or their performances, might be sent to *The St. James's Chronicle*; the compiler of these Anecdotes transmitted a few hasty lines, which were printed in that paper *April* 29, 1762. They are not worth transcribing: but a short extract will preserve the ASSUMED names of some of the artists—

> "And *Masmore, Lester's, Ward's,* and *Fishbourne's* name,
> With thine, *Vandyck,* shall live to endless fame;
> In your collection Wit and Skill combine,
> And Humour flows in every well-chose Sign."

[84] She is still living, and has been loud in abuse of this work, a circumstance to which she owes a niche in it.

[85] Among the compliments *Hogarth* was disposed to pay his own genius, he asserted his ability to take a complete likeness in three quarters of an hour. This head of Mr. *Welsh* was painted within the compass of the time prescribed, but had afterwards the advantage of a second sitting.

[86] Mr. *Walpole* is now possessed of the portrait of his brother Sir *Edward*.

[87] This, and the preceding article, are now in the possession of *Peter Coxe*, esq. of *College Hill*, in the city, executor to Mr. *Forrest*, and brother to the Rev. *William Coxe*, who has obliged the world with his Travels through *Poland, Russia*, &c.

[88] The following brief Memoirs of Mr. *William Tothall*, F. A. S. were communicated by Dr. *Ducarel*, who was personally acquainted with Mr. *Tothall*, and received the intelligence in a letter from the Rev. Mr. *Lyon*, Minister of *St. Mary's* at *Dover*, to whom the particulars in it were related by Captain *Bulstrode* of that town.

"*Dover, June* 11, 1781.

"Sir,

"The following narrative of your friend *Tothall* may be depended upon, as Captain *Bulstrode* informs me he frequently heard it from *Tothall* himself. His father was an apothecary in *Fleet-street*; but dying, as Captain *Bulstrode* thinks, while his son was young, and in but indifferent circumstances (as his mother afterwards practised as a midwife), he was taken by an uncle, who was a fishmonger. He lived with his uncle some time; but, not approving of the business, ran away from him, and entered on board a merchant-ship going to *The West Indies*. He also went several times to *Newfoundland*. During the time of his being in *The West Indies*, though so early in life, he was indefatigable in the collecting of shells, and brought home several utterly unknown in *England*. He continued at sea till he was almost 30 years of age. In one of his voyages he was taken by the *Spaniards*, and marched a considerable way up the country, without shoe or stocking, with only a woollen cap on his head, and a brown waistcoat on, with a large staff in his hand. He had afterwards his picture drawn in this dress. He continued a prisoner till exchanged.

"When he was about 30 years of age, he went as shopman to a woollen-draper at the corner of *Tavistock Court, Covent Garden,* with whom he continued some years; and his master, finding him a faithful servant, told him, 'as he dealt only in cloth, and his customers were taylors, he would lend him money to buy shalloons and trimmings, and recommend him to his chapmen, if he liked to take the trouble and the profit of the branch upon himself.' He readily accepted the proposal.

"About the same time an acquaintance in *The West Indies* sent him a puncheon of rum. Before he landed it, he consulted his master what he should do with it; who advised him to sell it out in small quantities, and lent him a cellar in his house. He followed this advice; and, finding the profits considerable, wrote to his correspondent in *The West Indies* to send him another supply; and from this time he commenced rum, brandy, and shalloon merchant.

"I cannot learn how long he continued in this way; but his master having acquired a fortune, and being desirous of retiring from business, left him in possession of his whole stock at prime cost, and he was to pay him as he sold it. He now commenced woollen-draper, and continued in this business till he acquired a sum sufficient, as he thought, to retire upon; and he left his business to his shopman, the late Mr. *Job Ray*, on the same conditions his master left it to him.

"During his residence in *Covent Garden*, he became a member of the club at the *Bedford Coffee-house*, and of course contracted an acquaintance with *Hogarth, Lambert,* and other men eminent in their way; and *Hogarth* lived some time in his house on the footing of a most intimate friend.

"On quitting his business (being troubled with an asthmatical complaint) he came and settled at *Dover*; where, soon becoming connected with certain persons in the smuggling branch, he fitted out a bye-boat, which was designed (as is supposed) to promote their business; but in this branch Fortune, which had hitherto smiled upon his endeavours, now frowned upon his attempts. The vessel, in going over with horses either to *Ostend* or *Flushing*, was lost. This, with some other losses, so reduced him, that he was rather straitened in his circumstances, and he could not live as he had done previous to the losses he sustained.

"His residence was near the Rope-walk at *Dover* (since pulled down), where his old friend *Hogarth* frequently visited him: but being in a decline, and his asthma increasing, he bought a very small cottage at *West Langdon*, about three miles from *Dover*, to which he used to go on horseback. Digging in a very small garden belonging to this cottage, he had the good fortune to find some valuable fossils; which to a man of his taste was a singular treasure. He died *January* 9, 1768, at the age of 70 (possessed of about 1500 *l.*), and was buried at *St. Mary's Church* at *Dover*. His collection of shells and fossils were sold by auction at *Longford's*, the following year.

"The foregoing is the substance of what I have gathered from Capt. *Bulstrode*. If there should be any other particular which you are desirous of knowing, I shall be happy to make the inquiry, and to communicate it; and am, Sir, your most obedient humble servant,

"J. LYON."

[89] *William Gostling*, M. A. a minor canon of *Canterbury* cathedral for fifty years, and vicar of *Stone* in the isle of *Oxney, Kent*, well known to all lovers of antiquity by his truly original "Walk in and about *Canterbury*," first printed in 1774, of which there have been three editions. He died *March* 9, 1777, in the 82d year of his age. Of his father, who was first a minor canon of *Canterbury*, and afterwards one of the priests of the chapel-royal and sub-dean of *St. Paul's*, there are several anecdotes, communicated by his son, in Sir *John Hawkins's* "History of Music." To which may be added what King *Charles* II. is reported to have said of him, "You may talk as much as you please of your nightingales, but I have a *Gostling* who excels them all." Another time, the same merry monarch presented him with a silver egg filled with guineas, saying, "that he had heard that eggs were good for the voice."

[90] See the Catalogue, under the year 1782.

CATALOGUE OF HOGARTH'S PRINTS.[1]

I am now engaged in an undertaking, which from its nature will be imperfect. While *Hogarth* was yet an apprentice, and worked on his master's account, we may suppose he was not at liberty to affix his name to his own performances. Nay, afterwards, when he appeared as an independent artist, he probably left many of them anonymous, being sometimes obliged to measure out his exertions in proportion to the scanty prices paid for them. For reasons like these, we may be sure that many of his early plates must have eluded search; and, if gradually discovered, will serve only to swell the collections they will not adorn.—The judicious connoisseur, perhaps, would be content to possess the pictures of *Raffaelle*, without aiming at a complete assemblage of the Roman *Fayence* that passes under his name.

In settling the dates of his pieces there is also difficulty. Sometimes, indeed, they have been inferred from circumstances almost infallible; as in respect to the *Rabbit-breeder*,&c. which would naturally have been published in the year 1726. On other occasions they are determined within a certain compass of time. Thus the *Ticket for Milward*, then a player at *Lincoln's-Inn Fields*, must have preceded 1733, when he removed with *Rich* to *Covent Garden*; and it is equally sure, that *Orator Henley christening an Infant*, and *A Girl swearing a child to a grave citizen*, came out before 1735, in which year we know that *J. Y. Schley*, one of *Picart's* coadjutors, had re-engraved them both for the use of the fourth volume of the *Religious Ceremonies*, published at *Amsterdam* in 1736. But how are we to guess at the period that produced *Sancho at Dinner*, or *The Discovery*?

The merits and demerits of his performances would prove deceitful guides in our researches. As our artist grew older, he did not regularly advance in estimation; for neither the frontispieces to *Tristram Shandy*, the *Times*, the *Bathos*, or the *Bear*, can be said to equal many of his earliest productions.— Under such difficulties is the following chronological list of our author's pieces attempted.

The reader is likewise entreated to observe, that throughout the annexed catalogue of plates, variations, &c. *J. N.* has mentioned only such as he has seen. Alike unwilling to deceive or be deceived, he has suppressed all intelligence he could not authenticate from immediate inspection. He might easily have enlarged his work by admitting particulars of doubtful authority, sometimes imperfectly recollected by their several communicators, and sometimes offered as sportive impositions on an author's credulity. Of this weakness every one possesses some; but perhaps no man more than he who ambitiously seeks opportunities to improve on the labours of another. *J. N.* is sure, however, that Mr. *Walpole*, whom none can exceed in taste and judgment, will be little concerned about the merits of a performance that founds its claim to notice only on the humbler pretences of industry and correctness.

[1] It is proper to acknowledge, that all such short strictures and annotations on these performances as are distinguished by being printed both in *Italics* and between inverted commas, are copied from the list of *Hogarth's* works published by Mr. *Walpole*.

1720.

1. *W. Hogarth*, engraver, with two figures and two *Cupids, April* 28, 1720.

1721.

1. An emblematic print on the *South Sea. W. Hogarth inv. & sc. Sold by Mrs. Chilcot in Westminster-hall, and B. Caldwell, Printseller in Newgate-street.* "Persons riding on wooden horses. The Devil cutting Fortune into collops. A man broken on the wheel, &c. A very poor performance." Under it are the following verses:

> See here the causes why in *London*
> So many men are made and undone;
> That arts and honest trading drop,
> To swarm about the Devil's shop (A),
> Who cuts out (B) Fortune's golden haunches,
> Trapping their souls with lots and chances,
> Sharing 'em from blue garters down
> To all blue aprons in the town.
> Here all religions flock together,
> Like tame and wild fowl of a feather,
> Leaving their strife religious bustle,
> Kneel down to play at pitch and hustle (C):
> Thus when the shepherds are at play;
> Their flocks must surely go astray;
> The woeful cause that in these times
> (E) Honour and Honesty (D) are crimes
> That publickly are punish'd by
> (G) Self-Interest and (F) Vilany;
> So much for mony's magic power,
> Guess at the rest, you find out more.
> *Price One Shilling.*[1]

It may be observed, that *London* always affords a set of itinerant poets, whose office it is to furnish inscriptions for satirical engravings. I lately overheard one of these unfortunate sons of the Muse making a bargain with his employer. "Your print," says he, "is a taking one, and why won't you go to the price of a half-crown Epigram?" From such hireling bards, I suppose, our artist purchased not a few of the wretched rhimes under his early performances, unless he himself be considered as the author of them.

Of this print emblematic of the *South Sea*, there are, however, two impressions. The second, printed for *Bowles*, has been retouched.

[1] For some further account of this design, see the article *Man of Taste*, under the year 1732, N° 7.

2. The Lottery.[1] *W. Hogarth inv. & sculp. Sold by Chilcot and Caldwell. "Emblematic, and not good."* This plate is found in four different states. In one there is no publisher's name under the title. Another was *sold by Chilcot, &c.* A third was printed and sold by S. *Sympson*, in *Maiden-lane*, near *Covent Garden*. A fourth was printed for *John Bowles*, in whose possession the plate, which he has had retouched, remains. The following explanation accompanies this plate: "1. Upon the pedestal, National Credit leaning on a pillar, supported by Justice. 2. *Apollo* shewing *Britannia* a picture representing the Earth receiving enriching Showers drawn from herself (an emblem of state lotteries). 3. Fortune drawing the blanks and prizes. 4. Wantonness drawing the numbers. 5. Before the pedestal, Suspence turned to and fro by Hope and Fear. 6. On one hand, Good Luck being elevated is seized by Pleasure and Folly, Fame persuading him to raise sinking Virtue, Arts, &c. 7. On the other hand, Misfortune oppressed by Grief, *Minerva* supporting him points to the sweets of Industry. 8. Sloth hiding his head in the curtain. 9. On the other side, Avarice hugging his money. 10. Fraud tempting Despair with money at a trap-door in the pedestal." *Price One Shilling.*—Had not *Hogarth*, on this occasion, condescended to explain his own meaning, it must have remained in several places inexplicable.

[1] It appears, from the following notice in the *General Advertiser, Dec.* 12, 1751, that this and the foregoing print were re-published by *Bowles* during the life of *Hogarth*.

"Lately reprinted, designed, and engraved by Mr. *William Hogarth*.

"Two Prints on the Lottery. One of them showing the drawing of the Lottery by Wantonness and Fortune; and by suitable emblems represents the suspence of the adventurers, the situation of the fortunate and unfortunate.

"The other print is a burlesque representation of the folly and madness which inspires all ranks of people after lottery-gaming, with the pernicious consequences thereof. *Price One Shilling.*

"Sold by *J. Bowles*, at the *Black-horse*, in *Cornhill.*"

1723.

1. Fifteen plates to *Aubry de la Motraye's* "Travels through *Europe*, *Asia*, and Part of *Africa*." *W. Hogarth sculp.* on fourteen of them; viz. plates V. IX. X.[1] XI. XV. XVII. b. XVIII. XXVI. XXX.[2] XXXII. XXXIII. 1. XXXIII. 2. XXXV. XXXVIII. One of these (viz. XXX.) contains a portrait of *Charles* the XIIth of *Sweden*. Several of the pictures, from which the Seraglio, &c. were engraved, are still in being, and are undoubtedly authentic, being painted in *Turkey*, and brought home by *De la Motraye*, at his return from his travels. They were sold about twenty-five years ago at *Hackney*, for a mere trifle, together with the plates to the present work. The latter, in all probability, are destroyed. This book was originally published in *English* at *London*, 1723; afterwards in *French* at *The Hague*, in 1727; and again in *English*[3] at *London*, revised by the author; with the addition of two new cuts, in 1730. In the *French* edition, Plate V. Tom. I. is engraved by *R. Smith*, instead of *Hogarth*, so that this intermediate copy contains only fourteen plates by him. It is probable also, that some other anonymous ones, in all the editions, were by the same engraver. His reputation, indeed, will save more than it loses by the want of his signature to establish their authenticity.

[1] At the bottom of this plate, in one copy of the *English* edition, the name of *Hogarth*, though erased, is sufficiently legible.

[2] In some of the *English* copies of this work, instead of Plate XXX. by *Hogarth*, we only find a very small and imperfect copy of it by another hand.

[3] This, strictly speaking, was not a re-publication; it is the identical edition of 1723, with the addition of a Preface and an Appendix. New title-pages were again printed to it, and a third volume added, in 1732.

2. Five *Muscovites*. This small print appears at the corner of one of the maps to the second volume of the foregoing work. It has no intelligible reference; but, in the *English* copy now before me, is the last plate but one, and is marked. C—T. II. In a former edition of the present catalogue, it was enumerated as a separate article, but must now be reckoned as one of the fifteen plates to *Motraye's* Travels.

To these I might add three plates more. If *Hogarth* engraved the *Muscovites* at the corner of the map already mentioned, he likewise furnished the figures in the corner of another, marked T. I.—B. And Plate T. I.—XVI. and T. I.—XXXVII. I have likewise reason to suppose were the works of our artist; eighteen plates in all; though the three latter being only conjectural, I have not ventured to set them down as indisputed performances. Of the *Muscovites* there is a modern copy.[1]

I have just been assured by a gentleman of undoubted veracity, that he was once possessed of a set of plates engraved by *Hogarth* for some treatise on mathematicks; but, considering them of little value, disposed of them at the price of the copper. As our artist could have displayed no marks of genius in representations of cycloids, diagrams, and equilateral triangles, the loss of these plates is not heavily to be lamented.

[1] Mr. *Walpole* enumerates only 12 plates.

1724.

1. Seven small prints to "The New Metamorphosis of *Lucius Apuleius* of *Medaura. London*, printed for *Sam. Briscoe*, 1724." 12mo. 2 vol. I. Frontispiece. II. Festivals of Gallantry, which the noblemen of *Rome* make in the churches for the entertainment of their mistresses. III. The banditti's bringing home a beautiful virgin, called *Camilla*, from her mother's arms, the night before she was to have been married. Vol. I. p. 113. No name to this plate. IV. *Fantasio's* arrival at the house of an old witch, who is afterwards changed into a beautiful young lady. V. The provincial of the Jesuits' recovery of his favourite dog from the cooper's wife. VI. *Psyche's* admission of her unknown husband in the dark, who always departed before the return of light. VII. Cardinal *Ottoboni* and his niece's visit to an Hermitage in the holy desert, called *Camaldule*; the Cardinal's discourse against solitude to the hermit, who had not been out of his cell, nor spoke a word, for forty years together. Plate IV. is the only one that has the least trait of character in it.

2. Masquerades and operas. *Burlington-gate. W. Hogarth inv. & sculp*. Of the three small figures in the center of this plate, the middle one is Lord *Burlington*, a man of considerable taste in Painting and Architecture, but who ranked Mr. *Kent* (an indifferent artist) above his merit. On one side of the peer is Mr. *Campbell*, the architect; on the other, his lordship's postilion. On a show-cloth in this plate is also supposed to be the portrait of King *George* II. who gave 1000 *l*. towards the masquerade; together with that of the Earl of *Peterborough*, who offers *Cuzzoni*, the *Italian* singer, 8000 *l*. and she spurns at him.[1] Mr. *Heidegger*, the regulator of the Masquerade, is also exhibited, looking out at a window, with the letter *H*. under him. The substance of the

foregoing remarks is taken from a collection lately belonging to Captain *Baillie*,[2] where it is said that they were furnished by an eminent Connoisseur.[3] A board is likewise displayed, with the words—"Long Room. *Fawks's* dexterity of hand." It appears front the following advertisement in *Mist's Weekly Journal* for *Saturday, December* 25, 1725, that this artist was a man of great consequence in his profession. "Whereas the town hath lately been alarmed, that the famous *Fawks* was robbed and murdered, returning from performing at the Dutchess of *Buckingham's* house at *Chelsea*; which report being raised and printed by a person to gain money to himself, and prejudice the above mentioned Mr. *Fawks*, whose unparalleled performances have gained him so much applause from the greatest of quality, and most curious observers: We think, both in justice to the injured gentleman, and for the satisfaction of his admirers, that we cannot please our readers better than to acquaint them he is alive, and will not only perform his usual surprizing dexterity of hand, posture-master, and musical clock; but for the greater diversion of the quality and gentry, has agreed with the famous *Powell* of *The Bath* for the season, who has the largest, richest, and most natural figures, and finest machines in *England*, and whose former performances in *Covent Garden* were so engaging to the town, as to gain the approbation of the best judges, to show his puppet-plays along with him, beginning in the *Christmas* holidays next, at the old *Tennis-court* in *James-Street*, near *The Haymarket*; where any incredulous persons may be satisfied he has not left this world, if they please to believe their hands, though they can't believe their eyes."—*May* 25," indeed, "1731, died Mr. *Fawkes*, famous for his dexterity of hand, by which he had honestly acquired a fortune of above 10,000 *l.* being no more than he really deserved for his great ingenuity, by which he had surpassed all that ever pretended to that art." Political State, vol. XLI. p. 543.

This satirical performance of *Hogarth*, however, was thought to be invented and drawn at the mitigation of Sir *James Thornhill*, out of revenge, because Lord *Burlington* had preferred Mr. *Kent* before him to paint for the king at his palace at *Kensington*. Dr. *Faustus* was a pantomime performed to crowded houses throughout two seasons, to the utter neglect of plays, for which reason they are cried about in a wheel-barrow.[4] We may add that there are three prints of this small masquerade, &c. one a copy from the first. The originals have *Hogarth's* name within the frame of the plate, and the eight verses are different from those under the other. It is sometimes found without any lines at all; those in the first instance having been engraved on a separate piece of copper, so that they could either be retained, dismissed, or exchanged, at pleasure. In the first copy of this print, instead of *Ben Jonson's* name on a label, we have *Pasquin*, N° XI. This was a periodical paper published in 1722-3, and the number specified is particularly severe on operas, &c. The verses to the first impression of this plate, are,

> Could now dumb *Faustus*, to reform the age,
> Conjure up *Shakespear's* or *Ben Johnson's* ghost,
> They'd blush for shame, to see the *English* stage
> Debauch'd by fool'ries, at so great a cost.
> What would their manes say? Should they behold
> Monsters and masquerades, where useful plays
> Adorn'd the fruitfull theatre of old,
> And rival wits contended for the bays.
> *Price* 1 *shilling* 1724.

To the second impression of it:

> O how refin'd, how elegant we're grown!
> What noble Entertainments charm the town!
> Whether to hear the Dragon's roar we go,
> Or gaze surpriz'd on *Fawks's* matchless show,
> Or to the Operas, or to the Masques,
> To eat up ortelans, and t' empty flasques,
> And rifle pies from *Shakespear's* clinging page,
> Good gods! how great's the gusto of the age.

In this print our artist has imitated the engraving of *Callot*.

To the third impression, i. e. the copy:

> Long has the stage productive been
> Of offsprings it could brag on,
> But never till this age was seen
> A Windmill and a Dragon.
>
> O *Congreve*, lay thy pen aside,
> *Shakespear*, thy works disown,
> Since monsters grim, and nought beside,
> Can please this senseless town.

I should have observed, that the idea of the foregoing plate was stolen from an anonymous one on the same subject. It represents *Hercules* chaining follies and destroying monsters. He is beating *Heidegger*, till the money he had amassed falls out of his pocket. The situation of the buildings, &c. on the sides, &c. has been followed by our artist. *Mercury* aloft sustains a scroll, on which is written "The Mascarade destroy'd." The inscription under this print is "Hei Degeror. O! I am undone." *Price One Shilling*.

[1] She is rather drawing the money towards her with a rake.

[2] This collection, consisting of 241 prints, in three portfeuilles, was sold at *Christie's, April* 7, 1781, for 59 guineas, to Mr. *Ingham Foster*, a wealthy ironmonger, since dead. A set, containing only 100 prints, had been sold some time before, at the same place, for 47 guineas. The Hon. *Topham Beauclerk's* set, of only 99 prints, was sold in 1781 (while this note was printing off for the first edition) for 34*l.* 10*s.*

[3] It is not, indeed, inconvenient for the reputation of this famous connoisseur, that his name continues to be a secret. Either he could not spell, or his copier was unable to read what he undertook to transcribe. *Postilion* must be a mistake for some other word. The whole note, in the original, appears to have been the production of a male *Slip-slop*, perhaps of high fashion. His petulant invective against Lord *Burlington* is here omitted.

[4] Dr. *Faustus* was first brought out at *Lincoln's-Inn Fields* in 1723, and the success of it reduced the rival theatre to produce a like entertainment at their house in 1725. From a scarce pamphlet in octavo, without date, called "Tragi-comical Reflections, of a moral and political Tendency, occasioned by the present State of the two Rival Theatres in *Drury-Lane* and *Lincoln's-Inn Fields*, by *Gabriel Rennel*, Esq." I shall transcribe an illustration of these plates: "A few years ago, by the help of *Harleykin*, and Dr. *Faustus*, and *Pluto* and *Proserpine*, and other infernal persons, the New-House was raised to as high a pitch of popularity and renown as ever it had been known to arrive at. Tho' the actors there consisted chiefly of *Scotch*, and *Irish*, and *French* Strollers, who were utterly unacquainted with the *English* Stage, and were remarkably deficient in elocution and gesture: yet so much was the art of juggling at that time in vogue, and so extreamly was the nation delighted with Raree-Shows, and foreign representations, that all people flocked to the New-House, whilst the Old one was altogether deserted, tho' it then could glory in as excellent a set of *English* actors as ever had trod upon any stage. In the midst of this joyful prosperity and success, the Managers of the New-House were not without secret uneasiness and discontent, whenever they considered how slippery a ground they stood upon, and how much a juster title their rivals had to the favour and affections of the people. They were therefore always intent upon forming designs and concerting measures for the entire subversion of the Old-House. For this purpose, they constantly kept in pay a standing army of Scaramouches, who were sent about the town to possess it with aversion and resentment against the Old Players, whose virtues had rendered them formidable, and whose merit was their greatest crime. These Scaramouches, in so corrupt and degenerate a time, when blindness and folly, and a false taste every where reigned, were every where looked on as men of a superior skill to all other actors, and consequently had a greater influence than the rest, and could lead after them a larger number of followers. It was by means of the incessant clamour and outcry that these

miscreants raised, and of the lies and forgeries which they scattered about the nation, that the common people were spirited up to commit the most extravagant acts of insolence and outrage on the Managers of the Old-House. They were made the sport and derision of fools, and were delivered up to an enraged and deluded populace, as a prey to the fury of wild beasts. Their enemies were continually plotting and conspiring their destruction, and yet were continually prosecuting them for Sham-Plots and pretended Conspiracies, and suborning witnesses to prove them guilty of attempts to undermine and blow up the New-House.

"During the course of those violent and illegal proceedings, the New Actors were not wanting in any pains or expence to gratify and increase the then popular taste for Raree-Shows, and Hocus-Pocus Tricks. Scenes and Machines, and Puppets, and Posture-Masters, and Actors, and Singers, with a new set of Heathen Gods and Goddesses, and several other foreign Decorations and Inventions, were sent for from *France and Italy*, and were ready to be imported with the first fair wind. But quarrels falling out among the Managers of the House, and one or two of the principal Actors happening to quit the Stage, and the people growing tired with so much foul play, and with the same *deceptio visus* so often repeated, the scene changed at once, the *vox populi* turned against the New-House, which sunk under a load of infamy and contempt, and was deserted not only by the Spectators, but even by its Actors, who, to save themselves from the justice of an abused and enraged people, were forced to fly out of the nation, and to beg for protection and subsistence from their wicked Confederates and Fellow-Jugglers abroad."

1725.

1. Five small prints for the translation of *Cassandra*, in five volumes duodecimo. *W. Hogarth inv. & sculp.*

2. Fifteen head pieces for "The *Roman* Military Punishments, by *John Beaver*, Esq. *London*. From the happy Revolution, Anno xxxvii." (i. e. 1725.) Small quarto, pp. 155. From the preface it should seem that the author had been Judge Advocate. The book is divided into seventeen chapters, each of which, except the second, third, seventh, and twelfth, have small head-pieces prefixed, of ancient military punishments, in the manner of *Callot's* Small Miseries of War. *W. Hogarth inv. & sculp.* In 1779, were first sold by a printseller ten of these prints, together with two others not in the book, being scenes of modern war; a pair of drums being in one, and a soldier armed with a musket in the other. Thus are there three prints in the book not in this set; viz. Chap. 9. Soldiers sold for slaves. 10. Degradation. 16. Banishment. There

is also in the title-page a little figure of a *Roman* General sitting; probably done by *Hogarth*, though his name is not under it.

In the year 1774, these plates were in the possession of a Button-manufacturer at *Birmingham*. There are only eleven, one of them being engraved on both sides. They were given by him, however, to my informant, who parted with them to *S. Harding* an engraver, who sold them to *Humphry* the printseller near *Temple-Bar*, their present proprietor. How they fell into the hands of the *Birmingham* manufacturer (who took off a few impressions from them), is unknown.

Query. Does the plate engraved on both sides contain the two modern designs?

In a Catalogue of Books sold by *W. Bathoe*, was included "Part of the Collection of the late ingenious *W. Hogarth*, Esq. Serjeant Painter to his Majesty;" in which was *Beaver's* "*Roman* Military Punishments," with *twelve plates* by *Hogarth*.

The plate to Chap. XVII. viz. "Pay stopt wholly, or in part, by way of punishment"—"Barley given to offenders instead of wheat, &c." differs in many instances from that sold with the set. At the bottom of the former, in the book, we read, "*W. Hogarth, Invent. sculpt.*" The latter has "*W. Hogarth, invent. & fec.*" The former has a range of tents behind the pay-table. These are omitted in the latter; which likewise exhibits an additional soldier attendant on the measuring out of the corn, &c.

I do not mean to say that the plate sold with the set is spurious. Had it been a copy, it would naturally have been a servile one. Some reason, now undiscoverable, must have prevailed on our artist to re-engrave it with variations.

N. B. The two "scenes of modern war," mentioned also in p. 134, were designed for a continuation of the same work, which was never printed, as I guess from the conclusion of the Author's preface. "This regularly divided my book into two parts; one treating of the *Roman*, the other of the *Modern Military Punishments*. The first I now send into the world, as a man going into the water dips his foot to feel what reception he is like to meet with; by that rule resolving, either to publish the second part, or sit down contented with the private satisfaction of having, by my studies, rendered myself more able worthily to discharge the duties of my office."

I have since been assured, that our Author's heir was a pastry-cook, who used all the copies of this book for waste-paper.

3. A burlesque on *Kent's* altar piece at *St. Clement's*, with notes. "*It represents angels very ill drawn, playing on various instruments.*" Speaking of this print, Mr. *Walpole* in one place calls it a *parody*; and in another, a *burlesque* on *Kent's* Altar-piece. But, if we may believe *Hogarth* himself, it is neither, but a very fair and honest representation of a despicable performance. The following is our artist's inscription to it, transcribed *verbatim & literatim*.

"This Print is exactly Engraiv'd after ye celebrated Altar-Piece in St. *Clements* Church which has been taken down by Order of ye Lord Bishop of *London* (as tis thought) to prevent Disputs and Laying of wagers among the Parrshioners about ye Artists meaning in it. for publick Satisfaction here is a particular Explanation of it humbly Offerd to be writ under the Original, that it may be put up again by which means ye Parish'es 60 pounds which thay nifely gave for it, may not be Entirely lost.

"1st. Tis not the Pretenders Wife and Children as our weak brethren imagin.

"2dly. Nor St. *Cecilia* as the Connoisseurs think but a choir of Angells playing in Consort.

"A   an Organ

B   an Angel playing on it

C   the shortest Ioint of the Arm.

D   the longest Ioint

E   An Angel tuning an harp

F   the inside of his Leg but whether right or Left is yet undiscover'd

G   a hand Playing on a Lute

H   the other leg judiciously Omitted to make room for the harp

I&K 2 Smaller Angells as appears by their wings"

This picture produced a tract, intituled, "A Letter from a Parishioner of *St. Clement Danes* to *Edmund [Gibson]* Lord Bishop of *London*, occasion'd by his lordship's causing the picture over the altar to be taken down: with some observations on the use and abuse of Church-paintings in general, and of that picture in particular, 1725." 8vo. See Appendix II. The proofs of this plate are commonly on blue paper, though I have met with more than one on white. The original, after it was removed from the church, was for some years one of the ornaments of the music-room at *The Crown and Anchor* in the

Strand. As this house has frequently changed its tenants, &c. I am unable to trace the picture in question any further. There is a good copy of this print by *Livesay*.

4. A scene in *Handel's* opera of *Ptolomeo*, performed in 1728, with *Farinelli, Cuzzoni*, and *Senesino*, in the characters of *Ptolemy, Cleopatra*, and *Julius Cæsar*. Those who are inclined to doubt the authenticity of this performance, will do well to consult the representation on a painted canvas in the small print on masquerades and operas, where the same figures occur in almost the same attitudes. I do not, however, vouch for the genuineness of this plate. In *Southwark Fair*, our artist has borrowed the subject of his show-cloth from *Laguerre*; and might, in the present instance, have adopted it from another hand.

The appearance *Farinelli* makes on this occasion may be justified by the following quotation from a Pamphlet, intituled, *Reflections upon Theatrical Expression in Tragedy, &c.* printed for *W. Johnston*, &c. 1755. "I shall therefore, in my further remarks upon this article, go back to the *Old Italian Theatre*, when *Farinelli* drew every body to the *Haymarket*. What a pipe! what modulation! what extasy to the ear! But, heavens! what clumsiness! what stupidity! what offence to the eye! Reader, if of the city, thou mayest probably have seen in the fields of *Islington* or *Mile-end*, or if thou art in the environs of *St. James's*, thou must have observed in the park, with what ease and agility a Cow, heavy with Calf, has rose up at the command of the Milk-woman's foot. Thus from the mossy bank sprung up the *Divine Farinelli*. Then with long strides advancing a few paces, his left hand settled upon his hip, in a beautiful bend like that of the handle of an old-fashioned caudle-cup, his right remained immoveable across his manly breast, till numbness called its partner to supply its place; when it relieved itself in the position of the other handle to the caudle-cup." p. 63, &c.

Under a copy of the print abovementioned, which must have been made soon after its publication, appear the following inscription, and wretched ungrammatical lines:

The three most Celebrated Singers at the Opera.

Scire tuum nihil est, nisi te scire hoc sciat alter.

Sigra the great, harmoniously inclin'd,
Who charms the ear and captivates the mind.

Cuzzoni.
Thou little slave an emblem is of those
Whose hearts are wholly att ye worlds dispose.

Great *Barrenstadt*[1] encomiums great and true
is very short of whats your right and due.

The characters in the print under consideration, might have been new-christen'd by the copier of it.

Either the dignity of *Senesino* must have been wonderful, or the following passage in Dr. *Warburton's* "Enquiry into the Cause of Prodigies and Miracles," (printed in 1727) affords a most notorious example of the Bathos. "Observe," says he, p. 60. "Sir *Walter Raleigh's* great manner of ending the *first part of the History of the World*. 'By this which we have already set down is seen the beginning and end of the Three first Monarchies of the World; whereof the founders and erectors thought that they could never have ended: that of *Rome*, which made the fourth, was also at this time almost at the highest. We have left it flourishing in the middle of the field; have rooted up, or cut down, all that kept it from the eyes and admiration of the world; but after some continuance, it shall begin to lose the beauty it had; the storms of ambition shall beat her great boughs and branches one against another; her leaves shall fall off; her limbs wither, and a rabble of barbarous nations enter the field and cut her down.' What strength of colouring! What grace, what nobleness of expression! With what a majesty does he close his immortal labour! It puts one in mind of the so much admired exit of the late famed ITALIAN SINGER."

[1] *Berenstadt*; a castrato engaged by *Handel* in the operas.

5. A just View of the *British* Stage, or three heads better than one, scene *Newgate*, by *M. D. V—to*.[1] This print represents the rehearsing a new farce, that will include the two famous entertainments *Dr. Faustus* and *Harlequin Shepherd*.[2] To which will be added, *Scaramouch Jack Hall* the Chimney-sweeper's Escape from *Newgate* through the Privy, with the comical Humours of *Ben Johnson's Ghost*, concluding with the Play Dance, performed in the air by the figures A. B. C. [*Wilks, Booth,* and *Cibber*] assisted by ropes from the Muses. Note, there are no Conjurors concerned in it, as the Ignorant imagine. The Bricks, Rubbish, &c. will be real; but the Excrements upon *Jack Hall* will be made of chewed Gingerbread, to prevent Offence. *Vivat Rex. Price Sixpence.* Such is the inscription on the plate; but I may add, that the *ropes* already mentioned are no other than *halters*, suspended over the heads of the three managers;[3] and that labels issuing from their respective mouths have the following characteristic words. The airy *Wilks*, who dangles the effigy of *Punch*, is made to exclaim—"Poor *R-ch*! faith I pitty him." The laureat *Cibber*, with *Harlequin* for his playfellow, invokes the Muses painted on the cieling—"Assist, ye sacred Nine;" while the solemn *Booth*, letting down the image of *Jack Hall* into the forica, is most tragically blaspheming—"Ha! this will do,

G-d d-m me." On a table before these gentlemen lies a pamphlet, exhibiting a print of *Jack Shepherd*, in confinement; and over the forica is suspended a parcel of waste paper, consisting of leaves torn from *The Way of the World—Hamlet—Macbeth*, and *Julius Cæsar*. Ben Jonson's Ghost, in the mean while, is rising through the stage, and p———g on a pantomimic statue tumbled from its base. A fidler is also represented hanging by a cord in the air, and performing, with a scroll before him, that exhibits—*Music for the What*— [perhaps the *What d' ye call it*] *entertainment*. The countenances of Tragedy and Comedy, on each side of the stage, are hoodwinked by the bills for *Harlequin Dr. Faustus* and *Harlequin Shepherd*, &c. &c. There is also a dragon preparing to fly; a dog thrusting his head out of his kennel; a flask put in motion by machinery, &c. *Vivetur Ingenio* is the motto over the curtain. In Mr. *Walpole's* catalogue the description of this plate is, "*Booth, Wilks, and Cibber, contriving a pantomime. A satire on farces. No name.*"

[1] Mr. *Devoto* was scene-painter to *Drury-Lane* or *Lincoln's-Inn Fields*, and also to *Goodman's Fields* Theatre. There is a mezzotinto of him with the following title: "*Johannes Devoto* Historicus Scenicusque Pictor." *Vincenso Damini* pinxit. *J. Faber* fecit, 1736.

[2] Dr. *Faustus* and *Harlequin Shepherd* were pantomimes contrived by *Thurmond* the dancing-master, and acted at *Drury-Lane* in 1725.

[3] —*Halters*, &c.; The same idea is introduced in the 9th plate of the apprentices.

1726.

1. Frontispiece to *Terræ-filius*. *W. Hogarth fec*. This work was printed in two volumes 12°, at *Oxford*, and is a satire on the Tory principles of that University. It was written by *Nicholas Amherst*, author of *The Craftsman*, and was originally published in one volume.

2. Twelve prints for *Hudibras*; the large set. *W. Hogarth inv. pinx. et sculp*. Under the head of *Butler*: "The basso relievo of the pedestal represents the general design of Mr. *Butler*, in his incomparable poem of *Hudibras*; viz. *Butler's* Genious in a Car lashing around Mount *Parnassus*, in the persons of *Hudibras* and *Ralpho*, Rebellion, Hypocrisy, and Ignorance, the reigning vices of his time." This set of prints was published by subscription, by *P. Overton* and *J. Cooper*. Mr. *S. Ireland* has seven of the original drawings; three others are known to be preserved in *Holland*; and two more were lately existing in this kingdom. The plates, as has been mentioned already in p. 11, are now the property of Mr. *Sayer*, whose name, as publisher, is subjoined. The Rev. Mr.

Bowle, F. A. S. had a set with the list of the subscribers, which he purchased at the Duke of *Beaufort's* sale in *Wiltshire*. The printed title to them is, "Twelve excellent and most diverting Prints; taken from the celebrated Poem of *Hudibras*, wrote by Mr. *Samuel Butler*. Exposing the Villany and Hypocrisy of the Times. Invented and Engraved on Twelve Copper-plates, by *William Hogarth*, and are humbly dedicated to *William Ward*, Esq. of *Great Houghton* in *Northamptonshire*; and Mr. *Allan Ramsay*, of *Edinburgh*.

> "What excellence can Brass or Marble claim!
> These Papers better do secure thy Fame:
> Thy Verse all Monuments does far surpass,
> No Mausoleum's like thy *Hudibras*.

"Printed and sold by *Philip Overton*, Print and Map-seller, at the *Golden Buck* near *St. Dunstan's Church* in *Fleet-street*; and *John Cooper*, in *James-street*, Covent Garden, 1726."

Allan Ramsay subscribed for 30 sets. The number of subscribers in all amounts to 192. On the print of *Hudibras* and the *Lawyer* is *W. Hogart delin. et sculp.* a proof that our artist had not yet disused the original mode in which he spelt his name. In the scene of the *Committee*, one of the members has his gloves on his head. I am told this whimsical custom once prevailed among our sanctified fraternity; but it is in vain, I suppose, to ask the reason why. In plate XI. (earliest impressions) the words "Down with the Rumps" are wanting on the scroll.—Memorandum. At the top of the proposals for this set of Prints, is a small one representing *Hudibras* and *Ralpho*, engraved by *Pine*. The original drawing for it by *Hogarth* is in the possession of Mr. *Betew*, Silversmith, in *Compton-street, Soho*.

3. Seventeen small prints for *Hudibras*, with *Butler's* head. There certainly must have been some mistake concerning this portrait. It never could have been designed for the author of *Hudibras*; but more strongly resembles *John Baptist Monnoyer*, the flower-painter. There is a print of him by *White*, from a picture of Sir *Godfrey Kneller*. This I suppose to have been the original of *Hogarth's* small *Butler*.

The same designs engraved on a larger scale, and with some slight variations, by *J. Mynde*, for *Grey's* edition of *Hudibras*, published in 1744.

Previous, however, to both, appeared another set of plates, eighteen in number, for an edition in *eighteens* of this celebrated poem. To these it is manifest that *Hogarth* was indebted for his ideas of several of the scenes and personages both in his larger and smaller performances on the same subject. That the collector may know the book when he meets with it, the following is a transcript of the title-page. "*Hudibras*. In three Parts. Written in the time of the late Wars. Corrected and amended, with Additions. To which is added,

Annotations to the third Part, with an exact Index to the whole; never before printed. Adorned with cuts. London. Printed for R. *Chiswel*, J. *Tonson*, T. *Horne*, and R. *Willington*, 1710."

Copies from the smaller plates are likewise inserted in *Townly's* translation of *Hudibras* into *French*, with the *English* on the opposite page. He was, I believe, an officer in the *Irish* brigade. The following is the title-page to his work. "*Hudibras*, Poeme ecrit dans les tems des troubles d'*Angleterre*; et traduit en vers *François*, avec des remarques et des figures. 3 tom. 12mo. A *Londres*, 1757." It seems rather to have been printed at *Paris*. The plates have no name subscribed to them.

4. *Cunicularii*, or the Wise Men of *Godliman* in Consultation.

> "They held their talents most adroit
> For any mystical exploit." HUDIB.

This print was published in the year 1726, i. e. about the same time that Lord *Onslow* wrote the following letter:

> "To the Hon[ble]. Sir *Hans Sloane*. To be left at the *Grecian* Coffe House, in *Devereux Court* near *Temple Bar London*.
>
> "Sir, The report of a woman's breeding of rabbits has almost alarmed *England*, and in a manner persuaded several people of sound judg[t] of that truth. I have been at some pains to discover the affair, and think I have conquerd my poynt, as you will se by the Depotition taken before me, which shall be published in a day or two. I am
>
> "Y[r] humble Servant,
>
> "ONSLOW.
>
> "*Clandon, Dec. 4th*, 1726."

Soon after, Mr. *St. André* also addressed this note to Sir *Hans Sloane*.

> "Sir, I have brought the woman from *Guilford* to ye Bagnio in *Leicester-fields*, where you may if you please have the opportunity of seeing her deliver'd. I am Sr Your Hum Servt
>
> "ST. ANDRÉ.[1]
>
> "To Sir *Hans Sloane* in *Bloomsbury Square*."

In the plate already mentioned, figure A represents *St. André*. [He has a kitt under his arm, having been at first designed by his family for a fencing and dancing-master, though he afterwards attached himself to music of a higher order than that necessary for one of the professions already mentioned.] B is

Sir *Richard Manningham*, C Mr. *Sainthill* a celebrated surgeon here in *London*, D is *Howard* the surgeon at *Guildford*, who was supposed to have had a chief hand in the imposture. The rest of the characters explain themselves.

Perhaps my readers may excuse me, if I add a short account of another design for a print on the same subject; especially as some collectors have been willing to receive it as a work of *Hogarth*.

In *Mist's Weekly Journal, Saturday, Jan.* 11th, 1726-7, was the following advertisement:

"The Rabbit affair made clear in a full account of the whole matter; with the pictures engraved of the pretended Rabbit-breeder herself, *Mary Tofts*, and of the Rabbits, and of the persons who attended her during her pretended deliveries, shewing who were and who were not imposed on by her. 'Tis given gratis no where, but only up one pair of stairs at the sign of the celebrated Anodyne Necklace recommended by Doctor *Chamberlen* for Children's teeth, &c."

The original drawing from which the plate promised in *Mist's* Journal was taken, remained in the possession of Mr. *James Vertue*, and was probably designed by his brother *George*. It was sold in 1781 in the collection of *George Scott*, Esq. of *Chigwell* in *Essex*, together with eight tracts relative to the same imposture, for three guineas, and is now in the collection of Mr. *Gough*.

St. André's Miscarriage, a ballad, published in 1727, has the following stanza on this subject:

> "He dissected, compar'd, and distinguish'd likewise
> The make of these rabbits, their growth and their size.
> He preserv'd them in spirits, and—a little too late
> Preserv'd (*Vertue sculpsit*) a neat copper plate."

There is also a copper-plate, consisting of twelve compartments, on the same story. It exhibits every stage throughout this celebrated fraud. *St. André* appears in the habit of a *Merry-Andrew*. The general title of it is, "The Doctors in Labour; or a new Whim-wham from *Guilford*. Being a representation of the frauds by which the *Godliman* woman carried on her pretended Rabbit breeding; also of the simplicity of our Doctors, by which they assisted to carry on that imposture, discovered their skill, and contributed to the mirth of his Majesty's liege subjects."

In *Mist's* Journal for *Saturday, Dec.* 17, 1726, is also the following paragraph, which shews that the playhouse joined in the general ridicule of *St. André*. "Last week the entertainment called *The Necromancer* was performed at the Theatre in *Lincoln's-Inn Fields*, wherein a new *Rabbit-scene* was introduced by way of episode; by which the Public may understand as much of that affair, as by the present controversy among the Gentlemen of the faculty, who are flinging their bitter pills at one another, to convince the world that none of them understand any thing of the matter." I am told by one of the spectators still alive, that in this new scene, *Harlequin*, being converted into a woman, pretended to be in labour, and was first delivered of a large pig, then of a sooterkin, &c. &c.

From the same paper of *Saturday, Jan.* 21, 1727, we learn, that "The pretended Rabbit-breeder, in order to perpetuate her fame, has had her picture done in a curious mezzotinto print by an able hand." It was painted by *Laguerre*, and scraped by *Faber*. She has a rabbit on her lap, and displays a countenance expressive of the utmost vulgarity. In *Hogarth's* comic representation, the remarkable turn-up of the nose is preserved. This, perhaps, was the only feature in her face that could not be altered by the convulsions of her pretended agony, or our artist would have given her resemblance with greater exactness.

Mr. *Dillingham*, an apothecary in *Red-Lion-Square*, laid a wager of ten guineas with *St. André*, that in a limited time the cheat would be detected. The money was paid him, and he expended it on a piece of plate, with three rabbits engraved by way of arms.

I learn from *The Weekly Miscellany*, for *April* 19, 1740, that a few days before, "The celebrated Rabbit-woman of *Godalmin* in *Surry* was committed to *Guildford Gaol*, for receiving stolen goods."

In *The Gazetteer, or Daily London Advertiser, Jan.* 21, 1763, was this paragraph, which closes the story of our heroine: "Last week died at *Godalming* in *Surry*, *Mary Tofts*, formerly noted for an imposition of breeding Rabbits."

[1] Both these letters are in *The British Museum*. See MS. Sloan. 3312. XXVI. G. and MS. Sloan. 3316. XXVI. G.

1727.

1. Music introduced to *Apollo* by *Minerva*. Hogarth fecit. *"Frontispiece to some book of music, or ticket for a concert."* I can venture to affirm, on unquestionable authority, that this print is a mere copy from the frontispiece to a more ancient book of music. The composer's name has escaped my memory.

2. Masquerade Ticket. A. a sacrifice to *Priapus*. B. a pair of Lecherometers shewing the companys inclinations as they approach em. Invented for the use of ladies and gentlemen, by the ingenious Mr. H———r *[Heidegger]*. Price One Shilling. *"There is much wit in this print."* The attentive observer will find, that *Hogarth* has transplanted several circumstances from hence into the first plate to the *Analysis of Beauty*, as well as into his Satire on the Methodists. See

the ornaments of an altar composed of a concatenation of different periwigs, and the barometers expressing the different degrees of animal heat. At the corners of the dial on the top of this print is the date of the year (1727), and the face of *Heidegger* appears under the figure XII. In the earliest impressions, the word Provocatives has, instead of V the open vowel U. This incorrectness in spelling was afterwards amended, though in a bungling manner, the round bottoms of the original letters being still visible.[1]

Concerning *John James Heidegger*, whose face has been more than once introduced by our artist, the reader may express some curiosity. The following account of him is therefore appended to the foregoing article.

"This extraordinary man, the son of a clergyman, was a native of *Zurich* in *Switzerland*, where he married, but left his country in consequence of an intrigue. Having had an opportunity of visiting the principal cities of *Europe*, he acquired a taste for elegant and refined pleasures, which, united to a strong inclination for voluptuousness, by degrees qualified him for the management of public amusements. In 1708, when he was near 50 years old, he came to *England* on a negotiation from the *Swiss* at *Zurich*; but, failing in his embassy, he entered as a private soldier in the guards for protection.[2] By his sprightly, engaging conversation, and insinuating address, he soon worked himself into the good graces of our young people of fashion; from whom he obtained the appellation of 'the *Swiss* Count.'[3] He had the address to procure a subscription, with which in 1709 he was enabled to furnish out the opera of '*Thomyris*,'[4] which was written in *English*, and performed at the Queen's theatre in the *Haymarket*. The music, however, was *Italian*; that is to say, airs selected from sundry of the foreign operas by *Bononcini, Scarlatti, Stefani, Gasparini,* and *Albinoni*. Most of the songs in '*Thomyris*' were excellent, those by *Bononcini* especially: *Valentini, Margarita,* and Mrs. *Tofts* sung in it; and *Heidegger* by this performance alone was a gainer of 500 guineas.[5] The judicious remarks he made on several defects in the conduct of our operas in general, and the hints he threw out for improving the entertainments of the royal theatre, soon established his character as a good critic. Appeals were made to his judgement; and some very magnificent and elegant decorations, introduced upon the stage in consequence of his advice, gave such satisfaction to *George* II. who was fond of operas, that, upon being informed to whose genius he was indebted for these improvements, his majesty was pleased from that time to countenance him, and he soon obtained the chief management of the Opera-house in *The Haymarket*. He then set about improving another species of diversion, not less agreeable to the king, which was the masquerades, and over these he always presided at the king's theatre. He was likewise appointed master of the revels. The nobility now caressed him so much, and had such an opinion of his taste, that all splendid and elegant entertainments given by them upon particular occasions, and all private assemblies by subscription, were submitted to his direction.[6]

"From the emoluments of these several employments, he gained a regular considerable income, amounting, it is said, in some years, to 5000 *l.* which he spent with much liberality: particularly in the maintenance of perhaps a somewhat too luxurious table; so that it may be said, he raised an income, but never a fortune. His foibles, however, if they deserve so harsh a name, were completely 'covered' by his 'charity,' which was boundless.[7]

"That he was a good judge of music, appears from his opera: but this is all that is known of his mental abilities;[8] unless we add, what we have good authority for saying in honour to his *memory*, that he walked from *Charing-Cross* to *Temple-bar*, and back again; and when he came home, wrote down every sign on each side the *Strand.*

"As to his person, though he was tall and well made, it was not very pleasing, from an unusual hardness of features.[9] But he was the first to joke upon his own ugliness; and he once laid a wager with the earl of *Chesterfield*, that, within a certain given time, his lordship would not be able to produce so hideous a face in all *London*. After strict search, a woman was found, whose features were at first sight thought stronger than *Heidegger's*; but, upon clapping her head-dress upon himself, he was universally allowed to have won the wager. *Jolly*, a well-known taylor, carrying his bill to a noble duke, his grace, for evasion said, 'Damn your ugly face, I never will pay you till you bring me an uglier fellow than yourself!' *Jolly* bowed and retired, wrote a letter, and sent it by a servant to *Heidegger;* saying, 'his grace wished to see him the next morning on particular business.' *Heidegger* attended, and *Jolly* was there to meet him; and in consequence, as soon as *Heidegger's* visit was over, *Jolly* received the cash.

"The late facetious duke of *Montagu* (the memorable author of the bottle-conjuror at the theatre in *The Haymarket*) gave an entertainment at *The Devil-tavern, Temple-bar,* to several of the nobility and gentry, selecting the most convivial, and a few hard-drinkers, who were all in the plot. *Heidegger* was invited, and in a few hours after dinner was made so dead drunk that he was carried out of the room, and laid insensible upon a bed. A profound sleep ensued; when the late Mrs. *Salmon's* daughter was introduced, who took a mould from his face in plaster of Paris. From this a mask was made, and a few days before the next masquerade (at which the king promised to be present, with the countess of *Yarmouth*), the duke made application to *Heidegger's* valet de chambre, to know what suit of cloaths he was likely to wear; and then procuring a similar dress, and a person of the same stature, he gave him his instructions. On the evening of the masquerade, as soon as his majesty was seated (who was always known by the conductor of the entertainment and the officers of the court, though concealed by his dress from the company), *Heidegger*, as usual, ordered the music to play 'God save the King;' but his back was no sooner turned, than the false *Heidegger* ordered them to strike up '*Charly* over the Water.' The whole company were instantly thunderstruck, and all the courtiers, not in the plot, were thrown into a stupid consternation. *Heidegger* flew to the music-gallery, swore, stamped, and raved, accused the musicians of drunkenness, or of being set on by some secret enemy to ruin him. The king and the countess laughed so immoderately, that they hazarded a discovery. While *Heidegger* stayed in the gallery, 'God save the King' was the tune; but when, after setting matters to rights, he retired to one of the dancing-rooms, to observe if decorum was kept by the company, the counterfeit stepping forward, and placing himself upon the floor of the theatre, just in front of the music-gallery, called out in a most audible voice, imitating *Heidegger*, damned them for blockheads, had he not just told them to play '*Charly* over the Water.' A pause ensued; the musicians, who knew his character, in their turn thought him either drunk or mad; but, as he continued his vociferation, '*Charly*' was played again. At this repetition of the supposed affront, some of the officers of the guards, who always attended upon these occasions, were for ascending the gallery, and kicking the musicians out; but the late duke of *Cumberland*, who could hardly contain himself, interposed. The company were thrown into great confusion. 'Shame! Shame!' resounded from all parts, and *Heidegger* once more flew in a violent rage to that part of the theatre facing the gallery. Here the duke of *Montagu*, artfully addressing himself to him, told him, 'the king was in a violent passion; that his best way was to go instantly and make an apology, for certainly the music were mad, and afterwards to discharge them.' Almost at the same instant, he ordered the false *Heidegger* to do the same. The scene now became truly comic in the circle before the king. *Heidegger* had no sooner made a genteel apology for the insolence of his musicians, but the false *Heidegger* advanced, and, in a plaintive tone, cried out, 'Indeed, Sire, it was not my fault, but that devil's in my likeness.' Poor *Heidegger* turned round, stared, staggered, grew pale, and could not utter a word. The duke then humanely whispered in his ear the sum of his plot, and the counterfeit was ordered to take off his mask. Here ended the frolick; but *Heidegger* swore he would never attend any public amusement, if that witch the wax-work woman did not break the mould, and melt down the mask before his face.[10]

"Being once at supper with a large company, when a question was debated, which nationalist of *Europe*, had the greatest ingenuity; to the surprise of all present, he claimed that character for the *Swiss*, and appealed to himself for the truth of it. 'I was born a *Swiss*, said he, 'and came to *England* without a farthing, where I have found means to gain 5000 *l.* a year, and to spend it. Now I defy the most able *Englishman* to go to *Switzerland*, and either to gain that income, or to spend it there.' He died *Sept.* 4, 1749, at the advanced age of 96 years, at his house at *Richmond* in *Surrey*, where he was buried. He left behind him one natural daughter, Miss *Pappet*, who was married *Sept.* 2, 1750, to Captain (afterwards Sir *Peter*) *Denis*.[11] Part of this lady's fortune was a house at the north west corner of *Queen-square, Ormond-street*, which Sir *Peter* afterwards sold to the late Dr. *Campbell*, and purchased a seat in *Kent*, pleasantly situated near *Westram*, then called *Valence*, but now (by its present proprietor, the earl of *Hillsborough*) *Hill Park*."

[1] In this print our artist has likewise imitated the manner of *Callot*.

[2] See N° 48, among the prints of uncertain date.

[3] See Sir *John Hawkins's* History of Music, Vol. V. p. 142. He is twice noticed under this title in the "Tatler," Nos. 12. and 18.; and in Mr. *Duncombe's* "Collection of Letters of several eminent Persons deceased," is a humourous dedication of Mr. *Hughes's* "Vision of *Chaucer*," to "the *Swiss* Count."

[4] There was another opera of the same name, by *Peter Motteux*, in 1719.

[5] "*Thomyris*" and "*Camilla*" were both revived in 1726; but neither of them then succeeded.

[6] J. N. has been favoured with the sight of an amethyst snuff-box set in gold, presented to *Heidegger* in 1731, by the duke of *Lorrain*, afterwards emperor of *Germany*, which *Heidegger* very highly valued, and bequeathed to his executor *Lewis Way*, esq. of *Richmond*, and which is now (1785) in the possession of his son *Benjamin Way*, esq.

[7] After a successful masquerade, he has been known to give away several hundred pounds at a time. "You know poor objects of distress better than I do," he would frequently observe to Mr. *Way*, "Be so kind as to give away this money for me." This well-known liberality, perhaps, contributed much to his carrying on that diversion with so little opposition as he met with.

[8] *Pope* (Dunciad, I. 289.) calls the bird which attended on the goddess

"————————a monster of a fowl,
Something betwixt a *Heidegger* and owl."

and explains *Heidegger* to mean "a strange bird from *Switzerland*, and not (as some have supposed) the name of an eminent person, who was a man of parts, and, as was said of *Petronius*, Arbiter Elegantiarum."

The author of *The Scandalizade* has also put the following description of our hero into the mouth of *Handel*:

"Thou perfection, as far as e'er nature could run,
Of the ugly, quoth H—d-l, in th' ugliest baboon,
Human nature's, and even thy Maker's disgrace,

> So frightful thy looks, so grotesque is thy face!
> With a hundred deep wrinkles impress'd on thy front,
> Like a map with a great many rivers upon't;
> Thy lascivious ridottos, obscene masquerades,
> Have unmaided whole scores ev'ry season of maids."

Fielding also has introduced him in the Puppet-show, with which the *Author's Farce* (acted at the *Haymarket* 1729), concludes, under the title of *Count Ugly*.

> "*Nonsense.*
> Too late, O mighty Count, you came.
>
> *Count.*
> I ask not for myself, for I disdain
> O'er the poor ragged tribe of bards to reign.
> Me did my stars to happier fates prefer,
> Sur-intendant des plaisirs d'*Angleterre.*
> If masquerades you have, let those be mine,
> But on the Signor let the laurel shine.
>
> *Tragedy.*
> What is thy plea? Half written?
>
> *Count.*
> No nor read.
> Put it from dulness any may succeed,
> To that and nonsense I good title plead,
> Nought else was ever in my masquerade."

[9] In a Dedication to "The Masquerade, a Poem, inscribed to Count *Heidegger*," (which is the production of Mr. *Fielding*, though foisted into the works of Dr. *Arbuthnot,*) the facetious writer says, "I cannot help congratulating you on that gift of Nature, by which you seem so adapted to the post you enjoy. I mean that natural masque, which is too visible a perfection to be here insisted on——and, I am sure, never fails of making an impression on the most indifferent beholder. Another gift of Nature, which you seem to enjoy in no small degree, is that modest confidence supporting you in every act of your life. Certainly, a great blessing! For I always have observed, that brass in the forehead draws gold into the pocket. As for what mankind calls virtues, I shall not compliment you on them: since you are so wise as to keep them secret from the world, far be it from me to publish them; especially since they are things which lie out of the way of your calling. Smile then (if you can smile) on my endeavours, and this little poem, with candour——for which the author desires no more gratuity than a ticket for your next ball." There is a mezzotinto of *Heidegger* by *J. Faber*, 1742, (other

copies dated 1749) from a painting by *Vanloo*, a striking likeness, now (1785) in the possession of *Peter Crawford*, esq. of *Cold Bath Fields*.

[10] To this occurrence the following imperfect stanzas, transcribed from the hand-writing of *Pope*, are supposed to relate. They were found on the back of a page containing some part of his translation, either of the "Iliad" or "Odyssey," in the *British Museum*.

> XIII.
> "Then he went to the side-board, and call'd for much liquor,
> And glass after glass he drank quicker and quicker;
> So that *Heidegger* quoth,
> Nay, faith on his oath,
> Of two hogsheads of Burgundy, *Satan* drank both.
> Then all like a —— the Devil appear'd,
> And strait the whole tables of dishes he clear'd;
> Then a friar, then a nun,
> And then he put on
> A face all the company took for his own.
> Even thine, O false *Heidegger!* who wert so wicked
> To let in the Devil——"

[11] Who died *June* 12, 1778, being then vice-admiral of the red. See Memoirs of him in Gent. Mag. 1780, p. 268.

---

3. Frontispiece to a Collection of Songs, with the Music by Mr. *Leveridge*, in two vols. 8vo. *London*, engraved and printed for the author, in *Tavistock-street, Covent-Garden*, 1727. This design consists of a *Bacchus* and a *Venus* in the Clouds, and a figure with musical instruments, &c. on the earth, soliciting their attention, &c. The ornaments round the engraved title-page seem likewise to be *Hogarth's*.

1728.

1. Head of *Hesiod*, from the bust at *Wilton*. The frontispiece to *Cook's* translation of *Hesiod*, in 2 vols. 4to. printed by *N. Blandford* for *T. Green*.

2. *Rich's* Glory, or his Triumphant Entry into *Covent Garden*. W. H. I. E^t. SULP. Price Sixpence.

The date of the print before us has been conjectured from its reference to the *Beggar's Opera,* and *Perseus* and *Andromeda,*[1] both of which were acted in the year already mentioned.

This plate represents the removal of *Rich* and his scenery, authors, actors, &c. from *Lincoln's-Inn Fields* to the *New House*; and might therefore be as probably referred to the year 1733, when that event happened. The scene is the area of *Covent Garden,* across which, leading toward the door of the Theatre, is a long procession, consisting of a cart loaded with thunder and lightning; performers, &c. and at the head of them Mr. *Rich* (invested with the skin of the famous dog in *Perseus* and *Andromeda*) riding with his mistress in a chariot driven by *Harlequin,* and drawn by Satyrs. But let the verses at bottom explain our artist's meaning:

>   Not with more glory through the streets of *Rome,*
>   Return'd great conquerors in triumph home,
>   Than, proudly drawn with Beauty by his side,
>   We see gay *R——*[2] in gilded chariot ride.
>   He comes, attended by a num'rous throng,
>   Who, with loud shouts, huzza the Chief along.
>   Behold two bards, obsequious, at his wheels,
>   Confess the joy each raptur'd bosom feels;
>   Conscious that wit by him will be receiv'd,
>   And on his stage true humour be retriev'd.
>   No *sensible* and *pretty* play will fall[3]
>   Condemn'd by him as not theatrical.
>   The players follow, as they here are nam'd,
>   Dress'd in each character for which they're fam'd.
>   *Quin* th' *Old Bachelour,* a *Hero Ryan* shows,
>   Who *stares* and stalks majestick as he goes.
>   *Walker,*[4] in his lov'd character we see
>   A Prince, tho' once a fisherman was he,
>   And *Massanelo* nam'd; in this he prides,
>   Tho' fam'd for many other parts besides.
>   Then *Hall,*[5] who tells the bubbled countrymen
>   That *Carolus* is *Latin* for *Queen Anne.*
>   Did ever mortal know so clean a bite?
>   Who else, like him, can copy *Serjeant Kite!*
>   To the *Piazza* let us turn our eyes,
>   See *Johnny Gay* on porters shoulders rise,
>   Whilst a bright Man of Tast his works despise.[6]
>   Another author wheels his works with care,
>   In hopes to get a market at this fair;
>   For such a day he sees not ev'ry year.

By the *Man of Taste*, Mr. *Pope* was apparently designed. He is represented, in his tye-wig, at one corner of the *Piazza*, wiping his posteriors with the *Beggar's Opera*. The letter P is over his head. His little sword is significantly placed, and the peculiarity of his figure well preserved.

The reason why our artist has assigned such an employment to him, we can only guess. It seems, indeed, from Dr. *Johnson's* Life of *Gay*, that *Pope* did not *think* the *Beggar's Opera* would succeed. *Swift*, however, was of the same opinion; and yet the former supported the piece on the first night of exhibition, and the latter defended it in his *Intelligencer* against the attacks of Dr. *Herring*,[7] then preacher to the Society of *Lincoln's-Inn*, afterwards archbishop of *Canterbury*. *Hogarth* might be wanton in his satire; might have founded it on idle report; or might have sacrificed truth to the prejudices of Sir *James Thornhill*, whose quarrel, on another occasion, he is supposed to have taken up, when he ridiculed *The Translator of Homer* in a view of "The Gate of *Burlington-house*."

There are besides some allusions in the verses already quoted, as well as in the piece they refer to, which I confess my inability to illustrate. Those who are best acquainted with the theatric and poetical history of the years 1728, &c. would prove the most successful commentators on the present occasion; but not many can possibly be now alive who were at that period competent judges of such matters.

This print, however, was not only unpublished, but in several places is unfinished. It was probably suppressed by the influence of some of the characters represented in it. The style of composition, and manner of engraving, &c. &c. would have sufficiently proved it to be the work of *Hogarth*, if the initials of his name had been wanting at the bottom of the plate.

[1] The *Perseus* and *Andromeda*, for which *Hogarth* engraved the plates mentioned in p. 170, was not published till 1730; but there was one under the same title at *Drury-Lane* in 1728. As both houses took each other's plans at that time, perhaps the *Lincoln's-Inn Fields Perseus* might have been acted before it was printed.

[2] *Rich*.

[3] No *sensible* and *pretty* play, &c. This refers to *Cibber's* decision on the merits of some piece offered for representation, and, we may suppose, rejected. In a copy of verses addressed to *Rich* on the building of *Covent Garden* Theatre, are the following lines, which seem to allude to the rejection already mentioned:

> "Poets no longer shall submit their plays
> To learned *Cibber's* gilded withered bays;

> To such a judge the labour'd scene present,
> Whom *sensible* and *pretty* won't content:
> But to thy theatre with pleasure bear
> The comic laughter and the tragic tear."

[4] The original *Macheath*. He used, however, to perform the heroes, particularly *Alexander*. From these lines it appears that *Massanello*, was a favourite part with him. From *Chetwood's* History of the Stage, p. 141, I learn that *Walker* had contracted the two parts of *Durfey's Massanello* into one piece, which was acted with success at *Lincoln's-Inn Fields*.

[5] The original *Lockit*, who was also celebrated for his performance of Serjeant *Kite*.

[6] The grammar and spelling of this line are truly *Hogarthian*.

[7] "A noted preacher near *Lincoln's-Inn* playhouse has taken notice of the *Beggar's Opera* in the pulpit, and inveighed against it as a thing of very evil tendency." *Mist's Weekly Journal, March* 30, 1728.

3. The Beggar's Opera. The title over it is in capitals uncommonly large.

> *Brittons* attend—view this harmonious stage,
> And listen to those notes which charm the age.
> Thus shall your tastes in *sounds* and *sense* be shown,
> And *Beggar's Op'ras* ever be your own.

No painter or engraver's name. The plate seems at once to represent the exhibition of *The Beggar's Opera*, and the rehearsal of an *Italian* one. In the *former*, all the characters are drawn with the heads of different animals; as *Polly*, with a Cat's; *Lucy*, with a Sow's; *Macheath*, with an Ass's; *Lockit*, and Mr. and Mrs. *Peachum*, with those of an Ox, a Dog, and an Owl. In the *latter*, several noblemen appear conducting the chief female singer forward on the stage, and perhaps are offering her money, or protection from a figure that is rushing towards her with a drawn sword. Harmony, flying in the air, turns her back on the *English* playhouse, and hastens toward the rival theatre. Musicians stand in front of the former, playing on the Jew's-harp, the salt-box, the bladder and string, bagpipes, &c. On one side are people of distinction, some of whom kneel as if making an offer to *Polly*, or paying their adorations to her. To these are opposed a butcher, &c. expressing similar applause. *Apollo*, and one of the Muses, are fast asleep beneath the stage. A man is easing nature under a wall hung with ballads, and shewing his contempt of such compositions, by the use he makes of one of them. A sign of the star, a gibbet, and some other circumstances less intelligible, appear in the back ground.

4. The same. The lines under it are engraved in a different manner from those on the preceding plate. Sold at the Print-Shop in *The Strand*, near *Catherine Street*.

5. A copy of the same, under the following title, &c.

> The Opera House, or the *Italian* Eunuch's Glory. Humbly inscribed to those Generous Encouragers of Foreigners, and Ruiners of *England*.
>
> From *France*, from *Rome* we come,
> To help Old *England* to *to* b' undone.

Under the division of the print that represents the *Italian Opera*, the words—*Stage Mutiny*—are perhaps improperly added.

On the two sides of this print are scrolls, containing a list of the presents made to *Farinelli*. The words are copied from the same enumeration in the second plate of the Rake's Progress.[1]

At the bottom are the following lines:

> "*Brittains* attend—view this harmonious stage,
> And listen to those notes which charm the age.
> How sweet the sound where cats and bears
> With brutish noise offend our ears!
> Just so the foreign singers move
> Rather contempt than gain our love.
> Were such discourag'd, we should find
> Musick at home to charm the mind!
> Our home-spun authors must forsake the field,
> And *Shakespear* to the *Italian Eunuchs* yield."[2]

Perhaps the original print was the work of *Gravelot*, *Vandergucht*, or some person unknown.[3] The idea of it is borrowed from a *French* book, called *Les Chats*, printed at *Amsterdam* in 1728. In this work, facing p. 117, is represented an opera performed by cats, superbly habited. The design is by *Coypel*; the engraving by *T. Otten*. At the end of the treatise, the opera itself is published. It is improbable that *Hogarth* should have met with this *jeu d'esprit*; and, if he did, he could not have read the explanation to it.

[1] The following paragraph appeared in the *Grub-street Journal* for *April* 10, 1735; and to this perhaps *Hogarth* alluded in the list of donations already mentioned: "His Royal Highness the Prince hath been pleased to make a present of a fine wrought gold snuff-box, richly set with brilliants and rubies,

in which was inclosed a pair of brilliant diamond knee buckles, as also a purse of 100 guineas, to the famous Signor *Farinelli*, &c."

[2] These two last lines make part of *Addison's* Prologue to *Phædra and Hippolytus*, reading only "the soft *Scarlatti*," instead of *Italian Eunuchs*.

[3] At the back of an old impression of it, in the collection of the late Mr. *Rogers*, I meet with the name of *Echerlan*, but am unacquainted with any such designer or engraver.——I have since been told he came over to *England* to dispose of a number of foreign prints, and was himself no mean caricaturist. Having drawn an aggravated likeness of an *English* nobleman, whose figure was peculiarly unhappy, he was forced to fly in consequence of a resentment which threatened little short of assassination.

1729.

1. King *Henry* the Eighth, and *Anna Bullen*. "*Very indifferent.*" This plate has very idly been imagined to contain the portraits of *Frederick* Prince of *Wales* and Miss *Vane*;[1] but the stature and faces, both of the lady and *Percy*, are totally unlike their supposed originals. Underneath are the following verses by *Allan Ramsay*:

> Here struts old pious *Harry*, once the great
> Reformer of the *English* church and state:
> 'Twas thus he stood, when *Anna Bullen's* charms
> Allur'd the amorous monarch to her arms;
> With his right hand he leads her as his own,
> To place this matchless beauty on his throne;
> Whilst *Kate* and *Piercy* mourn their wretched fate,
> And view the royal pair with equal hate,
> Reflecting on the pomp of glittering crowns,
> And arbitrary power that knows no bounds.
> Whilst *Wolsey*, leaning on his throne of state,
> Through this unhappy change foresees his fate,
> Contemplates wisely upon worldly things,
> The cheat of grandeur, and the faith of kings.

Mr. *Charlton*, of *Canterbury*, has a copy of this print, with the following title and verses: "King *Henry* VIII. bringing to court *Anne Bullen*, who was afterwards his royal consort." *Hogarth design. &. sculp.*

> See here the great, the daring *Harry* stands,
> Peace, Plenty, Freedom, shining in his face,
> With lovely *Anna Bullen* joining hands,

Her looks bespeaking ev'ry heav'nly grace.

See *Wolsey* frowning, discontent and sour,
Feeling the superstitious *structure* shake:
While *Henry's* driving off the *Roman* whore,
For *Britain's* weal, and his *Lutherian's* sake.

Like *Britain's* Genius our brave King appears,
Despising Priestcraft, Avarice, and Pride;
Nor the loud roar of *Babel's* bulls he fears,
The Dagon falls before his beauteous bride.

Like *England's* Church, all sweetness and resign'd,
The comely queen her lord with calmness eyes;
As if she said, If goodness guard your mind,
You ghostly tricks and trump'ry may despise.

[1] To the fate of this lady Dr. *Johnson* has a beautiful allusion in his *Vanity of Human Wishes*:

"Yet *Vane* could tell what ills from beauty spring,
And *Sedley* curs'd the form that *pleas'd a king*."

Perhaps the thought, that suggested this couplet, is found in *Loveling's* Poems, a work already quoted:

-------nec *Gwynnam* valebat
Angliaco placuisse regi.

Mersa est acerbo funere sanguinis
Vanella clari: nec grave spiculum
Averteret fati *Machaon*,
Nec madido *Fredericus* ore.

2. The same plate without any verses, but with an inscription added in their room. *Ramsay* seems to have been particularly attached to *Hogarth*. He subscribed, as I have already observed, for thirty copies of the large *Hudibras*.

The original picture was at *Vauxhall*, in the portico of the old great room on the right-hand of the entry into the garden. See p. 29.

3. Frontispiece to the "Humours of *Oxford*," a comedy by *James Miller*, acted at *Drury-Lane*, and published in 8vo, 1729.[1] *W. Hogarth inv. G. Vandergucht sc.* The Vice-chancellor, attended by his beadle, surprizing two Fellows of a College, one of them much intoxicated, at a tavern.

[1] It met with but moderate success in the theatre; but drew on Mr. *Miller* the resentment of some of the heads of the colleges in *Oxford*, who looked on themselves as satirized in it.

1730.

1. *Perseus*, and *Medusa* dead, and *Pegasus*. Frontispiece to *Perseus* and *Andromeda*. *W. H. fec.*

2. Another print to the same piece, of *Perseus* descending. Mr. *Walpole* mentions only one.

3. A half-starved boy. (The same as is represented in the print of *Morning.*) *W. H. pinx. F. Sykes sc. Sykes* was a pupil of *Thornhill* or *Hogarth*. This print bears the date of 1730; but I suspect the 0 was designed for an 8, and that the upper part of it is wanting, because the aqua fortis failed; or, that the pupil copied the figure from a sketch of his master, which at that time was unappropriated. No one will easily suspect *Hogarth* of such plagiarism as he might justly be charged with, could he afterwards have adopted this complete design as his own; neither is it probable that any youth could have produced a figure so characteristic as this; or, if he could, that he should have published it without any concomitant circumstances to explain its meaning. The above title, which some collector has bestowed on this etching, is not of a discriminative kind. Who can tell from it whether he is to look for a boy emaciated by hunger, or shivering with cold? It is mentioned here, only that it may be reprobated. If every young practitioner's imitation of a single figure by *Hogarth* were to be admitted among his works, they would never be complete.

4. *Gulliver* presented to the Queen of *Babilary*. *W. Hogarth inv. Ger. Vandergucht sc. "It is the frontispiece to the Travels of Mr.* John Gulliver," son of Capt. *Lemuel Gulliver*, a translation from the *French* by Mr. *Lockman*. There is as much merit in this print as in the work to which it belongs.

1731.

1. Two frontispieces to a translation of two of *Moliere's* plays, viz. *L'Avare*[1] and *Le Cocû imaginaire*. These are part of a select collection of *Moliere's* Comedies in *French* and *English*. They were advertised in *The Grub-street Journal*, with designs by "Monsieur *Coypel*, Mr. *Hogarth*, Mr. *Dandridge*, Mr. *Hamilton*," &c. in eight pocket volumes.

[1] Of this one, Mr. *S. Ireland* has the original drawing.

2. Frontispiece to "The Tragedy of Tragedies, or the Life and Death of *Tom Thumb*," in three acts;[1] by *Henry Fielding. W. Hogarth inv. Ger. Vandergucht sc.* *"There is some humour in this print."*

[1] This piece had before made its appearance in 1730 in one act only.

3. Frontispiece to the Opera of *The Highland Fair, or the Union of the Clans*, by *Joseph Mitchell. W. Hogarth inv. Ger Vandergucht sculp.*

"Forsan et hæc olim meminisse juvabit." VIRG.

The date of this piece is confirmed by the following paragraph in *The Grub-street journal*, March 4, 1731: "We hear from the Theatre-Royal in *Drury-lane*, that there is now in rehearsal, and to be performed on *Tuesday, March* 16, a new *Scots* Opera, called *The Highland Fair, or Union of the Clans*, &c." The subject being too local for the *English* stage, it met with little or no success.

1732.

1. *Sarah Malcolm*,[1] executed *March* 7, 1732, for murdering Mrs. *Lydia Duncombe* her mistress, *Elizabeth Harrison*, and *Anne Price*, drawn in *Newgate. W. Hogarth (ad vivum) pinxit & sculpsit.*[2] Some copies are dated 1733, and have only *Hogarth pinx*. She was about twenty-five years of age.[3] *"This woman put on red to sit to him for her picture two days before her execution."*[4] Mr. *Walpole* paid *Hogarth* five guineas for the original. Professor *Martyn* dissected this notorious murderess, and afterwards presented her skeleton, in a glass case, to the Botanic Garden at *Cambridge*, where it still remains.

[1] On *Sunday* morning, the 4th of *February*, Mrs. *Lydia Duncombe*, aged 80, *Elizabeth Harrison*, her companion, aged 60, were found strangled, and *Ann Price*, her maid, aged 17, with her throat cut, in their beds, at the said Mrs. *Duncombe's* apartments in *Tanfield-Court* in *The Temple. Sarah Malcolm*, a chare-woman, was apprehended the same evening on the information of Mr. *Kerrol*, who had chambers on the same stair-case, and had found some bloody linen under his bed, and a silver tankard in his close-stool, which she had hid there. She made a pretended confession, and gave information against *Thomas Alexander, James Alexander*, and *Mary Tracey*, that they committed the murder and robbery, and she only stood on the stairs as a watch; that they took away three hundred pounds and some valuable goods, of which she had not more than her share; but the coroner's inquest gave their verdict *Wilful Murder* against *Malcolm* only.—On the 23d her trial came on at *The Old Bailey*: when it appeared that Mrs. *Duncombe* had but 54 *l.* in her box, and 53 *l.* 11 *s.* 6 *d.* of

it were found upon *Malcolm* betwixt her cap and hair. She owned her being concerned in the robbery, but denied she knew any thing of the murder till she went in with other company to see the deceased. The jury found her guilty of both. She was strongly suspected to have been concerned in the murder of Mr. *Nesbit* in 1729, near *Drury-lane*, for which one *Kelly*, alias *Owen*, was hanged; the grounds for his conviction being only a bloody razor found under the murdered man's head that was known to be his. But he denied to the last his being concerned in the murder; and said, in his defence, he lent the razor to a woman he did not know.—On *Wednesday, March 7*, she was executed on a gibbet opposite *Mitre-court, Fleet-street*, where the crowd was so great, that a Mrs. *Strangways*, who lived in *Fleet-street*, near *Serjeant's-Inn*, crossed the street, from her own house to Mrs. *Coulthurst's* on the opposite side of the way, over the heads and shoulders of the mob. She went to execution neatly dressed in a crape mourning gown, holding up her head in the cart with an air, and looking as if she was painted, which some did not scruple to affirm. Her corpse was carried to an undertaker's upon *Snow-hill*, where multitudes of people resorted, and gave money to see it: among the rest a gentleman in deep mourning, who kissed her, and gave the people half a crown. She was attended by the Rev. Mr. *Pedington*, lecturer of *St. Bartholomew* the Great, seemed penitent, and desired to see her master *Kerrol*; but, as she did not, protested all accusations against him were false. During her imprisonment she received a letter from her father at *Dublin*, who was in too bad circumstances to send her such a sum as 17 *l.* which she pretended he did. The night before her execution, she delivered a paper to Mr. *Pedington* (the copy of which he sold for 20 *l.*), of which the substance is printed in *The Gentleman's Magazine*, 1733, p. 137. She had given much the same account before, at her trial, in a long and fluent speech.

[2] The words "*& sculpsit*" are wanting in the copies. In the three last of them the figure also is reversed.

[3] "This woman," said *Hogarth*, after he had drawn *Sarah Malcolm*, "by her features, is capable of any wickedness."

[4] "*Monday Sarah Malcolm* sat for her picture in *Newgate*, which was taken by the ingenious Mr. *Hogarth*: Sir *James Thornhill* was likewise present." *Craftsman, Saturday, March* 10, 1732-3.

2. An engraved copy of ditto.

3. Ditto, mezzotinto.

4. Ditto, part graven, part mezzotinto.

The knife with which she committed the murder is lying by her.

5. Another copy of this portrait[1] (of which only the first was engraved by *Hogarth*), with the addition of a clergyman holding a ring in his hand, and a motto, "No recompence but Love."[2]

In *The Grub-street Journal* of *Thursday, March* 8, 1732, appeared the following epigram:

> "To *Malcolm Guthrie*[3] cries, confess the murther;
> The truth disclose, and trouble me no further.
> Think on both worlds; the pain that thou must bear
> In that, and what a load of scandal here.
> Confess, confess, and you'll avoid it all:
> Your body shan't be hack'd at *Surgeons Hall*:
> No *Grub-street* hack shall dare to use your ghost ill,
> *Henly* shall read upon your post a postile;
> *Hogarth* your charms transmit to future times,
> And *Curll* record your life in prose and rhimes.
>
> "*Sarah* replies, these arguments might do
> From *Hogarth, Curll*, and *Henly*, drawn by you,
> Were I condemn'd at *Padington* to ride:
> But now from *Fleet-street Pedington's* my guide."

The office of this *Pedington*[4] may be known from the following advertisement in *The Weekly Miscellany*, N° 37. *August* 25, 1733. "This day is published, Price Six-pence, (on occasion of the Re-commitment of the two *Alexanders*; with a very neat effigies of *Sarah Malcolm* and her *Reverend Confessor*, both taken from the Life) The Friendly Apparition: Being an account of the most surprising appearance of *Sarah Malcolm's* Ghost to a great assembly of her acquaintance at a noted Gin-shop; together with the remarkable speech she then made to the whole company."

[1] A copy of it in wood was inserted in *The Gentleman's Magazine*, 1733, p. 153.

[2] This print was designed as a frontispiece to the pamphlet advertised in *The Weekly Miscellany*. (See text, above.)

[3] The Ordinary of *Newgate*.

[4] Mr. *Pedington* died September 18, 1734. He is supposed to have made some amorous overtures to *Sarah*.

6. The Man of TASTE. The Gate of *Burlington-house. Pope* white-washing it, and bespattering the Duke of *Chandos's* coach. "*A satire on* Pope's *Epistle on Taste. No name.*" It has been already observed that the plate was suppressed;

and if this be true, the suppression may be accounted for from the following inscription, lately met with at the back of one of the copies.

"Bo^t this book of Mr. *Wayte*, at *The Fountain Tavern*, in *The Strand*, in the presence of Mr. *Draper*, who told me he had it of the Printer, Mr. *W. Rayner*.[1]

"J. Cosins."

On this attested memorandum a prosecution seems meant to have been founded. *Cosins* was an attorney, and *Pope* was desirous on all occasions to make the law the engine of his revenge.

[1] *Rayner* was at that time already under prosecution for publishing a pamphlet called, "*Robin's* Game, or Seven's the Main." Neglecting to surrender himself, he was taken by a writ of execution from the crown, and confined to the *King's Bench*; where he became connected with Lady *Dinely*, whole character was of equal infamy with his own.

7. The same, in a smaller size; prefixed to a pamphlet, intituled, "A Miscellany of Taste, by Mr. *Pope*," &c. containing his Epistles, with Notes and other poems. In the former of these Mr. *Pope* has a tie-wig on, in the latter a cap.

8. The same, in a size still smaller; very coarsely engraved. Only one of them is noted by Mr. *Walpole*.

A reader of these Anecdotes observes, "That the total silence of *Pope* concerning so great an artist, encourages a suspicion that his attacks were felt though not resented. The thunders of the poet were usually pointed at inglorious adversaries; but he might be conscious of a more equal match in our formidable caricaturist. All ranks of people have eyes for pencil'd ridicule, but of written satire we have fewer judges. It may be suspected, that the 'pictured shape' would never have been complained of, had it been produced only by a bungler in his art. But from the powers of *Hogarth, Pope* seems to have apprehended more lasting inconvenience; and the event has justified his fear. The frontispiece to *Smedley's Gulliveriana* has been long forgotten; but the *Gate of Burlington house* is an object coveted by all who assemble prints of humour.—It may be added, that our painter's reputation was at the height ten years before the death of *Pope*, who could not therefore have overlooked his merit, though, for some reason or other, he has forborne to introduce the slightest allusion to him or his performances. Yet these, or copies from them, were to be met with in almost every public and private house throughout the kingdom; nor was it easy for the bard of *Twickenham* to have mixed in the conversation of the times, without being obliged to hear repeated praises of the author of *The Harlot's Progress*."

The sheet containing this page having been shewn to a friend, produced from him the following remark: "That *Pope* was silent on the merits of *Hogarth* (as one of your readers has observed) should excite little astonishment, as our artist's print on the *South Sea* exhibits the translator of *Homer* in no very flattering point of view. He is represented with one of his hands in the pocket of a fat personage, who wears a hornbook at his girdle. For whom this figure was designed, is doubtful. Perhaps it was meant for *Gay*, who was a fat man, and a loser in the same scheme."—"*Gay*," says Dr. *Johnson*, "in that disastrous year had a present from young *Craggs* of some *South-sea* stock, and once supposed himself to be master of twenty-thousand pounds. His friends persuaded him to sell his share; but he dreamed of dignity and splendour, and could not bear to obstruct his own fortune. He was then importuned to sell as much as would purchase an hundred a year for life, which, says *Fenton*, will make you sure of a clean shirt and a shoulder of mutton every day. This counsel was rejected; the profit and principal were lost, and *Gay* sunk under the calamity so low that his life became in danger.—The Hornbook appended to his girdle, perhaps, refers to the Fables he wrote for the Duke of *Cumberland*. Some of your ingenious correspondents, or Mr. *Walpole*, who is *instar omnium*, may be able to give a further illustration. The conclusion to the inscription under this plate—*Guess at the rest, you'll find out more*—seems also to imply a consciousness of such personal satire as it was not prudent to explain. I may add, that the print before us exhibits more than one figure copied from *Callot*. Among the people going along the gallery to raffle for husbands, the curious observer will recognize the *Old Maid* with lappets flying, &c. afterwards introduced into the scene of *Morning*. Dr. *Johnson*, however, bears witness to the propriety of our great poet's introduction into a satire on the 'disastrous year of national infatuation, when more riches than *Peru* can boast were expected from the *South Sea*; when the contagion of avarice tainted every mind; and *Pope*, being seized with the universal passion, ventured some of his money. The stock rose in its price; and he for a while thought himself *The Lord of Thousands*. But this dream of happiness did not last long: and he seems to have waked soon enough to get clear with the loss only of what he once thought himself to have won, and perhaps not wholly that.'"

It appears from *Pope's* correspondence with *Atterbury*, that the stock he had was at one time valued at between twenty and thirty thousand pounds; and that he was one of the lucky few who had "the good fortune to remain with half of what they imagined they had."—"Had you got all you have lost beyond what you ventured," said the good Bishop in reply, "consider that your superfluous gains would have sprung from the ruin of several families that now want necessaries."[1]

[1] Letters to and from Bishop *Atterbury*, 1782, vol. I. p. 71.

1733.

1. The Laughing Audience. "1733. Rec^d. Dec^{br}. 18 *of the Right Honn^{ble}. Lord Biron Half a Guinea being the first Payment for nine Prints 8 of which Represent a Rakes Progress and the 9*th *a Fair, Which I promise to Deliver at Michaelmass Next on Receiving one Guinea more. Note the Fair will be Deliver'd next Christmass at Sight of this receipt the Prints of the Rake*^s*. Progress alone will be 2 Guineas each set after the Subscription is over.*"

The words printed in *Italicks* are in the hand-writing of *Hogarth*.

2. The *Fair*[1] [at *Southwark*]. *Invented, painted, and engraved by W. Hogarth*.. The show-cloth, representing the Stage Mutiny, is taken from a large etching by *John Laguerre* (son of *Louis Laguerre*, the historical painter), who sung at *Lincoln's-Inn Fields* and *Covent-Garden* Theatres, painted some of their scenes, and died in 1748. *The Stage-Mutineers*, or *A Playhouse to be let*, a tragi-comi farcical-ballad-opera, which was published in 1733, will throw some light on the figures here represented by *Hogarth*. See also the *Supplement* to *Dodsley's* Preface to his Collection of Old Plays, and the "Biographia Dramatica, 1782."

It is remarkable that, in our artist's copy of this etching, he has added a paint-pot and brushes at the feet of the athletic figure *with a cudgel in his hand*, who appears on the side of *Highmore*.[2] From these circumstances it is evident that *John Ellis* the painter (a pupil of Sir *James Thornhill*, a great frequenter of *Broughton's* gymnasium, the stages of other prize-fighters, &c.) was the person designed. *Ellis* was deputy-manager for Mrs. *Wilks*, and *took up the cudgels* also for the new patentee. Mr. *Walpole* observes that *Rysbrack*, when he produced that "exquisite summary of his skill, knowledge, and judgment," the *Hercules* now in Mr. *Hoare's* Temple at *Stourhead*, modelled the legs of the God from those of *Ellis*. This statue was compiled from the various limbs and parts of seven or eight of the strongest and best-made men in *London*, chiefly the bruisers, &c. of the then famous amphitheatre in *Tottenham Court road*.

In *Banks's* Works, vol. I. p. 97. is a Poetical Epistle on this print, which alludes to the disputes between the managers of *Drury-Lane*, and such of the actors as were spirited up to rebellion by *Theophilus Cibber*, and seceded to *The Haymarket* in 1733. *Cibber* is represented under the character of *Pistol*;[3] *Harper* under that of *Falstaff*. The figure in the corner was designed for *Colley Cibber* the Laureat, who had just sold his share in the play-house to Mr. *Highmore*, who is represented holding a scroll, on which is written "it cost £.6000." A monkey is exhibited sitting astride the iron that supports the sign of *The Rose*, a well-known tavern. A label issuing from his mouth contains the words: "*I am a gentleman*."[4] *The Siege of Troy*, upon another show-cloth, was a celebrated droll, composed by *Elkanah Settle*, and printed in 1707; it was a great favourite at fairs. A booth was built in *Smithfield* this year for the use of *T. Cibber, Griffin, Bullock*, and *H. Hallam*; at which the Tragedy of *Tamerlane*, with *The Fall of Bajazet*, intermixed with the Comedy of *The Miser*, was actually represented. The figure vaulting on the rope was designed for Signor *Violante*, who signalized himself in the reign of *Geo.* I.; and the tall man exhibited on a showcloth, was *Maximilian*, a giant from *Upper Saxony*. The man flying from the steeple was one *Cadman*, who, within the recollection of some persons now living, descended in the manner here described from the steeple of *St. Martin's* into *The Mews*. He broke his neck soon after, in an experiment of the like kind, at *Shrewsbury*, and lies buried there in the churchyard of *St. Mary Friars*, with the following inscription on a little tablet inserted in the church-wall just over his grave.[5] The lines are contemptible, but yet serve to particularize the accident that occasioned his death.

> Let this small monument record the name
> Of *Cadman*, and to future times proclaim
> How, by an attempt to fly from this high spire
> Across the *Sabrine* stream, he did acquire
> His fatal end. 'Twas not for want of skill,
> Or courage, to perform the task, he fell:
> No, no,—a faulty cord, being drawn too tight,
> Hurry'd his soul on high to take her flight,
> Which bid the body here beneath, good night.

A prelate being asked permission for a line to be fixed to the steeple of a cathedral church, for this daring adventurer, replied, the man might fix *to* the church whenever he pleased, but he should never give his consent to any one's flying *from* it. It seems that some exhibitor of the same kind met with a similar inhibition here in *London*. I learn from *Mist's* Journal for *July* 8, 1727, that a sixpenny pamphlet, intituled, "The Devil to pay at *St. James's*, &c."[6] was published on this occasion, Again, in *The Weekly Miscellany* for *April* 17, 1736. "*Thomas Kidman*, the famous Flyer, who has flown from several of the highest precipices in *England*, and was the person that flew off *Bromham* steeple in *Wiltshire* when it fell down, flew, on *Monday* last, from the highest of the rocks near *The Hot-well* at *Bristol*, with fire-works and pistols; after which he went up the rope, and performed several surprising dexterities on it, in sight of thousands of spectators, both from *Somersetshire* and *Gloucestershire*." In this print also is a portrait which has been taken for that of Dr. *Rock*, but was more probably meant for another Quack, who used to draw a crowd round him by seeming to eat fire, which, having his checks puffed up with tow, he blew out of his mouth.[7] Some other particulars are explained in the notes to the poetical epistle already mentioned.

[1] In the Craftsman, 1733, was this advertisment; "Mr. *Hogarth* being now engraving nine copper-plates from pictures of his own painting, one of which represents the Humours of a Fair, the other eight the Progress of a Rake, intends to publish the prints by subscription, on the following terms: each subscription to be one guinea and a half: half-a-guinea to be paid at the time of subscribing, for which a receipt will be given on a new-etched print, and the other payment of one guinea on delivery of all the prints when finished, which will be with all convenient speed, and the time publicly advertised. The Fair, being already finished, will be delivered at the time of subscribing. Subscriptions will be taken in at Mr. *Hogarth's*, the *Golden Head*, in *Leicester Fields*, where the pictures are to be seen."

[2] *Highmore* was originally a man of fortune; but *White's* gaming-house, and the patent of *Drury-Lane* theatre, completely exhausted his finances. Having proved himself an unsuccessful actor as well as manager, in 1743 he published *Dettingen*, a poem which would have disgraced a Bell-man. In 1744 he appeared again in the character of *Lothario*, for the benefit of Mrs. *Horten*. From this period his history is unknown. If *Hogarth's* representation of him, in the print entitled *The Discovery*, was a just one, he had no external requisites for the stage.

[3] In a two-shilling pamphlet, printed for *J. Mechell* at *The King's Arms* in *Fleet street*, 1740, entitled "An Apology for the life of Mr. T—— C——, comedian; being a proper sequel to the apology for the life of Mr. *Colley Cibber*, comedian; with a historical view of the stage to the present year; supposed to be written by himself in the stile and manner of the Poet Laureat," but in reality the work of *Harry Fielding*; the following passages, illustrative of our subject, occur. "In that year when the stage fell into great commotions, and the *Drury Lane* company, asserting the glorious cause of liberty and property, made a stand against the oppressions in the patentees—in that memorable year when the Theatric Dominions fell in labour of a revolution under the conduct of *myself*, that revolt gave occasion to several pieces of wit and satirical flirts at the conductor of the enterprize. I was attacked, as my father had been before me, in the public papers and journals; and the burlesque character of *Pistol* was attributed to me as a real one. Out came a *Print* of *Jack Laguerre's*, representing, in most vile designing, this expedition of ours, under the name of *The Stage Mutiny*, in which, gentle reader, *your humble servant*, in the *Pistol* character, was the principal figure. This I laughed at, knowing it only a proper embellishment for one of those necessary structures to which persons out of necessity repair." p. 16, &c.—Again, p. 88.—"At the Fair of *Bartholomew*, we gained some recruits; but, besides those advantages over the enemy, I myself went there in person, and publickly *exposed* myself. This was done to fling defiance in the Patentee's teeth; for, on the booth where I exhibited, I hung out *The Stage Mutiny*, with *Pistol* at the head of his troop,

our standard bearing this motto,—*We eat*."—Whether this account which *Cibber* is made to give of his own conduct is entirely jocular, or contains a mixture of truth in it, cannot now be ascertained. *Hogarth* might have transplanted a circumstance from *Bartholomew* to *Southwark* Fair; or *Fielding*, by design, may have misrepresented the matter, alluding at the same time to *Hogarth's* print.

[4] Mr. *Victor*, speaking of this transaction, observes, that "the general observation was, what business had *a gentleman* to make the purchase?"

[5] In *The Gentleman's Magazine* for 1740, p. 89, is no bad copy of verses "on the death of the famous *Flyer* on the Rope at *Shrewsbury*". It is therefore here inserted.

    ——————-*Magnis tamen excidit ausis.*
Fond *Icarus* of old, with rash essay,
In air attempted a forbidden way;
Too thin the medium for so cumb'rous freight,
Too weak the plumage to support the weight.
Yet less he dar'd who soar'd on waxen wing,
Than he who mounts to æther on a string.
Just as *Arachne*, when the buzzing prey
Entangled flutter, and would wing away,
From watchful ambuscade insidious springs,
And to a slender twine, ascending, clings.
So on his rope, th' advent'rer climbs on high,
Bounds o'er cathedral heights, and seeks the sky;
Fix but his cable, and he'll tell you soon,
What sort of natives cultivate the moon.
An army of such wights to cross the main,
Sooner than *Haddock's* fleet, shou'd humble *Spain*.
As warring cranes on pigmies thund'ring fall,
And, without scaling ladders, mount the wall,
The proudest spire in *Salop's* lofty town
Safely he gains, and glides as safely down;
Then soars again aloft, and downward springs,
Swift as an eagle, without aid of wings;
Shews anticks, hangs suspended by his toe;
Undazzled, views th' inverted chasm below.
Invites with beat of drum brave voluntiers,
Defies *Jack Spaniard*, nor invasion fears,
Land when they will, they ne'er cou'd hurt *his ears*.
Methink I see as yet his flowing hair
And body, darting like a falling star:
Swifter than what "with fins or feathers fly

Thro' the ærial or the wat'ry sky."
Once more he dares to brave the pathless way,
Fate now pursuing, like a bird of prey;
And, comet-like, he makes his latest tour,
In air excentric (oh! ill-omen'd hour!)
Bar'd in his shirt to please the gazing crowd,
He little dreamt, poor soul! of winding shroud!
Nothing could aught avail but limbs of brass,
When ground was iron, and the *Severn* glass.
As quick as lightning down his line he skims,
Secure in equal poize of agile limbs.
But see the trusted cordage faithless prove!
Headlong he falls, and leaves his soul above:
The gazing town was shock'd at the rebound
Of shatter'd bones, that rattled on the ground;
The broken cord rolls on in various turns,
Smokes in the whirl, and as it runs it burns.
So when the wriggling snake is snatch'd on high
In eagle's claws, and hisses in the sky,
Around the foe his twirling tail he flings,
And twists her legs, and writhes about her wings.
Cadman laid low, ye rash, behold and fear,
Man is a reptile, and the ground his sphere.
Unhappy man! thy end lamented be;
Nought but thy own ill fate so swift as thee,
Were metamorphoses permitted now,
And tuneful *Ovid* liv'd to tell us how;
His apter Muse shou'd turn thee to a daw,
Nigh to the fatal steeple still to kaw;
Perch on the cock, and nestle on the ball,
In ropes no more confide, and never fall. *J. A.*

[6] Supposed to have been written by Dr. *Arbuthnot,* and as such preserved in the Collection of his Works. The full title is, "The Devil to pay at *St. James's*: or, a full and true Account of a most horrid and bloody Battle between Madam *Faustina* and Madam *Cuzzoni.* Also of a hot Skirmish between Signor *Boschi* and Signor *Palmerini.* Moreover, how *Senesino* has taken Snuff, is going to leave the Opera, and sings Psalms at *Henley's Oratory.* Also about the Flying Man, and how the Doctor of *St. Martin's* has very unkindly taken down the Scaffold, and disappointed a World of good Company. As also how a certain Great Lady is gone mad for the Love of *William Gibson,* the Quaker. And how the *Wild Boy* is come to Life again, and has got a Dairy Maid with Child. Also about the great Mourning, and the Fashions, and the Alterations, and what not. With other material Occurrences, too many to insert."

In this pamphlet our artist is incidentally mentioned, but in such a manner as shews that he had attained some celebrity so early as 1727. Speaking of some *Lilliputian* swine, supposed to be in the possession of Dean *Swift*, Dr. *Arbuthnot* adds, "But *Hogarth* the Engraver is making a print after them, which will give a juster idea of them than I can."

[7] Perhaps he was only a fire-eater.

3. *Judith* and *Holofernes*. "Per vulnera servor, morte tuâ vivens." *W. Hogarth inv. Ger. Vandergucht sc.* A frontispiece to the Oratorio of *Judith*.—Our heroine, instead of holding the sword by its handle, grasps it by its edge, in such a manner as should seem to have endangered her fingers. (*Judith* was an Oratorio by *William Huggins*, Esq. set to musick by *William De Fesch*[1] late Chapel-master of the cathedral church of *Antwerp*. This piece was performed with scenes and other decorations, but met with no success. It was published in 8vo, 1733.)—The original plate of the frontispiece is in the possession of Dr. *Monkhouse*. This design has little of *Hogarth*; yet if he furnished other engravers with such slight undetermined sketches as he himself is sometimes known to have worked from, we cannot wonder if on many occasions his usual characteristics should escape our notice. Whoever undertakes to perfect several of his unpublished drawings, will be reduced to the necessity of inventing more than presents itself for imitation.

[1] *William Defesch*, a *German*, and some time chapel-master at *Antwerp*, was in his time a respectable professor on the violin, and leader of the band for several seasons at *Marybone-gardens*. His head was engraved as a frontispiece to some musical compositions published by him; and his name is to be found on many songs and ballads to which he set the tunes for *Vauxhall* and *Marybone-gardens*. He died, soon after the year 1750, at the age of 70.

The following lines were written under a picture of *Defesch*, painted by *Soldi*, 1751.

> Thou honor'st verse, and verse must lend her wing,
> To honor thee, the priest of *Phœbus*' quire,
> That *tun'st* her happiest lines in hymn or song. MILTON.

Defesch was the patriotic Mr. *Hollis's* music-master.

4. Boys peeping at Nature. "*The subscription-ticket to the Harlot's Progress.*" A copy in aqua-tinta from this receipt was made by *R. Livesay* in 1781, and is to be had at Mrs. *Hogarth's* house in *Leicester-square*.

1733 and 1734.

1.[1] The Harlot's Progress,[2] in six plates. In the first is a portrait of Colonel *Chartres*. "Cette figure de viellard (says *Rouquet*) est d'aprés nature; c'est le portrait d'un officier très riche, fameux dans ce tems-là pour de pareilles expéditions, grand séducteur de campagnardes, et qui avoit toujours à ses gages des femmes de la profession de celle qui cajole ici la nouvelle débarquée." Behind him is *John Gourlay* a Pimp, whom he always kept about his person. The next figure that attracts our notice, is that of Mother *Needham*. To prove this woman was sufficiently notorious to have deserved the satire of *Hogarth*, the following paragraphs in *The Grub-street Journal* are sufficient.

March 25, 1731. "The noted Mother *Needham* was yesterday committed to *The Gatehouse* by Justice *Railton*."

Ibid. "Yesterday, at the quarter-sessions for the city and liberties of *Westminster*, the infamous Mother *Needham*, who has been reported to have been dead for some time, to screen her from several prosecutions, was brought from *The Gatehouse*, and pleaded not guilty to an indictment found against her for keeping a lewd and disorderly house; but, for want of sureties, was remanded back to prison."

Ibid. *April* 29, 1731. "Oh *Saturday* ended the quarter-sessions for *Westminster*, &c. The noted Mother *Needham*, convicted for keeping a disorderly house in *Park Place, St. James's*, was fined One Shilling, to stand twice in the pillory, and find sureties for her good behaviour for three years."

Ibid. *May* 6, 1731. "Yesterday the noted Mother *Needham* stood in the pillory in *Park Place*, near *St. James's-street*, and was roughly handled by the populace. She was so very ill that she lay along, notwithstanding which she was so severely &c. that it is thought she will die in a day or two."—Another account says—"she lay along on her face in the pillory, and so evaded the law which requires that her face should be exposed."—"Yesterday morning died Mother *Needham*. She declared in her last words,[3] that what most affected her was the terror of standing in the pillory to-morrow in *New Palace-yard*, having been so ungratefully used by the populace on *Wednesday*."

The memory of this woman is thus perpetuated in *The Dunciad*, I. 323.

"To *Needham's* quick lthe voice triumphal rode,
But pious *Needham* dropt the name of God."

The note on this passage says, she was "a matron of great fame, and very religious in her way; whose constant prayer it was, that she might 'get enough by her profession to leave it off in time, and make her peace with God.'[4] But her fate was not so happy; for being convicted, and set in the pillory, she was (to the lasting shame of all her great Friends and Votaries) so ill used by the populace, that it put an end to her days."

Rouquet has a whimsical remark relative to the clergyman just arrived in *London*. "Cet ecclesiastique monté sur un cheval blanc, *comme ils affectent ici de l'être*."—The variations in this plate are; shade thrown by one house upon another; *London* added on the letter the parson is reading; change in one corner of the fore-ground; the face of the Bawd much altered for the worse, and her foot introduced.

Plate II. *Quin* compared *Garrick* in *Othello* to the black boy with the tea-kettle,[5] a circumstance that by no means encouraged our *Roscius* to continue acting the part. Indeed, when his face was obscured, his chief power of expression was lost; and then, and not till then, was he reduced to a level with several other performers. In a copy of this set of plates, one of the two small portraits hanging up in the *Jew's* bedchamber, is superscribed, *Clarke*; but without authority from *Hogarth*. *Woolston* would likewise have been out of his place, as he had written against the *Jewish* tenets. Of this circumstance, *Hogarth* was probably told by some friend, and therefore effaced a name he had once ignorantly inserted.

In Plate III.[6] (as already observed) is the portrait of Sir *John Gonson*. That Sir *John Gonson* was the person intended in this print, is evident from a circumstance in the next, where, on a door in *Bridewell*, a figure hanging is drawn in chalk, with an inscription over it, "Sir *J. G.*" as well as from the following explanation by *Rouquet*: "La figure, qui paroit entrer sans bruit avec une partie de guet, est un commissaire qui se distinguoit extrêmement par son zèle pour la persecution des filles de joye."

Respecting another circumstance, however, in the third plate, *Rouquet* appears to have met with some particular information that has escaped me. "L'auteur a saisi l'occasion d'un morceau de beurre qui fait partie du déjeuné, pour l'enveloper plaisamment dans le titre de la lettre pastorale qu'un grand prelat[7] addressa dans ce tems-là à son diocese, & dont plusieurs exemplaires eurent le malheur d'être renvoyés à l'epicier."—The sleeve of the maid-servant's gown in this plate is enlarged, and the neck of a bottle on the table is lengthened.

For variations in Plate IV. see the roof of the room. Shadow on the principal woman's petticoat, and from the hoop-petticoat hanging up in the back ground. The dog made darker. The woman next the overseer has a high cap, which in the modern impressions is lowered.

In Plate V. Roof of the room. Back of the chair. Table. Dr. *Misaubin's* waistcoat. Name of Dr. *Rock* on the paper lying on the close-stool. Dish at the fire.

In a despicable poem published in 1732, under the fictitious name of *Joseph Gay*, and intituled "*The Harlot's Progress*, which is a key to the six prints lately published by Mr. *Hogarth*," the two quacks in attendance on the dying woman are called *Tan—r* and *G—m*. It is evident from several circumstances, that this Mr. *J. Gay* became acquainted with our author's work through the medium of a copy.

In Plate VI. the woman seated next the clergyman was designed for *Elizabeth Adams*, who, at the age of 30, was afterwards executed for a robbery, *September* 10, 1737. The common print of her will justify this assertion.

If we may trust the wretched metrical performance just quoted, the Bawd in this sixth plate was designed for Mother *Bentley*.

The portrait hanging up in the *Jew's* apartment was originally subscribed "Mr. *Woolston*." There was a scriptural motto to one of the other pictures; and on the cieling of the room in which the girl is dying, a certain obscene word was more visible than it is at present. The former inscription on the paper now inscribed Dr. *Rock*, was also a gross one. I should in justice add, that before these plates were delivered to the subscribers, the offensive particulars here mentioned were omitted.

The following paragraph in *The Grub-street Journal* for *September* 24, 1730, will sufficiently justify the splendid appearance the Harlot makes in *Bridewell*. See Plate IV. Such well-dressed females are rarely met with in our present houses of correction.

"One *Mary Muffet*, a woman of great note in the hundreds of *Drury*, who, about a fortnight ago, was committed to hard labour in *Tothill-fields Bridewell*, by nine justices, brought his Majesty's writ of *Habeas Corpus*, and was carried before the right honourable the lord chief justice *Raymond*, expecting to have been either bailed or discharged; but her commitment appearing to be legal, his lordship thought fit to remand her back again to her former place of confinement, where *she is now beating hemp in a gown very richly laced with silver*."

Rouquet concludes his illustration of the fifth plate by observing, that the story might have been concluded here. "L'auteur semble avoir rempli son dessein. Il a suivi son heroine jusques au dernier soupir. Il l'a conduite de l'infamie à la pauvreté, par les voies séduisantes du libertinage. Son intention de tâcher de retenir, ou de corriger celles qui leur foiblesse, ou leur ignorance exposent tous les jours à de semblables infortunes, est suffisament executée; on peut donc dire que la tragedie finit à cette planche, et que la suivante est comme le petite piece. C'est une farce done la defunte est plustôt l'occasion que le sujet."—Such is the criticism of *Rouquet*; but I cannot absolutely concur in the justness of it. *Hogarth* found an opportunity to convey admonition, and enforce his moral, even in this last plate. It is true that the exploits of our heroine are concluded, and that she is no longer an agent in her own story. Yet as a wish prevails, even among those who are most humbled by their own indiscretions, that some respect should be paid to their remains, that they should be conducted by decent friends to the grave, and interred by a priest who feels for the dead that hope expressed in our Liturgy, let us ask whether the memory of our Harlot meets with any such marks of social attention, or pious benevolence. Are not the preparations for her funeral licentious, like the course of her life, as if the contagion of her example had reached all the company in the room? Her sisters in iniquity alone surround her coffin. One of them is engaged in the double trade of seduction and thievery. A second is admiring herself in a mirror. A third gazes with unconcern on the corpse. If any of the number appear mournful, they express at best but a maudlin sorrow, having glasses of strong liquor in their hands. The very minister, forgetful of his office and character, is shamefully employed; nor does a single circumstance occur, throughout the whole scene, that a reflecting female would not wish should be alienated from her own interment.—Such is the plate which our illustrator, with too much levity, has styled a farce appended to a tragic representation.

He might, however, have exercised his critical abilities with more success on *Hogarth's* neglect of propriety, though it affords him occasion to display his wit. At the burial of a wanton, who expired in a garret, no escutcheons were ever hung up, or rings given away; and I much question if any bawd ever chose to avow that character before a clergyman, or any infant was ever habited as chief mourner to attend a parent to the grave.—I may add, that when these pictures were painted (a time, if news-papers are to be credited, when, having no established police, every act of violence and licentiousness was practised with impunity in our streets, and women of pleasure were brutally persecuted in every quarter of the town), a funeral attended by such a sisterhood would scarcely have been permitted to reach the place of interment. Much however must be forgiven to the morality of *Hogarth's* design, and the powers with which it is executed. It may also, on the present occasion, be observed, that in no other scene, out of the many he has painted, has he so widely deviated from *vraisemblance*.

The following verses, however wretched, being explanatory of the set of plates already spoken of, are here re-printed. They made their appearance under the earliest and best of the pirated copies published by *Bowles*. Hogarth, finding that such a metrical description had its effect, resolved that his next series of prints should receive the same advantage from an abler hand.

> PLATE I.
> See there, but just arriv'd in town,
> The *Country Girl* in home-spun gown,
> Tho' plain her dress appears, how neat!
> Her looks how innocent and sweet!
> Does not your indignation rise,
> When on the bawd you cast your eyes?
> Fraught with devices to betray;
> She's hither come in quest of prey;
> Screens her designs with godly airs,
> And talks of homilies and pray'rs,
> Till, by her arts, the wretched Maid
> To vile *Francisco* is betray'd.
> And see, the lewd old rogue appears,
> How at the fresh young thing thing he leers!
> In lines too strong, too well exprest
> The lustful satyr stands confest.
>
> On batter'd jade, in thread-bare gown,
> The *Rural Priest* is come to town—
> Think what his humble thought engages;
> Why—lesser work and greater wages.
>
> PLATE II.
> Debauch'd, and then kick'd out of doors,
> The fate of all *Francisco's* whores,
> Poor *Polly's* forc'd to walk the streets,
> Till with a wealthy *Jew* she meets.
> Quickly the man of circumcision
> For her reception makes provision.
> You see her now in all her splendour,
> A Monkey and a Black t' attend her.
> How great a sot's a keeping cully,
> Who thinks t' enjoy a woman solely!
> Tho' he support her grandeur, Miss
> Will by the bye with others kiss.
> Thus Polly play'd her part; she had
> A *Beau* admitted to her bed;
> But th' *Hebrew* coming unexpected,
> Puts her in fear to be detected.
> This to prevent, she at breakfast picks

A quarrel, and insulting kicks
The table down: while by her *Maid*
The *Beau* is to the door convey'd.

PLATE III.
Molly discarded once again,
Takes lodgings next in *Drury-lane*;
Sets up the business on her own
Account, and deals with all the town.
At breakfast here in deshabille,
While *Margery* does the tea-pot fill,
Miss holds a watch up, which, by slight
Of hand, was made a prize last night.
From chandler's shop a dab of butter,
Brought on his lordship's *Pastoral Letter*,
A cup, a saucer, knife, and roll,
Are plac'd before her on a stool.
A chair behind her holds a cloak,
A candle in a bottle stuck,
And by't a bason—but indecent
T'would be in me to say what is in't.
At yonder door, see there Sir *John's*
Just ent'ring with his *Myrmidons*,
To *Bridewell* to convey Miss *Molly*,
And *Margery* with her to Mill Dolly.[8]

PLATE IV.
See *Polly* now in *Bridewell* stands,
A galling mallet in her hands,
Hemp beating with a heavy heart,
And not a soul to take her part.
The *Keeper*, with a look that's sourer
Than *Turk* or Devil, standing o'er her:
And if her time she idles, thwack
Comes his rattan across her back.
A dirty, ragged, saucy Jade,
Who sees her here in rich brocade
And *Mechlin* lace, thumping a punny,
Lolls out her tongue, and winks with one eye.
That other *Maux* with half a nose,
Who's holding up her tatter'd cloaths,
Laughs too at Madam's working-dress,
And her grim Tyrant's threat'ning face,

A *Gamester* hard by *Poll* you see,
In coat be-lac'd and smart toupee.
Kate vermin kills—chalk'd out upon
A window-shutter, hangs *Sir John*.

PLATE V.
Released from *Bridewell*, *Poll* again
Drives on her former trade amain;
But who e'er heard of trading wenches
That long escap'd disease that *French* is?
Our *Polly* did not—Ills on ills,
Elixirs, boluses and pills,
Chatarticks and emeticks dreary,
Had made her of her life quite weary;
At last thrown into salivation
She sinks beneath the operation.
A snuffling whore in waiting by her
Screams out to see the wretch expire.
The *Doctors* blame each other; *Meagre*,
With wrath transported, hot and eager,
Starts up, throws down the chair and stool,
And calls her brother *Squab* a fool.
Your pills, quoth *Squab*, with cool disdain,
Not my elixir, prov'd her bane.
While they contend, a muffled Punk
Is rummaging poor *Polly's* trunk.

PLATE VI.
The sisterhood of *Drury-lane*
Are met to form the funeral train.
Priss turns aside the coffin lid,
To take her farewell of the dead.
Kate drinks dejected; *Peggy* stands
With dismal look, and wrings her hands.
Beck wipes her eyes; and at the glass
In order *Jenny* sets her face.
The ruin'd *Bawd* roars out her grief;
Her bottle scarcely gives relief.
Madge fills the wine; his castle-top
With unconcern the *Boy* winds up.
The *Undertaker* rolls his eyes
On *Sukey*, as her glove he tries:
His leering she observes, and while he

Stands thus, she picks his pocket slily.
The *Parson* sits with look demure
By *Fanny's* side, but leaning to her.
His left hand spills the wine; his right—
I blush to add—is out of sight.

Over the figure of the *Parson* is the letter A, which conducts to the following explanation underneath the plate. "A. The famous *Couple-Beggar* in *The Fleet*, a wretch who there screens himself from the justice due to his *villainies*, and daily repeats them."

All but the first impressions of this set of plates are marked thus †. None were originally printed off except for the 1200 subscribers. Immediately after they were served, the plates were retouched, and some of the variations introduced.

[1] In *The Craftsman* of *Nov.* 25, 1732, we read, "This day is published, six prints in chiaro oscuro, of *The Harlot's Progress*, from the designs of Mr. *Hogarth*, in a beautiful green tint, by Mr. *E. Kirkall*, with proper explanations under each print. Printed and sold by *E. Kirkall*, in *Dockwell-court, White-Fryars; Phil. Overton*, in *Fleet-street; H. Overton* and *J. Hoole*, without *Newgate; J. King*, in the *Poultry*; and *T. Glass*, under the *Royal Exchange*."

Lest any of our readers should from hence suppose we have been guilty of an innacuracy in appropriating this set of prints to the year 1733, &c. it is necessary to observe, that the plates advertised as above, were only a pirated copy of *Hogarth's* work, and were published before their original.

[2] In *The Grub-street Journal* for *December* 6, 1733, appeared the following advertisement: "Lately published, (illustrated with six prints, neatly engraven from Mr. *Hogarth's* Designs,) *The Lure of Venus*; or a Harlot's Progress. An heroi-comical Poem, in six Cantos, by Mr. *Joseph* Gay.

"To Mr. *Joseph* Gay.

"Sir,

"It has been well observed, that a great and just objection to the Genius of Painters is their want of invention; from whence proceeds so many different designs or draughts on the same history or fable. Few have ventured to touch upon a new story; but still fewer have invented both the story and the execution, as the ingenious Mr. *Hogarth* has done, in his six prints of a *Harlot's Progress*; and, without a compliment, Sir, your admirable Cantos are a true key and lively explanation of the painter's hieroglyphicks.

"I am, Sir, yours, &c.

"A. PHILLIPS."

This letter, ascribed to *Ambrose Phillips*, was in all probability a forgery, like the name of *Joseph Gay*.

[3] "Mother *Needham's* Lamentation," was published in *May* 1731, price 6d.

[4] It seems agreed on by our comic-writers, not to finish the character of a Bawd without giving her some pretence to Religion. In *Dryden's* Wild Gallant, *Mother du Lake*, being about to drink a dram, is made to exclaim, "'Tis a great way to the bottom; but heaven is all-sufficient to give me strength for it." The scene in which this speech occurs, was of use to *Richardson* in his *Clarissa*, and perhaps to *Foote*, or *Foote's* original of the character of Mother *Cole*.

[5] So in *Hill's Actor*, pp. 69, 70. "If there be any thing that comes in competition with the unluckiness of this excellent player's figure in this character, it is the appearance he made in his new habit for *Othello*. We are used to see the greatest majesty imaginable expressed throughout that whole part; and though the joke was somewhat prematurely delivered to the publick, we must acknowledge, that his appearance in that tramontane dress made us rather expect to see a tea-kettle in his hand, than to hear the thundering speeches *Shakspeare* has thrown into that character, come out of his mouth."

[6] See the back ground of this plate, for a circumstance of such unpardonable grossness as admits of no verbal interpretation.

[7] Bishop *Gibson*.

[8] Beat hemp.

2. Rehearsal of the Oratorio of *Judith*. Singing men and boys. Ticket for "A Modern Midnight Conversation." This Oratorio of *Judith*, which was performed in character, was written by Mr. *Huggins*, as has been already observed in p. 187; and the line taken from it,

"The world shall bow to the *Assyrian* throne,"

inscribed on the book, is a satire on its want of success.—The corner figure looking over the notes, was designed for Mr. *Tothall*.

3. A Midnight Modern Conversation. *W. Hogarth inv. pinx. & sculp*. Hogarth soon discovered that this engraving was too faintly executed; and therefore, after taking off a few impressions in red as well as black, he retouched and strengthened the plate. Under this print are the following verses:

Think not to find one meant resemblance here,
We lash the Vices, but the Persons spare.
Prints should be priz'd, as Authors should be read,

Who sharply smile prevailing Folly dead.
So *Rabilaes* laught, and so *Cervantes* thought,
So Nature dictated what Art has taught.

Most of the figures, however, are supposed to be real portraits. The Divine and the Lawyer,[1] in particular, are well known to be so.

A pamphlet was published about the same time, under the same title as this plate. In *Banks's* Poems, vol. I. p. 87. the print is copied as a head-piece to an Epistle to Mr. *Hogarth*, on this performance. In a note, it is said to have appeared after *The Harlot's Progress*; and that in the original, and all the larger copies, on the papers that hang out of the politician's pocket at the end of the table, was written *The Craftsman*, and *The London Journal*.

Of this print a good, but contracted copy, was published (perhaps with *Hogarth's* permission), and the following copy of verses engraved under it.

The Bacchanalians; or a Midnight Modern Conversation. A Poem addressed to the Ingenious Mr. *Hogarth*.

Sacred to thee, permit this lay
Thy labour, *Hogarth*, to display!
Patron and theme in one to be!
'Tis great, but not too great for thee;
For thee, the Poet's constant friend,
Whose vein of humour knows no end.
This verse which, honest to thy fame,
Has added to thy praise thy name!
Who can be dull when to his eyes
Such various scenes of humour rise?
Now we behold in what unite
The Priest, the Beau, the Cit, the Bite;
Where Law and Physick join the Sword,
And Justice deigns to crown the board:
How *Midnight Modern Conversations*
Mingle all faculties and stations!

Full to the sight, and next the bowl,
Sits the physician of the soul;
No loftier themes his thought pursues
Than Punch, good Company, and Dues:
Easy and careless what may fall,
He hears, consents, and fills to all;

Proving it plainly by his face
That cassocks are no signs of grace.

Near him a son of *Belial* see;
(That Heav'n and *Satan* should agree!)
Warm'd and wound up to proper height
He vows to still maintain the fight,
The brave surviving Priest assails,
And fairly damns the first that fails;
Fills up a bumper to the Best
In Christendom, for that's his taste:
The parson simpers at the jest,
And puts it forward to the rest.

What hand but thine so well could draw
A formal Barrister at Law?
Fitzherbert, Littleton, and *Coke,*
Are all united in his look.
His spacious wig conceals his ears,
Yet the dull plodding beast appears.
His muscles seem exact to fit
Much noise, much pride, and not much wit.

Who then is he with solemn phiz,
Upon his elbows pois'd with ease?
Freely to speak the Muse is loth—
Justice or knave—he may be both—
Justice or knave—'tis much the same:
To boast of crimes, or tell the shame,
Of raking talk or reformation,
'Tis all good *Modern Conversation.*

What mighty *Machiavel* art thou,
With patriot cares upon thy brow?
Alas, that punch should have the fate
To drown the pilot of the state!
That while both sides thy pocket holds,
Nor *D'Anvers* grieves, nor *Osborne* scolds,
Thou sink'st the business of the nation
In *Midnight Modern Conversation!*

The Tradesman tells with wat'ry eyes
How Credit sinks, how Taxes rise;

At Parliaments and Great Men pets,
Counts all his losses and his debts.

The puny Fop, mankind's disgrace,
The ladies' jest and looking-glass;
This he-she thing the mode pursues,
And drinks in order—till he sp—s.

See where the Relict of the Wars,
Deep mark'd with honorary scars,
A mightier foe has caus'd to yield
Than ever *Marlbro'* met in field!
See prostrate on the earth he lies;
And learn, ye soldiers, to be wise.

Flush'd with the fumes of gen'rous wine
The Doctor's face begins to shine:
With eyes half clos'd, in stamm'ring strain,
He speaks the praise of rich champaign.
'Tis dull in verse, what from thy hand
Might even a *Cato's* smile command.
Th' expiring snuffs, the bottles broke,
And the full bowl at four o'clock.

March 22, 1742, was acted at *Covent-Garden*, a new scene, called *A Modern Midnight Conversation*, taken from *Hogarth's* celebrated print; in which was introduced, *Hippisley's Drunken Man*, with a comic tale of what really passed between himself and his old aunt, at her house on *Mendip-Hills*, in *Somersetshire*. For Mr. *Hippisley's* benefit.

[1] These, in my first edition, I had ventured, on popular report, to say were parson *Ford*, and the first Lord *Northington*, when young. But I am now enabled to identify their persons, on the authority of Sir *John Hawkins*: "When the Midnight Modern Conversation came out, the general opinion was, that the Divine was the portrait of Orator *Henley*; and the Lawyer of *Kettleby*, a vociferous bar orator, remarkable, though an utter barrister, for wearing a full-bottom'd wig, which he is here drawn with, as also for a horrible squint."

In that once popular satire, *The Causidicade*, are the following lines on this lawyer:

"Up *Kettleby* starts with a *horrible stare!*
'Behold, my good Lord, your old friend at the bar,
Or rather old foe, for foes we have been,
As treason fell out, and poor traitors fell in.

Strong opposites e'er, and not once of a side,
Attornies will always great counsel divide.
You *for* persecutions, I always *against*,
How oft with a joke 'gainst your law have I fenc'd?
How oft in your pleadings I've pick'd out a hole,
Thro' which from your pounces my culprit I've stole;
I've puzzled against you now eight years or nine,
You, my Lord, for your King, I a ——l for mine.
But what is all this? Now your Lordship will say,
To get at the office this is not the way.
I own it is not, so I make no request
For myself, still firm to my party and test:
But if 'tis your pleasure to give it my son,
He shall take off his coif t'accept of the boon;
That coif I, refusing, transferr'd upon him,
For who'd be a serjeant where P——r was Prime?
That my son is a lawyer no one can gainsay,
As witness his getting off *W——te* t'other day.'
Quo' my Lord, 'My friend *Abel*, I needs must allow
You have puzzled me oft, as indeed you do now;
Nay, have puzzled yourself, the court and the law,
And chuckled most wittily over a flaw;
For your nostrums, enigmas, conundrums, and puns,
Are above comprehension, save that of your son's.
To fling off the coif! Oh fye, my friend *Abel*,
'Twould be acting the part of the Cock in the Fable!
'Tis a badge of distinction! and some people buy it;
Can you doubt on't, when *Skinner* and *Hayward* enjoy it?
Tho' I own you have spoil'd (but I will not enlarge on't)
A good Chancery draftsman to make a bad Serjeant.'"

Lord *Northington* did not come into notice till many years after the publication of this print.

1735.

1. The Rake's Progress, in eight plates.

Extract from the *London Daily Post*, May 14, 1735:

"The nine prints from the paintings of Mr. *Hogarth*, one representing a Fair, and the others a Rake's Progress, are now printing off, and will be ready to be delivered on the 25th of *June* next.

"Subscriptions will be taken at Mr. *Hogarth's*, the *Golden-Head*, in *Leicester-fields*, till the 23d of *June*, and no longer, at half a guinea to be paid on subscribing, and half a guinea more on delivery of the prints at the price above-mentioned, after which the price will be two guineas.

"N. B. Mr. *Hogarth* was, and is, obliged to defer the publication and delivery of the abovesaid prints till the 25th of *June* next, in order to secure his property, pursuant to an act lately passed both houses of parliament, now waiting for the royal assent, to secure all new invented prints that shall be published after the 24th of *June* next, from being copied without consent of the proprietor, and thereby preventing a scandalous and unjust custom (hitherto practised with impunity) of making and vending base copies of original prints, to the manifest injury of the author, and the great discouragement of the arts of painting and engraving."

In *The Craftsman*, soon afterwards, appeared the following advertisement:

"Pursuant to an agreement with the subscribers to the Rake's Progress, not to sell them for less than two guineas each set after publication thereof, the said original prints are to be had at Mr. *Hogarth's*, the *Golden-Head*, in *Leicester-fields*; and at *Tho. Bakewell's*, print-seller, next *Johnson's Court*, in *Fleet-street*, where all other print-sellers may be supplied.

"In four days will be published, copies from the said prints, with the consent of Mr. *Hogarth*, according to the act of parliament, which will be sold at 2 *s.* 6 *d.* each set, with the usual allowance to all dealers in town and country; and, that the the publick may not be imposed on, at the bottom of each print will be inserted these words, *viz.* 'Published with the consent of Mr. *William Hogarth*, by *Tho. Bakewell*, according to act of parliament.'

"N. B. Any person that shall sell any other copies, or imitations of the said prints, will incur the penalties in the late act of parliament, and be prosecuted for the same."

This series of plates, however, as Mr. *Walpole* observes, was pirated by *Boitard* on one very large sheet of paper, containing the several scenes represented by *Hogarth*. It came out a fortnight before the genuine set, but was soon forgotten. The principal variations in these prints are the following:

Plate I. The girl's face who holds the ring is erased, and a worse is put in.[1] The mother's head, &c. is lessened. The shoe-sole, cut from the cover of an ancient family Bible, together with a chest, is added; the memorandum-book removed into another place; the woollen-draper's shop bill,[2] appended to a roll of black cloth, omitted; the contents of the closet thrown more into shade.

In Plate II. are portraits of *Figg*, the prize-fighter;[3] *Bridgeman*, a noted gardener; and *Dubois*, a master of defence, who was killed in a duel by one of the same name, as the following paragraphs in *The Grub-street Journal* for *May* 16, 1734, &c. will testify: "Yesterday (*May* 11) between two and three in the afternoon, a duel was fought in *Mary-le-bone Fields*, between Mr. *Dubois* a *Frenchman*, and Mr. *Dubois* an *Irishman*, both fencing-masters, the former of whom was run through the body, but walked a considerable way from the place, and is now under the hands of an able surgeon, who has great hopes of his recovery."

May 23, 1734, "Yesterday morning died Mr. *Dubois*, of a wound he received in a duel."

The portrait of *Handel* has been supposed to be represented in the plate before us; but "this," as Sir *John Hawkins* observes to me, "is too much to say. Mr. *Handel* had a higher sense of his own merit than ever to put himself in such a situation; and, if so, the painter would hardly have thought of doing it. The musician must mean in general any composer of operas." On the floor lies a picture representing *Farinelli*, seated on a pedestal, with an altar before him, on which are several flaming hearts, near which stand a number of people with their arms extended, offering him presents: at the foot of the altar is one female kneeling, tendering her heart. From her mouth a label issues, inscribed, "One God, one *Farinelli*;" alluding to a lady of distinction, who, being charmed with a particular passage in one of his songs, uttered aloud from the boxes that impious exclamation. On the figure of the captain, *Rouquet* has the following remark: "Ce caractere ne paroit plus *Italien* qu'*Anglois*." I am not sufficiently versed in *Alsatian* annals to decide on the question; but believe that the bully by profession (not assassin, as *Rouquet* seems to interpret the character) was to be found during the youth of our artist. More have heard and been afraid of these vulgar heroes, than ever met with them. This set of prints was engraved by *Scotin* chiefly; but several of the faces were touched upon by *Hogarth*. In the second plate the countenance of the man with the quarter-staves was wholly engraved by *Hogarth*. In some early proofs of the print, there is not a single feature on this man's face; there is no writing either in the musician's book, or on the label; nor is there the horse-race cup, the letter, or the poem that lies at the end of the label, that being entirely blank. I mention these circumstances to shew that our artist would not entrust particular parts of his work to any hand but his own; or perhaps he had neither determined on the countenance or the inscription he meant to introduce, till the plate was far advanced. With unfinished proofs, on any other account, this catalogue has nothing to do. As the rudiments of plates, they may afford instruction to young engravers; or add a fancied value to the collections of connoisseurs.

In the third plate is *Leather-coat*,[4] a noted porter belonging to *The Rose* Tavern, with a large pewter dish in his hand, which for many years served as a sign to the shop of a pewterer on *Snow-Hill*. In this utensil the posture-woman, who is undressing, used to whirl herself round, and display other feats of indecent activity: "Il suffit" (I transcribe from *Rouquet*, who is more circumstantial) "de vous laisser à deviner la destination de la chandelle. Ce grand plat va servir a cette femme comme à une poularde. Il sera mis au milieu de la table; elle s'y placera sur le dos; et l'ivresse et l'esprit de débauche feront trouver plaisant un jeu, qui de sang-froid ne le paroit guères." *Rouquet*, in his description of an *English* tavern, such as that in which our scene lies, mentions the following as extraordinary conveniencies and articles of magnificence: "Du linge toujours blanc[5]—de tables de bois qu'on appelle ici mahogani—grand feu et gratis." Variations: *Pontac's* head is added in the room of a mutilated *Cæsar*. Principal woman has a man's hat on. Rake's head altered. Undrest woman's head altered. Woman who spirts the wine, and she who threatens her with a drawn knife, have lower caps, &c.

So entirely do our manners differ from those of fifty years ago, that I much question if at present, in all the taverns of *London*, any thing resembling the scene here exhibited by *Hogarth* could be found. That we are less sensual than our predecessors, I do not affirm; but may with truth observe, we are more delicate in pursuit of our gratifications.—No young man, of our hero's fortune and education, would now think of entertaining half a score of prostitutes at a tavern, after having routed a set of feeble wretches, who are idly called our Guardians of the Night.

Plate IV. *Rakewell* is going to court on the first of *March*, which was Queen *Caroline's* birth-day, as well as the anniversary of *St. David*. In the early impressions a shoe-black steals the Rake's cane. In the modern ones, a large group of blackguards[6] [the chimney-sweeper peeping over the poll boy's cards, and discovering that he has two honours, by holding up two fingers, is among the luckiest of *Hogarth's* traits] are introduced gambling on the pavement; near them a stone inscribed BLACK'S, a contrast to *White's* gaming-house, against which a flash of lightning is pointed. The curtain in the window of the sedan chair is thrown back. This plate is likewise found in an intermediate state;[7] the sky being made unnaturally obscure, with an attempt to introduce a shower of rain, and lightning very aukwardly represented. It is supposed to be a first proof after the insertion of the group of black-guard gamesters; the window of the chair being only marked for an alteration that was afterwards made in it. *Hogarth* appears to have so far spoiled the sky, that he was obliged to obliterate it, and cause it to be engraved over again by another hand.[8] Not foreseeing, however, the immense demand for his prints, many of them were so slightly executed, as very early to stand in need of retouching. The seventh in particular was so much more slightly executed than the rest, that it sooner wanted renovation, and is therefore to be found in three different states. The rest appear only in two.

In Plate V. is his favourite dog *Trump*. In this, also the head of the maid-servant is greatly altered, and the leg and foot of the bridegroom omitted.

From the antiquated bride, and the young female adjusting the folds of her gown, in this plate, is taken a *French* print of a wrinkled harridan of fashion at her toilet, attended by a blooming coëffeuse. It was engraved by *L. Surugue* in 1745, from a picture in crayons by *Coypel*, and is entitled, *La Folie pare la Decrepitude des ajustemens de la Jeunesse*. From the *Frenchman*, however, the *Devonshire-square* dowager of our artist has received so high a polish, that she might be mistaken for a queen mother of *France*.

Mr. *Gilpin*, in his remarks on this plate, appears not to have fully comprehended the extent of the satire designed in it. Speaking of the church, he observes, that "the wooden post, which seems to have no use, divides the picture disagreeably." *Hogarth*, however, meant to expose the insufficiency of such ecclesiastical repairs as are confided to the superintendance of parish-officers. We learn, from an inscription on the front of a pew, that "This church was beautified in the Year 1725. *Tho. Sice, Tho. Horn*, Churchwardens."[9] The print before us came out in 1735 (i. e. only ten years afterwards), and by that time the building might have been found in the condition here exhibited, and have required a prop to prevent part of its roof from falling in.—As a proof that this edifice was really in a ruinous state, it was pulled down and rebuilt in the year 1741.

Fifty years ago, *Marybone* church was considered at such a distance from *London*, as to become the usual resort of those who, like our hero, wished to be privately married.

In Plate VI. the fire breaking out, alludes to the same accident which happened at *White's, May* 3, 1733. I learn from a very indifferent poem descriptive of this set of plates (the title is unfortunately wanting), that some of the characters in the scene before us were real ones:

> "But see the careful plain old man,
> M———[10], well-known youth to trepan,
> To C———*sh*[11] lend the dear bought pence,
> C———*sh* quite void of common sense,
> Whose face, unto his soul a sign,
> Looks stupid, as does that within.
> A quarrel from behind ensues,
> The sure retreat of those that lose.
> An honest *'Squire* smells the cheat,
> And swears the villain shall be beat:

>   But *G——dd* wisely interferes,
>   And dissipates the wretch's fears."

The original sketch in oil for this scene is at Mrs. *Hogarth's* house in *Leicester-fields*. The principal character was then sitting, and not, as he is at present, thrown upon his knees in the act of execration.

The thought of the losing gamester pulling his hat over his brows is adopted from a similar character to be found among the figures of the principal personages in the court of *Louis* XIV. folio. This work has no engraver's name, but was probably executed about the year 1700.

Plate VII. The celebrated *Beccaria*, in his "Essay on Public Happiness," vol. II. p. 172, observes, "I am sensible there are persons whom it will be difficult for me to persuade: I mean those profound contemplators, who, secluding themselves from their fellow-creatures, are assiduously employed in framing laws for them, and who frequently neglect the care of their domestic and private concerns, to prescribe to empires that form of government, to which they imagine that they ought to submit. The celebrated *Hogarth* hath represented, in one of his moral engravings, a young man who, after having squandered away his fortune, is, by his creditors, lodged in a gaol. There he sits, melancholy and disconcerted, near a table, whilst a scroll lies under his feet, and bears the following title: 'being a new scheme for paying the debt of the nation. By *T. L.* now a prisoner in *The Fleet*.'"

The Author of the poem already quoted, intimates that the personage in the night-gown was meant for some real character:

>   "His wig was full as old as he,
>   In which one curl you could not see.
>   His neckcloth loose, his beard full grown,
>   An old torn night-gown not his own.
>   *L———*, great schemist, that can pay,
>   The nation's debt an easy way."

In Plate VIII. (which appears in three different states) is a half-penny reversed (struck in the year 1763) and fixed against the wall, intimating, that *Britannia* herself was fit only for a mad-house. This was a circumstance inserted by our artist (as he advertises) about a year before his death. I may add, that the man drawing lines against the wall just over the half-penny, alludes to *Whiston's* proposed method of discovering the Longitude by the firing of bombs, as here represented. The idea of the two figures at each corner of the print appears to have been taken from *Cibber's* statues at *Bedlam*. The faces of the two females are also changed. That of the woman with a fan, is entirely altered; she has now a cap on, instead of a hood, and is turned, as if speaking to the other.

Mr. *Gilpin's* opinion concerning this set of prints is too valuable to be omitted, and is therefore transcribed below.[12] The plates were thus admirably illustrated by Dr. *John Hoadly*.

PLATE I.
O Vanity of *Age*, untoward,
Ever spleeny, ever froward!
Why these Bolts, and massy chains,
Squint suspicions, jealous Pains?
Why, thy toilsome Journey o'er,
Lay'st thou in an useless store?
Hope along with *Time* is flown,
Nor canst thou reap the field thou'st sown.

Hast thou a son? in time be wise—.
He views thy toil with other eyes.
Needs must thy kind, paternal care,
Lock'd in thy chests be buried there?
Whence then shall flow that friendly ease,
That social converse, home-felt peace,
Familiar duty without dread,
Instruction from example bred,
Which youthful minds with freedom mend,
And with the *father* mix the *friend*?

Uncircumscrib'd by prudent rules,
Or precepts of expensive schools
Abus'd at home, abroad despis'd,
Unbred, unletter'd, unadvis'd;
The headstrong course of youth begun,
What comfort from this darling son?

PLATE II.
Prosperity (with harlot's smiles,
Most pleasing when she most beguiles)
How soon, sweet foe, can all thy train
Of false, gay, frantic, loud, and vain,
Enter the unprovided mind,
And Memory in fetters bind;
Load *Faith* and *Love* with golden chain,
And sprinkle *Lethe* o'er the brain!

Pleasure, in her silver throne,
Smiling comes, nor comes alone;
Venus comes with her along,
And smooth *Lyæus* ever young;
And in their train, to fill the press,
Come apish *Dance*, and swol'n *Excess*,
Mechanic *Honour*, vicious *Taste*,
And *Fashion* in her changing vest.

PLATE III.
O vanity of youthful blood,
So by misuse to poison *good!*
Woman, fram'd for social love,
Fairest gift of powers above;
Source of every houshold blessing,
All charms in innocence possessing—
But turn'd to Vice, all plagues above,
Foe to thy Being, foe to Love!
Guest divine to outward viewing,
Ablest Minister of Ruin!

And thou, no less of gift divine,
"Sweet poison of misused wine!"
With freedom led to every part,
And secret chamber of the heart;
Dost thou thy friendly host betray,
And show thy riotous gang the way
To enter in with covert treason,
O'erthrow the drowsy guard of reason,
To ransack the abandon'd place,
And revel there in wild excess?

PLATE IV.
O vanity of youthful blood,
So by misuse to poison *good!*
Reason awakes, and views unbarr'd
The sacred gates he watch'd to guard;
Approaching sees the harpy, *Law*,
And *Poverty*, with icy paw,
Ready to seize the poor remains—
That Vice has left of all his gains.
Cold *Penitence*, lame *After-thought*,
With fears, despair, and horrors fraught,

Call back his guilty pleasures dead,
Whom he hath wrong'd, and whom betray'd.

PLATE V.
New to the School of hard *Mishap*,
Driven from the ease of Fortune's lap,
What schemes will Nature not embrace
T' avoid less shame of drear distress!
Gold can the charms of youth bestow,
And mask deformity with show:
Gold can avert the sting of *Shame*,
In winter's arms create a flame;
Can couple youth with hoary age,
And make antipathies engage.

PLATE VI.
Gold, thou bright son of *Phœbus*, source
Of universal intercourse;
Of weeping Virtue soft redress,
And blessing those who live to bless!
Yet oft behold this sacred truth,
The tool of avaricious Lust:
No longer bond of human kind,
But bane of every virtuous mind.

What chaos such misuse attends!
Friendship stoops to prey on friends;
Health, that gives relish to delight,
Is wasted with the wasting night;
Doubt and mistrust is thrown on *Heaven*,
And all its power to *Chance* is given.
Sad purchase of repentant tears,
Of needless quarrels, endless fears,
Of hopes of moments, pangs of years!
Sad purchase of a *tortur'd mind*
To an *imprison'd body* join'd!

PLATE VII.
Happy the man, whose constant thought
(Though in the school of hardship taught)
Can send *Remembrance* back to fetch
Treasures from life's earliest stretch;
Who, self-approving, can review

Scenes of past virtues, which shine through
The gloom of age, and cast a ray
To gild the evening of his day!

Not so the guilty wretch confin'd:
No pleasures meet his conscious mind;
No blessings brought from early youth,
But broken faith and wrested truth,
Talents idle and unus'd,
And every trust of Heaven abus'd.

In seas of sad reflection lost,
From horrors still to horrors toss'd,
Reason the vessel leaves to steer,
And gives the helm to mad *despair*.

PLATE VIII.
Madness! thou chaos of the brain;
What art, that pleasure giv'st and pain?
Tyranny of Fancy's reign!
Mechanic *Fancy!* that can build
Vast labyrinths and mazes wild,
With rule disjointed, shapeless measure,
Fill'd with *horror*, fill'd with *pleasure!*
Shapes of *horror*, that would even
Cast doubt of mercy upon Heaven!
Shapes of *pleasure*, that but seen
Would split the shaking sides of *spleen*.

O vanity of age! here see
The stamp of Heaven effac'd by thee!
The headstrong course of youth thus run,
What comfort from this darling son?
His rattling chains with terror hear;
Behold Death grappling with despair;
See him by thee to ruin sold,
And curse *Thyself*, and curse thy *Gold*.

On this occasion also appeared an 8vo pamphlet, intituled, "The Rake's Progress, or the Humours of *Drury-Lane*, a poem in eight canto's, in *Hudibrastick* verse, being the ramble of a modern *Oxonian*, which is a compleat key to the eight prints lately published by the celebrated Mr. *Hogarth*." The second edition with additions, particularly an "epistle to Mr. *Hogarth*" was "printed for *J. Chetwood*, and sold at *Inigo Jones's-Head* against

Exeter Change in *The Strand*, 1735." This is a most contemptible and indecent performance. Eight prints are inserted in some copies of it; but they are only the designs of *Hogarth* murdered, and perhaps were not originally intended for the decoration of the work already described.

The original paintings, both of the Rake's and Harlot's Progress, were at *Fonthill*, in *Wiltshire*, the seat of Mr. *Beckford*,[13] where the latter were destroyed by a fire, in the year 1755; the former set was happily preserved. Mr. *Barnes*, of *Rippon*, in *Yorkshire*, has the Harlot's Progress in oil. It must, however, be a copy. Mr. *Beckford* has also twenty-five heads from the Cartoons by *Hogarth*, for which he paid twenty-five guineas.

There is reason to believe that *Hogarth* once designed to have introduced the ceremony of a *Marriage Contract* into the Rake's Progress, instead of the *Levee*. An unfinished painting of this scene is still preserved. We have here the Rake's apartment as now exhibited in Plate II. In the anti-room, among other figures, we recognize that of the poet who at present congratulates our hero on his accession to wealth and pleasure. The bard is here waiting with an epithalamium in his hand. The Rake has added connoisseurship to the rest of his expensive follies. One of his purchases is a canvas containing only the representation of a human foot. [Perhaps this circumstance might allude to the dissection of *Arlaud's Leda*. See Mr. *Walpole's* Anecdotes, &c. vol. IV. p. 39.] A second is so obscure, that no objects in it are discernible. [A performance of the same description is introduced in our artist's *Piquet, or Virtue in Danger*.] A third presents us with a *Madona* looking down with fondness on the infant she holds in her arms. [This seems intended as a contrast to the grey headed bride who sits under it, and is apparently past child-bearing.] The fourth is emblematical, and displays perhaps too licentious a satire on transubstantiation. The Blessed Virgin is thrusting her Son down the hopper of a mill, in which he is ground by priests till he issues out in the shape of the consecrated *wafer*, supposed by Catholicks to contain the *real presence*. At a table sits a toothless decrepit father, guardian, or matchmaker, joining the hand of the rake with that of the antiquated female, whose face is highly expressive of eagerness, while that of her intended husband is directed a contrary way, toward a groom who is bringing in a piece of plate won at a horse-race.[14] On the floor in front lie a heap of mutilated busts, &c. which our spendthrift is supposed to have recently purchased at an auction. The black boy, who is afterwards met with in Plate IV. of Marriage Alamode, was transplanted from this canvas. He is here introduced supporting such a picture of *Ganymede* as hangs against the wall of the lady's dressing-room in the same plate of the same work.

[1] The face of this female has likewise been changed on the last plate. In the intermediate ones it remains as originally designed. To give the same

character two different casts of countenance, was surely an incongruity without excuse.

[2] The inscription on this bill is—"*London*, bought of *William Tothall*, Woollen-draper in *Covent-Garden*." See the corner figure looking over the music in the *Rehearsal of the Oratorio of Judith*; and note 88 above.

[3] Of whom a separate portrait, by *Ellis*, had been published by *Overton*. Figg died in the year 1734. As the taste of the publick is much changed about the importance of the *noble* Science of Defence, as it was called, and as probably it will never again revive, it may afford some entertainment to my readers, to see the terms in which this celebrated prize-fighter is spoken of by a professor of the art. "FIGG was the *Atlas* of the Sword; and may he remain the gladiating statue! In him strength, resolution, and unparalleled judgement, conspired to form a matchless master. There was a majesty shone in his countenance, and blazed in all his actions, beyond all I ever saw. His right leg bold and firm, and his left, which could hardly ever be disturbed, gave him the surprising advantage already proved, and struck his adversary with despair and panic. He had that peculiar way of stepping in I spoke of, in a parry; he knew his arm, and its just time of moving; put a firm faith in that, and never let his adversary escape his parry. He was just as much a greater master than any other I ever saw, as he was a greater judge of time and measure." *Captain John Godfrey's Treatise upon the Useful Science of Defence*, 4to, 1747, p. 41. "Mr. *Figg*," says *Chetwood*, History of the Stage, p. 60, "informed me once, that he had not bought a shirt for more than twenty years, but had sold some dozens. It was his method, when he fought in his amphitheatre (his stage bearing that superb title), to send round to a select number of his scholars, to borrow a shirt for the ensuing combat, and seldom failed of half a dozen of superfine Holland from his prime pupils (most of the young nobility and gentry made it a part of their education to march under his warlike banner). This champion was generally conqueror, though his shirt seldom failed of gaining a cut from his enemy, and sometimes his flesh, though I think he never received any dangerous wound. Most of his scholars were at every battle, and were sure to exult at their great master's victories, every person supposing he saw the wounds his shirt received. Mr. *Figg* took his opportunity to inform his lenders of linen of the chasms their shirts received, with a promise to send them home. But, said the ingenious courageous *Figg*, I seldom received any other answer than D-mn you, keep it!" A Poem by Dr. *Byrom*, on a battle between *Figg* and *Sutton*, another prize-fighter, is in the 6th Volume of *Dodsley's* Collection of Poems.

[4] *Fielding* has introduced this porter, under the name of *Leathersides*, into *The Covent-Garden Tragedy*, acted in 1732.

Leath.
Two whores, great Madam, must be straight prepar'd,
A fat one for the Squire, and for my Lord a lean.

Mother.
Thou, *Leathersides*, best know'st such nymphs to find,
To thee their lodgings they communicate.
Go thou procure the girl.

[5] The cleanliness of the *English* seems to have made a similar impression on the mind of M. *De Grosley*, who, in his "Tour to *London*," observes, that "The plate, hearth-stones, moveables, apartments, doors, stairs, the very street-doors, their locks, and the large brass knockers, are every day washed, scowered, or rubbed. Even in lodging-houses, the middle of the stairs is often covered with carpeting, to prevent them from being soiled. All the apartments in the house have mats or carpets; and the use of them has been adopted some years since by the *French*;" and that "The towns and villages upon the road have excellent inns, but somewhat dear; at these an *English* lord is as well served as at his own house, and with a cleanliness much to be wished for in most of the best houses of *France*. The innkeeper makes his appearance only to do the honours of his table to the greatest personages, who often invite him to dine with them."

[6] The chief of these, who wears something that seems to have been a tie-wig, was painted from a *French* boy, who cleaned shoes at the corner of *Hog-Lane*.

[7] In the collection of Mr. *Steevens* only.

[8] He had meditated, however, some additional improvements in the same plate. When he had inserted the storm, he began to consider the impropriety of turning the girl out in the midst of it with her head uncovered; and therefore, on a proof of this print, from which he designed to have worked, he sketched her hat in with *Indian* ink.

[9] It appears, on examination of the Registers, &c. that *Tho. Sice* and *Tho. Horn* are not fictitious names. Such people were really churchwardens when the repairs in 1725 were made. The following inscription on the pew, denoting a vault beneath, is also genuine, and, as far as can be known at present, was faithfully copied in regard to its obsolete spelling.

> THESE PEWES VNSCRVD AND TANE IN SVNDER
> IN STONE THERS GRAVEN WHAT IS VNDER
> TO WIT A VALT FOR BURIAL THERE IS
> WHICH EDWARD FORSET MADE FOR HIM AND HIS.

Part of these words, in raised letters, at present form a pannel in the wainscot at the end of the right-hand gallery, as the church is entered from the street.—No heir of the *Forset* family appearing, their vault has been claimed and used by his Grace the Duke of *Portland*, as lord of the manor. The mural monument of the *Taylors*, composed of lead gilt over, is likewise preserved. It is seen, in *Hogarth's* print, just under the window. The bishop of the diocese, when the new church was built, gave orders that all the ancient tablets should be placed, as nearly as possible, in their former situations.

[10] Old *Manners*, brother to the late *Duke of Rutland*.

[11] The old Duke of *Devonshire* lost the great estate of *Leicester* abbey to him at the gaming-table. *Manners* was the only person of his time who had amassed a considerable fortune by the profession of a gamester.

[12] "The first print of this capital work is an excellent representation of a young heir, taking possession of a miser's effects. The passion of avarice, which hoards every thing, without distinction, what is and what is not valuable, is admirably described.—The *composition*, though not excellent, is not unpleasing. The principal group, consisting of the young gentleman, the taylor, the appraiser, the papers, and chest, is well shaped: but the eye is hurt by the disagreeable regularity of three heads nearly in a line, and at equal distances.—The *light* is not ill disposed. It falls on the principal figures: but the effect might have been improved. If the extreme parts of the mass (the white apron on one side, and the memorandum-book on the other) had been in shade, the *repose* had been less injured. The detached parts of a group should rarely catch a strong body of light.—We have no striking instances of *expression* in this print. The principal figure is unmeaning. The only one, which displays the true *vis comica* of *Hogarth*, is the appraiser fingering the gold. You enter at once into his character.—The young woman might have furnished the artist with an opportunity of presenting a graceful figure; which would have been more pleasing. The figure he *has* introduced, is by no means an object of allurement.—The *perspective* is accurate, but affected. So many windows, and open doors, may shew the author's learning; but they break the back ground, and injure the simplicity of it.

"The second print introduces our hero into all the dissipation of modish life. We became first acquainted with him, when a boy of eighteen. He is now of age; has entirely thrown off the clownish school-boy; and assumes the man of fashion. Instead of the country taylor, who took measure of him for his father's mourning, he is now attended by *French* barbers, *French* taylors, poets, milleners, jockies, bullies, and the whole retinue of a fine gentleman.—The *expression*, in this print, is wonderfully great. The dauntless front of the bully; the keen eye, and elasticity of the fencing-master; and the simpering importance of the dancing-master, are admirably expressed. The last is perhaps a little *outré*. The architect[A] is a strong copy from nature.—The *composition* seems to be entirely subservient to the expression. It appears, as if *Hogarth* had sketched, in his memorandum-book, all the characters which he has here introduced; but was at a loss how to group them; and chose rather to introduce them in detached figures, as he had sketched them, than to lose any part of the expression by combining them.—The *light* is ill distributed. It is spread indiscriminately over the print; and destroys the *whole*—We have no instance of *grace* in any of the figures. The principal figure is very deficient. There is no contrast in the limbs; which is always attended with a degree of ungracefulness.—The *execution* is very good. It is elaborate, and yet free.—The satire on operas, though it may be well directed, is forced and unnatural.

"The third plate carries us still deeper into the history. We meet our hero engaged in one of his evening amusements. This print, on the whole, is no very extraordinary effort of genius.—The *design* is good; and may be a very exact description of the humours of a brothel.—The *composition* too is not amiss. But we have few of those masterly strokes which distinguish the works of *Hogarth*. The whole is plain history. The lady setting the world on fire is the best thought: and there is some humour in furnishing the room with a set of *Cæsars*; and not placing them in order.—The *light* is ill managed. By a few alterations, which are obvious, particularly by throwing the lady dressing into the shade, the disposition of it might have been tolerable. But still we should have had an absurdity to answer, whence comes it? Here is light in abundance; but no visible source.—*Expression* we have a little through the whole print. That of the principal figure is the best. The ladies have all the air of their profession; but no variety of character. *Hogarth's* women are, in general, very inferior to his men. For which reason I prefer the *Rake's Progress* to the *Harlot's*. The female face indeed has seldom strength of feature enough to admit the strong markings of expression.

"Very disagreeable accidents often befall gentlemen of pleasure. An event of this kind is recorded in the fourth print; which is now before us. Our hero going, in full dress, to pay his compliments at court on St. *David's* day, was accosted in the rude manner which is here represented.—The *composition* is good. The form of the group, made up of the figures in action, the chair, and the lamp-lighter, is pleasing. Only, here we have an opportunity of remarking, that a group is disgusting when the extremities of it are heavy. A group in some respect should resemble a tree. The heavier part of the foliage (the *cup* as the landscape painter calls it) is always near the middle; the outside branches, which are relieved by the sky, are light and airy. An inattention to this rule has given a heaviness to the group before us. The two bailiffs, the woman, and the chairman, are all huddled together in that part of the group which should have been the lightest; while the middle part, where the hand holds the door, wants strength and consistence. It may be added too, that the four heads, in the form of a diamond, make an unpleasing shape. All regular figures should be studiously avoided.—The *light* had been well distributed, if the bailiff holding the arrest, and the chairman, had been a little lighter, and the woman darker. The glare of the white apron is disagreeable.—We have, in this print, some beautiful instances of *expression*. The surprise and terror of the poor gentleman is apparent in every limb, as far as is consistent with the fear of discomposing his dress. The insolence of power in one of the bailiffs, and the unfeeling heart, which can jest with misery, in the other, are strongly marked. The self-importance too of the honest *Cambrian* is not ill portrayed; who is chiefly introduced to settle the chronology of the story.—In point of *grace*, we have nothing striking. *Hogarth* might have introduced a degree of it in the female figure: at least he might have contrived to vary the heavy and unpleasing form of her drapery.—The *perspective* is good, and makes an agreeable shape.—I cannot leave this print without remarking the *falling band-box*. Such representations of quick motion are absurd; and every moment the absurdity grows stronger. You cannot deceive the eye. The falling body *must* appear *not* to fall. Objects of that kind are beyond the power of representation.

"Difficulties crowd so fast upon our hero, that at the age of twenty-five, which he seems to have attained in the fifth plate, we find him driven to the necessity of marrying a woman, whom he detests, for her fortune. The *composition* here is very good; and yet we have a disagreeable regularity in the climax of the three figures, the maid, the bride, and the bride-groom.—The *light* is not ill distributed. The principal figure too is *graceful*; and there is strong *expression* in the seeming tranquillity of his features. He hides his contempt of the object before him as well as he can; and yet he cannot do it. She too has as much meaning as can appear thro' the deformity of her features. The clergyman's face we are all well acquainted with, and also his wig; tho' we cannot pretend to say, where we have seen either. The clerk too is an admirable fellow.—The *perspective* is well understood; but the church is too small;[B] and the wooden post, which seems to have no use, divides the picture very disagreeably.—The creed lost, the commandments broken, and the poor's-box obstructed by a cobweb, are all excellent strokes of satirical humour.

"The fortune, which our adventurer has just received, enables him to make one push more at the gaming-table. He is exhibited, in the sixth print, venting curses on his folly for having lost his last stake.—This is upon the whole, perhaps, the best print of the set. The horrid scene it describes was never more inimitably drawn. The *composition* is artful, and natural. If the shape of the whole be not quite pleasing, the figures are so well grouped, and with so much ease and variety, that you cannot take offence.—In point of light, it is more culpable. There is not shade enough among the figures to balance the glare. If the neck-cloth and weepers of the gentleman in mourning had been removed, and his hands thrown into shade, even that alone would have improved the effect.—The *expression*, in almost every figure, is admirable; and the whole is a strong representation of the human mind in a storm. Three stages of that species of madness, which attends gaming, are here described. On the first shock, all is inward dismay. The ruined gamester is representing leaning against a wall, with his arms across, lost in an agony of horror. Perhaps never passion was described with so much force. In a short time this horrible gloom bursts into a storm of fury: he tears in pieces what comes next him; and, kneeling down, invokes curses upon himself. He next attacks others; every one in his turn whom he imagines to have been instrumental in his ruin.—The eager joy of the winning gamesters, the attention of the usurer, the vehemence of the watchman, and the profound reverie of the highwayman, are all admirably marked. There is great coolness too expressed in the little we see of the fat gentleman at the end of the table. The figure opposing the mad-man is bad: it has a drunken appearance; and drunkenness is not the vice of a gaming table.—The principal figure is *ill-drawn*. The *perspective* is formal; and the *execution* but indifferent: in heightening his expression, *Hogarth* has lost his spirit.

"The seventh plate, which gives us the view of a jail, has very little in it. Many of the circumstances, which may well be supposed to increase the misery of a confined debtor, are well contrived; but the fruitful genius of *Hogarth*, I should think, might have treated the subject in a more copious manner. The episode of the fainting woman might have given way to many circumstances more proper to the occasion. This is the same woman, whom the rake discards in the first print; by whom he is rescued in the fourth; who is present at his marriage; who follows him into jail; and, lastly, to *Bedlam*. The thought is rather unnatural, and the moral certainly culpable.—The *composition* is bad. The group of the woman fainting is a round heavy mass: and the other group is very ill-shaped. The *light* could not be worse managed, and, as the groups are contrived, can hardly be improved.—In the principal figure there is great *expression*; and the fainting scene is well described. A scheme to pay off the national debt, by a man who cannot pay his own; and the attempt of a silly rake, to retrieve his affairs by a work of genius; are admirable strokes of humour.

"The eighth plate brings the fortune of our hero to a conclusion. It is a very expressive representation of the most horrid scene which human nature can exhibit.—The *composition* is not bad. The group, in which the lunatic is chained, is well managed; and if it had been carried a little further towards the middle of the picture, and the two women (who seem very oddly introduced) had been removed, both the composition, and the distribution of light, had been good.—The *drawing* of the principal figure is a more accurate piece of anatomy than we commonly find in the works of this master. The *expression* of the figure is rather unmeaning; and very inferior to the strong characters of all the other lunatics. The fertile genius of the artist has introduced as many of the causes of madness, as he could well have collected; but there is some tautology. There are two religionists, and two astronomers. Yet there is variety in each; and strong *expression* in all the characters. The self-satisfaction, and conviction, of him who has discovered the longitude; the mock majesty of the monarch; the moody melancholy of the lover; and the superstitious horror of the popish devotee; are all admirable.—The *perspective* is simple and proper.

"I should add, that these remarks are made upon the first edition of this work. When the plates were much worn, they were altered in many parts. They have gained by the alterations, in point of *design*; but have lost in point of *expression*."

[A] The *architect*. Mr. *Gilpin* means—the *gardener*.

[B] I am authorized to observe, that this is no fault in our artist. The old church at *Marybone* was so little, that it would have stood within the walls of the present one, leaving at the same time sufficient room for a walk round it.

[13] Afterwards twice lord mayor of *London*. See p. 44.

[14] The same as that introduced in Plate II.

1736.

1. Two prints of Before and After. The two pictures, from which these prints are taken, were painted at the particular request of a certain vicious nobleman, whose name deserves no commemoration. The hero of them is said to have been designed for Chief Justice *Willes*. *Hogarth* repented of having engraved them; and almost every possessor of his works will wish they had been with-held from the public, as often as he is obliged to shew the volume that contains them to ladies. To omit them, is to mutilate the collection; to pin the leaves, on which they are pasted, together, is a circumstance that tends only to provoke curiosity; and to display them, would be to set decency at defiance. The painter who indulges himself, or his employers, in such representations, will forfeit the general praise he might have gained by a choice of less offensive subjects. We have an artist of no common merit, who has frequently disgraced his skill by scenes too luxuriant to appear in any situation but a brothel; and yet one of the most meretricious of his performances, but a few years ago, was exhibited by the Royal

Academy. These prints, however, display almost the only instance in which *Hogarth* condescended to execute a subject proposed to him; for I am assured by one who knew him well, that his obstinacy on these occasions has often proved invincible. Like *Shakspeare's Tully*,

> "———he would never follow any thing
> That other men began."

In the later impressions from these plates, the scroll-work on the head-cloth, &c. of the bed, is rendered indistinct, by an injudicious attempt to strengthen the engraving. Mr. *S. Ireland* has the first sketch in oil of "Before."[1]

[1] The originals of both are at the earl of *Besborough's* seat at *Roehampton*.

2. The Sleeping Congregation. The preacher was designed as the representative of Dr. *Desaguliers*. This print was first published in 1736. It was afterwards retouched and *improved*[1] by the author in 1762, and is found in three different states. In the first, *Dieu & Mon Droit* is wanting under the King's Arms; the angel with one wing and two pair of thighs, that supports this motto, is smoking a pipe; and the lion has not his present magnificent genitals. In the second, the words already mentioned are added; the angel's pipe is obliterated; the insignia of the lion's sex rendered ostentatiously conspicuous; and the lines of the triangle under the angel are doubled. The other distinctions are chiefly such as a reiteration of engraving would naturally produce, by adding strength to the fainter parts of the composition. Changes of this slender kind are numberless in all the repaired prints of our artist. There is also a pirated copy of this plate. It is not ill executed, but in size is somewhat shorter than its predecessor, and has no price annexed. In the original picture, in the collection of Sir *Edward Walpole*, the clerk's head is admirably well painted, and with great force; but he is dozing, and not leering at the young woman near him, as in the print.

[1] I wish, for the sake of some future edition of the present work, these *improvements* could be ascertained. To me they are invisible, like those in the re-published *March to Finchley*.

3. The Distressed Poet.[1] In a back ground, a picture of *Pope* threshing *Curll*. Over the head of *Pope* we read, *Pope's Letters*; out of his mouth comes *Veni, vidi, vici*; and under *Curll* lies a letter, directed—*to Curll*. The distressed bard is composing *Poverty*, a poem. At the bottom of the plate are the following lines from *The Dunciad*, I. iii.

> Studious he sate, with all his books around,
> Sinking from thought to thought, a vast profund!

Plung'd for his sense, but found no bottom there;
Then writ, and flounder'd on in mere despair.

In the subsequent impressions, dated *December* 15, 1740, the triumphs of *Pope* are changed to a view of the gold mines of *Peru*; and our hero of the garret is employed in celebrating the praise of *Riches*. The lines already quoted are effaced. The original painting is at lord *Grosvenor's* house at *Milbank, Westminster*.

[1] In *The Craftsman, March* 12, 1736-7, occurs, "This day is published, price 3s. a print representing a *Distressed Poet*. Also, five etchings, of different characters of heads in groups, viz. a Chorus of Singers; a pleased Audience at a Play; Scholars at a Lecture; and Quacks in Consultation; price 6d. each. To be had either bound together with all Mr. *Hogarth's* late engraved works (except the Harlot's Progress), or singly, at the *Golden Head*, in *Leicester Fields*; and at Mr *Bakewell's*, printseller, next the *Horn Tavern, Fleet-street.*" And *April* 2 and 9, 1737, "Just published, price 3s. A print representing a *Distressed Poet*. Designed and engraved by Mr. *Hogarth*. Also four etchings, viz. A pleased Audience; a Chorus of Singers; Scholars at a Lecture; and a Consultation of Quacks, price 6d. each. To be had at the *Golden Head*, in *Leicester Fields*; and at Mr. *Bakewell's*, print-seller, next the *Horn Tavern*, in *Fleet-street*. Where may be had, bound or otherwise, all Mr. *Hogarth's* late engraved works, viz. A *Midnight Conversation; Southwark Fair*, the *Rake's Progress*, in eight prints; a sleepy Congregation in a Country Church; Before and After, two prints."

4. Right Hon. *Frances* Lady *Byron*. Whole length, mezzotinto. *W. Hogarth pinxit. J. Faber fecit.* The most beautiful impressions of this plate were commonly taken off in a brown colour.

5. The same, shortened into a three-quarters length.

6. Consultation of Physicians. Arms of the Undertakers. In this plate, amongst other portraits, is the well-known one of Dr. *Ward*[1] (who was called *Spot Ward*, from the left side of his face being marked of a claret colour); and that of the elder *Taylor*,[2] a noted oculist, with an eye on the head of his cane; Dr. *Pierce Dod*,[3] Dr. *Bamber*,[4] and other physicians of that time. The figure with a bone in its hand, between the two demi-doctors (i. e. *Taylor* and *Ward*), is said to have been designed for Mrs. *Mapp*, a famous masculine woman, who was called the bone-setter, or shape-mistress. I am told, that many of her advertisements may be found in *Mist's Journal*, and still more accounts of her cures in the periodical publications of her time. Her maiden name was *Wallin*. Her father was also a bone-setter at *Hindon, Wilts*; but quarrelling with him, she wandered about the country, calling herself *crazy Sally*. On her success in her profession she married, *August* 11, 1736,[5] one *Hill Mapp*, a

servant to Mr. *Ibbetson*, mercer on *Ludgate-Hill*. In most cases her success was rather owing to the strength of her arms, and the boldness of her undertakings, than to any knowledge of anatomy or skill in chirurgical operations. The following particulars relative to her are collected from the *The Grub-street Journal*, &c. and serve at least to shew, that she was a character considerable enough to deserve the satire of *Hogarth*.

August 19, 1736, "We hear that the husband of Mrs. *Mapp*, the famous bone-setter at *Epsom*, ran away from her last week, taking with him upwards of 100 guineas, and such other portable things as lay next hand."

"Several letters from *Epsom* mention, that the footman, whom the female bone-setter married the week before, had taken a sudden journey from thence with what money his wife had earned; and that her concern at first was very great: but soon as the surprize was over, she grew gay, and seemed to think the money well disposed of, as it was like to rid her of a husband. He took just 102 guineas."

The following verses were addressed to her in *August* 1736.

> "Of late, without the least pretence to skill,
> *Ward's* grown a fam'd physician by a pill;[6]
> Yet he can but a doubtful honour claim,
> While envious Death oft blasts his rising fame.
> Next travell'd *Taylor* fill'd us with surprize,
> Who pours new light upon the blindest eyes;
> Each journal tells his circuit thro' the land;
> Each journal tells the blessings of his hand:
> And lest some hireling scribbler of the town
> Injures his history, he writes his own.
> We read the long accounts with wonder o'er;
> Had he wrote less, we had believ'd him more.
> Let these, O *Mapp!* thou wonder of the age!
> With dubious arts endeavour to engage:
> While you, irregularly strict to rules,
> Teach dull collegiate pedants they are fools:
> By merit, the sure path to fame pursue;
> For all who see thy art, must own it true."

September 2, 1736, "On *Friday* several persons, who had the misfortune of lameness, crowded to *The White-hart Inn*, in *White-chapel*, on hearing Mrs. *Mapp* the famous bone-setter was there. Some of them were admitted to her, and were relieved as they apprehended. But a gentleman, who happened to come by, declared Mrs. *Mapp* was at *Epsom*, on which the woman thought proper to move off."

September 9, 1736. "Advertisement.

"Whereas it has been industriously (I wish I could say truly) reported, that I had found great benefit from a certain female bone-setter's performance, and that it was to a want of resolution to undergo the operation, that I did not meet with a perfect cure: this is therefore to give notice, that any persons afflicted with lameness (who are willing to know what good or harm others may receive, before they venture on desperate measures themselves) will be welcome any morning to see the dressing of my leg, which was sound before the operation, and they will then be able to judge of the performance, and to whom I owe my present unhappy confinement to my bed and chair.

"*Thomas Barber*, Tallow-chandler, *Saffron-hill.*"

September 16, 1736. "On *Thursday*, Mrs. *Mapp's* plate of ten guineas was run for at *Epsom*. A mare, called 'Mrs. *Mapp*,' won the first heat; when Mrs. *Mapp* gave the rider a guinea, and swore if he won the plate she would give him 100; but the second and third heat was won by a chestnut mare."

"We hear that the husband of Mrs. *Mapp* is returned, and has been kindly received."

September 23, 1736. "Mrs. *Mapp* continues making extraordinary cures: she has now set up an equipage, and on *Sunday* waited on her Majesty."

Saturday, October 16, 1736. "Mrs. *Mapp*, the bone-setter, with Dr. *Taylor*, the oculist, was at the play-house, in *Lincoln's-Inn Fields*, to see a comedy called 'The Husband's Relief, with the Female Bone-setter and Worm Doctor;' which occasioned a full house, and the following epigram:

> "'While *Mapp* to th'actors shew'd a kind regard,
> On one side *Taylor* sat, on the other *Ward*:
> When their mock persons of the Drama came,
> Both *Ward* and *Taylor* thought it hurt their *fame*;
> Wonder'd how *Mapp* cou'd in good humour be—
> Zoons! cries the manly dame, it hurts not me;
> Quacks without art may either blind or kill;
> But[7] *demonstration* shews that mine is *skill*.'

"And the following was sung upon the stage:

> "'You surgeons of *London*, who puzzle your pates,
> To ride in your coaches, and purchase estates,
> Give over, for shame, for your pride has a fall,
> And the doctress of *Epsom* has outdone you all.
> *Derry down*, &c.

> "'What signifies learning, or going to school,

When a woman can do, without reason or rule,
What puts you to nonplus, and baffles your art?
For petticoat-practice has now got the start.

"'In physics, as well as in fashions, we find,
The newest has always the run with mankind;
Forgot is the bustle 'bout *Taylor* and *Ward*;
Now *Mapp's* all the cry, and her fame's on record.

"'Dame Nature has given her a doctor's degree,
She gets all the patients, and pockets the fee;
So if you don't instantly prove it a cheat,
She'll loll in her chariot, whilst you walk the street.
Derry down, &c.'"

October 19, 1736, *London Daily Post.* "Mrs. *Mapp*, being present at the acting of *The Wife's Relief*, concurred in the universal applause of a crowded audience. This play was advertised by the desire of Mrs. *Mapp*, the famous bone-setter from *Epsom*."

October 21, 1736, "On *Saturday* evening there was such a concourse of people at the Theatre-royal in *Lincoln's-Inn Fields*, to see the famous Mrs. *Mapp*, that several gentlemen and ladies were obliged to return for want of room. The confusion at going out was so great, that several gentlemen and ladies had their pockets picked, and many of the latter lost their fans, &c. Yesterday she was elegantly entertained by Dr. *Ward*, at his house in *Pall-Mall*."

"On *Saturday* and yesterday Mrs. *Mapp* performed several operations at *The Grecian Coffee-house*, particularly one upon a niece of Sir *Hans Sloane*, to his great satisfaction and her credit. The patient had her shoulder-bone out for about nine years."

"On *Monday* Mrs. *Mapp* performed two extraordinary cures; one on a young lady of *The Temple*, who had several bones out from the knees to her toes, which she put in their proper places: and the other on a butcher, whose knee-pans were so misplaced that he walked with his knees knocking one against another. Yesterday she performed several other surprizing cures; and about one set out for *Epsom*, and carried with her several crutches, which she calls trophies of honour."

November 18, 1736, "Mrs. *Mapp*, the famous bone-setter, has taken lodgings in *Pall-Mall*, near Mr. *Joshua Ward's*, &c."

November 25, 1736,

"In this bright age three wonder-workers rise,
Whose operations puzzle all the wise.
To lame and blind, by dint of manual slight,
Mapp gives the use of limbs, and *Taylor* sight.
But greater *Ward*, &c."

December 16, 1736, "On *Thursday*, *Polly Peachum* (Miss *Warren*, that was sister to the famous Mrs. *Mapp*) was tried at *The Old Bailey* for marrying Mr. *Nicholas*; her former husband, Mr. *Somers*, being living, &c."

December 22, 1737, "Died last week, at her lodgings near *The Seven Dials*, the much-talked-of Mrs. *Mapp*, the bone-setter, so miserably poor, that the parish was obliged to bury her."

The plate is thus illustrated by the engraver: "The Company of Undertakers beareth Sable, an Urinal proper, between twelve Quack Heads of the second, and twelve Cane Heads, Or, Consultant. On a Chief,[8] Nebulæ,[9] Ermine, one compleat Doctor[10] issuant, checkie, sustaining in his right hand a baton of the second. On his dexter and sinister sides two *demi*-doctors issuant of the second, and two Cane Heads issuant of the third; the first having one eye couchant, towards the dexter side of the escutcheon; the second faced per pale proper and gules, guardant, with this motto—*Et plurima mortis imago*."

[1] *Joshua Ward* was one of the younger sons of an ancient and respectable family settled at *Guisborough* in *Yorkshire*, where he was born some time in the last century. He seems, from every description of him, to have had small advantages from education, though he indisputably possessed no mean natural parts. The first account we have of him is, that he was a associated in partnership with a brother named *William*, as a dry-salter, in *Thames-street*. After they had carried on this business some time, a fire broke out in an adjoining house, which communicated itself to their warehouses, and entirely destroyed all their property. On this occasion Mr. *Ward*, with a gentleman from the country who was on a visit to him, escaped over the tops of the houses in their shirts. In the year 1717 he was returned member for *Marlborough*; but, by a vote of the House of Commons, dated *May* 13, was declared not duly elected. It is imagined that he was in some measure connected with his brother *John Ward* (who is stigmatized by Mr. *Pope*, Dunciad III. 34.) in secreting and protecting illegally the property of some of the *South Sea* directors. Be this as it may, he soon after fled from *England*, resided some years abroad, and has been frequently supposed to have turned *Roman* Catholic. While he remained in exile, he acquired that knowledge of medicine and chemistry, which afterwards was the means of raising him to a state of affluence. About the year 1733 he began to practise physic, and combated, for some time, the united efforts of Wit, Learning, Argument,

Ridicule, Malice, and Jealousy, by all of which he was opposed in every shape that can be suggested. At length, by some lucky cures, and particularly one on a relation of Sir *Joseph Jekyl* Master of the Rolls, he got the better of his opponents, and was suffered to practise undisturbed. From this time his reputation was established: he was exempted, by a vote of the House of Commons, from being visited by the censors of the college of physicians, and was even called in to the assistance of King *George* the Second, whose hand he cured, and received, as a reward, a commission for his nephew the late General *Gansel*. It was his custom to distribute his medicines and advice, and even pecuniary assistance, to the poor, at his house, *gratis*; and thus he acquired considerable popularity. Indeed, in these particulars his conduct was entitled to every degree of praise. With a stern outside, and rough deportment, he was not wanting in benevolence. After a continued series of success, he died *Dec.* 21, 1761, at a very advanced age, and left the secret of his medicines to Mr. *Page*, member for *Chichester*, who bestowed them on two charitable institutions, which have derived considerable advantages from them. His will is printed in *The Gentleman's Magazine*, 1762, p. 208.

[2] I was assured by the late Dr. *Johnson*, that *Ward* was the weakest, and *Taylor* the most ignorant, of the whole empiric tribe. The latter once asserted, that when he was at *St. Petersburg*, he travelled as far as *Archangel* to meet Prince *Herculaneum*. Now *Archangel* being the extreme point from *European Asia*, had the tale been true, the oculist must have marched so far backwards out of the route of Prince *Heraclius*, whose name he had blundered into *Herculaneum*.

The present likeness of our oculist, however, we may suppose to have been a strong one, as it much resembles a mezzotinto by *Faber*, from a picture painted at *Rome* by the Chevalier *Riche*. Under it is the following inscription: "*Joannes Taylor*, Medicus in Optica expertissimus multisque in Academiis celeberrimis Socius." Eight *Latin* verses follow, which are not worth transcription. *Taylor* made presents of this print to his friends. It is now become scarce.

[3] One of the physicians to *St. Bartholomew's* Hospital. He died *August* 6, 1754. His merits were thus celebrated by Dr. *Theobald*, a contemporary physician:

> "O raro merito quem juncta scientia dudum
> Illustrem sacris medico stellam addidit orbi
> Auspiciis, pura nunquam non luce corusce!
> Utcunque incolumem virtutum aversa tueri
> Gens humana solet, non ni post fata corona
> Donandam merita, potitus melioribus astris,
> Invidia major, tu præsens alter haberis
> *Hippocrates*, pleno jam nunc cumulatus honore.

> Te seu, corporea tandem compage soluta,
> Accipiet, doctis clarescentem artibus, alta
> *Coi* sphæra senis; seu tu venerabilis aureo
> *Romani Celsi* rite effulgebis in orbe;
> O sit adhuc tarda illa dies, sit tarda, precamur,
> Illa dies, nostris et multum ferior annis,
> Cum tua mens, membris seducta fluentibus, almas
> Advolet, angelicis immixta cohortibus, arces!
> Hic potius Musas, thematis dulcedine captas,
> Delecta, atque audi laudes vel *Apolline* dignas."

[4] A celebrated anatomist, physician, and man-midwife, to whose estate the present *Gascoyne* family succeeded, and whose surname has been given as a Christian name to two of them.

[5] Some indifferent verses on this event were printed in *The Gentleman's Magazine*, 1736, p. 484.

[6] General *Churchill* was "the primary puffer of *Ward's* pill at court;" and Lord Chief Baron *Reynolds* soon after published "its miraculous effects on a maid servant," as I learn by some doggrel verses of Sir *William Browne*, addressed to "Dr. *Ward*, a Quack, of merry memory," under the title of "The Pill-Plot. On *The Daily Courant's* miraculous Discovery, upon the ever-memorable 28th day of *November* 1734, from the Doctor himself being a Papist, and distributing his Pills to the poor *gratis*, by the hands of the Lady *Gage* also a Papist, that the Pill must be beyond all doubt a deep-laid Plot, to introduce popery."

[7] "This alludes to some surprizing cures she performed before Sir *Hans Sloane* at *The Grecian Coffee-house* (where she came once a week from *Epsom* in her chariot with four horses): viz. a man of *Wardour-street*, whose back had been broke nine years, and stuck out two inches; a niece of Sir *Hans Sloane* in the like condition; and a gentleman who went with one shoe heel six inches high, having been lame twenty years of his hip and knee, whom she set strait, and brought his leg down even with the other." *Gent. Mag.* 1756, p. 617.

[8] A chief betokeneth a senator, or honourable personage borrowed from the *Greeks*, and is a word signifying a head; and as the head is the chief part of a man, so the chief in the escutcheon should be a reward of such only whose high merits have procured them chief place, esteem, or love amongst men.

[9] The bearing of clouds in armes (saith *Upton*) doth import some excellencie.

[10] Originally printed *docter*, but afterwards altered in this print.

1737.

1. The Lecture. "Datur vacuum." The person reading is well known to be the late Mr. *Fisher*, of *Jesus College, Oxford*, and Registrar of that University. This portrait was taken with the free consent of Mr. *Fisher*, who died *March* 18, 1761. There are some impressions in which "Datur vacuum" is not printed, that leaf being entirely blank; published *January* 20, 1736-7; the other *March* 3, 1736. *Hogarth* at first marked these words in with a pen and ink.

2. *Æneas* in a Storm. The following advertisement appeared in *The London Daily Post, January* 17, 1736-7.

"This day is published, price sixpence, a hieroglyphical print called *Æneas in a Storm*.

"Tanta hæc mulier potuit suadere malorum.

"Sold by the booksellers and printsellers in town and country. Of whom may be had, a print called *Tartuff's Banquet*, or *Codex's* Entertainment. Price one shilling.

"—populus me sibilat, at mihi plaudo
Ipse domi."

The same paper mentions the King's arrival at *Loestoff* on the 16th of *January*, and afterwards at *St. James's* on the 17th.

The author of this print, whoever he was, did not venture to put his name to so ludicrous a representation of the tempest which happened on King *George* the Second's return from *Hanover*. His Majesty is supposed to have kicked his hat overboard. This, it seems, was an action customary to him when he was in a passion. To the same circumstance *Loveling* has alluded in his Sapphic Ode ad *Carolum B*———.[1]

Concinet majore poeta plectro
Georgium,[2] quandoque calens furore
Gestiet circa thalamum ferire
Calce galerum.

I have been told, that Mr. *Garrick*, when he first appeared in the character of *Bayes*, taking the same liberty, received instantly such a message from one of the stage boxes, as prevented him from practising so insolent a stroke of mimickry a second time.

In spite of the confidence with which this plate has been attributed to *Hogarth*, I by no means believe it was his performance. It more resembles the manner of *Vandergucht*, who was equally inclined to personal satire, however his talents might be inadequate to his purposes. Witness several scattered designs of his in the very same style of engraving. I may add, that he always exerted his talents in the service of the Tory faction. Besides, there is nothing in the plate before us which might not have been expected from the hand of any common artist. The conceit of the blasts issuing from the posteriors of the *Æolian* tribe, is borrowed from one of the prints to *Scarron's Travesty of Virgil*; and the figure of *Britannia* is altogether insipid and unworthy of *Hogarth*. Our artist also was too much accustomed to sailing parties, and too accurate an observer of objects on *The Thames*, not to have known that our Royal Yachts are vessels without three masts, &c.

[1] *Bunbury*.

[2] The author had here left a blank, which I have ventured to fill up with the royal name.

1738.

1. The Four Parts of the Day.[1] *Invented, painted, engraved, and published by W. Hogarth.* Mr. *Walpole* observes that these plates, "except the last, are inferior to few of his works." We have been told that *Hogarth's* inclination to satire once cost him a legacy. It seems that the figure of the Old Maid, in the print of *Morning*, was taken either from an acquaintance or relation of his. At first she was well enough satisfied with her resemblance; but some designing people teaching her to be angry, she struck the painter out of her will, which had been made considerably in his favour. This story we have heard often related by those whom, on other occasions, we could readily believe. In the same print is a portrait of Dr. *Rock*, who formerly attended *Covent-Garden* market every morning.

To the propriety of *Hogarth's* having introduced a scene of riot within *King's Coffee-house*, the following quotation from *The Weekly Miscellany* for *June* 9, 1739, bears sufficient testimony: "*Monday* Mrs. *Mary King* of *Covent-Garden* was brought up to the King's Bench Bar at *Westminster*, and received the following sentence, for keeping a disorderly house; viz. to pay a fine of £.200, to suffer three months imprisonment, to find security for her good behaviour for three years, and to remain in prison till the fine be paid." As it was impossible she could carry on her former business, as soon as the time of her imprisonment was ended, she retired with her savings, built three houses on *Haverstock* hill, near *Hampstead*, and died in one of them, *September* 1747. Her own mansion was afterwards the last residence of the celebrated *Nancy Dawson*;[2] and the three together are still distinguished by the appellation of *Moll King's Row*. Perhaps the use of the mirror in reversing objects was not yet understood by our engravers, for in *Hogarth's* painting the late Mr. *West's* house (now *Lowe's* Hotel) is properly situated on the left of *Covent-garden* church. In the print it appears on the contrary side.

The *Crying Boy* in *Noon* was sketched by *Hogarth* from a picture by *N. Poussin* of the Rape of the *Sabines*, at Mr. *Hoare's* at *Stourhead*. The school boy's kite lodged on the roof of a building, was introduced only to break the disagreeable uniformity of a wall.

Our artist, in the scene of *Evening*, inserted the little girl with the fan, as an after-thought, some friend having asked him what the boy cried for. He therefore introduced the girl going to take the play-thing from her brother. Nothing is more common than to see children cry without reason. The circumstance, however, shews that this great Genius did not always think himself above advice, as some have alledged to have been the case with him. In the early impressions of this plate, the face and neck of the woman are coloured with red, to express heat; and the hand of her husband is tinged with blue, to intimate that he was by trade a *Dyer*. The purchasers of the plate, intituled *Evening*, are hereby cautioned against imposition. In a modern copy of it, sold to the late Mr. *Ingham Foster*, the face of the woman had been washed over with vermilion, that it might pass (as it chanced to do) for a first impression. In the true ones, and none but these, the face and bosom were *printed* off with red, and the hand with blue ink. Only the traces of the graver, therefore, ought to be filled by either colour, and not the whole surface of the visage, &c. as in the smeary counterfeit. I have been told that a few copies of plate III. were taken off before the fan was inserted, but have not hitherto met with one of them. In *Night*, the drunken Free-mason has been supposed to be Sir *Thomas de Veil*; but Sir *John Hawkins* assures me, it is not the least like him. The *Salisbury Flying-Coach* implies a satire on the right honourable inventor of that species of carriage. The two first of these pictures were sold to the Duke of *Ancaster*, for 57 Guineas; the remaining pair to Sir *William Heathcote* for 64.

[1] *Hogarth* advertises in *The London Daily Post, January* 20, 1737-8, five copper plates, viz. Morning, Noon, Evening and Night, and a Company of Strolling Actresses dressing in a barn, for *one guinea*, half to be paid at the time of subscribing, half on the delivery. After the subscription, to be raised to five shillings a plate.

[2] A hornpipe dancer at *Covent Garden*. She was mistress to *Shuter* the comedian, &c. &c. &c.

2. Strolling Actresses[1] dressing in a Barn. *Invented, painted, engraved, and published by W. Hogarth.* Mr. *Walpole* observes that this piece, "for wit and

imagination, without any other end," is the best of all our artist's works. Mr. *Wood* of *Littelton* has the original, for which he paid only 26 Guineas.

Dr. *Trusler*, in his explanation of this plate, is of opinion, that some incestuous commerce among the performers is intimated by the names of *Oedipus* and *Jocasta* appearing above the heads of two figures among the theatrical lumber at the top of the barn. But surely there is no cause for so gross a supposition. Painted prodigies of this description were necessary to the performance of *Lee's Oedipus*. See Act II. where the following stage direction occurs; "The cloud draws, that veiled the heads of the figures in the sky, and shews them crowned, with the names of *Oedipus* and *Jocasta* written above, in great characters of gold." The magazine of dragons, clouds, scenes, flags, &c. or the woman half naked, was sufficient to attract the notice of the rustick peeping through the thatch he might be employed to repair. Neither is the position of the figures at all favourable to the Doctor's conceit. Incest was also too shocking an idea to have intruded itself among the comic circumstances that form the present representation. When this plate was retouched a second time, a variety of little changes were made in it. In the two earliest impressions the actress who personates *Flora*, is greasing her hair with a tallow candle, and preparing to powder herself, after her cap, feathers, &c. were put on. This solecism in the regular course of dress is removed in the third copy, the cap and ornaments being there omitted. The coiffure of the female who holds the cat, is also lowered; and whereas at first we could read in the play-bill depending from the truckle-bed, that the part of *Jupiter* was to be performed by Mr. *Bilk-village*, an additional shade in the modern copy renders this part of the inscription illegible. Several holes likewise in the thatch of the barn are filled up; and the whole plate has lost somewhat of its clearness. The same censure is due to the reparations of the *Harlot's* and *Rake's Progresses*. Had *Hogarth* lived, he would also have gradually destroyed much of that history of dress, &c. for which his designs have been justly praised by Mr. *Walpole*. In the first and last scenes of the *Rake's Progress*, he began to adorn the heads of his females in the fashion prevalent at the time he retraced the plates. In short, the collector, who contents himself with the later impressions of his work, will not consult our artist's reputation. Those who wish to be acquainted with the whole extent of his powers, should assemble the first copies, together with all the varieties of his capital works.

[1] I know not why this print should have received its title only from its female agents. Not to dwell on the *Jupiter* pointing with *Cupid's* bow to a pair of stockings, whoever will examine the linen[A] of the weeping figure receiving a dram-glass from the *Syren*, and look for the object that attracts her regard, may discover an indication that the other sex has also a representative in this theatrical parliament.

[A] Non sic præcipiti carbasa tensa noto.

1739.

1. Several children of *The Foundling Hospital*; the boys with mathematical instruments; the girls with spinning wheels. Over the door of the house they come out of, are the King's-arms. A porter is bringing in a child, followed by Capt. *Coram*, whose benevolent countenance[1] is directed towards a kneeling woman. On the right hand is a view of a church; near it a woman lifting a child from the ground; at a little distance another infant exposed near a river. In the back of the picture, a prospect of ships sailing. *W. Hogarth inv. F. Morellon la Cave sculp. London.*

This is prefixed to an engraved Power of Attorney, from the trustees of *The Foundling Hospital*, to those gentlemen who were appointed to receive subscriptions towards the building, &c. The whole together is printed on a half sheet.

[1] See p. 261.

1741.

1. The Enraged Musician, *Designed, engraved, and published by W. Hogarth.* "Mr. *John Festin*,[1] the first hautboy and *German* flute of his time, had numerous scholars, to each of whom he devoted an hour every day. At nine in the morning he attended Mr. *Spencer*, grandfather to the earl of that name. If he happened to be out of town on any day, he devoted that hour to another. One morning at that hour he waited on Mr. *V———n*, afterwards Lord *V———n*. He was not up. Mr. *Festin* went into his chamber, and opening the shutter of a window, sat down in it. The figure with the hautboy was playing under the window. A man, with a barrow full of onions, came up to the player, and sat on the edge of his barrow, and said to the man, 'if you will play the *Black Joke*, I will give you this onion.' The man played it. When he had so done, the man again desired him to play some other tune, and then he would give him another onion. 'This,' said *Festin* to me, 'highly angered me; I cried out, Z———ds, sir, stop here. This fellow is ridiculing my profession: he is playing on the hautboy for onions.' Being intimate with Mr. *Hogarth*, he mentioned the circumstance to him; which, as he said, was the origin of 'The enraged Musician.' The fact may be depended upon. Mr. *Festin*[2] was himself the Enraged Performer." The story is here told just as he related it to a clergyman, in whose words the reader now receives it.

Of this print[3] it has been quaintly said, that it deafens one to look at it. Mr. *Walpole* is of opinion that it "tends to farce." *Rouquet* says of it, "Le Musicien est un *Italien* que les cris de *Londres* font enrager." The wretched figure playing on a hautbois, was at that time well known about the streets. For variations, see the horse's head, originally white, but now black.—Sleeve of the child with a rattle, at first smaller, as well as of a lighter hue—the milk-woman's face, cloak, &c. boy's dragg, cutler's hatchet, dog, &c. &c. more darkened than in the first impressions. These, however, can scarcely be termed varieties, as they were occasioned only by retouching the plate, and adding a few shadows.

Hogarth, however, made several alterations and additions in this plate when it appeared to be finished. He changed in some measure all the countenances, and indeed the entire head and limbs of the chimney-sweeper, who had originally a grenadier's cap on. Miss had also a *Doll*, significantly placed under the trap composed of bricks, near which some sprigs from a tree are set in the ground, the whole contrivance being designed by some boy for the purpose of taking birds; but when occupied by Miss's Play-thing, became emblematic of the art of catching men. What relates, however, to this young lady from a boarding-school, was gross enough without such an amplification. The play-bill, sow-gelder, cats, dragg, &c. were not introduced, nor the pewterer's advertisement, nor the steeple in which the ringers are supposed. It is remarkable that the dustman was without a nose. The proofs of the plate in this condition are scarce. I have seen only one of them.[4] Mr. *S. Ireland* has the original sketch.

[1] "Mr. *Festin* has not been dead ten years. He was brother to the *Festin* who led the band at *Ranelagh*."

[2] In the second edition of these anecdotes, I had said "the musician was undoubtedly *Castrucci*;" though one gentleman assured me it was *Veracini*. The error is here acknowledged, to shew the danger of receiving information upon trust. In the first edition, I had fallen into a less pardonable mistake, by supposing it was *Cervetto*, whom I described to be then lately dead. But "*Hogarth's* musician," as a friend on that occasion suggested to me, "is represented with a violin; whereas *Cervetto's* instrument was the violoncello; but, however that may be, he is now certainly living. He lodges at *Friburg's* snuff-shop, in *The Haymarket*, and may be seen every day at *The Orange Coffeehouse*, although he completed his 101st. year in *November* 1781." This extraordinary character in the musical world came to *England* in the hard frost, and was then an old man. He soon after was engaged to play the bass at *Drury-lane* theatre, and continued in that employment till a season or two previous to Mr. *Garrick's* retiring from the stage. He died *June* 14, 1783, in his 103d year. One evening when Mr. *Garrick* was performing the character of Sir *John Brute*, during the drunkard's muttering and dosing till he falls fast asleep in the chair (the audience being most profoundly silent and attentive

to this admirable performer), *Cervetto* (in the orchestra) uttered a very loud and immoderately-lengthened yawn! The moment *Garrick* was off the stage, he sent for the musician, and with considerable warmth reprimanded him for so ill-timed a symptom of somnnolency, when the modern *Naso*, with great address, reconciled *Garrick* to him in a trice, by saying, with a shrug, "I beg ten tousand pardon! but I alvays do so ven I am *ver much please*!" Mr. *Cervetto* was distinguished among his friends in the galleries by the name of *Nosey*. See *Gentleman's Magazine*, 1783, p. 95.

[3] *London Daily Post*, November 24, 1740. "Shortly will be published, a new print called *The Provoked Musician*, designed and engraved by Mr *William Hogarth*; being a companion to a print representing a *Distressed Poet*, published some time since. To which will be added, a *Third on Painting*, which will compleat the set; but as this subject may turn upon an affair depending between the right honourable the L—d M—-r and the author, it may be retarded for some time."

Query to what affair does *Hogarth* allude? *Humphrey Parsons* was then Lord Mayor.

[4] In the collection of Mr. *Crickitt*.

1742.

1. *Martin Folks*, Esq. half length. *W. Hogarth pinxit & sculpsit*. An engraving. To some impressions of this print, which are not proofs, the name of *Hogarth* is wanting.

2. The same, half length mezzotinto. *W. Hogarth pinx.* 1741; *J. Faber fecit.* 1742. The original of both is now in the meeting-room of the Royal Society, in *Somerset Place*.

3. Charmers of the Age.[1] "*A sketch. No name.*" It was intended to ridicule Mons. *Desnoyer*[2] and Signora *Barberini*, the two best dancers that ever appeared in *London*. This plate exhibits the internal prospect of a theatre. The openings between the side scenes are crowded with applauding spectators. The two performers are capering very high. A sun over head (I suppose the emblem of public favour) is darting down its rays upon them. The representatives of Tragedy and Comedy are candle-holders on the occasion. Underneath is the following inscription: "The prick'd lines show the rising height." There are also a few letters of direction, so situated as to convey no very decent innuendo. The whole is but a hasty outline, executed, however, with spirit, and bitten uncommonly deep by the aqua fortis. I ascribe it to *Hogarth* without hesitation. Of this print there is a copy by *Livesay*.

All the three pieces of our artist that satirize the stage, &c. are peculiarly scarce. We may suppose them, therefore, to have been suppressed by the influence of the managers for the time being, who were not, like our present ones, become callous through the incessant attacks of diurnal criticks in the news-papers.

[1] *Hogarth* designed to have published this print, with some explanation at the bottom of it in 1741-2.—See the inscription almost effaced, a circumstance to which the copier did not attend.

[2] I learn from *The Grub-street Journal* for *October* 17, 1734, that Monsieur *Desnoyer* was just arrived from *Poland*, together with Mademoiselle *Roland* from *Paris* (this lady is still alive). Again, from the same paper, *August* 19, 1756, that "Monsieur *Desnoyer*, the famous dancer at *Drury-lane*, is gone to *Paris*, by order of Mr. *Fleetwood*, to engage Mademoiselle *Sallee* for the ensuing winter." In some future expedition, we may suppose, he prevailed on Signora *Barberini* to come over for the same purpose.

4. Taste in High Life. A beau, a fashionable old lady, a young lady, a black boy, and a monkey. Painted by Mr. *Hogarth*. It was sold by Mr. *Jarvis*, in Bedford-street, Covent-Garden. Published May 24th, [no year]. The original picture is in the possession of Mr. *Birch*, surgeon, *Essex-street*, in *The Strand*.

It displays (as we learn from an inscription on the pedestal under a *Venus* dressed in a hoop-petticoat) the reigning modes of the year 1742. It was painted for the opulent Miss *Edwards*, who paid our artist sixty guineas for it. Her reason for choosing such a subject was rather whimsical. By her own singularities having incurred some ridicule, she was desirous, by the assistance of *Hogarth*, to recriminate on the publick. As he designed after her ideas, he had little kindness for his performance, and never would permit a print to be taken from it. The present one was from a drawing made by connivance of her servants. The original was purchased by the father of its present owner, at her sale at *Kensington*.

The figure of the beau holding the china-saucer is said to have been that of Lord *Portmore*, dressed as he first appeared at court after his return from *France*. The young female was designed for a celebrated courtezan, who was the *Kitty Fisher* of her time. Her familiarity with the black boy alludes to a similar weakness in a noble duchess, who educated two brats of the same colour. One of them afterwards robbed her, and the other was guilty of some offence equally unpardonable. The pictures with which the room is adorned, contain many strokes of temporary satire. See the *Venus* with stays, a hoop, and high-heel'd shoes; *Cupid* burning all these parts of dress, together with a modish wig, &c.; a second *Cupid* paring down a plump lady to the fashionable standard; and [in a framed picture classed with a number of insects] the figure of *Desnoyer* the dancing-master in a grand ballet. The ridicule on the folly of collecting old china, &c. &c. are alike circumstances happily introduced, and explanatory of the fashions then in vogue. The colouring is better than that in most of *Hogarth's* pictures. The plate is now the property of Mr. *Sayer*.

1743.

1. *Benjamin Hoadly*, bishop of *Winchester*. *W. Hogarth pinx. B. Baron sculp.* The plate belongs to Mrs. *Hoadly*.

2. Captain *Thomas Coram*, who obtained the charter[1] for *The Foundling Hospital.* Mezzotinto; a three-quarters. The first print published by *M'Ardell.* The original is a whole length. The captain has the seal of the charter in his hand. Before him is a globe; at a distance a prospect of the sea. This is perhaps the best of all *Hogarth's* portraits, and is thus described in the *Scandalizade*, a satire published about 1749.

> "Lo! old Captain *Coram*,[2] so round in the face,
> And a pair of good chaps plump'd up in good case,
> His amiable locks hanging grey on each side
> To his double-breast coat o'er his shoulders so wide," &c.

[1] In which the name of *William Hogarth* stands enrolled as one of the earliest governors of the charity.

[2] Mr. *Coram* was bred to the sea, and spent the first part of his life as master of a vessel trading to our colonies. While he resided in that part of the metropolis which is the common residence of seafaring people, business often obliging him to come early into the city and return late; he had frequent occasions of seeing young children exposed, through the indigence or cruelty of their parents. This excited his compassion so far, that he projected *The Foundling Hospital*; in which humane design he laboured 17 years, and at last, by his sole application, obtained the royal charter for it.[A] He died at his lodgings near *Leicester-Square, March* 29, 1751, in his 84th year: and was interred under the chapel of the *Foundling Hospital*, where the following inscription perpetuates his memory:

> "Captain THOMAS CORAM,
> whose Name will never want a Monument
> so long as this Hospital shall subsist, was born about
> the year 1668; a Man eminent in that most eminent
> Virtue, the Love of Mankind;
> little attentive to his private Fortune, and refusing
> many Opportunities of encreasing it, his Time and Thoughts

were continually employed in endeavours to promote the
public Happiness,
both in this Kingdom and elsewhere, particularly
in the Colonies of North America; and his Endeavours
were many Times crowned with the desired Success. His
unwearied Solicitation, for above Seventeen Years together,
(which would have battled the Patience and Industry of any
Man less zealous in doing Good)
and his Application to Persons of Distinction of both Sexes,
obtained at Length the Charter of the Incorporation
(bearing Date the 17th of *October*, 1739)
FOR THE MAINTENANCE AND EDUCATION
OF EXPOSED AND DESERTED YOUNG CHILDREN,
by which many Thousands of Lives may be preserved to the
Public, and employed in a frugal and honest Course of
Industry. He died the 29th of *March*, 1731, in the
84th Year of his Age, poor in worldly Estate, rich in good
Works; was buried, at his own Desire, in the Vault
underneath this Chapel;
(the first here deposited)
at the East End thereof; many of the Governors
and other Gentlemen attending the Funeral, to do
Honour to his Memory.
Reader, thy Actions will shew whether thou art sincere
in the Praises thou may'st bestow on him; and if thou hast
Virtue enough to commend his Virtues, forget not to
add also the Imitation of them."

[A] For his other charitable projects, see Biog. Dict. 1784, vol. IV. p. 120.

3. The same engraving, for the *London Magazine*.

4. Characters and Caricaturas, "*to show that Leonardo da Vinci exaggerated the latter.*" The subscription-ticket to Marriage à la Mode.

1745.

1. Marriage à la Mode.[1] Six plates. In 1746 was published, "Marriage à la Mode: an Humourous Tale, in Six Canto's, in Hudibrastic Verse; being an Explanation of the Six Prints lately published by the ingenious Mr. *Hogarth. London*: printed for *Weaver Bickerton*, in *Temple-Exchange Passage*, in *Fleet-Street*, 1746. Price One Shilling." Of this pamphlet it will be sufficient to extract the

Preface and the arguments of the several Canto's; the poem itself (if such it may be called) being extended to the length of 59 pages.

"The prints of Marriage à la Mode, being the latest production of that celebrated Artist who had before obliged the town with several entertaining pieces, have, ever since their publication, been very justly admired; the particular vein of humour, that runs through the whole of his works, is more especially preserved in this.

"If the Comic Poet who draws the characters of the age he lives in, by keeping strictly up to their manners in their speeches and expressions; if satirizing vice and encouraging virtue in dialogue, to render it familiar, is always reckoned amongst the liberal arts; and the authors, when dead, dignified with busts and monuments sacred to their memory; sure the master of the pencil, whose traits carry, not only a lively image of the persons and manners, but whose happy genius has found the secret of so disposing the several parts, as to convey a pleasing and instructive moral through the history he represents, may claim a rank in the foremost class, and acquire, if the term is allowable, the appellation of the Dramatic Painter.

"The Modish Husband, incapable of relishing the pleasures of true happiness, is here depicted in his full swing of vice, 'till his mistaken conduct drives his wife to be false to his bed, and brings him to a wretched end; killed in revenging the loss of that virtue which he would never cherish. The Lady is equally represented as a true copy of all the fine ladies of the age, who, by indulging their passions, run into all those extravagances, that at last occasion a shameful exit. If the gentlemen of the long robe, who ought to know the consequences, are guilty of committing such a breach of hospitality as is here described, they are properly reprimanded: the penurious Alderman, and the profligate old Nobleman, are a fine contrast; the Quack Doctor, the *Italian Singer*, &c. are proofs of the Inventor's judgement and distinction, both in high and low life.

"Though these images are pleasing to the eye, yet many have complained that they wanted a proper explanation, which we hope will plead an excuse for publication of the following Canto's, as the desire to render these pieces more extensive may atone for the many faults contained in this poem, for which the *Hudibrastic* style was thought most proper."

THE ARGUMENTS.

CANTO I.
"The joys and plagues that wedlock brings,
The Limner paints, the Poet sings;

How the old dads weigh either scale,
And set their children up to sale;
How, void of thought, the Viscount weds
The nymph, who such a marriage dreads;
And, whilst himself the Fop admires,
M——y with love her soul inspires."

CANTO II.
"The wedding o'er, the ill-match'd pair
Are left at large, their fate to share;
All public places he frequents,
Whilst she her own delight invents;
And, full of love, bewails her doom,
When drunk i'th' morning he comes home;
The pious stew'rd, in great surprize,
Runs from them with uplifted eyes."

CANTO III.
"My Lord now keeps a common Miss,
Th' effects describ'd of amorous bliss,
Venereal taints infect their veins,
And fill them full of aches and pains;
Which to an old *French* Doctor drives 'em,
Who with his pill, a grand p—x gives 'em;
A scene of vengeance next ensues,
With which the Muse her tale pursues."

CANTO IV.
"Fresh honours on the Lady wait,
A Countess now she shines in state;
The toilette is at large display'd,
Where whilst the morning concert's play'd,
She listens to her lover's call,
Who courts her to the midnight-ball."

CANTO V.
"The dismal consequence behold,
Of wedding girls of *London* mould;
The Husband is depriv'd of life,
In striving to detect his Wife;
The Lawyer naked, in surprize,
Out of the Bagnio window flies:
Whilst Madam, leaping from the bed,

Doth on her knee for pardon plead."

CANTO VI.
"The Lawyer meets his just reward,
Nor from the triple tree is spar'd;
The Father takes my Lady home,
Where, when she hears her Lover's doom,
To desperate attempts she flies,
And with a dose of poison dies."

In these plates only a single variation is detected. In the very first impressions of the second of them (perhaps a few only were taken off) a lock of hair on the forehead of the lady is wanting. It was added by our artist, after *Baron* had finished the plate. In the early copies he inserted it with *Indian* ink. A passage in the *Analysis*[2] will perhaps account for this supplemental ornament: "A lock of hair falling cross the temples, and by that means breaking the regularity of the oval, has an effect too alluring to be strictly decent." The room represented in this plate is adorned with a *melange* of pictures on wanton and devotional subjects.

Mr. *Walpole* has remarked, that the works of *Hogarth* have little obscurity. This position is true in general, though *Marriage à la Mode* may supply an exception to it; no two persons, perhaps, having hitherto agreed in their explanation of Plate the third.[3]

When this set of plates was to be engraved, *Ravenet*, a young artist, then just coming into employ, was recommended to Mr. *Hogarth*; and a hard bargain was made. *Ravenet* went through two of the plates, but the price proved far inadequate to the labour. He remonstrated, but could obtain no augmentation. When the *Sigismunda* was to be engraved, Mr. *Ravenet* was in a different sphere of life. The painter, with many compliments, solicited his assistance as an engraver, but *Ravenet* indignantly declined the connexion.

In the fourth of these plates[4] are the following portraits: Mrs. *Lane* (afterwards Lady *Bingley*) adoring *Carestini*; her husband *Fox Lane* asleep. *Rouquet* only calls him "Un gentilhomme campagnard, fatigué d'une course après quelque renard ou quelque cerf, s'endort." This idea seems to be countenanced by the whip in his hand. The same explainer adds, speaking of the two next figures, "Ici on voit en papillotes un de ces personages qui passent toute leur vie à tâcher de plaire sans y reüssir; la, un eventail au poing, on reconnoît un de ces hérétiques en amour, un sectateur d'*Anacreon*." The former of these has been supposed to represent Monsieur *Michel*, the *Prussian* ambassador. *Weideman* is playing on the *German* flute.—The pictures in the room are properly suited to the bed-chamber of a profligate pair—*Jupiter* and *Io*, *Lot* with his Daughters, *Ganymede* and the Eagle, and the Young Lawyer who debauches the Countess. The child's coral, hanging from the back of the chair she sits in, serves to shew she was already a mother; a circumstance that renders her conduct still more unpardonable. Some of her new-made purchases, exposed on the floor, bear witness to the warmth of her inclinations. These will soon be gratified at the fatal masquerade, for which her paramour is offering her a ticket.

The pompous picture on the right hand of the window in the nobleman's apartment, Plate I. also deserves attention. It appears to be designed as a ridicule on the unmeaning flutter of *French* portraits, some of which (particularly those of *Louis* XIV.) are painted in a style of extravagance equal at least to the present parody by *Hogarth*. This ancestor of our peer is invested with several foreign orders. At the top of one corner of the canvas, are two winds blowing across each other, while the hero's drapery is flying quite contrary directions. A comet is likewise streaming over his head. In his hand he grasps the lightning of *Jove*, and reposes on a cannon going off, whose ball is absurdly rendered an object of sight. A smile, compounded of self-complacency and pertness, is the characteristic of his face.

On the cieling of this magnificent saloon is a representation of *Pharaoh* and his Host drowned in the Red Sea. The pictures underneath are not on the most captivating subjects—*David* killing *Goliath*—*Prometheus* and the Vulture—the Murder of the *Innocents*—*Judith* and *Holofernes*—St. *Sebastian* shot full of Arrows—*Cain* destroying *Abel*—and St. *Laurence* on the Gridiron.

Among such little circumstances in this plate as might escape the notice of a careless spectator, is the Thief in the Candle, emblematic of the mortgage on his Lordship's estate.

When engravings on a contracted scale are made from large pictures, a few parts of them will unavoidably become so small, as almost to want distinctness. It has fared thus with a number of figures that appear before the unfinished edifice,[5] seen through a window in the first plate of this work. *Hogarth* designed them for the lazy vermin of his Lordship's hall, who, having nothing to do, are sitting on the blocks of stone, or staring at the building;[6] for thus *Rouquet* has described them, "Une troupe de lacquais oisifs, qui sont dans le cour de ce batiment, acheve de caracteriser le faste ruineux qui environne le comte." The same illustrator properly calls the *Citizen* Echevin (i. e. sheriff) of *London*, on account of the chain he wears.

Plate II. From the late Dr. *Ducarel* I received the following anecdote; but there must be some mistake in it, as *Herring* was not archbishop till several years after the designs for *Marriage à la Mode* were made.

"*Edward Swallow*, butler to Archbishop *Herring*, had an annuity of ten pounds given to him in his Grace's will. For the honesty and simplicity of his physiognomy, this old faithful servant was so remarkable, that *Hogarth*, wanting such a figure in *Marriage à la Mode*, accompanied the late dean of *Sarum*, Dr. *Thomas Greene*, on a public day, to *Lambeth*, on purpose to catch the likeness. As they were coming away, he whispered, 'I have him!' And he may now be seen to the life preserved in the old steward, in Plate II. with his hands held up, &c."

In Plate V. the back ground, which is laboured with uncommon delicacy (a circumstance that will be remarked by few except artists), was the work of Mr. *Ravenet's* wife. *Solomon's* wise judgement is represented on the tapestry. When *Ravenet's* two plates were finished, *Hogarth* wanted much to retouch the faces,[7] and many disputes happened between him and the engraver on this subject. The first impressions, however, escaped without correction. Those who possess both copies, may discover evident marks of *Hogarth's* hand in the second. See particularly the countenance of the dying nobleman, which is fairly ploughed up by his heavier burin.

I have been told that our artist took the portrait of the female, who is so placed, that the legs of a figure in the tapestry supply the want of her own, from a coarse picture of a woman called *Moll Flanders*.

Plate the sixth of this set, affords *Rouquet* an opportunity of illustrating the following remark, which he had made at the outset of his undertaking: "Ce qu'un *Anglois* lit, pour ainsi dire, en jettant les yeux sur ces estampes, va exiger de vous la lecture de plusieurs pages." Speaking of our citizen's parsimony, says he—"Voyez-vous ces pipes conservées dans le coin d'un armoire? Vous ne devineriez pas, vous qui n'êtes pas jamais venu en *Angleterre*, qu'elles sont aussi une marque d'economie; mais il faut vous dire que les pipes sont si communes ici, qu'on ne fume jamais deux fois dans la même. La païsan, l'artizan le plus vil prend une pipe gratis dans le premier cabaret où il arrête: il continue son chemin en achevant de la fumer, et la jette à ses pieds."

As *Rouquet* observes, "Ce qui sert à garnir cet apartement ne contribue pas à l'orner. Tout y indique une économie basse." The scarcity of the real dinner—the picture exhibiting plenty of provision—the starved dog—the departing physician—the infected and ricketty condition of the child who is brought to take a last kiss of its dying mother—are circumstances too striking to be overlooked.

The Daily Advertiser of 1750 affords the following illustration of our artist's history: "Mr. *Hogarth* proposes to publish by subscription two large prints, one representing *Moses* brought to *Pharaoh's* daughter; the other *Paul* before *Felix*; engraved after the pictures of his painting which are now hung up in *The Foundling Hospital* and *Lincoln's-Inn Hall*. Five Shillings to be paid at the time of subscribing, and Five Shillings more on the delivery of the print. On the first payment a receipt will be given, which receipt will contain a new print (in the true *Dutch* taste) of *Paul* before *Felix*. Note, The above two prints will be Seven Shillings and Six Pence each after the subscription is over; and the receipt-print will not be sold at a less price than One Guinea each. Subscriptions are taken in till the 6th of *June* next, and no longer, at *The Golden-Head* in *Leicester-Fields*, where the drawings may be seen; as likewise the author's six pictures of *Marriage-à-la-Mode*, which are to be disposed of in the following manner: That every bidder sign a note with the sum he intends to give. That such note be deposited in the drawer of a cabinet, which cabinet shall be constantly kept locked by the said *William Hogarth*; and in the cabinet, through a glass door, the sums bid will be seen on the face of the drawer, but the names of the bidders may be concealed till the time of bidding shall be expired. That each bidder may, by a fresh note, advance a further sum if he is outbid, of which notice shall be sent him. That the sum so advanced shall not be less than Three Guineas. That the time of bidding shall continue till twelve o'clock the 6th of *June* next, and no longer. That no dealer in pictures will be admitted a bidder.

"As (according to the standard of judgement, so righteously and laudably established by picture-dealers, picture-cleaners, picture-frame-makers, and other connoisseurs) the works of a painter are to be esteemed more or less valuable as they are more or less scarce, and as the living painter is most of all affected by the inferences resulting from this and other considerations equally uncandid and edifying; Mr. *Hogarth*, by way of precaution, not puff, begs leave to urge, that, probably, this will be the last suit or series of pictures he may ever exhibit, because of the difficulty of vending such a number at once to any tolerable advantage, and that the whole number he has already exhibited of the historical or humourous kind does not exceed fifty, of which the three sets called *The Harlot's Progress, The Rake's Progress*, and that now to be sold, make twenty; so that whoever has a taste of his own to rely on, not too squeamish for the production of a Modern, and courage enough to own it, by daring to give them a place in his collection (till Time, the supposed finisher, but real designer of paintings, has rendered them fit for those more sacred repositories where Schools, Names, Heads, Masters, &c. attain their last stage of preferment), may from hence be convinced that multiplicity at least of his (Mr. *Hogarth's*) pieces will be no diminution of their value."

Mr. *Lane*, of *Hillingdon* near *Uxbridge*, bought the six original pictures for 120 guineas, at *Hogarth's* auction.[8]

[1] *London Daily Post, April* 7, 1743. "Mr. *Hogarth* intends to publish by subscription Six Prints from copper plates, engraved by the best masters in *Paris*, after his own paintings (the heads, for the better preservation of the

characters and expressions, to be done by the author), representing a variety of modern occurrences in high life, and called *Marriage a-la-mode*.

"Particular care is taken that the whole work shall not be liable to exception on account of any *indecency* or *inelegancy*, and that none of the characters represented shall be *personal*. The subscription will be one guinea; half, &c."

[2] See p. 325.

[3] In the third plate of this work, the figure of the female unclasping a penknife, is said to have been designed for the once celebrated *Betty Careless*. This remark is supposed to be countenanced by the initials E. C. on her bosom. From being in a state to receive company, this woman had been long reduced to show it, and, after repeated confinements in various prisons, was buried from the poor's house of St. *Paul, Covent Garden, April* 22, 1752, about seven years after this set of prints had been published. Such a representation of her decline from beauty, as may be given in the plate before us, is justified by various passages in *Loveling's* poems, *Latin* and *English*, written about the year 1738, and published in 1741. Thus in his ode, "Ad *Sextum*,"

> *Carlesis* turpis macies decentem
> Occupat vultum——

Again more amply in his Elegiac Epistle, "Ad *Henricum*:"

> Nympha *Coventini* quæ gloria sulferat Horti,
> Cui vix vidisset *Druria* vestra parem,
> Exul, inops, liquit proprios miseranda Penates,
> Fortunæ extremas sustinuitque vices,
> Nunc trahit infaustam tenebroso in carcere vitam,
> Et levat insolito mollia membra toro.
> *Carlesis*, ah! quantum, quantum mutaris ab illâ,
> *Carlese*, quæ *Veneris* maxima cura fuit!
> Æde tua risêre olim Charitesque Jocique,
> Hic fuerant *Paphiæ* currus & arma Deæ;
> Arsêrunt Cives, arsit *Judæus Apella*,
> Et te Bellorum deperiêre chori.
> Jam sordes, pallensque genas, & flaccida mammas,
> Non oculi, quondam qui micuere, micant.
> Heu! ubi formosæ referentes lilia malæ!
> Labra ubi purpureis quæ rubuére rosis!
> Te puer *Idalius*, te fastiditque juventus
> Tam marcescentem, dissimilemque tui.
> Siccine tam fidam curas *Erycina* ministram?
> Hæccine militiæ praemia digna tuæ?
> O *Venus!* ô nimium, nimiumque oblita tuarum!

> *Carlesis* an meruit sortis acerba pati?
> Quæ posthàc arisve tuis imponet honorem,
> Ardebit posthàc vel tua castra sequi?
> Omnigenas æquo circumspice lumine mœchas
> Quas tua pellicibus *Druria* dives alit,
> Quæ cellas habitant, vicos peditesve peragrant,
> Aut quæ *Wappinios* incoluêre lares;
> Invenienda fuit nusquam lascivior, artus
> Mobilior, sacris vel magis apta tuis.
> *Carlesis* ah nostris & flenda & fleta Camœnis!
> Accedat vestris nulla medela malis?
> Te vereor miseram fortuna tenaciter anget,
> Nec veniet rebus mollior aura tuis.

Again in his Ode, "Ad *Carolum B.......*"

> ----------------relinquent
> *Carlesis* quondam miseræ Penates
> *Douglasa & Johnson*, duo pervicacis
> Fulmina linguæ.

Again in a "Copy of Verses on *Betty Close's* coming to Town, &c."

> *Roberts* will curse all whores—
> From worn-out *Careless* to fair *Kitty Walker*.

Again in an Ode intituled "Meretrices *Britannicæ*."

> Alma scortorum *Druriæque* custos
> Orta *Neptuno!* tibi cura pulchræ;
> *Carlesis* satis data, tu secundà
> *Carlesis* regnes.

These lines will serve to enforce the moral of *The Harlot's Progress*, while they aim at the illustration of a single circumstance in *Marriage à la Mode*; where if this female is introduced at all, it seems to be in the character of an opulent procuress, either threatening the peer for having diseased her favourite girl, or preparing to revenge herself on the quack whose medicines had failed to eradicate his lordship's disorder. That heroine must have been notorious, who could at once engage the pencil of *Hogarth* and the pens of *Loveling* and *Fielding*, who in the sixth chapter of the first book of *Amelia* has the following story: "I happened in my youth to sit behind two ladies in a side-box at a play, where, in the balcony on the opposite side was placed the inimitable *Betty Careless*, in company with a young fellow of no very formal, or indeed sober, appearance. One of the ladies, I remember, said to the other—'Did you ever see any thing look so modest and so innocent as that girl over the way? What pity it is such a creature should be in the way of ruin, as I am afraid she is, by her being alone with that young fellow!' Now this lady was no bad physiognomist; for it was impossible to conceive a greater appearance of modesty, innocence, and simplicity, than what nature had displayed in the countenance of that girl; and yet, all appearances notwithstanding, I myself (remember, critic, it was in my youth) had a few mornings before seen that very identical picture of those engaging qualities in bed with a rake at a bagnio, smoking tobacco, drinking punch, talking obscenity, and swearing and cursing with all the impudence and impiety of the lowest and most abandoned trull of a soldier." We may add, that one of the mad-men in the last plate of *The Rake's Progress* has likewise written "charming *Betty Careless*" on the rail of the stairs, and wears her portrait round his neck. Perhaps between the publication of *The Rake's Progress* and *Marriage à la Mode*, she sunk from a wanton into a bawd. Mrs. *Heywood's Betsey Thoughtless* was at first entitled *Betsey Careless*, but the name was afterwards changed for obvious reasons.

The London Daily Post, Nov. 28, 1735, contains the following advertisement from this notorious female:

"Mrs. *Careless*, from the *Piazza* in *Covent-Garden*, not being able to make an end of her affairs so soon as she expected, intends on *Monday* next to open a coffee-house in *Prujean's-Court*, in *The Old Bailey*, where she hopes her friends will favour her with their company, notwithstanding the ill situation of the place; since her misfortunes oblige her still to remain there.

"N. B. It is the uppermost house in the court, and coaches and chairs may come up to the door."

Again in *The London Daily Post*, Oct. 21, 1741, Mrs. *Careless* advertises *The Beggar's Opera*, at the theatre in *James-Street, Haymarket*, for her benefit, *Oct.* 27. At the bottom of the advertisement she says, "Mrs. *Careless* takes this benefit because she finds a small pressing occasion for one: and as she has the happiness of knowing she has a great many friends, hopes not to find an instance to the contrary by their being absent the above-mentioned evening; and as it would be entirely inconvenient, and consequently disagreeable, if they should, she ventures to believe they won't fail to let her have the honour of their company." In the bill of the day she says—"N. B. Mrs. *Careless* hopes her friends will favour her according to their promise, to relieve her from terrible fits of the vapours proceeding from bad dreams, though the comfort is they generally go by the contraries.

"Tickets to be had at Mrs. *Careless's* Coffee-house, the *Playhouse-Passage, Bridges-Street*."

Would the public, at this period of refinement, have patiently endured the familiar address of such a shameless, superannuated, advertising strumpet?

The reader will perhaps smile, when, after so much grave ratiocination, and this long deduction of particulars, he is informed that the letters are not E. C. but F. C. the initials of *Fanny Cock*, daughter to the celebrated auctioneer of that name, with whom our artist had had some casual disagreement.

The following, somewhat different, explanation has also been communicated to me by *Charles Rogers*, esq. who says it came from *Sullivan*, one of *Hogarth's* engravers: "The nobleman threatens to cane a quack-doctor for having given pills which proved ineffectual in curing a girl he had debauched; and brings with him a woman, from whom he alledges he caught the infection; at which she, in a rage, is preparing to stab him with her clasp knife. This wretch is one of the lowest class, as is manifest by the letters of her name marked with gunpowder on her breast. She, however, is brought to the *French* barber-surgeon for his examination and inspection, and for which purpose he is wiping his spectacles with his coarse muckender."

The explanation given by *Rouquet*, however, ought not to be suppressed, as in all probability he received it from *Hogarth*. "Il falloit indiquer la mauvaise conduite du héros de la piece. L'auteur pour cet effet l'introduit dans l'appartement d'un empirique, où il ne peut guères se trouver qu'en consequence de ses débauches; il fait en même tems rencontrer chez cet empirique une de ces femmes qui perdues depuis long-tems, font enfin leur métier de la perte des autres. Il suppose un démêlé entre cette femme et son héros, dont le sujet paroît être la mauvaise santé d'un petite fille, du commerce de laquelle il ne s'est pas bien trouvé. La petite fille au reste fait ici contraste par son âge, sa timidité, sa douceur, avec le caractère de l'autre femme, qui paroît un composé de rage, de fureur, et de tous les crimes qui accompagnent d'ordinaire les dernières débauches chez celles de son sexe.

"L'empirique et son appartement sont des objets entièrement épisodiques. Quoique jadis barbier,[A] il est aujourdhui, si l'on en juge par l'etalage, non seulment chirurgien, mais naturaliste, chimiste, mechanicien, medecin, apoticaire; et vous remarquerez qu'il est *François* pour comble de ridicule. L'auteur pour achever de le caracteriser suivant son idée, lui fait inventer des machines extrèmement composées pour les opérations les plus simples, comme celles de remettre un membre disloqué, ou de déboucher une bouteille.

"Je ne deciderai pas si l'auteur est aussi heureux dans le choix des objets de sa satire, quand il les prend parmi nous, que lorsqu'il les choisit parmi ceux de sa nation; mais il me semble qu'il doit mieux connoître ceux-ci; et je crois que cette planche vous en paroîtra un exemple bien marqué. Il tourne ici en ridicule ce que nous avons de moins mauvais; que deviendroit le reste s'il étoit vrai qu'il nous connût assez pour nous depeindre?"

[A] This circumstance seems to be implied by the broken comb, the pewter bason, and the horn so placed as to resemble a barber's pole, all which are exhibited either above, or within the glass case, in which the skeleton appears whispering a man who had been exsiccated by some mode of embalming at present unknown. About the time of the publication of this set of prints, a number of bodies thus preserved were discovered in a vault in *Whitechapel* church.—Our Quack is likewise a virtuoso. An ancient spur, a high-crowned hat, old shoes, &c. together with a model of the gallows, are among his rarities.—On his table is a skull, rendered carious by the disease he is professing to cure.—These two last objects are monitory as well as characteristic.

[4] *Scotin* engraved the first and sixth; *Baron* the second and third; *Ravenet* the fourth and fifth.

[5] The blunders in architecture in this unfinished nobleman's seat, on the same account, are seen to disadvantage.

[6] This edifice seems at a stand for want of money, no workman appearing on the scaffolds, or near them.

[7] In his advertisement for this set of plates, he had engaged to engrave all the faces with his own hand. See note 1 above.

[8] The account given in a former edition of this volume concerning the sale of the original pictures of *Marriage-à-la-mode*, being somewhat erroneous, I am happy in the present opportunity of acknowledging my obligations to Mr. *Lane* abovementioned, who has corrected my mistakes by a communication of the following particulars relative to the purchase:

"Some time after they had been finished, perhaps six or seven years, during which period Mr. *Hogarth* had been preparing and publishing prints from them, in the year 1750 he advertised the sale of the originals by a kind of auction not carried on by personal bidding, but by a written ticket on which every one was to put the price he would give, with his name subscribed to it. These papers were to be received by Mr. *Hogarth* for the space of one month; and the highest bidder, at twelve o'clock on the last day of the month, was to be the purchaser: and none but those who had in writing made their biddings were to be admitted on the day that was to determine the sale. This nouvelle method of proceeding probably disobliged the public; and there seemed to be at that time a combination against poor *Hogarth*, who perhaps, from the extraordinary and frequent approbation of his works, might have imbibed some degree of vanity, which the town in general, friends and foes, seemed resolved to mortify. If this was the case (and to me it is very apparent), they fully effected their design; for on the memorable sixth of *June* 1750, which was to decide the fate of this capital work, about eleven o'clock

Mr. *Lane*, the fortunate purchaser, arrived at the *Golden Head*: when, to his great surprize, expecting (what he had been a witness to in 1745, when *Hogarth* disposed of many of his pictures) to have found his painting-room full of noble and great personages, he only found the painter and his ingenious friend Dr. *Parsons*, secretary to the Royal Society, talking together, and expecting a number of spectators at least, if not of buyers. Mr. *Hogarth* then produced the highest bidding, from a gentleman well known, of £120. Nobody coming in, about ten minutes before twelve, by the decisive clock in the room, Mr. *Lane* told Mr. *Hogarth* he would make the pounds guineas. The clock then struck twelve, and *Hogarth* wished Mr. *Lane* joy of his purchase, hoping it was an agreeable one. Mr. *Lane* answered, Perfectly so. Now followed a scene of disturbance from *Hogarth's* friend the Doctor, and, what more affected Mr. *Lane*, a great appearance of disappointment in the painter, and truly with great reason. The Doctor told him, he had hurt himself greatly by fixing the determination of the sale at so early an hour, when the people at that part of the town were hardly up. *Hogarth*, in a tone and manner that could not escape observation, said, Perhaps it may be so! Mr. *Lane*, after a short pause, declared himself to be of the same opinion, adding, that the artist was very poorly rewarded for his labour, and, if he thought it would be of service to him, would give him till three o'clock to find a better purchaser. *Hogarth* warmly accepted the offer, and expressed his acknowledgements for the kindness in the strongest terms. The proposal likewise received great encomiums from the Doctor, who proposed to make it public. This was peremptorily forbidden by Mr. *Lane*, whose concession in favour of our artist was remembered by him to the time of his death.— About one o'clock, two hours sooner than the time appointed by Mr. *Lane*, *Hogarth* said he would no longer trespass on his generosity, but that, if he was pleased with his purchase, he himself was abundantly so with the purchaser. He then desired Mr. *Lane* to promise that he would not dispose of the pictures without previously acquainting him of his intention, and that he would never permit any person, under pretence of cleaning, to meddle with them, as he always desired to take that office on himself. This promise was readily made by Mr. *Lane*, who has been tempted more than once by *Hogarth* to part with his bargain at a price to be named by himself. When Mr. *Lane* bought the pictures, they were in Carlo Marratt frames which cost the painter four guineas apiece."

The memory of this occurrence ought always to attend the work which afforded Mr. *Lane* an opportunity of displaying so much disinterested generosity.

Another correspondent begins the same story as follows—A little time before the auction, *Hogarth* publickly declared, that no picture-dealer should be allowed to bid. He also called on his friends, requesting them not to appear at the sale, as his house was small, and the room might be over crowded. They obeyed his injunctions. Early in this mortifying day he dressed himself, put on his tye-wig, strutted away one hour, and fretted away two more, no bidder appearing, &c. &c.

2. A small print of Archbishop *Herring*, at the head of the speech he made to the clergy of *York*, September 24, 1745. *William Hogarth pinx. C. Moseley sculp.*

3. The same head cut out of the plate, and printed off without the speech.

4. The Battle of the Pictures. "*Ticket to admit persons to bid for his works at an auction.*" On the plate called *The Battle of the Pictures* is written, "The bearer hereof is entitled (if he thinks proper) to be a bidder for Mr. *Hogarth's* pictures, which are to be sold on the last day of this month [*February,* 1744-5.]."

5. A festoon, with a mask, a roll of paper, a palette, and a laurel. Subscription ticket for *Garrick* in *Richard* the Third. A very faithful copy from this receipt was made by R. *Livesay,* 1781. It is to be sold at Mrs. *Hogarth's* house in *Leicester-square.*

1746.

1. *Simon* Lord *Lovat*.[1] *Drawn from the life, and etched in aquafortis by William Hogarth.*—Hogarth said himself, that Lord *Lovat's* portrait was taken (at the *White-Hart,* at *St. Alban's*) in the attitude of relating on his fingers the numbers of the rebel forces.—"Such a general had so many men, &c." and remarked, that the muscles of *Lovat's* neck appeared of unusual strength, more so than he had ever seen. When the painter entered the room, his lordship, being under the barber's hands, received his old friend with a salute, which left much of the lather on his face.—The second impressions are marked, *Price One Shilling.* When *Hogarth* had finished this plate, a printseller offered its weight in gold for it. The impressions could not be taken off so fast as they were wanted, though the rolling-press was at work all night for a week together. For several weeks afterwards he is said to have received at the rate of 12 *l.* per day.

[1] "This powerful laird, it has been observed, was one of the last Chieftains that preserved the rude manners and barbarous authority of the early feudal ages. He resided in a house which would be esteemed but an indifferent one for a very private, plain country gentleman in *England*; as it had, properly,

only four rooms on a floor, and those not large. Here, however, he kept a sort of court, and several public tables; and had a numerous body of retainers always attending. His own constant residence, and the place where he received company, even at dinner, was in the very same room where he lodged; and his lady's sole apartment was her bed-room; and the only provision for the lodging of the servants, and retainers, was a quantity of straw, which they spread every night, on the floors of the lower rooms, where the whole inferior part of the family, consisting of a very great number of persons, took up their abode." See Mr. *King's* observations on ancient Castles, in the *Archæologia*, vol. IV.

Sir *William Young*, one of the managers appointed by the Commons of *Great Britain*, for conducting the prosecution against this Nobleman for High Treason, in the year 1745, makes the following observation: "Your Lordships have already done national justice on some of the principal traitors, who appeared in open arms against his Majesty, by the ordinary course of law; but this noble Lord, who, in the whole course of his life, has boasted of his superior cunning in wickedness, and his ability to commit frequent treasons with impunity, vainly imagined that he might possibly be a traitor in private, and rebel only in his heart, by sending his son and his followers to join the Pretender, and remaining at home himself, to endeavour to deceive his Majesty's faithful subjects; hoping *he* might be rewarded for his son's services, if successful; or his *son* alone be the sufferer for *his* offences, if the undertaking failed: diabolical cunning! monstrous impiety!" See *State Trials*, vol. IX. p. 627.

2. Mr. *Garrick*[1] in the character of *Richard* III. *Painted by Wm. Hogarth; engraved by Wm. Hogarth and C. Grignion.* The late Mr. *Duncombe*, of *Duncombe Park* in *Yorkshire*, gave 200 *l.* for the original picture, which is now in the possession of his family. The expression of the countenance is happily hit off, but the figure is abundantly too large and muscular. This print was afterwards, by *Hogarth's* permission, copied for a watch-paper.

[1] "Mr. *Garrick* had several of *Hogarth's* paintings; and the latter designed for him, as president of the *Shakespeare* club, a mahogany chair richly carved, on the back of which hangs a medal of the poet carved by *Hogarth* out of the mulberry-tree planted at *Stratford* by *Shakespeare*." Anecdotes of Painting, vol. IV. p. 180. edit. 8vo, 1782.

3. A stand of various weapons, bag-pipes, &c. and a pair of scissars cutting out the arms of *Scotland*. A subscription-ticket for the March to *Finchley*; of

which the original price was only 7 *s.* 6 *d.* It was to be raised to 10 *s.* 6 *d.* on closing the subscription. The additional three shillings afforded the subscriber a chance for the original picture.

1747.

1. Stage-coach. An election procession in the yard. *Designed and engraved by William Hogarth.* In this plate there is a variation. The early impressions have a flag behind the wheel of the coach, inscribed NO OLD BABY, which was the cry used by the opponents of the honourable *John Child Tylney* (then Viscount *Castlemain* and now Earl *Tylney*[1]) when he stood member for the county of *Essex,* against Sir *Robert Abdy* and Mr. *Bramston.* The figure still carries a horn-book, and a rattle in its hands. At the election, a man was placed on a bulk with an *infant* in his arms, and exclaimed, as he whipt the child, "What, you little *Child,* must you be a member?" The family name was changed from *Child* to *Tylney* by an act of parliament in 1735. In this disputed election, it appeared from the register-book of the parish where Lord *Castlemain* was born, that he was but 20 years of age. Some pains have been taken to ascertain the particular inn-yard in which the scene is laid, but without success, so many of the publick-houses between *Whitechapel* and *Chelmsford* in *Essex* having been altered, or totally rebuilt.

[1] Since dead.—*Inter Socraticos notissima fossa cinædos.*

2. Industry and Idleness, in twelve plates.[1] Mr. *Walpole* observes, that "they have more merit in the intention than execution." At first they were printed off on very thin paper. Plate V. The scene is *Cuckold's Point,* below *London Bridge.* Plate VI. In a few first impressions, "*Goodchild* and *West*" is written under the sign, instead of "*West* and *Goodchild.*" *Hogarth* had inadvertently placed the name of the junior partner first. Some mercantile friend, however, pointing out the mistake, when as yet only a few copies were taken off, our artist corrected it, to avoid the criticisms of *Cheapside* and *Cornhill.* In this plate is a figure of *Philip in the Tub,* a well-known beggar and cripple, who was a constant epithalamist at weddings in *London,* and had visited *Ireland* and *The Seven Provinces.* The *French* clergyman in Plate VIII. was designed for Mr. *Platell,* curate of *Barnet.* Plate XI. The scene is in a cellar of a noted house that went by the name of "The Blood Bowl House," from the various scenes of blood that were there almost daily exhibited, and where there seldom passed a month without the commission of a murder. *Blood Bowl-alley* is down by the fishmonger's, near *Water-lane, Fleet-street;* and I am assured, that the house and event, that gave rise to the name, were there. In Plate XI. is *Tiddy Doll,* the well-known vender of gingerbread. Just behind him, in a cart, to bring away

the body of the criminal, is his mother. Though her face is concealed, she is distinguished by her excess of sorrow, and the black hood she has worn throughout the foregoing representations of her. Plate XII. *Frederick* Prince of *Wales*, and the Princess of *Wales*, in the balcony. The standards of the Blacksmiths' and Stationers' Companies appear in the procession. The flag, at the corner of one of the stands, belongs to the Pinners and Needlers. The hint for this series of prints was evidently taken from the old comedy of *Eastward-hoe*, by *Jonson, Chapman,* and *Marston*, reprinted in *Dodsley's* Collection of Old Plays. "The scenes of *Bedlam* and the gaming-house," as Mr. *Walpole* well observes, "are inimitable representations of our serious follies, or unavoidable woes; and the concern shown by the lord-mayor, when the companion of his childhood is brought before him as a criminal, is a touching picture, and big with humane admonition and reflection." The late comedian Mr. *James Love* (otherwise *Dance*, and brother to the painter of that name) dramatized this series of prints; and Mr. *King*, now deputy-manager of *Drury-lane*, performed the character of the Good 'Prentice.

These Plates were retouched by *Hogarth*; but, as usual, whatever they gained in respect to force, they lost in the article of clearness. They offer no variations, except such as are occasioned by his having thrown a few of the figures into shade, that others might appear more prominent. Dr. *Ducarel* informed me, that the passages of Scripture applicable to the different scenes were selected for Mr. *Hogarth*, by his friend the Rev. Mr. *Arnold King*.

In the following year was published, price one shilling (being an explanation of the moral of twelve celebrated prints lately published, and designed by the ingenious Mr. *Hogarth*), "The Effects of Industry and Idleness, illustrated in the Life, Adventures, and various Fortunes of Two Fellow 'Prentices of the City of *London*: shewing the different Paths, as well as Rewards of Virtue and Vice; how the good and virtuous 'Prentice, by gradual Steps of Industry, rose to the highest Pitch of Grandeur; and how, by contrary Pursuits, his Fellow-'Prentice, by Laziness and Wickedness, came to die an ignominious Death at the Gallows. ¶ This little book ought to be read by every 'Prentice in *England*, to imprint in their hearts these two different examples, the contrary effects each will produce on their young minds being of more worth than a hundred times the price, *i. e.* an abhorrence of the vice and wickedness they perceive in the one boy, and, on the contrary, an endeavour after an imitation of the actions of the other. And is a more proper present to be given to the Chamber of *London*, at the binding and enrolling an apprentice, than any other book whatever. Printed by *Charles Corbett*, at *Addison's* Head in *Fleet street*."

[1] The following description of *Hogarth's* design is copied from his own hand-writing: "Industry and Idleness exemplified in the conduct of two Fellow 'Prentices: where the one, by taking good courses, and pursuing

points for which he was put apprentice, becomes a valuable man and an ornament to his country; the other, by giving way to idleness, naturally falls into poverty, and ends fatally, as is expressed in the last print. As the prints were intended more for use than ornament, they were done in a way that might bring them within the purchase of whom they might most concern; and, lest any print should be mistaken, the description of each print is engraved at top."

3. *Jacobus Gibbs*, architectus. *W. Hogarth delin. B. Baron sculp.*

4. *Jacobus Gibbs*, architectus. *W. Hogarth delin. J. McArdell fec.* Partly mezzotinto, partly graved. No date.

5. To this period may be referred the arms of *The Foundling Hospital*, printed off on the tops of the indentures; together with

6. The same, but smaller; employed as a frontispiece to "Psalms, Hymns, and Anthems; for the Use of the Children of the Hospital for the Maintenance and Education of exposed and deserted Young Children."

They are both classed here, because the original drawing (see under the year 1781) is dated in 1747.

1748.

1. A monk leading an ass with a *Scotch* man and woman on it, &c. A wooden cut. Head-piece to the "Jacobite's Journal." This was a news-paper set up and supported by *Henry Fielding*, and carried on for a few months with some success. The wooden-cut was only prefixed to six or seven of the papers. Being faintly executed, it was soon worn out, and has lately been copied in aqua tinta by Mr. *Livesay*.

2. Pool of *Bethesda*, from the picture[1] he painted for *St. Bartholomew's Hospital. Engraved by Ravenet for S. Austen*, as a frontispiece for *Stackhouse's* Bible. In this plate, I am assured by an old acquaintance of Mr. *Hogarth*, is a faithful portrait of *Nell Robinson*, a celebrated courtezan, with whom, in early life, they had both been intimately acquainted.

[1] Of this picture Mr. *S. Ireland* has a large sketch in oil.

1749.

1.[1] The Gate of *Calais*.[2] Engraved by C. *Mosley* and *W. Hogarth*. *"His own head sketching the view. He was arrested when he was making the drawing, but set at liberty when his purpose was known."* See above, p. 49. Mr. *Walpole* also observes, that in this piece, though it has great merit, "the caricatura is carried to excess." Mr. *Pine* the engraver sat for the portrait of the Friar, a circumstance of which he afterwards repented;[3] for, thereby obtaining the nick-name of *Friar Pine*, and being much persecuted and laughed at, he strove to prevail on *Hogarth* to give his Ghostly father another face. Indeed, when he sat to our artist, he did not know to what purpose his similitude would afterwards be applied. The original picture is in the possession of the Earl of *Charlemont*. Soon after it was finished, it fell down by accident, and a nail ran through the cross on the top of the gate. *Hogarth* strove in vain to mend it with the same colour, so as to conceal the blemish. He therefore introduced a starved crow, looking down on the roast-beef, and thus completely covered the defect.

The figure of the half-starved *French* centinel has since been copied at the top of more than one of the printed advertisements for recruits, where it is opposed to the representation of a well-fed *British* soldier. Thus the genius of *Hogarth* still militates in the cause of his country.

A copy of this print was likewise engraved at the top of a Cantata, intituled, *The Roast Beef of Old England*. As it is probable that the latter was published under the sanction of our artist, I shall, without scruple, transcribe it.

   RECITATIVE.
   'Twas at the Gates of *Calais, Hogarth* tells,
   Where sad Despair and Famine always dwells,
   A meagre *Frenchman*, Madam *Grandsire's* cook,
   As home he steer'd his carcase, that way took,
   Bending beneath the weight of fam'd *Sir-loin*,
   On whom he often wish'd in vain to dine.
   Good Father *Dominick* by chance came by,
   With rosy gills, round paunch, and greedy eye;
   Who, when he first beheld the greasy load,
   His benediction on it he bestow'd;
   And while the solid fat his finger press'd,
   He lick'd his chaps, and thus the knight address'd:

   AIR.
   A lovely Lass to a Friar came, &c.
   O rare *Roast Beef!* lov'd by all mankind,
   If I was doom'd to have thee,
   When dress'd and garnish'd to my mind,
   And swimming in thy gravy,
   Not all thy country's force combin'd
   Should from my fury save thee.

Renown'd *Sir-loin*, oft-times decreed
The theme of *English* ballad,
E'en kings on thee have deign'd to feed,
Unknown to *Frenchman's* palate;
Then how much more thy taste exceeds
Soup-meagre, frogs, and sallad.

RECITATIVE.
A half-starv'd soldier, shirtless, pale and lean,
Who such a sight before had never seen,
Like *Garrick's* frighted *Hamlet*, gaping stood,
And gaz'd with wonder on the *British* food.
His morning's mess forsook the friendly bowl,
And in small streams along the pavement stole;
He heav'd a sigh, which gave his heart relief,
And then in plaintive tone declar'd his grief.

AIR.
Ah, sacre Dieu! vat do I see yonder,
Dat looks so tempting, red and white?
Begar I see it is de *Roast Beef* from *Londre*,
O grant to me one letel bite.
But to my guts if you give no heeding,
And cruel Fate dis boon denies,
In kind compassion to my pleading,
Return, and let me feast my eyes.

RECITATIVE.
His fellow guard, of right *Hibernian* clay,
Whose brazen front his country did betray,
From *Tyburn's* fatal tree had hither fled,
By honest means to get his daily bread;
Soon as the well-known prospect he espy'd,
In blubbering accents dolefully he cried:

AIR.
Ellen a Roon, &c.
Sweet *Beef*, that now causes my stomach to rise.
Sweet *Beef*, that now causes my stomach to rise,
So taking thy sight is,
My joy that so light is,
To view thee, by pailfuls runs out at my eyes.

While here I remain, my life's not worth a farthing,
While here I remain, my life's not worth a farthing,
Ah! hard-hearted *Lewy*,
Why did I come to ye?
The gallows, more kind, would have sav'd me from starving.

RECITATIVE.
Upon the ground hard by poor *Sawney* sate,
Who fed his nose, and scratch'd his ruddy pate;
But when *Old England's* bulwark he descry'd,
His dear-lov'd mull, alas! was thrown aside.
With lifted hands he bless'd his native place,
Then scrub'd himself, and thus bewail'd his case:

AIR.
The Broom of Cowdenknows, &c.
How hard, O *Sawney!* is thy lot,
Who was so blyth of late,
To see such meat as can't be got,
When hunger is so great!
O the Beef, the bonny bonny Beef!
When roasted nice and brown,
I wish I had a slice of thee,
How sweet it would gang down.
Ah, *Charley!* hadst thou not been seen,
This ne'er had hapt to me:
I would the De'el had pickt mine eyne
Ere I had gang'd with thee.
O the Beef, &c.

RECITATIVE.
But see! my Muse to *England* takes her flight,
Where *Health* and *Plenty* chearfully unite.
Where smiling *Freedom* guards great *George's* throne,
And chains, and racks, and tortures are not known;
Whose *Fame* superior bards have often wrote.—
An ancient fable give me leave to quote.

AIR.
The Roast Beef of Old England.
As once on a time a young *Frog*, pert and vain,
Beheld a large *Ox* grazing on the wide plain,

He boasted his size he could quickly attain.
Oh! the Roast Beef, &c.

Then eagerly stretching his weak little frame,
Mamma, who stood by, like a knowing old dame,
Cried, "Son, to attempt it you're greatly to blame."
Oh! the Roast Beef, &c.

But, deaf to advice, he for glory did thirst,
An effort he ventured, more strong than the first,
Till swelling and straining too hard, made him burst.
Oh! the Roast Beef, &c.

Then, *Britons,* be valiant; the moral is clear:
The *Ox* is *Old England,* the *Frog* is *Monsieur,*
Whose puffs and bravadoes we need never fear.
Oh! the Roast Beef, &c.

For while by our commerce and arts we are able
To see the brave *Ox* smoking hot on our table,
The *French* must e'en croak, like the *Frog* in the fable.
Oh! the Roast Beef, &c.

Printed for R. *Sayer,* at the *Golden Buck* in *Fleet-street;* and J. *Smith,* at *Hogarth's Head* in *Cheapside.*

At the end of a pamphlet which I shall have occasion to mention under the year 1755, was announced, as speedily to be published under the auspices of our artist, "A Poetical Description of Mr. *Hogarth's* celebrated print, *The Roast Beef of Old England,* or the *French* surprized at the Gate of *Calais.*"

[1] In *The General Advertiser, March* 9, 1748-9, appeared the following:

"This day is published, price 5*s*. A Print, designed and engraved by Mr. *Hogarth,* representing a PRODIGY which lately appeared before the Gate of *Calais.*

"O the Roast Beef of *Old England!*

"To be had at the *Golden-Head,* in *Leicester-Square,* and at the Print Shops."

[2] The following lines were written by the Rev. Mr. *Townley,* Master of *Merchant Taylors' School,* and spoken by one of the Scholars, *October* 22, 1767,

    ASSA BUBULA.
Littore in opposito, quâ turrim *Dubris* in altum
Ostentans, undas imperiosa regit,

Ferrea stat, multo cum milite, porta *Calesi*:
(Ingenium pinxit talia, *Hogarthe*, tuum).
Eo! sudans carnis portat latus ille bovile,
Quem, trepidis genibus, grande fatigat onus;
Obstupet hic fixis oculis atque ore patenti,
Et tenue, invitus, jus cito mittit humi:
Accedit monachus, digito tangente rubentem
Carnem, divinum prodigiumque colit.
Omnia visa placent animum; non pascis inani
Picturâ, pariter quæ placet atque docet.
Egregius patriæ proprios dat pictor honores;
Et palmam jussa est ferre bovina caro.

[3] Mr. *Walpole's* new edition of his "Anecdotes of Painting" having been published whilst the present page was preparing for the second edition, I took the earliest opportunity of letting that admirable writer speak for himself, in answer to a particular in which I had presumed to differ from him. "If *Hogarth* indulged his spirit of ridicule in personalities," (I now use the words of Mr. *Walpole*) "it never proceeded beyond sketches and drawings; his prints touched the folly, but spared the person. Early he drew a noted miser, one of the sheriffs, trying a mastiff that had robbed his kitchen, but the magistrate's son went to his house and cut the picture in pieces.[A] I have been reproved for this assertion," continues our agreeable Biographer, "and instances have been pointed out that contradict me. I am far from persevering in an error, and do allow that my position was too positive. Still some of the instances adduced were by no means caricaturas. Sir *John Gonson* and Dr. *Misaubin* in the *Harlot's Progress* were rather examples identified than satires. Others, as Mr. *Pine's*, were mere portraits, introduced by their own desire, or with their consent."

[A] See above, p. 69.

2. Portrait of *John Palmer*, esq. lord of the manor of *Cogenhoe* or *Cooknoe*, and patron of the church, of *Ecton* in *Northamptonshire*. *W. Hogarth pinx. B. Baron sculp*. This small head is inserted under a view of *Ecton* Church.

3. His own head in a cap, a pug-dog, and a palette with the line of beauty, &c. inscribed *Gulielmus Hogarth. Seipse pinxit & sculpsit*. Very scarce, because *Hogarth* erased his own portrait, and introduced that of Mr. *Churchill*, under the character of a bear, in its room. See under the year 1763.

On this print, in its original state, the *Scandalizade*, a satire published about 1749, has the following lines. The author represents himself as standing before the window of a print-shop.

"There elbowing in 'mong the crowd with a jog,
Lo! good father *Tobit*, said I, with his dog!
But the artist is wrong; for the dog should be drawn
At the heels of his master in trot o'er the lawn,—
To your idle remarks I take leave to demur,
'Tis not *Tobit*, nor yet his canonical cur,
(Quoth a sage in the crowd) for I'd have you to know, Sir,
'Tis *Hogarth* himself and his honest friend *Towser*,
Inseparate companions! and therefore you see
Cheek by jowl they are drawn in familiar degree;
Both striking the eye with an equal eclat,
The biped *This* here, and the quadruped *That*—
You mean—the great dog and the man, I suppose,
Or the man and the dog—be't just as you chuse.—
You correct yourself rightly—when much to be blam'd,
For the worthiest person you first should have nam'd,
Great dog! why great man I methinks you should say.
Split the difference, my friend, they're both great in their way.
Is't he then so famous for drawing a punk,
A harlot, a rake, and a parson so drunk,
Whom *Trotplaid*[1] delivers to praise as his friend?
Thus a jacknapes a lion would fain recommend.—
The very self same—how boldly they strike,
And I can't forbear thinking they're somewhat alike.—
Oh fie! to a dog would you *Hogarth* compare?—
Not so—I say only they're alike as it were,
A respectable pair! all spectators allow,
And that they deserve a description below
In capital letters, *Behold we are Two*."

[1] The name under which *Fielding* wrote a news-paper called *The Jacobite's Journal*, the frontispiece by *Hogarth*.

4. Portrait of *Hogarth*, small circle. Mr. *Basire* (to whom this plate has been ascribed) says it is much in our artist's manner. On enquiry, however, it appears to be no other than a watch-paper "Published according to Act of Parliament by *R. Sayer*, opposite *Fetter-lane*, *Sept.* 29, 1749," and certainly copied from the small portrait of our artist introduced in *The Roast Beef of Old England*. Another head of him, with a fur cap on, was also edited by the same printseller, at the same time. There is likewise a third head of *Hogarth*, in an oval, prefixed as a frontispiece to "A Dissertation" on his six prints, &c. *Gin Lane*, &c. which appeared in 1751.

1750.

1. *Thomas Herring*, Archbishop of *Canterbury*. *W. Hogarth p. B. Baron sculp.* Of this picture (which is preserved in *Lambeth-Palace*) the Archbishop, in a letter to Mr. *Duncombe*, says, "None of my friends can bear *Hogarth's* picture;" and Mr. *Duncombe*, the son, in a note to this epistle, observes, that "this picture (as appears by the print engraved by *Baron* in 1750) exhibits rather a caricature than a likeness, the figure being gigantic, the features all aggravated and *outrés*, and, on the whole, so far from conveying an idea of that *os placidum, moresque benigni*, as Dr. *Jortin* expresses it, that engaging sweetness and benevolence, which were characteristic of this prelate, that they seem rather expressive of a *Bonner*, who could burn a heretic.

> "*Lovat's* hard features *Hogarth* might command;
> A *Herring's* sweetness asks a *Reynolds'* hand."

Hogarth however made the following observation while the Archbishop was sitting to him: "Your Grace, perhaps, does not know that some of our chief dignitaries in the church have had the best luck in their portraits. The most excellent heads painted by *Vandyck* and *Kneller*, were those of *Laud* and *Tillotson*. The crown of my works will be the representation of your Grace."

2. *Jacobus Gibbs*, Architectus, A. M. and F. R. S. *Hogarth delin. Baron sculp.* The same face as that in 1747, but in an octagon frame, which admits more of the body to be shewn, as well as some architecture in the back ground. There is also a smaller head of *Gibbs*, in a circle, &c. but whether engraved by *Baron* from a picture by *Hogarth*, or any other hand, is uncertain. Perhaps it was designed as a vignette for some splendid edition of *Gibbs's* works.

3. The March to *Finchley*,[1] dedicated to the King of *Prussia*[2] [as "an Encourager of the Arts,"] "*in resentment for the late king's sending for the picture to St. James's, and returning it without any other notice.*" This print is *engraved by Luke Sullivan* but afterwards, as we learn from a note at the bottom of it, was "Retouched and *improved* by *Wm. Hogarth*, and republished *June* 12, 1761." The *improvements* in it, however, remain to be discovered by better eyes than mine.

I am authorized to add, that soon after the lottery described in a note at the beginning of this article, our artist waited on the treasurer to the *Foundling Hospital*, acquainting him that the trustees were at liberty to dispose of the picture by auction. Scarce, however, was the message delivered, before he changed his mind, and never afterwards would consent to the measure he had originally proposed. The late Duke of *Ancaster* offered the hospital 300 *l.* for it. The following complete explanation of it is in *The Student*, vol. II. p. 16. It is supposed to have been written by the ingenious Mr. *Bonnel Thornton*.

"The scene of this representation is laid at *Tottenham Court Turnpike*; the *King's-Head*, *Adam* and *Eve*, and the *Turnpike-house*, in full view; beyond which are discovered parties of the guards, baggage, &c. marching towards *Highgate*, and a beautiful distant prospect of the country; the sky finely painted. The picture, considered together, affords a view of a military march, and the humours and disorders consequent thereupon.

"Near the center of the picture, the painter has exhibited his principal figure, which is a handsome young grenadier, in whose face is strongly depicted repentance mixed with pity and concern; the occasion of which is disclosed by two females putting in their claim for his person, one of whom has hold of his right arm, and the other has *seized* his left. The figure upon his right hand, and perhaps placed there by the painter by way of preference (as the object of love is more desirable than that of duty), is a fine young girl in her person, debauched, with child, and reduced to the miserable employ of selling ballads, and who, with a look full of love, tenderness, and distress, casts up her eyes upon her undoer, and with tears descending down her cheeks, seems to say——*sure you cannot*——*will not leave me*! The person and deportment of this figure well justifies the painter's turning the body of the youth towards her. The woman upon the left is a strong contrast to this girl; for rage and jealousy have thrown the human countenance into no amiable or desirable form. This is the wife of the youth, who, finding him engaged with such an *ugly slut*, assaults him with a violence natural to a woman whose person and beauty is neglected. To the fury of her countenance, and the dreadful weapon her tongue, another terror appears in her hand, equally formidable, which is a roll of papers, whereon is wrote, *The Remembrancer*; a word of dire and triple import; for while it shews the occupation the *amiable bearer* is engaged in, it reminds the youth of an unfortunate circumstance he would gladly forget: and the same word is also a cant expression, to signify the blow she is meditating. And here, I value myself upon hitting the true meaning, and entering into the spirit of the great author of that celebrated *Journal* called *The Remembrancer*, or, *A weekly slap on the face for the Ministry*.

"It is easily discernible that the two females are of different parties. The ballad of *God save our noble King*, and a print of the *Duke of Cumberland*, in the basket of the girl, and the cross upon the back of the wife, with the implements of her occupation, sufficiently denote the painter's intention: and, what is truly beautiful, these incidents are applicable to the march.

"The hard-favoured serjeant directly behind, who enjoys the foregoing scene, is not only a good contrast to the youth, but also, with other helps, throws forward the principal figure.

"Upon the right of the grenadier is a drummer, who also has his *two Remembrancers*, a woman and a boy, the produce of their kinder hours; and who have laid their claim by a violent seizure upon his person. The figure of the woman is that of a complainant, who reminds him of her great applications, as well in sending him clean to guard, as other kind offices done, and his promises to make her an honest woman, which he, base and ungrateful, has forgot, and pays her affection with neglect. The craning of her neck shews her remonstrances to be of the shrill kind, in which she is aided by the howling of her boy. The drummer, who has a mixture of fun and wickedness in his face, having heard as many reproaches as suit his present inclinations, with a bite of his lip, and a leering eye, applies to the instrument of noise in his profession, and endeavours to drown the united clamour; in which he is luckily aided by the *ear-piercing fife* near him.

"Between the figures before described, but more back in the picture, appears the important but meagre phiz of a *Frenchman*, in close whisper with an *Independent*. The first I suppose a spy upon the motion of the army, the other probably drawn into the croud, in order to give intelligence to his brethren, at their next meeting, to commemorate their noble struggle in support of *Independency*. The *Frenchman* exhibits a letter, which he assures him contains positive intelligence, that 10000 of his countrymen are landed in *England*, in support of *liberty* and *independency*. The joy with which his friend receives these glorious tidings, causes him to forget the wounds upon his head, which he has unluckily received by a too free and premature declaration of his principles.

"There is a fine contrast in the smile of innocency in the child at the woman's back, compared with the grim joy of a gentleman by it; while the hard countenance of its mother gives a delicacy to the grenadier's girl.

"Directly behind the drummer's quondam spouse, appears a soldier pissing against a shed; and some distortions in his countenance indicate a malady too indelicate to describe; this conjecture is aided by a bill of Dr. *Rock's* for relief in like cases. Directly over him appears a wench at a wicket, probably drawn there to have a view of the march; but is diverted from her first intention by the appearance of another object directly under her eye, which seems to ingross her whole attention.

"Behind the drummer under the sign of the *Adam* and *Eve* are a group of figures; two of which are engaged in the fashionable art of bruising: their equal dexterity is shewn, by *sewed-up peepers* on one side, and *a pate well-sconced* on the other. And here the painter has shewn his impartiality to the merit of our *noble youths*, (whose minds, inflamed with love of glory, appear, not only encouragers of this truly laudable science, but many of them are also great proficients in the art itself,) by introducing a youth of quality, whose face is expressive of those boisterous passions necessary for forming a hero of this kind; and who, entering deep into the scene, endeavours to inspire the combatants with a noble contempt of bruises and broken bones. An old woman, moved by a foolish compassion, endeavours to force through the croud and part the fray, in which design she is stopped by a fellow, who prefers fun and mischief to humanity. Above their heads appears a little man[3] of meagre frame, but full of spirits, who enjoys the combat, and with fists clenched, in imagination deals blow for blow with the heroes. This figure is finely contrasted, by a heavy sluggish fellow just behind. The painter, with a stroke of humour peculiar to himself, has exhibited a figure shrinking under the load of a heavy box upon his back, who, preferring curiosity to ease, is a spectator, and waits in this uneasy state the issue of the combat. Upon a board next the sign, where roots, flowers, &c. were said to be sold, the painter has humorously altered the words, and wrote thereon, *Tottenham-Court Nursery*; alluding to a bruising-booth in this place, and the group of figures underneath.

"Passing through the turnpike, appears a carriage laden with the implements of war, as drums, halberts, tent-poles, and hoop-petticoats. Upon the carriage are two old women-campaigners, funking their pipes, and holding a conversation, as usual, in fire and smoke. These grotesque figures afford a fine contrast to a delicate woman upon the same carriage, who is suckling a child. This excellent figure evidently proves, that the painter is as capable of succeeding in the graceful style as in the humorous. A little boy laes at the feet of this figure; and the painter, to shew him of martial breed, has placed a small trumpet in his mouth.

"The serious group of the principal figures, in the center, is finely relieved by a scene of humour on the left. Here an officer has seized a milk-wench, and is kissing her in a manner excessively lewd, yet not unpleasing to the girl, if her eye is a proper interpreter of her affections: while the officer's ruffles suffer in this action, the girl pays her price, by an arch soldier, who in her absence of attention to her pails, is filling his hat with milk, and, by his waggish eye, seems also to partake of the kissing scene. A chimney-sweeper's boy with glee puts in a request to the soldier, to supply him with a cap full, when his own turn is served; while another soldier points out the fun to a fellow selling pyes, who, with an inimitable face of simple joy, neglects the care of his goods, which the soldier dexterously removes with his other hand. In the figure of the pye-man, the pencil has exceeded description——here the sounding epithets of *prodigious—excellent—wonderful—*and all the other terms used by Connoisseurs (when speaking of the beauties of an old picture, where the objects must have lain in eternal obscurity, if not conjured out to the apprehension of the spectator, by the magic of unintelligible description) are too faint to point out its real merit.

"The old soldier divested of one spatter-dash, and near losing the other, and knocked down by all-potent gin, upon calling for t'other cogue, his waggish comrade, supporting him with one hand, endeavours to pour water into his mouth with the other, which the experienced old one rejects with disdain, puts up his hand to his wife who bears the arms and gin-bottle, and who, well acquainted with his taste, is filling a quartern. And here the painter exhibits a sermon upon the excessive use of spirituous liquors, and the destructive consequences attending it: for the soldier is not only rendered incapable of his duty, but (what is shocking to behold) a child begot and conceived in gin, with a countenance emaciated, extends its little arms with great earnestness, and wishes for that liquor, which it seems well acquainted with the taste of. And here, not to dwell wholly upon the beauties of this print, I must mention an absurdity discovered by a professed connoisseur in painting—'Can there,' says he, 'be a greater absurdity than the introducing a couple of chickens so near such a croud—and not only so—but see—their direction is to go to objects it is natural for 'em to shun—is this is knowledge of nature?—absurd to the last degree!'——And here, with an air of triumph, ended our judicious critic. But how great was his surprize, when it was discovered to him, that the said chickens were in pursuit of the hen, which had made her escape into the pocket of a sailor.

"Next the sign-post is an honest tar throwing up his hat, crying 'God bless King *George*.' Before him is an image of drunken loyalty; who, with his shirt out of his breeches, and bayonet in his hand, vows destruction on the heads of the rebels. A fine figure of a speaking old woman, with a basket upon her head, will upon view tell you what she sells. A humane soldier perceiving a fellow hard-loaded with a barrel of gin upon his back, and stopped by the croud, with a gimblet bores a hole in the head of the cask, and is kindly easing him of a part of his burthen. Near him, is the figure of a fine gentleman in the army. As I suppose the painter designed him without character, I shall therefore only observe, that he is a very pretty fellow, and happily the contemplation of his own dear person guards him from the attempts of the wicked women on his right hand. Upon the right hand of this *petit maitre* is a licentious soldier rude with a girl, who screams and wreaks her little vengeance upon his face, whilst his comrade is removing off some linen which hangs in his way.

"You will pardon the invention of a new term—I shall include the whole *King's Head* in the word *Cattery*, the principal figure of which is a noted fat *Covent Garden* lady,[4] who, with pious eyes cast up to heaven, prays for the army's success, and the safe return of many of her babes of grace. An officer offers a letter to one of this lady's children, who rejects it; possibly not liking the cause her spark is engaged in, or, what is more probable, his not having paid for her last favour. Above her, a charitable girl is throwing a shilling to a cripple, while another kindly administers a cordial to her companion, as a sure relief against reflection. The rest of the windows are full of the like cattle; and upon the house-top appear three cats, just emblems of the creatures below, but more harmless in their amorous encounters."

There is likewise another explanation in *The Old Woman's Magazine*, vol. I. p. 182. To elucidate a circumstance, however, in this justly celebrated performance, it is necessary to observe, that near *Tottenham Court Nursery* was the place where the famous *Broughton's* amphitheatre for boxing was erected. It has been since taken down, having been rendered useless by the justices not permitting such kind of diversions. This will account for the appearance of the Bruisers at the left hand corner of the print. One of *Hogarth's* ideas in this performance also needs the assistance of colouring, to render it intelligible. The person to whom the *Frenchman* is delivering a letter, was meant for an old *Highlander* in disguise, as appears from the plaid seen through an opening in his grey coat; a circumstance in the print that escaped me, till after I had seen the picture, and perused *Rouquet's* explanation of this particular circumstance, which I shall add in his own words, with his reflections at the end of it. "A droite du principal group paroit une figure de *François*, qu'on a voulu representer comme un homme de quelque importance, afin de lui donner plus de ridicule; il parle à un homme dont la nation est indiquée par l'etoffe de sa veste, qui est celle dont s'habillent les habitans des montagnes *d'Ecosse*: le *François* semble communiquer à l'*Ecossois* des lettres qu'il vient de reçevoir, & qui ont rapport à l'evenement qui donne lieu à cette marche. Les *Anglois* ne se réjouissent jamais bien sans qu'il en coute quelque chose aux *François*; leur theatre, leur conversation, leurs tableaux, et sur tout ceux de notre peintre, portent toujours cette glorieuse marque de l'amour de la patrie; les romans même sont ornés de traits amusans sur cet ancien sujet; l'excellent auteur de *Tom Jones* a voulu aussi lâcher les siens. Mais le pretendu mépris pour les *François* dont le peuple de ce pais-ci fait profession, s'explique selon moi d'une façon fort équivoque. Le mépris suppose l'oubli; mais un objet dont on médit perpetuèllement est un objet dont on est perpetuèllement occupé: la satire constitue une attention qui me feroit soupconner qu'on fait aux *François* l'honneur de les haïr un peu."

All the off tracts from the faces in the original picture of the March to *Finchley*, in red chalk on oiled paper, are still preserved.

This representation may be said to contain three portraits, all of which were acknowledged by the artist: a noted *French* pye-man; one of the young fifers then recently introduced into the army by the Duke of *Cumberland*; and a chimney-sweeper with an aspect peculiarly roguish. The two latter were hired by *Hogarth*, who gave each of them half a crown, for his patience in sitting while his likeness was taken. Among the portraits in the *March to Finchley* (says a correspondent) that of *Jacob Henriques* may also be discovered. I wish it had been pointed out.

With this plate (of which the very few proofs in aqua-fortis, as well as the finished ones, are highly valuable) no unfair stratagems have been practised, that a number of the various impressions, taken off at different times, might be mistaken for the earliest. On copper nothing is more easy than to cover, alter, efface, or re-engrave an inscription, as often as temporary convenience may require a change in it.[5] Witness, the several copies of *The Lottery*, three of which exhibit the names of three different publishers: the fourth has none at all.

The possessors of this March to *Finchley* need not vehemently lament their want of the original. The spirit of it is most faithfully transfused on the copper. As to the colouring, it will hardly delight such eyes are are accustomed to the pictures of *Steen* or *Teniers*. To me the painting of the *March to Finchley* appears hard and heavy, and has much the air of a coloured print.

I should not, on this occasion, omit to add, that Mr. *Strange*, in his *Inquiry into the Rise and Establishment of the Royal Academy of Arts in London*, observes, that "the donations in painting which several artists presented to *The Foundling Hospital*," first led to the idea of those Exhibitions which are at present so lucrative to our Royal Academy, and so entertaining to the publick. *Hogarth* must certainly be considered as a chief among these benefactors.

[1] *General Advertiser, April* 14, 1750. Mr *Hogarth* is publishing, by subscription, a print representing the march to *Finchley* in the year 1746, engraved on a copper-plate, 22 inches by 17. The price 7 *s.* 6 *d.*

Subscriptions are taken in at *The Golden Head* in *Leicester-Fields*, till the 30th of this instant, and not longer, to the end that the engraving may not be retarded.

Note. Each print will be half a Guinea after the Subscription is over.

In the Subscription-book, are the particulars of a proposal whereby each subscriber of three shillings, over and above the said seven shillings and sixpence for the print, will, in consideration thereof, be entitled to a chance of having the original picture, which shall be delivered to the winning subscriber as soon as the engraving is finished.

General Advertiser, May 1, 1750.

Yesterday Mr. *Hogarth's* subscription was closed. 1843 chances being subscribed for, Mr. *Hogarth* gave the remaining 157 chances to *The Foundling Hospital*. At two o'clock the box was opened, and the fortunate chance was N° 1941, which belongs to the said Hospital; and the same night Mr. *Hogarth* delivered the picture to the Governors.

[2] PRUSIA, in the earliest impressions. I have been assured that only twenty-five were worked off with this literal imperfection, as *Hogarth* grew tired of adding the mark ~ with a pen over one S, to supply the want of the other. He therefore ordered the inscription to be corrected before any greater number of impressions were taken. Though this circumstance was mentioned by Mr. *Thane*, to whose experience in such matters some attention is due, it is difficult to suppose that *Hogarth* was fatigued with correcting his own mistake in so small a number of the first Impressions. I may venture to add, that I have seen, at least, five and twenty marked in the manner already described: and it is scarce possible, considering the multitudes of these plates dispersed in the world, that I should have met with all that were so distinguished.

[3] The real or nick name of this man, who was by trade a cobler, is said to have been *Jockey James*.

[4] This figure is repeated in the last print but one of *Industry*. and *Idleness*, and was designed for Mother *Douglas* of the Piazza.

[5] *Proofs* were anciently a few impressions taken off in the course of an engraver's process. He *proved* a plate in different states, that he might ascertain how far his labours had been successful, and when they were complete. The excellence of such early impressions, worked with care, and under the artist's eye, occasioning them to be greedily sought after, and liberally paid for, it has been customary among our modern printsellers to take off a number of them, amounting, perhaps, to hundreds, from every plate of considerable value; and yet their want of rareness has by no means abated their price. On retouching a plate, it has been also usual, among the same conscientious fraternity, to cover the inscription, which was immediately added after the first proofs were obtained, with slips of paper, that a number of secondary proofs might also be created. This device is notorious, and too often practised, without discovery, on the unskilful purchaser. A new print, in short, is of the same use to a crafty dealer, as a fresh girl to a politic bawd. In both instances *le fausse pucelage* is disposed of many times over.

1751.

1. *Beer-street*,[1] two of them, with variations, (the former price 1 *s.* the latter 1 *s.* 6 *d.*), and *Gin Lane*. The following verses under these two prints are by the Rev. Mr. *James Townley*, Master of *Merchant Taylors School*:

>BEER-STREET.
>Beer, happy product of our isle,
>Can sinewy strength impart,
>And, wearied with fatigue and toil,
>Can chear each manly heart.
>
>Labour and Art, upheld by thee,
>Successfully advance;
>We quaff thy balmy juice with glee,
>And water leave to *France*.
>
>Genius of Health, thy grateful taste
>Rivals the cup of *Jove*,
>And warms each *English* generous breast
>With Liberty and Love.
>
>GIN-LANE.
>Gin, cursed fiend! with fury fraught,
>Makes human race a prey;
>It enters by a deadly draught,
>And steals our life away.
>
>Virtue and Truth, driven to despair,
>Its rage compels to fly,
>But cherishes, with hellish care,
>Theft, Murder, Perjury.
>
>Damn'd cup! that on the vitals preys,
>That liquid fire contains,
>Which madness to the heart conveys,
>And rolls it thro' the veins.

Mr. *Walpole* observes, that the variation of the butcher lifting the *Frenchman* in his hand, was an after-thought;[2] but he is mistaken. This *butcher* is in reality a *blacksmith*; and the violent hyperbole is found in the original drawing, as well as in the earliest impressions of the plate. The first copies of *Beer-street*, *Gin Lane*, and *The Stages of Cruelty*, were taken off on very thin paper; but this being objected to, they were afterwards printed on thicker. The painter, who in the former of these scenes is copying a bottle from one hanging by him as a pattern, has been regarded as a stroke of satire on *John Stephen Liotard*, who (as Mr. *Walpole* observes) "could render nothing but what he saw before his eyes."[3]

It is probable that *Hogarth* received the first idea for these two prints from a pair of others by *Peter Breugel* (commonly called *Breugel d'enfer*, or *Hellish Breugel*), which exhibit a contrast of a similar kind. The one is entitled *La grasse*, the other *La maigre Cuisine*. In the first, all the personages are well-fed and plump; in the second, they are starved and slender. The latter of them also exhibits the figures of an emaciated mother and child, sitting on a straw-mat upon the ground, whom I never saw without thinking on the female, &c. in *Gin Lane*.[4] In *Hogarth*, the fat *English* blacksmith is insulting the gaunt *Frenchman*; and in *Breugel*, the plump cook is kicking the lean one out of doors. Our artist was not unacquainted with the works of this master, as will appear by an observation on the [Lilliputians giving Gulliver a clyster](#).

On the subject of these two plates, and the four following ones, was published a stupid pamphlet, intituled, "A Dissertation on Mr. *Hogarth's* Six Prints lately published, viz. *Gin-Lane, Beer-street,* and *The Four Stages of Cruelty*, Containing, I. A genuine narrative of the horrible deeds perpetrated by that fiery dragon, *Gin*; the wretched and deplorable condition of its votaries and admirers; the dreadful havock and devaluation it has made amongst the human species; its pernicious effects on the soldiers, sailors, and mechanicks of this kingdom; and its poisonous and pestilent qualities in destroying the health, and corrupting the morals of the people. II. Useful observations on wanton and inhuman cruelty, severely satirizing the practice of the common people in sporting with the lives of animals. Being a proper key for the right apprehension of the author's meaning in those designs. Humbly inscribed to the Right Honourable *Francis Cockayne*, Esq; Lord Mayor of the City of *London*, and the worshipful Court of Aldermen, who have so worthily distinguished themselves in the measures they have taken to suppress the excessive use of spirituous liquors. *London*: Printed for *B. Dickinson* on *Ludgate-Hill*. 1751. Price one shilling;" and eleven pence three farthings too dear, being compiled out of *Reynolds's* "God's Revenge against Murder," &c.

[1] *General Advertiser, February* 13, 1750-51.

On *Friday* next will be published, price one shilling each.

Two large Prints designed and etched by Mr. *Hogarth*, called *Beer-street* and *Gin-lane*.

A number will be printed in a better manner for the Curious at 1 *s.* 6 *d.* each.

And on *Thursday* following will be published,

Four Prints on the subject of Cruelty. Price and size the same.

N. B. As the subjects of these Prints are calculated to reform some reigning vices peculiar to the lower class of people, in hopes to render them of more extensive use, the author has published them in the cheapest manner possible.

To be had at the *Golden Head* in *Leicester Fields*, where may be had all his other works.

[2] I am sorry to perceive that this observation remains in the octavo edition of the "Anecdotes of Painting," vol. IV. p. 147.

[3] The opinion which *Hogarth* entertained of the writings of Dr. *Hill* may be discovered in his *Beer-Street*, where *Hill's* critique upon the Royal Society is put into a basket directed to the Trunk-Maker, in *St. Paul's Church-Yard*.

[4] This emaciated figure, who appears drunk and asleep at the corner of this print, was painted from nature.

2. The Stages of Cruelty, in four prints. *Designed by Wm. Hogarth, price* 4 *s.* Of the two latter of these there are wooden plates[1] on a large scale, *Inv^d. and published by Wm. Hogarth, Jan.* 1, 1750. *J. Bell sculp.* They were done by order of our artist, who wished to diffuse the salutary example they contain, as far as possible, by putting them within the reach of the meanest purchaser; but finding this mode of executing his design was expensive beyond expectation, he proceeded no further in it, and was content to engrave them in his own coarse, but spirited manner. Impressions from the wooden blocks are to be had at Mrs. *Hogarth's* house in *Leicester-fields*. This set of prints, however, is illustrated with the following verses:

> FIRST STAGE OF CRUELTY.
> While various scenes of sportive woe
> The infant race employ,
> And tortur'd Victims bleeding shew
> The tyrant in the boy;
> Behold! a *youth* of gentler heart,
> To spare the Creature's pain,[2]
> O take, he cries—take all my tart,
> But tears and tart are vain.
> Learn from this fair example—you,
> Whom savage sports delight,
> How Cruelty disgusts the view,
> While pity charms the sight.
>
> SECOND STAGE OF CRUELTY.

The generous *steed*, in hoary age,
Subdu'd by labour lies;
And mourns a cruel master's rage,
While *Nature* strength denies.
The tender *Lamb*, o'erdrove and faint,
Amidst expiring throes,
Bleats forth it's innocent complaint,
And dies beneath the blows.
Inhuman wretch! say whence proceeds
This coward Cruelty?
What int'rest springs from barb'rous deeds
What joy from misery?

III. CRUELTY IN PERFECTION.
To lawless *Love* when once betray'd,
Soon crime to crime succeeds;
At length beguil'd to *Theft*, the *maid*
By her *beguiler* bleeds.
Yet learn, seducing man, not night
With all its sable cloud,
Can skreen the guilty *deed* from sight:
Foul Murder cries aloud.
The gaping wounds, the blood-stain'd steel,
Now shock his trembling *soul*:
But oh! what pangs his breast must feel,
When Death his knell shall toll.

IV. THE REWARD OF CRUELTY.
Behold, the *Villain's* dire disgrace
Not death itself can end:
He finds no peaceful *burial-place*;
His breathless corse, no friend,
Torn from the root, that wicked *Tongue*,
Which daily swore and curst!
Those eye-balls, from their sockets wrung,
That glow'd with lawless lust.
His heart, exposed to prying eyes,
To pity has no claim;
But, dreadful! from his bones shall rise
His monument of shame.[3]

[1] N. B. The first of these wooden cuts differs in many circumstances from the engraving. In the former, the right hand of the murderer is visible; in the

latter it is pinioned behind him. Comparison will detect several other variations in this plate and its fellow.

[2] The thrusting an arrow up the fundament of a dog, is not an idea of *English* growth. No man ever beheld the same act of cruelty practised on any animal in *London*. *Hogarth*, however, met with this circumstance in *Callot's Temptation of St. Antony*, and transplanted it, without the least propriety, into its present situation.

[3] In the last of these plates, "how delicate and superior," as Mr. *Walpole* observes, "is *Hogarth's* satire, when he intimates, in the College of Physicians and Surgeons that preside at a dissection, how the legal habitude of viewing shocking scenes hardens the human mind, and renders it unfeeling. The president maintains the dignity of insensibility over an executed corpse, and considers it but as the object of a lecture. In the print of the Sleeping Judges, this habitual indifference only excites our laughter." To render his spectacle, however, more shocking, our artist has perhaps deviated from nature, against whose laws he so rarely offends. He has impressed marks of agony on the face of the criminal under dissection; whereas it is well known, that, the most violent death once past, the tumult of the features subsides for ever. But, in *Hogarth's* print, the wretch who has been executed, seems to feel the subsequent operation. Of this plate Mr. *S. Ireland* has the original drawing.

3. Boys peeping at Nature, with Variations.

Receipt for *Moses brought to Pharaoh's Daughter*, and St. *Paul before Felix*.

The burlesque *Paul*, &c. being the current receipt for these two prints, I know not why our artist should have altered and vamped up his *Boys peeping at Nature* (see p. 188.) for the same purpose. This plate was lately found at Mrs. *Hogarth's*, but no former impressions from it appear to have been circulated. It might have been a first thought, before the idea of its ludicrous successor occurred. *Hogarth*, however, with propriety, effaced all the wit in his original design, before he meant to offer it as a prologue to his uninteresting serious productions.

4. *Paul* before *Felix*, designed and scratched in the true *Dutch* taste, by *W. Hogarth*. This was the receipt for *Pharaoh's* daughter, and for the serious *Paul and Felix*; and is a satire on *Dutch* pictures. It also contains, in the character of a serjeant tearing his brief, a portrait of *Hume Campbell*, who was not over-delicate in the language he used at the bar to his adversaries and antagonists. This, however, is said by others to be the portrait of *William King*,[1] LL. D. Principal of *St. Mary Hall, Oxford*. In a variation of this print, the Devil is introduced sawing off a leg of the stool on which *Paul* stands. In the *third* impression, as is noted in the collection sold last at *Christie's*, "*Hogarth* has

again taken out the Devil. By these variations of *Devil and no Devil*, he glances at Collectors, who give great prices for such rarities; and perhaps he had in his eye the famous print of the Shepherd's Offering by *Poilly*, after *Guido*, which sells very dear, without the Angels." This, however, is erroneous. After the dæmon was once admitted, he was never discarded. The plate in Mrs. *Hogarth's* keeping confirms my assertion. In the first proof of *Poilly's Shepherd's Offering*, the angels are lightly sketched in; in the finished proof they are totally omitted; but were afterwards inserted. There are similar variations relative to the arms at the bottom of it.

Of this burlesque *Paul*, &c. none were originally intended for sale; but our artist gave them away to such of his acquaintance, &c. as begged for them. The number of these petitioners, however, increasing every day, he resolved at last to part with no copies of it at a less price than five shillings.[2] All the early proofs were stained by himself, to give them that tint of age which is generally found on the works of *Rembrandt*. Of this plate, however, there are *two* impressions. The inscription under the *first* is "*Paul* before *Felix*. Design'd and scratch'd in the true *Dutch* taste by &c." Under the *second*, "Designed and etch'd in the ridiculous manner of *Rembrant*, &c." From the former of these *Hogarth* took off a few reverses. He must have been severely mortified when he found his ludicrous representation of *Paul* before *Felix* was more coveted and admired than his serious painting on the same subject.

[1] Of Dr. *King*, who was "a tall, lean, well-looking man," there is a striking likeness in *Worlidge's* View of the Installation of Lord *Westmoreland* as chancellor of *Oxford* in 1761. Some particulars of his life and writings may be seen in the "Anecdotes of Mr. *Bowyer*," p. 594.

[2] Mr. *Walpole* has honoured a passage in the first edition of this hasty work, with the following stricture: (see Anecdotes of Painting, vol. IV. p. 149).

"I have been blamed for censuring the indelicacies of *Flemish* and *Dutch* painters, by comparing them with the *purity* of *Hogarth*, against whom are produced many instances of indelicacy, and some repetitions of the same indelicacy. I will not defend myself by pleading that these instances are thinly scattered through a great number of his works, and that there is at least humour in most of the incidents quoted, and that they insinuate some reflection, which is never the case of the foreigners—but can I chuse but smile when one of the nastiest examples specified is from the burlesque of *Paul* before *Felix*, professedly in ridicule of the gross images of the *Dutch*?"

In consequence of private remarks from Mr. *W.* this questionable position, as well as a few others, had been obviated in my second impression of the trifling performance now offered to the public: but as our author cannot *chuse but smile*, when the occasion of his mirth was no longer meant to be in his way, I would ask, in defence of my former observation, if moralists usually attempt to reform profligates by writing treatises of profligacy? or, if painters have a right to chastise indelicacy, by exhibiting gross examples of it in their own performances? To become indecent ourselves, is an unwarrantable recipe for curing indecency in others. The obscenities of *Juvenal* have hitherto met with no very successful vindication: "Few are the converts *Aretine* has made." According to our critic's mode of reasoning, a homicide might urge that the crime of which he stands accused was committed only as a salutary example of the guilt of murder; nay, thus indeed every human offence might be allowed to bring with it its own apology.—I forbear to proceed in this argument, or might observe in behalf of our "foreigners," that their incidents insinuate some reflections as well as *Hogarth's*. The evacuations introduced in *Dutch* pictures, most certainly inculcate the necessity of temperance, for those only who eat and drink too much at fairs, or in ale-houses, are liable to such public and unseemly accidents as *Heemskirk*, *Ostade*, and *Teniers*, have occasionally represented. If we are to look for "Sermons in stones, and good in everything," this inference is as fair as many which Mr. *W.* seems inclined to produce in honour of poor *Hogarth*, who, like *Shakspeare*, often sought to entertain, without keeping any moral purpose in view. But was there either wit or morality in *Hogarth's* own evacuation against the door of a church, a circumstance recorded by Mr. *Forrest* in his MS. tour, though prudently suppressed in his printed copy of it? Perhaps, following Uncle *Toby's* advice, he had better have wiped the whole up, and said nothing about the matter. Our worthy Tour-writer, however, was by no means qualified to be the author of a Sentimental Journey. He rather (and purposely, as we are told) resembles *Ben Jonson's* communicative traveller, who says to his companion,

> ——I went and paid a moccinigo
> For mending my silk stockings; by the way
> I cheapen'd sprats, and at *St. Mark's* I urin'd.
> Faith, these are politic notes!

1752.

1. *Paul* before *Felix*, from the original painting in *Lincoln's-Inn Hall*, painted by *W. Hogarth*. "*There is much less Dignity in this, than Wit in the preceding.*" Under the inscription to the first impressions of this plate is "Published *Feb.* 5, 1752. Engraved by *Luke Sullivan*." To the second state of it was added the quotation which, in p. <u>64</u>, I have printed from Dr. *Joseph Warton's* Essay on the Genius of *Pope*. It was covered with paper in the third impression, and entirely effaced in the fourth.

2. The same, "*as first designed, but the wife of* Felix *was afterwards omitted, because St.* Paul's *hand was very improperly placed before her.*" I have seen a copy of it, on which *Hogarth* had written, "A print off the plate that was set aside as

insufficient. Engraved by *W. H.*" On the appearance of Dr. *Warton's* criticism on this plate, *Hogarth* caused the whole of it to be engraved under both this and the next mentioned print, without any comment.

3. *Moses* brought to *Pharaoh's* daughter, from a picture at The Foundling Hospital. Engraved by *W.* Hogarth and *Luke Sullivan*.

In the early impressions from this plate (exclusive of its necessary and usual inscription) the words "Published *February* 5, 1752, according to Act of Parliament," and "*W. Hogarth pinxit*," are found. In subsequent copies they are obliterated; and we have only "Published as the Act directs" in their room. These were left out, however, only to make room for the quotation from Dr. *Warton's* book already mentioned.[1]

[1] It should here be remarked, that the heads of several of the figures in the original, differ widely from those in the engraving. The daughter of the *Egyptian* Monarch appears to more advantage in the print than on the canvas, for there she resembles a wanton under-actress, who, half-undrest, and waiting for her keeper, employs the interval of time in settling accounts with a washerwoman, who has her bastard at nurse, and has just brought him home to convince her that young *Curl-pated Hugh* has no shoes to his feet. The colouring of this piece is beneath criticism. I have just been told the head of *Pharaoh's* daughter was copied from one *Seaton*, a smock-faced youth of our artist's acquaintance: a proper model, no doubt, for an *Eastern* Princess! *Hogarth* could not, like *Guido*, draw a *Venus* from a common porter.

1753.

1. *Columbus* breaking the egg. "*The subscription-ticket to his Analysis.*" First payment 5 *s*. *Hogarth* published this print as a sarcasm on those artists who had been inclined to laugh at his boasted line of beauty, as a discovery which every one might have made.

2. Analysis of Beauty. Two plates. Mr. *Walpole* observes, that *Hogarth's* "samples of grace in a young lord and lady are strikingly stiff and affected. They are a *Bath* beau and a county beauty." The print is found in three different states. "In the original plate the principal figure represented the present king, then prince, but *Hogarth* was desired to alter it. The present figure was taken from the last duke of *Kingston*; yet, though like him, is stiff, and far from graceful."[1] In Plate I. Fig. 19. the fat personage drest in a *Roman* habit, and elevated on a pedestal, was designed, as *Hogarth* himself acknowledged, for a ridicule on *Quin* in the character of *Coriolanus*. *Essex* the

dancing-master is also represented in the act of endeavouring to reduce the graceful attitude of *Antinous* to modern stiffness. Fig. 20. was likewise meant for the celebrated *Desnoyer*, dancing in a grand ballet.

Dr. *Beattie*, speaking of the modes of combination, by which incongruous qualities may be presented to the eye, or the fancy, so as to provoke laughter, observes "A country dance of men and women, like those exhibited by *Hogarth* in his Analysis of Beauty, could hardly fail to make a beholder merry, whether he believed their union to be the effect of design or accident. Most of those persons have incongruities of their own in their shape, dress, or attitude, and all of them are incongruous in respect of one another; thus far the assemblage displays contrariety or want of relation: and they are all united in the same dance; and thus far they are mutually related. And if we suppose the two elegant figures removed, which might be done without lessening the ridicule, we should not easily discern any contrast of dignity and meanness in the group that remains.

"Almost the same remarks might be made on *The Enraged Musician*, another piece of the same great master, of which a witty author quaintly says, that it deafens one to look at it. This extraordinary group forms a very comical mixture of incongruity and relation; of incongruity, owing to the dissimilar employment and appearances of the several persons, and to the variety and dissonance of their respective noises; and of relation, owing to their being all united in the same place, and for the same purpose of tormenting the poor fidler. From the various sounds co-operating to this one end, the piece becomes more laughable, than if their meeting were conceived to be without any particular destination; for the greater number of relations, as well as of contrarieties, that take place in any ludicrous assembly, the more ludicrous it will generally appear. Yet, though this group comprehends not any mixture of meanness and dignity, it would, I think, be allowed to be laughable to a certain degree, merely from the juxta-position of the objects, even though it were supposed to be accidental." Essay on Laughter and Ludicrous Composition, 4to Edit. 608.

"I have no new books, alas! to amuse myself or you; so can only return yours of *Hogarth's* with thanks. It surprized me agreeably; for I had conceived the performance to be a set of prints only, whereas I found a book which I did not imagine *Hogarth* capable of writing; for in his pencil I always confided, but never imagined his pen would have afforded me so much pleasure. As to his not fixing *the precise degree of obliquity*, which constitutes beauty, I forgive him, because I think the task too hard to be performed literally: but yet he conveys an idea between his pencil and his pen, which makes one conceive his meaning pretty well." Lady *Luxborough's* Letters, p. 380.

I shall here transcribe as much from the *Analysis* as is necessary to communicate our artist's design relative to the various figures that compose the country-dance in the second plate. The reader who neither possesses the book, nor wishes to accompany the author throughout his technical explanations, may desire some intelligence concerning the present subject.

"CHAP. XIV.

"OF ATTITUDE.

"—As two or three lines at first are sufficient to shew the intention of an attitude, I will take this opportunity of presenting my reader with the sketch of a country-dance, in the manner I began to set out the design; in order to shew how few lines are necessary to express the first thoughts as to different attitudes [see fig. 71. T. p. 2.], which describe, in some measure, the several figures and actions, mostly of the ridiculous kind, that are represented in the chief part of plate II.

"The most amiable person may deform his general appearance by throwing his body and limbs into plain lines; but such lines appear still in a more disagreeable light in people of a particular make; I have therefore chose such figures as I thought would agree best with my first score of lines, fig. 71.

"The two parts of curves next to 71, served for the old woman and her partner at the farther end of the room. The curve and two strait lines at right angles gave the hint for the fat man's sprawling posture. I next resolved to keep a figure within the bounds of a circle, which produced the upper part of the fat woman between the fat man and the aukward one in a bag-wig, for whom I had made a sort of an X. The prim lady, his partner, in the riding habit, by pecking back her elbows, as they call it, from the waist upwards, made a tolerable D, with a straight line under it, to signify the scanty stiffness of her petticoat; and a Z stood for the singular position the body makes with the legs and thighs of the affected fellow in the tye-wig; the upper part of his plump partner was confined to an O, and this, changed into a P, served as a hint for the straight lines behind.[2] The uniform diamond of a card was filled by the flying dress, &c. of the little capering fellow in the Spencer wig; whilst a double L marked the parallel position of his poking partner's hands and arms [*N. B. This figure was copied from that of an uncouth young female whom* Hogarth *met with at* Isleworth *assembly*]: and, lastly, the two waving lines were drawn for the more genteel turns of the two figures at the hither end.

"The drawing-room is also ornamented purposely with such statues and pictures as may serve to a farther illustration. *Henry* VIII. [Fig. 72. P. 2] makes a perfect X with his legs and arms; and the position of *Charles* [Fig. 51. P. 2.] is composed of less-varied lines than the statue of *Edward* VI. [Fig. 73. P. 2.]; and the medal over his head is in the like kind of lines; but that over Q.

Elizabeth, as well as her figure, is in the contrary; so are also the two other wooden figures at the end. Likewise the comical posture of astonishment expressed by following the direction of one plain curve, as the dotted line in a *French* print of *Sancho*, where Don *Quixote* demolishes the puppet-show [Fig. 75. R. P. 2], is a good contrast to the effect of the serpentine lines in the fine turn of the *Samaritan* woman [Fig. 75. L. p. 2.] taken from one of the best pictures *Annibal Carache* ever painted."

Respecting the plate numbered I. there are no variations. In its companion the changes repeatedly made as to the two principal figures are more numerous than I had at first observed. It may, however, be sufficient for me to point out some single circumstance in each, that may serve as a mark of distinction. In the first, the principal female has scarce any string to her necklace; in the second it is lengthened; and still more considerably increased in the third. In the first and second editions also of this plate, between the young lord and his partner (and just under the figure of the man who is pointing out the stateliness of some of K. *Henry* VIIIth's proportions to a lady), is a vacant easy chair. In the third impression this chair is occupied by a person asleep. I have lately been assured that this country-dance was originally meant to have formed one of the scenes in the *Happy Marriage*. The old gentleman hastening away his daughter, while the servant is putting on his spatter-dashes, seems to countenance the supposition; and having since examined the original sketch in oil, which is in Mr. *Ireland's* possession, I observe that the dancing-room is terminated by a large old-fashioned bow-window, a circumstance perfectly consistent with the scenery of the wedding described in p. 46, &c.

I may add, that in this picture, the couple designed for specimens of grace, appear, not where they stand in the print, but at the upper end of the room: and so little versed was our painter in the etiquette of a wedding-ball, that he has represented the bride dancing with the bridegroom.[3]

When *Hogarth* shewed the original painting, from which this dance has been engraved, to my informant, he desired him to observe a pile of hats in the corner, all so characteristic of their respective owners, that they might with ease be picked out, and given to the parties for whom they were designed.

[1] Anecdotes of Painting, 8vo. vol. IV. p. 166.

[2] The idea of making human figures conform to the shape of capital letters, is by no means new. Several alphabets of this kind were engraved above 150 years ago.

[3] As different fashions, however, prevail at different times, this observation may be wrong.

3. The Political Clyster. *Nahtanoi Tfiws*.[1] *Dr. O'Gearth sculp. Nll Mrrg. Cht Nf. ndw Lps ec ple &c. &c. shd b. Prgd. See Gulliver's Speech to the Honble. House of Vulgaria in Lilliput.*

This was originally published about 1727, or 1728, under the title of "The punishment inflicted on *Lemuel Gulliver,* by applying a *Lilypucian* Fire Engine to his posteriors for his urinal profanation of the Royal Pallace at *Mildendo;* which was intended as a Frontispiece to his first volume, but omitted. *HogEarth sculp.*" The superiority of the impressions thus inscribed is considerable.[2]

More than the general idea of this print is stolen from another by *Hellish Breugel,* whom I have already mentioned in a remark on *Beer-street,* and *Gin-lane.* The *Dutchman* has represented a number of pigmies delivering a huge giant from a load of fæces. His postern is thrust out, like that of *Gulliver,* to favour their operations. *Breugel* has no less than three prints on this subject, with considerable variations from each other.

"When *Hogarth's* topics were harmless," says Mr. *Walpole,* "all his touches were marked with pleasantry and fun. He never laughed, like *Rabelais,* at nonsense that he imposed for wit; but, like *Swift,* combined incidents that divert one from their unexpected encounter, and illustrate the tale he means to tell. Such are the hens roosting on the upright waves in the scene of the Strollers, and the devils drinking porter on the altar." The print now before us is, however, no very happy exemplification of our critick's remark.

[1] Originally mistaken by Mr. *Walpole* for the name of a *Lilliputian* painter, but put right in his new edition.

[2] The present unmeaning title of this plate, was bestowed on it by its owner, Mr. *Sayer.*

1754.

1. Crowns, mitres, maces, &c. A subscription-ticket for the Election entertainment. This print has been already described. See p. 39. The engraved forms of a receipt annexed to it do not always agree. In one copy (which I suppose to be the eldest) it contains an acknowledgement for "Five Shillings, being the first payment for a print representing an Election Entertainment, which I promise to deliver, when finished, on the receipt of five shillings and sixpence more." The second is for "one guinea, being the first payment for four prints of an Election, which I promise, &c. on the receipt of one guinea more." The third for "fifteen shillings, being the first, &c. for three prints, &c. on the payment of sixteen shillings and sixpence more."

2. Frontispiece to *Kirby's* Perspective.[1] Engraved by *Sullivan*. Satire on false perspective. Motto, "Whoever maketh a design without the knowledge of Perspective, will be liable to such absurdities as are shewn in this frontispiece." The occasion of engraving the plate arose from the mistakes of Sir E. *Walpole*, who was learning to draw without being taught perspective. To point out in a strong light the errors which would be likely to happen from the want of acquaintance with those principles, this design was produced. It was afterwards given to *Kirby*, who dedicated Dr. *Brook Taylor's* Method of Perspective to Mr. *Hogarth*. The above anecdote is recorded on the authority of the gentleman already mentioned. The plate, after the first quantity of impressions had been taken from it, was retouched, but very little to its advantage. Mr. *S. Ireland* has the original sketch.

[1] "This work is in quarto, containing 172 pages, and 51 plates, in the whole; with a frontispiece designed and drawn by Mr. *Hogarth*. 'Tis a humourous piece, shewing the absurdities a person may be liable to, who attempts to draw without having some knowledge in perspective. As the production of that great genius, it is entertaining; and, though abounding with the grossest absurdities possible, may pass and please; otherwise I think it is a palpable insult offered to common sense, and tacitly calling the artists a parcel of egregious blockheads. There is not a finished piece in the book, but the mason's yard and the landscapes; so that I question if the whole of the plates were forty pounds expence. It was first printed for himself at *Ipswich*, dedicated to Mr. *Hogarth*, and published in the year 1754."

Malton, Appendix to Treatise on Perspective, p. 106.

1755.

1. Four prints of an Election.[1] These, by *Hogarth*, came out at different times, *viz*. Plate I. *Feb.* 24, 1755 (inscribed to the Right Hon. *Henry Fox*); Plate II. *Feb.* 20, 1757, (to his Excellency Sir *Charles Hanbury Williams*, Ambassador to the Court of *Russia*); Plate III. *Feb.* 20, 1758, (to the Hon. Sir *Edward Walpole*, Knight of the Bath); Plate IV. *Jan.* 1, 1758, (to the Hon. *George Hay*,[2] one of the Lords Commissioners of the Admiralty). The original pictures are now in the possession of Mrs. *Garrick*, at *Hampton*. The inscription on the banner, "Give us our eleven days," alludes to the alteration of the Style in 1752; in which year, from the 2d to the 14th of *September*, eleven days were not reckoned by act of parliament. In the election-dinner, Mr. *Hogarth* assured the writer of this paragraph, that there is but one at table intended for a real portrait and that is the *Irish* gentleman [the present Sir *John Parnell*, nephew to the poet, and remarkable for a very flat nose], who is diverting the company by a face drawn with a burnt cork upon the back of his hand, while he is supposed to be singing—*An old woman cloathed in grey*. This gentleman

(then an eminent attorney) begged it as a favour; declaring, at the same time, he was so generally known, that the introduction of his face would be of service to our artist in the sale of his prints at *Dublin*. Notwithstanding *Hogarth's* assertion, the handsome candidate is pronounced to be the late *Thomas Potter*, esq. and the effigy, seen through the window, with the words "*No Jews*" about its neck, to be meant for the late Duke of *Newcastle*. Of yet another real personage we receive notice, from a pamphlet intituled "The last Blow, or an unanswerable vindication of the Society of *Exeter College*, in reply to the Vice-chancellor Dr. *King*, and the writers of *The London Evening Post*." 4to. 1755. p. 21.—"The next character, to whose merits we would do justice, is the Rev. Dr. *C—ff—t (Cofferat)*. But as it is very difficult to delineate this fellow in colours sufficiently strong and lively, it is fortunate for us and the Doctor, that *Hogarth* has undertaken that task. In the print of an Election Entertainment, the publick will see the Doctor represented sitting among the freeholders, and zealously eating and drinking for the sake of the New Interest. His venerable and humane aspect will at once bespeak the dignity and benevolence of his heart. Never did alderman at *Guildhall* devour custard with half such an appearance of love to his country, or swallow ale with so much the air of a patriot. These circumstances the pencil of Mr. *Hogarth* will undoubtedly make manifest; but it is much to be lamented, that his words also cannot appear in this print, and that the artist cannot delineate that persuasive flow of eloquence which could prevail upon Copyholders to abjure their base tenures, and swear themselves Freeholders. But this oratory (far different from the balderdash of *Tully* and Dr. *King*, concerning liberty and our country) as the genius of mild ale alone could inspire, this fellow alone could deliver."—The very paper of tobacco, inscribed "*Kirton's* Best," has its peculiar significance. This man was a tobacconist by St. *Dunstan's* Church in *Fleet-street*, and ruined his health and constitution, as well as impaired his circumstances, by being busy in the *Oxfordshire* election of 1754. Plate II. In the painted cloth depending from the sign-post, the height of *The Treasury* is contrasted with the squat solidity of *The Horse-Guards*, where the arch is so low, that the state-coachman cannot pass through it with his head on; and the turret on the top is so drawn as to resemble a beer-barrel. *Ware* the architect very gravely remarked, on this occasion, that the chief defect would have been sufficiently pointed out by making the coachman only stoop. He was hurt by *Hogarth's* stroke of satire. Money is likewise thrown from *The Treasury* windows, to be put into a waggon, and carried into the country. *George Alexander Stevens*, in his celebrated "Lecture on Heads," exhibited the man with a pot of beer, explaining, with pieces of a tobacco-pipe, how *Porto Bello* was taken with six ships only. In Plate III. Dr. *Shebbeare*, with fetters on, is prompting the idiot; and in Plate IV. the old Duke of *Newcastle* appears at a window. A happy parody in the last of these plates may, perhaps, have escaped the notice of common observers. *Le Brun*, in his battle of the *Granicus*, has represented an eagle hovering above the laurel'd helmet of *Alexander*. *Hogarth* has painted a goose flying over the periwig'd head of the successful candidate. During the contested *Oxfordshire* election in 1754, an outrageous mob in the Old Interest had surrounded a post-chaise, and was about to throw it into the river; when Captain T——, within-side, shot a chimney-sweeper who was most active in the assault. The captain was tried and acquitted. To this fact *Hogarth* is supposed to allude in the Monkey riding on the Bear, with a cockade in his hat, and a carbine by his side, which goes off and kills the little sweep, who has clambered up on the wall. The member chaired is said to bear more than an accidental resemblance to Mr. *Dodington*, afterwards Lord *Melcombe*.

In 1759 appeared "A Poetical Description of Mr. *Hogarth's* Election Prints,[3] in four Cantos. Written under Mr. *Hogarth's* sanction and inspection," which I shall with the less scruple transcribe at large below,[4] as it was originally introduced by the following remarkable advertisement, dated *Cheapside, March 1*, 1759. "For the satisfaction of the reader, and in justice to the concealed author, I take the liberty, with the permission of Mr. *Hogarth*, to insert in this manner that gentleman's opinion of the following Cantos, which is, 'That the thoughts entirely coincide with his own; that there is a well-adapted vein of humour preserved through the whole; and that, though some of his works have been formerly explained by other hands, yet none ever gave him so much satisfaction as the present performance.' JOHN SMITH."

In the second state of the first of these plates few variations are discoverable. The perspective in the oval over the stag's horns is improved. A shadow on the wainscot, proceeding from a supposed window on the left side, is effaced; the hand of the beldam kissing the young candidate, is removed from under her apron, and now dangles by her side: a saltseller is likewise missing from the table. In the first impression also, the butcher who is pouring gin on the broken head of another man, has *For our Country* on his cockade; in the second we find *Pro Patria* in its stead. The lemons and oranges that once lay on a paper, by the tub in which the boy is making punch, are taken away; because *Hogarth*, in all probability, had been informed that vitriol, or cream of tartar, is commonly used, instead of vegetable acids, when a great quantity of such liquor is prepared at public houses on public occasions. In the third impression a hat is added to those before on the ground, and another on the bench. The whole plate has also lost much of its former clearness. The original inscription at one corner of it was—"Painted, and *the whole* engraved by *Wm. Hogarth*."[5] The two Words in *Italicks* were afterwards effaced.

I may here observe, that this performance, in its original state, is by far the most finished and laborious of all *Hogarth's* engravings. Having been two years on sale (from 1755 to 1757) it was considerably worn before the publication of Plate the second; and was afterwards touched and retouched till almost all the original and finer traces of the burin were either obliterated or covered by succeeding ones. In short, there is the same difference between the earliest and latest impressions, as there was between the first and second state of Sir *John Cutler's* stockings, which, by frequent mending, from silk degenerated into worsted.

I learn also, on the best authority, that our artist, who was always fond of trying to do what no man had ventured to do before him, resolved to finish this plate without taking a single proof from it as he proceeded in his operation. The consequence of his temerity was, that he almost spoiled his performance. When he discovered his folly, he raved, stamped, and swore he was ruined, nor could be prevailed on to think otherwise, till his passion subsided, and a brother artist assisted him in his efforts to remedy the general defect occasioned by such an attempt to perform an impossibility.

In Plate II. we meet with a fresh proof of our artist's inattention to orthography; *Party-tool* (used as a proper name) being here spelt parti-tool. This plate was engraved by *C. Grignion*, and has been retouched, as the upper-row of the lion's teeth are quite obliterated in the second impression.

Plate III. The militia (or, as *Hogarth* spells it, milicia) bill appearing out of the pocket of the maimed voter, is only found in the second impression. This print was engraved by *Hogarth* and *Le Cave*.[6]

The dead man, whom they are bringing up as a voter, alludes to an event of the same kind that happened during the contested election between *Bosworth* and *Selwyn*. "Why," says one of the clerks, "you have brought us here a dead man."—"Dead!" cries the bringer; "dead as you suppose him, you shall soon hear him vote for *Bosworth*." On this, a thump was given to the body, which, being full of wind, emitted a sound that was immediately affirmed to be a distinct, audible, and good vote for the candidate already mentioned.—This circumstance, however, might have reference to the behaviour of the late Dr. *Barrowby*, who persuaded a dying patient he was so much better, that he might venture with him in his chariot to go and poll for Sir *George Vandeput* in *Covent-Garden*. The unhappy voter took his physician's advice, but expired in an hour after his return from the hustings. "If *Hogarth*," says Mr. *Walpole*, "had an emblematic thought, he expressed it with wit, rather than by a symbol. Such is that of the whore setting fire to the world in *The Rake's Progress*. Once indeed he descended to use an allegoric personage, and was not happy in it.

In one of his Election prints [plate III.] *Britannia's* chariot breaks down, while the coachman and footman are playing at cards on the box."

In the second impressions of Plate IV.[7] (which was engraved by *W. Hogarth* and *F. Aviline*) the shadow on the sun-dial, denoting the hour, and the word indintur (commonly spelt indenture) on the scroll hanging out at the attorney's window, are both added. The fire from the gun is also continued farther; the bars of the church-gate are darkened; and the upper sprigs of a tree, which were bare at first, are covered with leaves.

By these marks, the unskilful purchaser may distinguish the early from the later impressions. I forbear therefore to dwell on more minute variations. The ruined house adjoining to the attorney's, intimating that nothing can thrive in the neighbourhood of such vermin, is a stroke of satire that should not be overlooked.

The publick were so impatient for this set of prints, that *Hogarth* was perpetually hastening his coadjutors, changing some, and quarrelling with others. Three of the plates therefore were slightly executed, and soon needed the reparations they have since received.

The following curious address appeared in the *Public Advertiser* of *Feb.* 28, 1757.

"Mr. *Hogarth* is obliged to inform the subscribers to his Election Prints, that the three last cannot be published till about *Christmas* next, which delay is entirely owing to the difficulties he has met with to procure able hands to engrave the plates; but that he neither may have any more apologies to make on such an account, nor trespass any further on the indulgence of the public by encreasing a collection already sufficiently large, he intends to employ the rest of his time in portrait-painting; chiefly this notice seems more necessary, as several spurious and scandalous prints[8] have lately been published in his name.

"All Mr. *Hogarth's* engraved works are to be had at his house in *Leicester-fields*, separate or together; as also his Analysis of Beauty, in 4to. with two explanatory prints, price 15*s*. With which will be delivered gratis, an eighteen-penny pamphlet published by *A. Miller*, called *The Investigator*, written in opposition to the principles laid down in the above Analysis of Beauty, by *A. R.*,[9] a friend to Mr. *Hogarth*, an eminent portrait-painter now of *Rome*."

The foregoing advertisement appears to have been written during the influence of a fit of spleen or disappointment, for nothing else could have dictated to our artist so absurd a resolution as that of quitting a walk he had trod without a rival, to re-enter another in which he had by no means distinguished himself from the herd of common painters.

[1] I learn from *The Grub-street Journal* for *June* 13, 1734, that the same subject had been attempted by an earlier hand, under the title of *The Humours of a Country Election*. The description of some of the compartments of this work (which I have not seen) bears particular resemblance to the scenes represented by *Hogarth*. "The candidates very complaisant to a *Country Clown*, &c."—"The candidates making an entertainment for the electors and their wives.—At the upper end of the table the *Parson* of the Parish, &c."

[2] The intimate friend of *Hogarth*, at that time a Commissioner of the Admiralty; afterwards Sir *George Hay*, knight, Dean of the Arches, Judge of the Prerogative Court, and also of the High Court of Admiralty, who died *October* 6, 1778, aged 63. He was possessed of several of *Hogarth's* paintings, which are now the property of Mr. *Edwards*, and have been mentioned in p. 98. Our honourable Judge has the following character in a work of great authority.

On the trial of her Grace the Duchess of *Kingston*, for bigamy, before the House of Lords, in *April* 1776, the present Lord Chancellor *Thurlow* (then Attorney-General) thus speaks of Sir *George* as a judge:—"The most loose and unconsidered notion, escaping in any manner from that able and excellent judge, should be received with respect, and certainly will; if the question were my own, with the choice of my court, I should refer it to his decision." State Trials, XI. 221.

[3] "Things unattempted yet in prose or rhime." MILTON.

[4]

    CANTO I.
The HUMOURS *of an* ELECTION ENTERTAINMENT.
Oh, born our wonder to engage!
HOGARTH, thou mirror of the age!
Permit a Bard, though screen'd his name,
To court the sanction of your fame;
Pursue your genius, taste, and art,
And knowledge of the human heart:
Just as your pencil, could my pen
But trace the various ways of men;
Express the tokens of the mind,
The humours, follies, of mankind;
Then might Thyself this verse regard,
Nor deem beneath the task the bard:
Yet, though unfit, perhaps unknown,
I supplicate thy aid alone:
Let others all the Nine inspire,
Do Thou, O *Hogarth*, tune my lyre!

Let o'er my thoughts thy spirit shine,
And thy vast fancy waken mine:
I feel the genuine influence now!
It glows!—my great *Apollo* Thou!

The Writs are issued:—to the Town
The future Members hasten down;
The merry bells their welcome sound,
And mirth and jollity abound,
The gay retinue now comes in,
The crouds, with emulative din,
Proclaim th' arrival, rend the sky,
And *Court* and *Country's* all the cry.
Each joyous house, of free access,
For patriot plebeians, more or less,
Is now reveal'd, in printed bills;
So quacks contrive to vend their pills.
So *Bayes* makes Earth, and Sun, and Moon,
Discourse melodiously in tune;
And, full of wit and complaisance,
Cry, "First of all we'll have a dance!"
So at Elections 'tis discreet
Still first of all to have a treat;
The pulse of every man to try,
And learn what votes they needs must *buy*;
No freeman well can tell his side,
Unless his belly's satisfied.

Behold the festive tables set,
The Candidates, the Voters met!
And lo, against the wainscot plac'd,
Th' escutcheon, with three guineas grac'd,
The motto and the crest explain,
Which way the gilded bait to gain.
There *William's* mangled portrait tells
What rage in party bosoms dwells;
And here the banner speaks the cry
For "Liberty and Loyalty."
While scratches dignify his face,
The tipsy Barber tells his case;
How well he for his Honour fought!
How many devilish knocks he got!
While, forc'd to carry on the joke,

The 'Squire's just blinded with the smoke;
And gives his hand (for all are free)
To one that's cunninger than he:
With smart cockade, and waggish laugh,
He thinks himself more wise by half.
See *Crispin*, and his blouzy *Kate*,
Attack the other Candidate!
What joy he feels her head to lug!
"Well done, my *Katy!* coaxing pug!"
But who is this pray?—*Abel Squatt*—
What has the honest Quaker got?
Why, presents for each voter's lady,
To make their interest sure and steady:
For right and well their Honours know
What things the Petticoat can do.
Discordant sounds now grate the ear,
For music's hir'd to raise the cheer;
And fiddling *Nan* brisk scrapes her strings,
While *Thrumbo's* bass loud echoing rings,
And *Sawney's* bagpipes squeaking trill
"God save the King," or what you will.
Music can charm the savage breast,
And lull the fiercest rage to rest;
But *Sawney's* face bespeaks it plain,
That vermin don't regard the strain;
A creature, well to *Scotchmen* known,
Now nips him by the collar-bone:
Ah, luckless louse! in ambush lie,
Or, by St. *Andrew*, you must die!

Ye vers'd in men and manners! tell
Why Parsons always eat so well!
Catch they the spirit from the Gown,
To cram so many plate-fulls down?
The feast is o'er with all the rest,
But Mayor and Parson still contest:
I'll hold a thousand!—Lay the bett—
The odds are on the Parson yet:
Huzza! the Black-gown wins the day!—
The Mayor with oysters dies away!—[A]
But softly, don't exult so fast,
His spirit's noble to the last;
His mouth still waters at the dish;

His hand still holds his favourite fish:
Bleed him the Barber-surgeon wou'd;
He breathes a vein, but where's the blood?
No more it flows its wonted pace,
And chilly dews spread o'er his face:
The Parson sweats; but be it told,
The sweat is more from heat than cold:
"Bring me the chafing-dish!" he cries;
'Tis brought; the savoury fumes arise:
"My last tit-bit's delicious so;
Can oysters vie with venison?"—No.

Behold, through sympathy of face,
(In life a very common case)
His Lordship gives the fidler wine!
"Come, brother *Chinny!* yours and mine:"
And o'er a pretty girl confest,
The Alderman, see! toasts "the best."
Ye hearty cocks! who feel the gout,
Yet briskly push the glass about,
Observe, with crutch behind his chair,
Your honest brother *Chalkstone* there!
His phiz declares he seems to strain;
Perhaps the gravel gives him pain:
But be it either that or this,
One thing is certain—he's at * * * *,
A wag, the merriest in the town,
Whose face was never meant to frown,
See, at his straining makes a scoff!
And, singing, takes his features off;
While clowns, with joy and wonder, stare,
"Gad-zookers! *Roger*, look ye there!"
The busy Clerk the Taylor plies,
"Vote for his Honour, and be wise:
These yellow-boys are all your own!"
But he, with puritanic tone,
Cries, "*Satan!* take thy bribes from me;
Why this were downright perjury!"
His wife, with all-sufficient tongue,
For rage and scandal glibly hung,
Replies, "Thou blockhead! gold refuse,
When here's your child in want of shoes!"

But hark! what uproar strikes the ear!
Th' opposing mob, incens'd, draw near:
Their waving tatter'd ensigns see!
Here "Liberty and Property:"
A label'd *Jew* up-lifted high;
There "Marry all, and multiply."
These, these, are patrotic scenes!
But not a man knows what he means.
The jordan drives their zeal to cool,
With added weight of three-legg'd stool;
But all in vain; and who can't eat,
Now sally out the foe to beat;
For glory be the battle try'd;
Huzza! my boys, the *yellow* side.
Observe the loyal work begin,
And stones and brick-bats enter in!
That knocks a rustic veteran down;
This cracks the Secretary's crown;
His minute-book, of special note,
For every sure, and doubtful vote,
Now tumbles; ink the table dyes,
And backward poor Pill-Garlick lies.
The Butcher, one who ne'er knew dread,
A Surgeon turns for t'other's head;
His own already broke and bound,
Yet with *pro patria* decked around.
Behold what wonders gin can do,
External and internal too!
He thinks a plaster but a jest;
All cure with what they like the best:
Pour'd on, it sooths the patient's pain;
Pour'd in, it makes him fight again.
His toes perchance pop out his shoe,
Yet he's a patriot through and through;
His lungs can for his party roar,
As loud as twenty men, or more.
Ye courtiers! give your *Broughton* praise;
The hero of your eleven days,
'Tis his to trim th'opposers round,
And bring their standard to the ground.
The waiting-boy, astonish'd, eyes
What gin the new-turn'd quack applies;
And fills a tub, that glorious punch

May make amends for blow and hunch.
But stop, my lad, put in no more,
For t'other side are near the door;
Nor will their conscience deem it sin,
To guzzle all, if once they're in.

Reader, perhaps thy peaceful mind
Is not to noise or blood inclin'd;
Then, lest some hurt should happen quick,
For see a sword! and many a stick!
We'll leave this inn, with all my heart,
And hasten to the second part.

CANTO II.
CANVASSING *for* VOTES.
Free'd from the madness of the throng,
Now, gentle Reader, come along;
A broken head's no clever joke—
Sir, welcome to *The Royal Oak*;
Together let us look about——
We'll find that Show-cloth's meaning out.

Satire! 'tis thine, with keenest dart,
To shoot the follies of the heart;
And, issuing from the press or stage,
Reclaim the vain, the culprit age!
From *Rich's* dome, of grand renown,
To thatch-torn barn, in country town;
From *Garrick*, monarch of his art,
To *Punch*, so comical and smart;
Satire delights, in every sphere,
To make men laugh at what they *are*:
"Walk in, the only show in town;
Punch candidate for *Guzzle-down*!"
There see the pile, in modern taste,
On top with tub-like turret grac'd!
Where the cramp'd entrance, like some shed,
Knocks off the royal driver's head;
Lives there a Wit but what will cry,
"An arch so *low* is mighty *high*!"
See from the Treasury flows the gold,
To shew that those who're *bought* are *sold*!
Come, Perjury, meet it on the road,

'Tis all your own; a waggon-load.
Ye party-tools, ye courtier-tribe,
Who gain no vote without a bribe,
Lavishly kind, yet insincere,
Behold in *Punch* yourselves appear!
And you, ye fools, who poll for pay,
Ye little great men of a day;
For whom your favourite will not care,
Observe how much bewitch'd you are!

Yet hush!—for see his Honour near;—
Truly, a pretty amorous leer:
The ladies both look pleasant too;
"Purchase some trinkets of the *Jew*."
One points to what she'd have him buy;
The other casts a longing eye;
And *Shylock*, money-loving soul,
Impatient waits to touch the cole:
But here's a Porter; what's the news?—
Ha, ha, a load of billet-doux!
Humbly to sue th' Electors' favour,
With vows of *Cato*-like behaviour;
And how the Borough he'll espouse,
When once a Member of the House:
Though wiser folks will lay a bet,
His promises he'll then forget.
But pray your Honour condescend
An eye on kneeling *Will* to lend;
Grant to the fair the toys they chuse,
And what the letter says, peruse:
"To *Timothy Parti-tool*, Esquire."—
Your title may in time be higher.

Ha, who stands here?—'Tis Farmer *Rye*,
A man of cunning, by the bye;
In times like this a mighty stirrer,—
Of some small interest in the Borough.
Which side? you ask—the question's well,
But more, as yet, than he can tell.
The *hosts* of either party try;
To both he casts a *knowing* eye.
"Sir, I'm commission'd by the 'Squire—
Your company they all desire:

My house contains near half the town—
'Tis just at hand, Sir;—'tis *The Crown*."
Then t'other cries, "Sure I first spoke—
This inn is mine!—*The Royal Oak*—
Sir, here's his Honour's invitation;
The greatest Patriot in the nation."

Which party shall the voter take,
Since both the same pretentions make?
The same?—sure not—for see each hand!
Aye, now he seems to understand:
The Crown Host fees him o'er his arm;
But t'other tips the stronger charm.
One, two, three, four—the jobb is done—
Troth, cunning *Fatty*, you have won;
Success in that sly glance is shown;
The honest Farmer's all your own:
But don't exult; for, being loth
To disoblige, he takes from both.

Oh, *Britain*! favourite Isle of Heaven,
When to thy Sons shall Peace be given?
The treachery of the *Gallic* shore
Makes even thy wooden lions roar.
That royal beast, who many a league
At sea hath sail'd with vengeance big!
And oft has scar'd the hostile coast,
Tho' fix'd in *Inn-Yard*, like a post,
Still keeps his furious power in use;
Devouring of the *Flower-de-luce*.
How certain those expanded paws!
How dreadful those extended jaws!
Behind him sits the Hostess fair,
Counting her cash with earned care;
While at the door the Grenadier
Inspects her with a cunning leer;
As who should say, "When we're alone,
Some part of that will be my own!"

But who are those two in the Bar?
Guttlers I fancy—that they are;
The fowl to Him's a noble feast;
He sure makes mouths, to mock the beast;

And t'other hopes to find relief,
By eating half the round of beef.

From *George*, who wears the *British* crown,
To the remotest country clown,
The love of politics extends,
And oft makes foes of nearest friends.
The Cobler and the Barber there,
That born to frown, and this to stare,
Both positive, you need not doubt,
Will argue till they both fall out.

"Well," says the Tonsor, "now we'll try,
Who's in the right, yourself or I:
One moment let your tongue be still,
Or else be judg'd by *Johnny Hill*:
Vernon he thought a glorious fellow,
Which made him put up *Porto Bello*.
I'll teach you reason, if I can—
I should though shave the Gentleman;
But never mind it, let him wait;—
These bits of pipe the case shall state"—

"Drink," cries the Cobler, "I'm adry;
Pshaw, damn your nonsense, what care I?
I told you first, and all along,
I'll lay this cole you're in the wrong;
I hope his worship will excuse,
I should, though, carry home his shoes."

"Well, well," the Barber makes reply,
"Election-time puts business by:
Only six ships our Admiral had;
A very slender force, egad;
What then? our dumplings gave them sport:—
Here stood one castle; there the fort."—

"'Sblood," cries the Cobler, "go to school,
You half-learn'd, half-starv'd, silly fool!
I tell you, Barber, 'tis not true;
Sure I can see as much as you."

But hark, what noise our ears assails!

A distant, loud huzza, prevails;
Ha, ha, they're at their wonted sport;
That was a gun, by the report:
Behold the rabble at *The Crown*!
"Damn, damn, th' Excise; we'll have it down."
And all the while, poor simple elves,
They little think 'twill crush themselves.
Danger again may wait our stay,
So, courteous Reader, come away.

CANTO III.
POLLING *at the* HUSTINGS.
Swift, reverend wag, *Ierne's* pride,
Who lov'd the comic rein to guide,
Has told us, "Gaolers, when they please,
Let out their flock, to rob for fees."
From this sage hint, in needful cases,
The wights, who govern other places,
Let out their crew, for private ends,
Ergo, to serve themselves and friends.
Behold, here gloriously inclin'd,
The Sick, and Lame, the Halt, and Blind!
From Workhouse, Gaol, and Hospital,
Submiss they come, true Patriots all!

But let's get nearer, while we stay,—
Good Master Constable, make way!
"Hoi! keep the passage clear and fair;—
I'll break your shins!—stand backward there;
What! won't you let the Pollers come:"—
Reader, they think us so—but *mum*.

Now praise and prejudice expand,
In printed bills, from hand to hand;
One tells, the 'Squire's a man of worth;
Generous and noble from his birth:
Another plainly makes appear,
"Some circumstance, in such a year."
The voice of Scandal's sure to wait,
Or true, or false, each Candidate.
Observe the waving flags applied,
To let Free-holders know their side!
Hark, at each vote exult the crew!

"*Yellow!* Huzza!—Huzza! the *Blue!*"

Whoe'er has walk'd through *Chelsea* town,
Which Buns and Charity renown,
Has many a College Veteran seen,
With scar-seam'd face, and batter'd mien,
But here's a theme for future story!
Survey that Son of *Mars* before ye!
Was ever Pensioner like him?—
What, almost robb'd of every limb!
Only one arm, one leg, one thigh;
Gods! was that man design'd to die?
Inspect his ancient, war-like face!
See, with what surly, manly grace,
He gives the Clerk to understand
His meaning, with his wooden hand!
Perhaps in *Anna's* glorious days,
His courage gain'd immortal praise:
Britons, a people brave and rough,
That time lov'd fighting well enough;
And, glad their native land to aid,
Leg-making was a thriving trade;
But now we from ourselves depart,
And war's conducted with new art;
Our Admirals, Generals, learn to run,
And Leg-makers are all undone.
Still he's an open, hearty blade,
Pleas'd with his sword, and gay cockade:
Unbrib'd he votes; and 'tis his pride;
He always chose the honest side.
You think he seems of man but half,
But, witty Clerk, suppress your laugh;
His heart is in its usual place,
And that same hook may claw your face.
How learnedly that Lawyer pleads!
"A vote like this, Sir, ne'er succeeds;
The naked hand should touch the book;
Observe h'as only got a hook."
"Sir," cries the other, "that's his hand;"
(Quibbles, like you, I understand)
"And be it either flesh or wood,
By Heavens! his vote is very good."
Wise Counsellor! you reason right,

You'll gain undoubted credit by't;
But please to turn your head about,
And find that Idiot's meaning out;
Dismiss the Whisperer from his chair,
'Tis quite illegal, quite unfair;
Though shackles on his legs are hung,
Those shackles can't confine his tongue;
Methinks I hear him tell the Nisey,
"Be sure to vote as I advise ye;
My writings shew I'm always right;
The nation sinks; we're ruin'd quite
America's entirely lost;
The *French* invade our native coast;
Our Ministers won't keep us free;——
You know all this as well as me.
All men of parts are out of place;
'Tis mine, 'tis many a wise man's case;
And though so *Cato*-like I write,
I ne'er shall get a farthing by't."
Good Clerk, dispatch them quick, I pray:
How easy fools are led astray!
He thinks th' insinuation's true,
As all the race of Idiots do.
But who comes here? Ha, one just dead,
Ravish'd from out th' infirmary's bed;
Through racking follies sad and sick,
Yet to the cause he'll ever stick;
Tie the groat favour on his cap,
And die True Blue, whate'er may hap.

Oh, Vice! through life extends thy reign:
When Custom fixes thy domain,
Not *Wesley's* cant, nor *Whitfield's* art,
Can chace thee from th' envelop'd heart!
Behold that wretch! whom *Venus* knows
Has in her revels lost his nose;
Still with that season'd Nurse he toys;
As erst indulges sensual joys;
Can drink, and crack a bawdy joke,
And still can quid, as well as smoke.
But, Nurse, don't smile so in his face;
Sure this is not a proper place;
Take from your duggs his hand away,

And mind your sick-charge better, pray;
Consider, if his faithful side
Should hear that in their cause he died,
They'd be so much enrag'd, I vow,
They'd punish you!—the Lord knows how.
Beside, you take up too much room,
That boy-led Blind-man wants to come;
And 'scap'd from wars, and foreign clutches,
An Invalid's behind on crutches.

The man whose fortune suits his wish,
A glutton at each favourite dish;
Who, when o'er venison, ne'er will spare it,
And washes down some rounds with claret;
That man will have a portly belly,
And be of consequence, they tell ye;
Grandeur shall 'tend his air and gait,
And make him like—that Candidate:
Observe him on the hustings sit!
Fatigu'd, he sweats, or seems to sweat;
Scratching his pate, with shook-back wig,
And puffs, and blows, extremely big:
Perhaps that paper hints about
Votes, whose legality's a doubt;
And will by scrutiny be try'd,
Unless they're on the proper side.
Stiff as if *Rackstraw*,[B] fam'd for skill,
For genius, taste, or what you will,
With temper'd plaister, stood in haste,
From his set face to form the cast;
Resting on oak-stick stedfastly,
The other would-be Member see!
Struck with his look, so fix'd and stout,
That Wag resolves to sketch it out;
Laughing, they view the pencil'd phiz.—
"'Tis very like him—that it is."
Hark to yon hawker with her songs!
"The Gallows shall redress our wrongs!"
I warrant, wrote in humourous style;
The hearers laugh; the readers smile.
And lo, although so thick the rout,
They've room to push the glass about!
Variety her province keeps;

One Beadle watches; t'other sleeps.

But see that chariot! who rides there?
Britannia, Sir, a lady fair:
To her celestial charms are given;
Ador'd on earth, beloved in heaven;
Her frown makes nations dread a fall;
Her smile gives joy and life to all.
Too generous, merciful, and kind;
Her Servants won't their duty mind;
Neither their Mistress' call regards;
Their study's how to cheat at cards;
The reins of power, oh, indiscreet!
They trample, careless, under feet;
Th' unguided coursers neigh and spurn,
And ah, the car must overturn!
Just gods, forbid!—there's comfort yet!
For, lo, how near that saving PITT!
Sure Heaven design'd her that resource,
To stop her venal servants course;
Her peace and safety to restore,
And keep from dangers evermore.

Ha! see, yon distant cavalcade!
Exulting crowds, and flags display'd!
Let's to the bridge our foot-steps bend—
So cheek by jole, along, my friend.

CANTO IV.
CHAIRING *the* MEMBERS.
"Huzza! the Country! not the Court!"—.
Your Honour can't have better sport;
In old arm-chair aloft you soar—
No Candidate can wish for more.
Th' election's got, the day's your own,
And be to all their member known!

Ye Moths of an exalted size!
Ye sage Historians, learn'd and wise!
Who pore on leaves of old tradition;
Vers'd in each prætor exhibition;
Tell me if, 'midst the spoils of age,
And relicks of the moulder'd page,

You e'er found why this aukward state
Must 'tend the man who'd fain be great!
When *Alexander*, Glory's son,
Enter'd in triumph *Babylon*,
Hear ancient annals make confession,
How aggrandiz'd was his procession!
But this is *Skymington*, I trow!——
Yet Time proclaims *We must*[C] do so.
It sure was meant to make folks stare,
"Like cloths hung out at country fair:
Where painted monsters rage and grin,
To draw the gaping bumpkins in."[D]
Minerva's sacred bird's an owl;
Our candidate's, behold, a fowl!
From which we readily suppose
(As now his generous Honour's chose)
His voice he'll in the Senate use;
And cackle, cackle, like—a goose.

But, hark ye! you who bear this load
Of patriot worth along the road,
Methinks you make his Honour lean;
Be careful, Sirs!—Zounds! what d' ye mean?
Off flies his hat, back leans his chair,
And dread of falling makes him stare.
His Lady, fond to see him ride,
With Nurse and *Black-moor* at her side,
In church-yard stands to view the sight,
And at his danger's in a fright.
"Alack, alack, she faints away!"
"The hartshorn, *Ora*—quick, I say!"
See, at yon house th' opposing party
Enjoy the joke, with laughter hearty!
"Well done, my boys—now let him fall;
Here's gin and porter for you all!"

But let's find whence this came about:
Ha, lo, that Thresher bold and stout!
How, like a hero, void of dread,
He aims to crack that sailor's head!
While, with the purchase of the stroke,
Behind, the bearer's pate is broke:
The sailor too resolves to drub,

Wrathful he sways the ponderous club;
Who to stir up his rage shall dare?
He'll fight for ever—for his Bear.

Sir *Hudibras* agreed, Bear-baiting
Was carnal, and of man's creating;
But, had he like that Thresher done,
I'll hold a wager, ten to one,
His knighthood had not kept him safe;
That Tar had trimm'd both him and *Ralph*.

In fighting *George's* glorious battles,
To save our liberties and chattels;
Commanded by some former *Howe*,
Ordain'd to make proud *Gallia* bow,
A cannon-ball took off his leg:
What then? he scorns, like some, to beg;
That muzzled beast is taught to dance,
That Ape to ape the beaux of *France*;
The countryfolks admire the sport,
And small collections pay him for't.
Sailors and Soldiers ne'er agree;—
There's difference twixt the Land and Sea;
He, willing not a jest shall 'scape,
In uniform riggs out his Ape:—
From which we reasonably infer
An Ape may be an Officer.
But, hey-day! more disasters still?
Turn quick thy head, bold sailor *Will*.
In vain that fellow, on his Ass,
Attempts to Hogs at home to pass,
The hungry Bear, who thinks no crime
To feast on guts at any time,
Arrests the garbage in the tub,
And with his snout begins to grub.
Pray is it friendly, honest brother,
That one Ass thus should ride another?
The beast seems wearied with his toil,
And, like the bear, would munch a while.
The good wife thought that every pig
Should in the wash, then coming, swig;
And went industriously to find
Her family of the hoggish kind;

But, oh, unhappy fate to tell!
Behind the Thresher down she fell:
Indeed the wonder were no more,
Had she, by chance, fall'n down before:
Away the sow affrighted runs,
Attended by her little ones:
Those gruntings to each other sounding;
This squeaking shrill, through fear of drowning.

"The lamb thou doom'st to bleed to-day,
Had he thy reason, wou'd he play?"[E]
And did that Bear know he'd be beat,
Would he from out that firkin eat?
The Ass's rider lifts his stick;
Take out your nose, old *Bruin*, quick;
A grin of vengeance arms his face,
Presaging torture, and disgrace.
The Ape, who dearly loves to ride
On *Bruin's* back, in martial pride,
Dejected at the sad occasion,
Looks up, with soft commiseration;
As if to speak, "Oh, spare my friend!
Avert that blow you now intend!"
'Tis complaisant, good-natur'd too;—
Much more than many Apes would do.

Observe the chimney-sweepers, there!
On gate-post, how they laugh and stare;
Those bones, and emblematic skull,
Have no effect to make them dull;
Pleas'd they adorn the death-like head
With spectacles of gingerbread.

When *London* city's bold train-band[F]
March, to preserve their track of land,
Each val'rous heart the *French* defying,
While drums are beating, colours flying,
How many accidents resound
From *Tower-hill* to th' *Artillery-ground!*
Perhaps some hog, in frisky pranks,
Unluckily breaks through their ranks,
And makes the captain storm and swear,
To *form* their soldiers, *as they were*:

Or else the wadding, which they ram,
Pop into some one's ear they jam;
Or not alert at gun and sword,
When their commander gives the word
To fire, amidst the dust and clamour,
Forget to draw their desperate rammer;
And one or two brave comrades hit,
As cooks fix larks upon a spit.
That Monkey's sure not of the reg'ment,
Yet still his arms should have abridgement;
The little, aukward, martial figure,
Will wriggle till he pulls the trigger:
'Tis done—and see the bullet fly!—
Pop down, you rogue! or else you'll die.

Survey, as merry as a grig,
The Fiddler dancing to his jig!
No goat, by good St. *David* rear'd,
Could ever boast more length of beard:
'Tis his to wait on Master *Bruin*,
And tune away to all he's doing;
You think this strange, but 'tis no more,
Than *Orpheus* did in days of yore;
With modern fiddlers so it fares;
They often scratch to dancing-bears.
He took to scraping in his prime,
And plays in tune, as well as time;
Elections cheer his merry heart;
Sure always then to *play* his *part*:
In toping healths as great a soaker
As executing *Ally Croaker*.
Tho' some Musicians scarce can touch
The strings, if drunk a glass too much;
Yet he'll tope ale, or stout *October*,
And scrape as well when drunk, as sober.

Lo, on yon stone which shows the way.
That travellers mayn't go astray;
And tells how many miles they lag on,
From *London*, in the drawling waggon,
A Soldier sits, in naked buff!
In troth, Sir, this is odd enough!
His head bound up, his sword-blade broken,

And flesh with many a bloody token,
Declare he fought extremely well;
But which had best on't, who can tell?
If he were victor, 'tis confest,
To be so maul'd makes bad the best:
What though he smart, he likes the jobb;
'Tis *great* to head a party-mob.
But what reward for all he did?—
Oh, Sir, he'll never want a—*quid*.

There's somewhat savory in the wind—
Those Courtiers, Friend, have not yet din'd:
Their true ally, grave *Puzzle-cause*,
A man right learned in the laws,
(Whose meagre clerk below can't venture,
And wishes damn'd the long indenture),
As custom bids, prepares the dinner,
For, though they've lost, yet he's the winner.
See, the domestic train appear!
Old *England* bringing up the rear!
Curse on their stomachs, who can't brook
Good *English* fare, from *English* cook!
Observe lank Monsieur, in amaze,
Upon the valiant soldier gaze!
"Morbleu! you love de fight, ve see,
But dat is no de dish for ve."
Behold, above, that azure garter—
Look, now he whispers, like a tartar;
By button fast he holds the other,
The lost election makes a pother.
"All this parade is idle stuff—
We know our interest well enough—
We still support what we espouse;
We'll bring the matter in the *House*."

Of some wise man, perhaps philosopher,
(If not, it flings the vice a gloss over)
I've read, who, Maudlin-like, would cry
Soon as he 'ad drunk his barrel dry:
Yon fellow, certain as a gun,
Of that Philosopher's a Son:
Long as the pot the beer could scoop,
He scorn'd, like swine, to trough to stoop;

But, now 'tis shallow, kneels devout,
Eager to suck the last drop out.
Vociferous Loyalty's a-dry,
And, lo, they bear a fresh supply!
That all the mob may roar applause,
And know they'll never starve the cause.

When grey-mare proves the better horse,
The man is mis'rable of course;
That Taylor leads a precious life—
Look at the termagant his wife,
She pays him sweetly o'er the head;—
"Get home, you dog, and get your bread;
Shall I have nothing to appear in,
While you get drunk electioneering?"

See from the Town-hall press the crowd,
While rustic Butchers ring aloud!
There, lo, their cap of liberty!
Here t'other side in effigy!
A notable device, to call
The Courtier party blockheads all:
Aloft True-Blue, their ensign, flies,
And acclamations rend the skies.
Reflect, my friend, and judge from thence.
How idle this extreme expence;
What mighty sums are thrown away,
To be the pageant of the day!
In vain Desert implores protections;
The Rich are fonder of Elections.
Th' ambitious Peer, the Knight, the 'Squire,
Can buy the Borough they desire;
Yet see, with unassisting eye,
Arts fade away, and Genius die.
Tir'd with the applauding, and the sneering,
And all that's styl'd Electioneering,
I think to take a little tour,
And likely tow'rd the *Gallic* shore;
The Muse, to whom we bear no malice,
Invites me to the Gate of *Calais*.[G]
That gate to which a knight of worth,
'Yclep'd *Sir Loin*, of *British* birth,
Advanc'd, though not in hostile plight,

And put their army in a fright.
But more it fits not, here to tell,
So, courteous Reader, fare thee well.

[A] In *The European Magazine* for the month of *Oct.* 1784, appears a letter on the subject of Painting, signed C. I. F. which contains the following extraordinary criticism on the circumstance here described.

"Our own inimitable *Hogarth* has, in some of his latter pieces, grossly violated this rule; and, for the sake of crowding his piece with incidents, has represented what could not happen at all.

"In his representation of an Election Feast, he has placed a man at the end of the table with an oyster still upon his fork, and his fork in his hand, though his coat must have been stripped up from his arm after he took it up, by the surgeon, who has made an ineffectual attempt to let him blood. Supposing gluttony to have so far absorbed all the persons present, even at the end of a feast, as that none of them should pay the least attention to this incident, which is, if not impossible, improbable in the highest degree, they must necessarily have been alarmed at another incident that is represented as taking place at the same moment: a great stone has just broke through the window, and knocked down one of the company, who is exhibited in the act of falling; yet every one is represented as pursuing his purpose with the utmost tranquillity."

I must entreat my reader to examine the print, before I can expect belief, when I assure him, that for this criticism there is not the slightest foundation.—The magistrate is bled in the right arm, which is bared for that purpose, by stripping the coat-sleeve from it.—It is in his left hand that he holds the fork with the oyster on it, his coat-sleeve being all the while on his left arm.—As to the attention of the company, it is earnestly engaged by different objects; and *Hogarth* perhaps designed to insinuate that accidents, arising from repletion or indigestion, are too common at election dinners to attract notice or excite solicitude.—The brickbat has not noisily forced its way through a window, but was thrown in at a casement already open; and a moment must have elapsed before an event so instantaneous could be perceived in an assembly, every individual of which had his distinct avocation. Of this moment our artist has availed himself. Till, therefore, the accident was discovered, he has, with the utmost propriety, left every person present to pursue his former train of thought or amusement.

[B] The ingenious artist in *Fleet-street*, well known to the learned and ingenious, by his excellence in taking Busts from the Life, and casts from Anatomical Dissections.

[C] See the Dial in Plate IV.

[D] See the Prologue to a farce called "The Male Coquette."

[E] See *Pope's* Essay on Man.

[F] This passage will, perhaps, be better illustrated by the following paragraph, printed in a daily paper called "The Citizen:"—"*Saturday* last, being the first day of *August* Old Stile, the Artillery Company marched according to custom once in three years (called *Barnes's March*, by which they hold an estate): they went to Sir *George Whitmore's*, and took a dunghill. As they were marching through *Bunhill-Row*, a large hog ran between a woman's legs and threw her down, by which accident the ranks were broke, which put the army in the utmost confusion before they could recover."

[G] See above, p. 295.

[5] The *earliest impressions* of this plate in its second state, have the same inscription.

[6] *Morellon Le Cave.* Mr. *Walpole*, in his catalogue of *English* engravers, (octavo edit.) professes to know no more of this artist than that he was "a scholar of *Picart*" and "did a head of Dr. *Pococke* before *Twells's* edition of the Doctor's works." In the year 1739, however, he engraved *Captain Coram*, &c. at the head of the Power of Attorney, &c. (a description of which see p. 254. of the present work) and afterwards was *Hogarth's* coadjutor in this third of his Election plates. At the bottom of it he is only styled *Le Cave*.

[7] Some of these scenes having been reversed by the engraver, the figures in them are represented as using their left hands instead of their right.

[8] Query, what were the scandalous prints to which he alludes?

[9] This *A. R.* was *Allan Ramsay*, but having never met with his performance, I can give no account of it.

1756.

1. *France* and *England*, two plates; both etched by himself. Under them are the following verses, by Mr. *Garrick*:

>PLATE I. FRANCE.
>With lanthern jaws, and croaking gut,
>See how the half-starv'd *Frenchmen* strut,
>And call us *English* dogs!
>But soon we'll teach these bragging foes,
>That beef and beer give heavier blows
>Than soup and roasted frogs.

The priests, inflam'd with righteous hopes,
Prepare their axes, wheels, and ropes,
To bend the stiff-neck'd sinner;
But, should they sink in coming over,
Old Nick may fish 'twixt *France* and *Dover*,
And catch a glorious dinner.

PLATE II. ENGLAND.
See *John* the Soldier, *Jack* the Tar,
With sword and pistol arm'd for war,
Should Mounseer dare come here!
The hungry slaves have smelt our food,
They long to taste our flesh and blood,
Old *England's* beef and beer!

Britons, to arms! and let 'em come,
Be you but *Britons* still, Strike home,
And lion-like attack 'em;
No power can stand the deadly stroke
That's given from hands and hearts of oak,
With Liberty to back 'em.

2. The Search Night, a copy. *J. Fielding sculp*. 21*st* March, 1756.[1] "*A very bad print, and I believe an imposition.*" On this plate are sixteen stupid verses, not worth transcribing. It was afterwards copied again in two different sizes in miniature, and printed off on cards, by *Darly*, in 1766. The original, in a small oval, was an impression taken from the top of a silver tobacco-box; engraved by *Hogarth* for one Captain *Johnson*, and never meant for publication.

[1] There is also a copy of this print, engraved likewise by *Fielding*, and dated *August* 11, 1746.

1758.

1. His own portrait,[1] sitting, and painting the Muse of Comedy; Head profile, in a cap. The Analysis of Beauty on the floor. *W. Hogarth, serjeant-painter to his Majesty.* The face engraved by *W. Hogarth*.

I should observe, that when this plate was left with the person employed to furnish the inscription, he, taking the whole for the production of our artist, wrote "Engraved by *W. Hogarth*" under it. *Hogarth*, being conscious that the face only had been touched by himself, added, with his own hand, "*The Face*" Engraved, &c.

In the second impression "The Face Engraved by *W. Hogarth*" is totally omitted.

In the third impression "Serjeant-painter, &c." is scratched over by the burin, but remains still sufficiently legible.

The fourth impression has "*the face retouched, but not so like as the preceding.*[2] *Comedy also has the face and mask marked with black,*[3] *and inscribed,* COMEDY, 1764. *No other inscription but his name,* William Hogarth, 1764."

The original from which this plate is taken, is in Mrs. *Hogarth's* possession at *Chiswick*. A whole-length of herself, in the same size, is its companion. They are both small pictures.

[1] Among the prints bequeathed by the late Mr. *Forrest* to his executor Mr. *Coxe*, is this head cut out of a proof, and touched up with *Indian* ink by *Hogarth*. Mr. *Forrest*, in an inscription on the back of the paper to which it is affixed, observes it was a present to him from Mrs. *Hogarth*.

With these prints are likewise several early impressions from other plates by our artist; and in particular a March to *Finchley* uncommonly fine, and with the original spelling of PRUSIA uncorrected even by a pen. I am told that both the head and this, with other engravings in the collection of the late Mr. *Forrest*, will be sold by auction in the course of the Winter 1786.

[2] i. e. the two first.

[3] So in both the third and fourth impressions.

2. The Bench. Over the top of this plate is written in capitals—CHARACTER. Under it "of the different meaning of the words *Character, Caracatura,* and *Outrè,* in painting and drawing," Then follows a long inscription on this subject. The original painting is in the collection of Mr. *Edwards*.

1759.

1. The Cockpit. *Designed and engraved by W. Hogarth.* In this plate is a portrait of *Nan Rawlins,* a very ugly old woman (commonly called *Deptford Nan,* sometimes the *Duchess of Deptford*), and well remembered at *Newmarket.* She was a famous cock-feeder, and did the honours of the *gentlemen's* ordinary at *Northampton*; while, in return, a single gentleman was deputed to preside at the table appropriated to the *ladies.* The figure with a hump-back, was designed for one *Jackson,* a once noted jockey at *Newmarket.* The blind president is Lord *Albemarle Bertie,* who was a constant attender of this

diversion. His portrait was before discoverable in the crowd round the bruisers in the March to *Finchley*.

By the cockpit laws, any person who cannot, or will not pay his debts of honour, is drawn up in a basket to the roof of the building. Without a knowledge of this circumstance, the shadow of the man who is offering his watch would be unintelligible.

The subject of The Cockpit had been recommended to *Hogarth* so long ago as 1747, in the following lines, first printed in *The Gentleman's Magazine* of that year, p. 292.

> "Where *Dudston's*[1] walks with vary'd beauties shine,
> And some are pleas'd with bowling, some with wine,
> Behold a generous train of Cocks repair,
> To vie for glory in the toils of war;
> Each hero burns to conquer or to die:
> What mighty hearts in little bosoms lie!

> "Come, *Hogarth*, thou whose art can best declare
> What forms, what features, human passions wear,
> Come, with a painter's philosophic sight,
> Survey the circling judges of the fight.
> Touch'd with the sport of death, while every heart
> Springs to the changing face, exert thy art;
> Mix with the smiles of Cruelty at pain
> Whate'er looks anxious in the lust of gain;
> And say, can aught that's generous, just, or kind,
> Beneath this aspect, lurk within the mind?
> Is lust of blood or treasure vice in all,
> Abhorr'd alike on whomsoe'er it fall?
> Are mighty states and gamblers still the same?
> And war itself a cock-fight, and a game?
> Are sieges, battles, triumphs, little things;
> And armies only the game-cocks of kings?
> Which fight, in Freedom's cause, still blindly bold,
> Bye-battles only, and the main for gold?

> "The crested bird, whose voice awakes the morn,
> Whose plumage streaks of radiant gold adorn,
> Proud of his birth, on fair *Salopia's* plain,
> Stalks round, and scowls defiance and disdain.
> Not fiercer looks the proud *Helvetians* wear,
> Though thunder slumbers in the arms they bear:
> Nor *Thracia's* fiercer sons, a warlike race!

Display more prowess, or more martial grace.
But, lo! another comes, renown'd for might,
Renown'd for courage, and provokes the fight.
Yet what, alas! avails his furious mien,
His ruddy neck, and breast of varied green?
Soon thro' his brain the foe's bright weapon flies,
Eternal darkness shades his swimming eyes;
Prostrate he falls, and quivering spurns the ground,
While life indignant issues from the wound.
Unhappy hero, had thy humbler life
Deny'd thee fame by deeds of martial strife,
Still hadst thou crow'd, for future pleasures spar'd,
Th' exulting monarch of a farmer's yard.

"Like fate, alas! too soon th' illustrious prove,
The great by hatred fall, the fair by love;
The wise, the good, can scarce preserve a name,
Expung'd by envy from the rolls of fame.
Peace and oblivion still through life secure,
In friendly glooms, the simple, homely, poor.
And who would wish to bask in glory's ray,
To buy with peace the laurel or the bay?
What tho' the wreath defy the lightning's fire,
The bard and hero in the storm expire.
Be rest and innocence my humbler lot,
Scarce known through life, and after death forgot!"

[1] A gentleman's seat, about a mile from *Birmingham*, fitted up for the reception of company, in imitation of *Vaux-hall Gardens*.

2. A small oval of Bishop *Hoadly*, ætat. 83. *Hogarth pinx. Sherlock sculp.*

1760.

1. Frontispiece to *Tristram Shandy*. Of this plate there are two copies; in the first of which the hat and clock are omitted. *S. Ravenet sculp.* In this plate is the portrait of Dr. *Burton*, of *York*, the Jacobite physician and antiquary, in the character of Dr. *Slop*.

Sterne probably was indebted for these plates (especially the first of them) to the following compliment he had paid our author in the first volume of *Tristram Shandy*. "Such were the outlines of Dr. *Slop's* figure, which, if you have read *Hogarth's Analysis of Beauty*, and, if you have not, I wish you would, you must know, may as certainly be caracatured, and conveyed to the mind by three strokes as three hundred."

2. Frontispiece to *Brook Taylor's* Perspective of Architecture.[1] With an attempt at a new order. *W. Hogarth, July* 1760. *W. Woollet sculp.* Lest any reader should suppose that this idea of forming a new capital out of the Star of St. *George*, the Prince of *Wales's* Feather,[2] and a regal Coronet, was hatched in the mind of *Hogarth* after he had been appointed Serjeant Painter, the following passage in the *Analysis* will prove that many years before he had conceived the practicability of such an attempt: see p. 40. "I am thoroughly convinced in myself, however it may startle some, that a completely new and harmonious order of architecture in all its parts might be produced, &c." Again, p. 46. "Even a capital, composed of the aukward and confined forms of hats and perriwigs, as Fig. 48. Plate I. in a skilful hand might be made to have some beauty." Mr. *S. Ireland* has the original sketch.

[1] Published in two volumes, folio, 1761, by *Joshua Kirby*, Designer in Perspective to his Majesty.—"Here is a curious frontispiece, designed by Mr. *Hogarth*; but not in the same ludicrous style as the former (see p. 333): it were to be wished that he had explained its meaning; for, being symbolical, the meaning of it is not so obvious as the other. To me it conveys the idea, which *Milton* so poetically describes, of the angel *Uriel* gliding down to Paradise on a sun-beam; but the young gentleman has dropped off before he had arrived at his journey's end, with *Palladio's* book of architecture on his knees. A ray of light from the sun, rising over a distant mountain, is directed to a scroll on the ground, on which are two or three scraps of perspective; over which, supported by a large block of stone, is the upper part of a sceptre, broke off; the shaft very obliquely and absurdly inclined, somewhat resembling the *Roman* fasces, and girt above with the Prince of *Wales's* coronet, as an astragal, through which the fasces rise, and swell into a crown, adorned with embroidered stars; this is the principal object, but most vilely drawn. The ray passes through a round temple, at a considerable distance, which is also falsly represented, the curves being for the distance too round, and consequently the diminution of the columns is too great. It appears to pass over a piece of water; on this side the ground is fertile and luxuriant with vegetation, abounding with trees and shrubs; on the other side it is rocky and barren.[A] What is indicated by this seems to be, that, where the arts are encouraged by the rays of royal favour, they will thrive and flourish; but where they are neglected, and do not find encouragement, they will droop and languish." *Malton's* Appendix to his Treatise on Perspective.

[A] The idea of this contrast between fertility and barrenness is an old one. *Hogarth* probably took it from the engraving known by the name of *Raffaelle's Dream.*

[2] Mr. *H. Emlyn* has lately realised this plan, by his Proposals for a new order of architecture, 1781.

3. Mr. *Huggins*. A small circular plate. *Hogarth pinx. Major sculp*. On the left, a bust, inscribed, "IL DIVINO ARIOSTO." "DANTE L'INFERNO, IL PURGATORIO, IL PARADISO." Mr. *Huggins* (of whom see p. 19.) had this portrait engraven, to prefix to his translation of *Dante*, of which no more than a specimen was ever published.

The bust of *Ariosto* was inserted by the positive order of Mr. *Huggins* (after the plate was finished), though much against the judgement of the engraver, who was convinced that a still ground would have shewn the countenance of the person represented to much greater advantage. Mr. *Major's* charge was only three guineas, and yet eleven years elapsed before he received even this trifling acknowledgement for his labour. Dr. *Monkhouse* has the plate.

1761.

1. Frontispiece and tail-piece to the catalogue of pictures exhibited at *Spring Gardens. W. Hogarth inv. C. Grignion sculp*. There is a variation of this print; a *Latin* motto under each in the second edition. In the earliest impressions *obit*, corrected afterwards to *obiit*. The same mark of ignorance, however, remains unamended over the monument of the Judge in the first plate of the *Analysis*.

2. *Time* blackening a picture. Subscription-ticket for his *Sigismunda*. "This, and the preceding tail-piece, are satires on Connoisseurs."

3. The Five Orders of Perriwigs at the Coronation of *George* III.[1] Many of the heads, as well as wigs, were known at the time. The first head of the second row was designed to represent Lord *Melcombe*; and those of Bishops *Warburton, Mawson,* and *Squire,* are found in the groupe. The advertisement annexed, as well as the whole print, is said to have been a ridicule on Mr. *Stewart's* Antiquities of *Athens*, in which, with minute accuracy, are given the measurements of all the members of the *Greek* Architecture. The inscription under the print affords a plentiful crop of false spellings—volumns—advertisment—baso—&c. The second *e* in advertisement was afterwards added on the neck of the female figure just over it. The first and subsequent impressions will be known by this distinction.

[1] A Dissertation on Mr. *Hogarth's* print of the Order of Perriwigs, viz. the Episcopal, Aldermanic, and Lexonic, is printed in *The Beauties of all the Magazines*, 1761, p. 52.

4. Frontispiece to the Farmer's Return from *London*, an Interlude by Mr. *Garrick*,[1] acted at *Drury Lane*. *W. Hogarth delin. J. Basire sculp*. In Mr. *Foster's* collection is a bad copy of this plate, no name, the figures reversed. The original drawing was given to Mr. *Garrick*, and is supposed to be in the possession of his widow at *Hampton*. Mr. *S. Ireland* has a sketch of it. An excellent copy of this plate is sometimes sold as the original.

[1] Mr. *Garrick'* publication was thus prefaced: "The following interlude was prepared for the stage, merely with a view of assisting Mrs. *Pritchard* at her benefit; and the desire of serving so good an actress is a better excuse for its defects, than the few days in which it was written and represented. Notwithstanding the favourable reception it has met with, the author would not have printed it, had not his friend, Mr. *Hogarth*, flattered him most agreeably, by thinking *the Farmer and his Family* not unworthy of a sketch of his pencil. To him, therefore, this trifle, which he has so much honoured, is inscribed, as a faint testimony of the sincere esteem which the writer bears him, both as a man and an artist."

5. Another frontispiece to *Tristram Shandy* (for the second volume). His christening. *F. Ravenet sculp*.

6. The same engraved by *Ryland*. This, as I am informed, was the first, but was too coarsely executed to suit that prepared for the first volume of the same work.

1762.

1. Credulity, Superstition, and Fanaticism. "*Satire on Methodists*." "For deep and useful satire," says Mr. *Walpole*, "the most sublime of all his works."

This print, however, contains somewhat more than a satire on Methodism. *Credulity* is illustrated by the figure of the Rabbit-breeder of *Godalming*, with her supposed progeny galloping from under her petticoats. St. *André's* folly furnished *Hogarth* with matter for one of his latest, as well as one of his earliest performances.

Primâ dicte mihi, summâ dicende Camœnâ.

2. The Times. Plate I. In one copy of this print *Henry* VIII. is blowing the flames; in another Mr. *Pitt* has the same employment: As this design is not illustrated in *Trusler's* Account of *Hogarth's* Works, I shall attempt its explanation, and subjoin, by way of note, a humourous description of it,

which was printed in a news-paper immediately after it's first appearance in the world.[1]

Europe on fire; *France, Germany, Spain,* in flames, which are extending to *Great Britain.* This desolation continued and assisted by Mr. *Pitt,* under the figure of King *Henry* VIII. with bellows increasing the mischief which others are striving to abate. He is mounted on the stilts of the populace. A *Cheshire* cheese depends from his neck, with 3000 *l.* on it. This alludes to what he had said in Parliament—that he would sooner live on a *Cheshire* cheese and a shoulder of mutton, than submit to the enemies of *Great Britain.* Lord *Bute,* attended by *English* soldiers, sailors, and *Highlanders,* manages an engine for extinguishing the flames, but is impeded by the Duke of *Newcastle,* with a wheel-barrow full of *Monitors* and *North Britons,* for the purpose of feeding the blaze. The respectable body under Mr. *Pitt* are the aldermen of *London,* worshiping the idol they had set up; whilst the musical King of *Prussia,* who alone is sure to gain by the war, is amusing himself with a violin amongst his miserable countrywomen. The picture of the *Indian* alludes to the advocates for retaining our *West Indian* conquests, which, it was said, would only increase excess and debauchery. The breaking down of the *Newcastle*-arms, and the drawing up the patriotic ones, refer to the resignation of that noble Duke, and the appointment of his successor. The *Dutchman* smoking his pipe, and a *Fox* peeping out behind him, and waiting the issue; the Waggon, with the treasures of the *Hermione;* the unnecessary marching of the *Militia,* signified by the *Norfolk* jig; the Dove with the olive-branch, and the miseries of war; are all obvious, and perhaps need no explication.

To those already given, however, may be added the following doggrel verses:

> Devouring flames with fury roll
> Their curling spires from Pole to Pole,
> Wide-spreading devastation dire,
> Three kingdoms ready to expire;
> Here realms convulsive pant for breath,
> And quiver in the arms of death.
> Ill-fated isle! *Britannia* bleeds;
> The flames her trait'rous offspring feeds:
> Now, now, they seize her vital parts—
> O save her from his murd'rous arts!
>
> In air exalted high, behold!
> Fierce, noisy, boisterous, and bold,
> Swol'n, like the king of frogs, that fed

On mangled limbs of victims dead,
With larger bellows in his hand,
Than e'er a blacksmith's in the land,
The flames that waste the world to blow,
He points unto the mob below:
'Look, *Britons*, what a bonfire there!
Halloo, be d———'d, and rend the air.'
Aldermen, marrow-bones and cleavers,
Brokers, stock-jobbers, and coal-heavers,
Templars, and knaves of ev'ry station,
The dregs of *London*, and the nation;
Contractors, agents, clerks, and all
Who share the plunder, great and small,
Join in the halloo at his call.
Higher they raise the stilts that bore
The shapeless idol they adore:
He, to increase his weight, had slung
A *Mill-stone* round his neck, which hung
With bulk enormous to the ground,
And adds thereto *Three Thousand Pound*;
That none may dare to say henceforth,
He wanted either weight or worth.
He blows,—the flames triumphant rise,
Devour the earth, and threat the skies.

When lo! in peaceful mien appears,
In bloom of life, and youthful years,
GEORGE, Prince of Men; a smile benign
That goodness looks, prognostic sign
Of soul etherial, seems to bode,
A world's deliv'rer sent from God.
Array'd in Majesty serene,
Like heav'nly spirits when they deign,
In pity to mankind, to come,
And stop avenging judgement's doom;
Behold, and bless! just not too late
T' avert a sinking nation's fate,
He comes, with friendly care to stay
Those flames that made the world their prey.
Born to reform and bless the age,
Fearless of *faction's* madd'ning rage,
Which, with united malice, throngs,
To reap the harvest of our wrongs,

He labours to defeat our foes,
Secure our peace, and ease our woes.
Before him *Faction* dare not shew
Her ghastly face and livid hue,
But back retires to *Temple-Bar*,
Where the spectator sees from far
Many a traitor's head erect,
To shew what traitors must expect.
Upon that *barefac'd* figure look,
With empty scull and full peruke;
For man or statue it might pass;
Cæsar would call't a golden ass.
Behold the vain malicious thing,
Squirting his poison at his king,
And pointing, with infernal art,
Th' envenom'd rancour of his heart.

Higher in parts and place appears
His venal race of Garretteers;
A starving, mercenary tribe,
That sell, for every bidder's bribe,
Their scantling wits to purchase bread
And always drive the briskest trade,
When *Faction* sounds with loudest din,
To bring some new Pretender in.
This tribe from their ærial station,
Deluge with scandal all the nation:
Below contempt, secure from shame,
Sure not to forfeit any fame,
Indifferent what part to choose,
With nothing but their ears to lose.
Not Virtue on a throne can be
From tongues below resentment free.
Of human things such the distraction,
With Liberty we must have Faction.

But look behind the *Temple-gate*,
Near the thick, clumsy, stinking seat,
Where *London's* pageant sits in state;
What wild, ferocious shape is there,
With raging looks and savage air?
Is that the monster without name,
Whom human art could never tame,

From *Indian* wilds of late brought o'er,
Such as no *Briton* saw before?
I mean the monster *P*** presented
To the late King, who quickly sent it,
Among his other beasts of prey,
Safe in a cage with lock and key.
Some said he was of *British* blood,
Though taken in an *Indian* wood.
If he should thus at large remain,
Without a keeper, cage, or chain,
Raging and roaming up and down,
He may set fire to half the town.
Has he not robb'd the *Bank?*—Behold,
In either hand, what bags of gold!
Monsters are dangerous things let loose:
Old *Cambrian*, guard thy mansion-house.

But here, what comes? A loaded car,
Stuff'd, and high pil'd, from *Temple-Bar*.
The labouring wretches hardly move
The load that totters from above.
By their wry faces, and high strains,
The cart some lumpish weight contains.
'*North Britons*—Gentlemen—come, buy,
There's no man sells so cheap as I.
Of the *North Briton* just a score,
And twenty *Monitors* or more,
For just one penny——
North Britons—*Monitors*—come, buy,
There's no man sells so cheap as I.'
'*North Britons! Monitors!* be d———'d!
Is that the luggage you have cramm'd
Into your stinking cart? Be gone,
Or else I'll burn them every one.'
'Good Sir, I'm sure they are not dear,
The paper's excellent, I swear—
You can't have better any where.
Come, feel this sheet, Sir—please to choose—
They're very soft, and fit for use.
All very good, Sir, take my word—
As cheap as any can afford.
The Curate, Sir, Lord! how he'll foam!
He cannot dine 'till we get home.

The Colonel too, altho' he be
So big, so loud, so proud, d'ye see,
Will have his share as well as he.'

While on a swelling sack of cheese
The frugal *Dutchman* sits at ease,
And smokes his pipe, and sees with joy
The flames, that all the world destroy,
Keep at a distance from his bales,
And sure thereby to raise the sales;
Good Mr. *Reynard*, wiser still,
Displays you his superior skill:
Behind the selfish miser's back,
He cuts a hole into the sack,
His paunch well cramm'd, he snugly lies,
And with himself the place supplies;
And now and then his head pops out,
To see how things go round about;
Prepar'd to run, or stand the fire,
Just as occasion may require,
But willing in the sack to stay,
And cram his belly while he may,
Regardless of the babbling town,
And every interest but his own.

On yonder plain behold a riddle,
That mighty warrior with his fiddle,
With sneering nose, and brow so arch,
A-scraping out the *German* march;
Bellona leading up the dance,
With flaming torch, and pointed lance,
And all the *Furies* in her train,
Exulting at the martial strain;
Pale *Famine* bringing up the rear,
To crown with woe the wasteful year.
There's nought but scenes of wretchedness.
Horror and death, and dire distress,
To mark their footsteps o'er the plains,
And teach the world what mighty gains
From *German* victories accrue
To th' vanquish'd and the victors too.
The fidler, at his ease reclin'd,
Enjoys the woes of human kind;

> Pursues his trade, destroys by rules,
> And reaps the spoils of Knaves and Fools.
> * * * * *Multa desunt.*

The first impressions of this print may be known by the following distinction. The smoke just over the Dove is left white; and the whole of the composition has a brilliancy and clearness not to be found in the copies worked off after the plate was retouched.

I am told that *Hogarth* did not undertake this political print merely *ex officio*, but through a hope the salary of his appointment as Serjeant Painter would be increased by such a show of zeal for the reigning Ministry.

He left behind him a second part, on the same subject; but hitherto it has been withheld from the public. The finished Plate is in the possession of Mrs. *Hogarth*.

There seems, however, no reason why this design should be suppressed. The widow of our artist is happily independent of a court; nor can aught relative to the politics of the year 1762 be of consequence to any party now existing. Our Monarch also, as the patron of arts, would rather encourage than prevent the publication of a work by *Hogarth*, even though it should recall the disagreeable ideas of faction triumphant, and a favourite in disgrace.

[1] The principal figure in the character of *Henry* VIII. appears to be not Mr. P. but another person whose power is signified by his bulk of carcase, treading on Mr. P. represented by 3000 *l*. The bellows may signify his well-meaning, though ineffectual, endeavours to extinguish the fire by wind, which, though it will put out a small flame, will cherish a large one. The guider of the engine-pipe, I should think, can only mean his M———, who unweariedly tries, by a more proper method, to stop the flames of war, in which he is assisted by all his good subjects, both by sea and land, notwithstanding any interruption from *Auditors* or *Britons, Monitors* or *North Britons*. The respectable body at the bottom can never mean the magistrates of *London*; Mr. H. has more sense than to abuse so respectable a body; much less can it mean the judges. I think it may as likely be the Court of Session in *Scotland*, either in the attitude of adoration, or with outspread arms intending to catch their patron, should his stilts give way. The *Frenchman* may very well sit at his ease among his miserable countrywomen, as he is not unacquainted that *France* has always gained by negociating what she lost in fighting. The fine gentleman at the window with his garretteers, and the barrow of periodical papers, refer to the present contending parties of every denomination. The breaking of the *Newcastle* arms alludes to the resignation of a great personage; and the replacing of them, by the sign of the four clenched fists, may be thought emblematical of the great œconomy of his successor. The *Norfolk* jig signifies, in a lively manner, the alacrity of all his

Majesty's forces during the war; and *G. T. [George Townshend] fecit*, is an opportune compliment paid to Lord *Townshend*, who, in conjunction with Mr. *Windham*, published "A Plan of Discipline for the Use of the *Norfolk* Militia," 4to. and had been the greatest advocate for the establishment of our present militia. The picture of the *Indian* alive from *America* is a satire on our late uncivilized behaviour to the three chiefs of the *Cherokee* nation, who were lately in this kingdom; and the bags of money set this in a still clearer point of view, signifying the sums gained by shewing them at our public gardens. The sly *Dutchman*, with his pipe, seems pleased with the combustion, from which he thinks he shall be a gainer. And the Duke of *Nivernois*, under the figure of a dove, is coming from *France* to give a cessation of hostilities to *Europe*.

3. *T. Morell*, S. T. P., S. S. A. *W. Hogarth delin. James Basire sculp*. From a drawing returned to Mr. *Hogarth*. Of this plate there is an admirable copy, though it has not yet been extensively circulated.

4. *Henry Fielding*, ætatis 48. *W. Hogarth delin. James Basire sculp*. From a drawing with a pen made after the death of Mr. *Fielding*. "That gentleman," says Mr. *Murphy*, "had often promised to sit to his friend *Hogarth*, for whose good qualities and excellent genius he always entertained so high an esteem, that he has left us in his writings many beautiful memorials of his affection. Unluckily, however, it so fell out that no picture of him was ever drawn; but yet, as if it was intended that some traces of his countenance should be perpetuated, and that too by the very artist whom our author preferred to all others, after Mr. *Hogarth* had long laboured to try if he could bring out any likeness of him from images existing in his own fancy, and just as he was despairing of success, for want of some rules to go by in the dimensions and outlines of the face, Fortune threw the grand *desideratum* in the way. A lady, with a pair of scissars, had cut a profile, which gave the distances and proportions of his face sufficiently to restore his lost ideas of him. Glad of an opportunity of paying his last tribute to the memory of an author whom he admired, Mr. *Hogarth* caught at this outline with pleasure, and worked, with all the attachment of friendship, till he finished that excellent drawing which stands at the head of this work, and recalls to all, who have seen the original, a corresponding image of the man." Notwithstanding this authentic relation of Mr. *Murphy*, a different account of the portrait has been lately given in one of the news-papers. Mr. *Garrick*, it is there said, dressed himself in a suit of his old friend's cloaths, and presented himself to the painter in the attitude, and with the features, of *Fielding*. Our *Roscius*, however, I can assert, interfered no farther in this business than by urging *Hogarth* to attempt the likeness, as a necessary adjunct to the edition of *Fielding's* works. I am assured that our artist began and finished the head in the presence of his wife

and another lady. He had no assistance but from his own memory, which, on such occasions, was remarkably tenacious.[1]

[1] To this sketch so great justice was done by the engraver, that Mr. *Hogarth* declared he did not know his own drawing from a proof of the plate before the ornaments were added. This proof is now in the collection of Mr. *Steevens*.

1763.

1. *John Wilkes*, Esq. *Drawn from the life, and etched in aquafortis by Wm. Hogarth.* Price 1*s*. It was published with the following oblique note. This is "a direct contrast to a print of SIMON LORD LOVAT."[1]

Mr. *Wilkes*, with his usual good humour, has been heard to observe, that he is every day growing more and more like his portrait by *Hogarth*.

In the second impressions of this plate there are a few slight variations, sufficient at least to shew that the face of the person represented had been retouched. I have been told, by a copper-plate printer, that near 4000 copies of this caricature were worked off on its first publication. Being kept up for two or three following nights on the occasion, he has reason to remember it.

[1] The original drawing, which was thrown by *Hogarth* into the fire, was snatched out of it by Mrs. *Lewis*, and is now in the possession of Mr. *S. Ireland*.

2. The Bruiser *C. Churchill*,[1] in the character of a *Russian Hercules*, &c. The *Russian Hercules* was thus explained, in *August*, 1763, by an admirer of *Hogarth*: "The principal figure is a *Russian Bear* (i. e. Mr. *Churchill*) with a club in his left paw, which he hugs to his side, and which is intended to denote his friendship to Mr. *Wilkes*: on the notches of the club are wrote, *Lye* 1, *Lye* 2, &c. signifying the falsities in *The North Briton*: in his other paw is a gallon pot of porter, of which (being very hot) he seems going to drink: round his neck is a clergyman's band, which is torn, and seems intended to denote the bruiser. The other figure is a *Pug-dog*, which is supposed to mean Mr. *Hogarth* himself, pissing with the greatest contempt on the epistle wrote to him by *C. Churchill*. In the centre is a prison begging-box, standing on a folio, the title of which is, *Great George-Street. A list of the Subscribers to the* North Briton: underneath is another book, the title of which is, *A New Way to pay Old Debts, a Comedy, by* Massinger. All of which allude to Mr. *Wilkes's* debts, to be defrayed by the subscriptions to *The North Briton*."

The same design is thus illustrated by a person who thought somewhat differently of our artist: "The *Bear*, with the shattered band, represents the former strength and abilities of Mr. *Hogarth*: the full pot of beer likewise shews that he was in a land of plenty. The stump of a headless tree with the notches, and on them wrote *Lye*, Signifies Mr. *Hogarth's* former art, and the many productions thereof, wherein he has excelled even Nature itself, and which of course must be but lies, flattery, and fallacy, the *Painter's Prerogative*; and the stump of the tree only being left, shews that there can be no more fruit expected from thence, but that it only stands as a record of his former services. The *Butcher's Dog* pissing upon Mr. *Churchill's* epistle, alludes to the present state of Mr. *Hogarth*; that he is arrived at such an age to be reduced so low, as, from the strength of a *Bear*, to a blind *Butcher's Dog*, not able to distinguish, but pissing upon his best friend; or, perhaps, giving the public a hint to read that Epistle, where his case is more fully laid before them. The next matter to be explained is the subscription-box, and under it is a book said to contain *a list of the Subscribers to the* North Briton, as well as one of *a New Way to pay Old Debts*. Mr. *Hogarth* mentioned *The North Briton*, to avoid the censure of the rabble in the street, who, he knew, would neither pity nor relieve him; and as Mr. *Churchill* was reputed to be the writer of that paper, it would seem to give a colour in their eyes of its being intended against Mr. *Churchill*. Mr. *Hogarth* meant only to shew his necessity, and that a book, entitled *A List of the Subscribers to the* North Briton, contained, in fact, a list of those who should contribute to the support of Mr. *Hogarth* in old age. By the book entitled *A New Way to pay Old Debts*, he can only mean this, that when a man is become disabled to get his livelihood, and much in debt, the only shift he has left is, to go a-begging to his creditors.

"There are likewise some of his old tools in this print, without any hand to use them."

On the same occasion were published the following verses, "on Mr. *Hogarth's* last delicate performance:"

> "What Merit could from native Genius boast,
> To civilize the age, and please us most,
> In lasting images each scene to grace,
> And all the soul to gather in the face,
> In one small sheet a volume to conceal,
> Yet all the story finely to reveal,
> Was once the glory of our *Hogarth's* name;
> But see, the short-liv'd eminence of fame
> Now dwindles like the exit of a flame,
> From which when once the unctuous juice is fled,
> A stinking vapour rises in its stead:
> So drops our Painter in his later day,
> His former virtue worn, alas! away,
> What busy dæmon, for thy cursed design'd,

> Could thus induce the rancour of thy mind
> To strike so boldly, with an impious hand,
> Against the blessings of thy native land?
> Open and unabash'd thy fury flies,
> And all regard for liberty denies.
>
> "When *Catiline*, with more than human hate,
> Resolv'd the ruin of the *Roman* state,
> In secret he pursu'd the hellish plan,
> Nor did his wickedness survive the man.
> His cruel arts are all by others shown,
> And thou the brave assertor of thy own:
> Nay, thy grim sheets thy principles will show,
> When *Charon* wafts thee to the realms below,
> Where all like thee shall unlamented go."

And also what the writer called,

> "*A* SLAP *at* BOTH SIDES."
> "Whilst *Bruin* and *Pug* contend for the prize
> Of merit in scandal, would parties be wise,
> And with honest derision contemn the dispute,
> The *Bear* would not roar, and the *Dog* would be mute:
> For they equally both their patrons betray,
> No sense of Conviction their reasons convey;
> So neither may hope one convert to gain,
> For the Rhime makes me sick, and the Print gives me pain."[2]

This plate, however, originally contained our artist's own portrait (see p. 295). To shew the contempt in which he held the "Poetical Epistle to *Hogarth*,[3] he makes the pug-dog water on it, but in a manner by no means natural to his species. Perhaps there is the same error relative to the Monkey in the print of the *Strollers*. This kind of *evacuation*, however, appears to have been regarded by *Hogarth* as a never-failing *joke*. On the palette he exhibits the *North Britons*, and a begging-box to collect subscriptions for them. *Designed and engraved by W. Hogarth.*

In the first impression of this print three of the upper knots on the club or ragged staff (viz. 1. 3. 5.) are left white. In the second impression they are completely shaded; the ruffle on the hand that clasps the pot of porter is likewise hatched over, and the shoulder of the animal made rounder. Minute differences occur in the other knots, &c. The inscription, instead of *Russian*, reads *Modern* Hercules.

[1] In a letter written to his friend Mr. *Wilkes*, dated *Aug.* 3, 1763, *Churchill* says: "I take it for granted you have seen *Hogarth's Print* against me. Was ever any thing so contemptible? I think he is fairly *felo de se*—I think not to let him off in that manner, although I might safely leave him to your NOTES. He has broke into my pale of private life, and set that example of illiberality which I wished—of that kind of attack which is ungenerous in the first instance, but justice in return. I intend an Elegy on him, supposing him dead; but * * tells me with a kiss, he will be really dead before it comes out: that I have already killed him, &c. How sweet is flattery from the woman we love! and how weak is our boasted strength when opposed to beauty and good sense with good nature!"—In Mr. *Churchill's* will is the following passage: "I desire my dear friend, *John Wilkes*, Esq. to collect and publish my Works, with the Remarks and Explanations he has prepared, and any others he thinks proper to make."

[2] In a few days after, the following Advertisement, for a satirical Print on *Hogarth*, was published:

Tara, Tan, Tara! Tara, Tan, Tara!

This Day made its appearance at the noted SUMPTER's Political Booth, next door to *The Brazen Head*, near *Shoe-Lane, Fleet-street*, which began precisely at twelve at noon, a new humourous performance, entitled, The BRUISER TRIUMPHANT: or, The Whole Farce of the *Leicester-fields* Pannel Painter. The principal parts by Mr. H[ogarth], Mr. W[ilkes], Mr. C[hurchill], &c. &c. &c. Walk in, Gentlemen, walk in! No more than 6 *d.* a-piece!

[3] The reader shall judge for himself of this Epistle's "power to hurt."

> "Amongst the sons of men, how few are known
> Who dare be just to merit not their own!
> Superior virtue, and superior sense,
> To knaves and fools will always give offence;
> Nay, men of real worth can scarcely bear,
> So nice is Jealousy, a rival there.
>
> "Be wicked as thou wilt, do all that's base,
> Proclaim thyself the monster of thy race;
> Let Vice and Folly thy Black Soul divide,
> Be proud with meanness, and be mean with pride!
> Deaf to the voice of Faith and Honour, fall
> From side to side, yet be of none at all;
> Spurn all those charities, those sacred ties,
> Which Nature in her bounty, good as wise,
> To work our safety, and ensure her plan,
> Contriv'd to bind, and rivet man to man;

> Lift against Virtue Power's oppressive rod,
> Betray thy Country, and deny thy God;
> And, in one general comprehensive line,
> To group, which volumes scarcely could define,
> Whate'er of Sin and Dulness can be said.
> Join to a F——'s heart a D——'s head.
> Yet mayst thou pass unnotic'd in the throng,
> And, free from Envy, safely sneak along.
> The rigid Saint, by whom no mercy's shewn
> To Saints whose lives are better than his own,
> Shall spare thy crimes; and WIT, who never once
> Forgave a Brother, shall forgive a Dunce."

After this nervous introduction, our satirist proceeds:

> "HOGARTH—I take thee, CANDOUR, at thy word,
> Accept thy proffer'd terms, and will be heard;
> Thee have I heard with virulence declaim,
> Nothing retain'd of Candour but the name;
> By thee have I been charg'd in angry strains
> With that mean falshood which my soul disdains—
> HOGARTH, stand forth—Nay hang not thus aloof—
> Now, CANDOUR, now Thou shalt receive such proof—
> Such damning proof, that henceforth Thou shalt fear
> To tax my wrath, and own my conduct clear—
> HOGARTH stand forth—I dare thee to be tried
> In that great Court, where Conscience must preside;
> At that most solemn bar hold up thy hand;
> Think before whom, on what account you stand—
> Speak, but consider well—from first to last
> Review thy life, weigh every action past—
> Nay, you shall have no reason to complain—
> Take longer time, and view them o'er again—
> Canst Thou remember from thy earliest youth,
> And as thy God must judge Thee, speak the truth,
> A single instance where, *Self* laid aside,
> And Justice taking place of fear and pride,
> Thou with an equal eye didst GENIUS view,
> And give to Merit what was Merit's due?
> Genius and Merit are a sure offence,
> And thy soul sickens at the name of Sense.
> Is any one so foolish to succeed?
> On ENVY'S altar he is doom'd to bleed.
> HOGARTH, a guilty pleasure in his eyes,

The place of Executioner supplies.
See how he glotes, enjoys the sacred feast,
And proves himself by cruelty a priest.

"Whilst the weak Artist, to thy whims a slave,
Would bury all those powers which Nature gave,
Would suffer blank concealment to obscure
Those rays, thy Jealousy could not endure;
To feed thy vanity would rust unknown,
And to secure thy credit blast his own,
In HOGARTH he was sure to find a friend;
He could not fear, and therefore might commend.
But when his Spirit, rous'd by honest Shame,
Shook off that Lethargy, and soar'd to Fame,
When, with the pride of Man, resolv'd and strong,
He scorn'd those fears which did his Honour wrong,
And, on himself determin'd to rely,
Brought forth his labours to the public eye,
No Friend in Thee, could such a Rebel know;
He had desert, and HOGARTH was his foe.

"Souls of a timorous cast, of petty name
In ENVY'S court, not yet quite dead to shame,
May some Remorse, some qualms of Conscience feel,
And suffer Honour to abate their Zeal:
But the Man, truly and compleatly great,
Allows no rule of action but his hate;
Through every bar he bravely breaks his way,
Passion his Principle, and Parts his prey.
Mediums in Vice and Virtue speak a mind
Within the pale of Temperance confin'd;
The daring Spirit scorns her narrow schemes,
And, good or bad, is always in extremes.

"Man's practice duly weigh'd, through every age
On the same plan hath ENVY form'd her rage.
'Gainst those whom Fortune hath our rivals made
In way of Science, and in way of Trade,
Stung with mean Jealousy she arms her spite,
First works, then views their ruin with delight.
Our HOGARTH here a grand improver shines,
And nobly on the general plan refines;
He like himself o'erleaps the servile bound;

Worth is his mark, wherever Worth is found.
Should Painters only his vast wrath suffice?
Genius in every walk is Lawful Prize.
'Tis a gross insult to his o'ergrown state:
His love to merit is to feel his hate.

"When WILKES, our Countryman, our common friend,
Arose, his King, his Country to defend,
When tools of power he bar'd to public view,
And from their holes the sneaking cowards drew;
When Rancour found it far beyond her reach
To soil his honour, and his truth impeach,
What could induce Thee, at a time and place,
Where manly Foes had blush'd to shew their face,
To make that effort, which must damn thy name,
And sink Thee deep, deep in thy grave with shame?
Did Virtue move Thee? no, 'twas Pride, rank Pride,
And if thou hadst not done it, Thou hadst dy'd.
MALICE (who, disappointed of her end,
Whether to work the bane of Foe or Friend,
Preys on herself, and, driven to the Stake,
Gives Virtue that revenge she scorns to take)
Had kill'd Thee, tottering on life's utmost verge,
Had WILKES and LIBERTY escap'd thy scourge.

"When that GREAT CHARTER, which our Fathers bought
With their best blood, was into question brought;
When, big with ruin, o'er each English head
Vile Slavery hung suspended by a thread;
When LIBERTY, all trembling and aghast,
Fear'd for the future, knowing what was past:
When every breast was chill'd with deep despair,
Till Reason pointed out that PRATT was there;
Lurking, most Ruffian-like, behind a screen,
So plac'd all things to see, himself unseen,
VIRTUE, with due contempt, saw HOGARTH stand,
The murderous pencil in his palsied hand.
What was the cause of Liberty to him,
Or what was Honour? Let them sink or swim,
So he may gratify, without controul,
The mean resentments of his selfish soul.
Let Freedom perish, if, to Freedom true,
In the same ruin WILKES may perish too.

"With all the symptoms of assur'd decay,
With age and sickness pinch'd, and worn away,
Pale quivering lips, lank cheeks, and faultering tongue,
The spirits out of tune, the nerves unstrung,
The body shrivel'd up, the dim eyes sunk
Within their sockets deep, the weak hams shrunk
The body's weight unable to sustain,
The stream of life scarce trembling through the vein,
More than half-kill'd by honest truths, which fell,
Through thy own fault, from men who wish'd thee well;
Canst thou, e'en thus, thy thoughts to vengeance give,
And, dead to all things else, to Malice live?
Hence, Dotard, to thy closet, shut thee in,
By deep repentance wash away thy sin,
From haunts of men to shame and sorrow fly,
And, on the verge of death, learn how to die.

"Vain exhortation! wash the Ethiop white,
Discharge the leopard's spots, turn day to night,
Controul the course of Nature, bid the deep
Hush at thy Pygmy voice her waves to sleep,
Perform things passing strange, yet own thy art
Too weak to work a change in such a heart.
That ENVY, which was woven in thy frame
At first, will to the last remain the same.
Reason may droop, may die; but Envy's rage
Improves by time, and gathers strength from age,
Some, and not few, vain triflers with the pen,
Unread, unpractis'd in the ways of men,
Tell us that ENVY, who with giant stride
Stalks through the vale of life by Virtue's side,
Retreats when she hath drawn her latest breath,
And calmly hears her praises after death.
To such observers HOGARTH gives the lie;
Worth may be hears'd, but Envy cannot die;
Within the mansion of his gloomy breast,
A mansion suited well to such a guest,
Immortal, unimpair'd, she rears her head,
And damns alike the living and the dead.

"Oft have I known Thee, HOGARTH, weak and vain,
Thyself the idol of thy aukward strain,

Through the dull measure of a summer's day,
In phrase most vile, prate long, long hours away,
Whilst Friends with Friends, all gaping sit, and gaze
To hear a HOGARTH babble HOGARTH'S praise.
But if athwart thee Interruption came,
And mention'd with respect some Ancient's name,
Some Ancient's name, who in the days of yore
The crown of Art with greatest honour wore,
How have I seen thy coward cheek turn pale,
And blank confusion seize thy mangled tale!
How hath thy Jealousy to madness grown,
And deem'd his praise injurious to thy own!
Then without mercy did thy wrath make way,
And Arts and Artists all became thy prey;
Then didst Thou trample on establish'd rules,
And proudly level'd all the ancient schools;
Condemn'd those works, with praise through ages grac'd,
Which you had never seen, or could not taste.
'But would mankind have true Perfection shewn,
It must be found in labours of my own.
I dare to challenge in one single piece,
Th' united force of ITALY and GREECE.'
Thy eager hand the curtain then undrew,
And brought the boasted Master-piece to view.
Spare thy remarks—say not a single word—
The Picture seen, why is the Painter heard?
Call not up Shame and Anger in our cheeks:
Without a Comment SIGISMUNDA speaks.

"Poor SIGISMUNDA! what a Fate is thine!
DRYDEN, the great High-Priest of all the Nine,
Reviv'd thy name, gave what a Muse could give,
And in his Numbers bade thy Memory live;
Gave thee those soft sensations, which might move
And warm the coldest Anchorite to Love;
Gave thee that Virtue, which could curb desire,
Refine and consecrate Love's headstrong fire;
Gave thee those griefs, which made the Stoic feel,
And call'd compassion forth from hearts of steel;
Gave thee that firmness, which our Sex may shame,
And make Man bow to Woman's juster claim,
So that our tears, which from compassion flow,
Seem to debase thy dignity of woe!

But O, how much unlike! how fall'n! how chang'd!
How much from Nature and herself estrang'd!
How totally depriv'd of all the powers
To shew her feelings, and awaken ours,
Doth SIGISMUNDA now devoted stand,
The helpless victim of a Dauber's hand!

"But why, *my* HOGARTH, such a progress made,
So rare a Pattern for the sign-post trade,
In the full force and whirlwind of thy pride,
Why was *Heroic* Painting laid aside?
Why is It not resum'd? Thy Friends at Court,
Men all in place and power, crave thy support;
Be grateful then for once, and, through the field
Of Politics, thy *Epic* Pencil wield;
Maintain the cause, which they, good lack! avow,
And would maintain too, but they know not how.

"Through ev'ry *Pannel* let thy Virtue tell
How BUTE prevail'd, how PITT and TEMPLE fell!
How ENGLAND'S sons (whom they conspir'd to bless
Against our Will, with insolent success)
Approve their fall, and with addresses run,
How got, God knows, to hail the SCOTTISH Sun!
Point out our fame in war, when Vengeance, hurl'd
From the strong arm of Justice, shook the world;
Thine, and thy Country's honour to increase,
Point out the honours of succeeding Peace;
Our *Moderation*, Christian-like, display,
Shew, what we got, and what we gave away.
In Colours, dull and heavy as the tale,
Let a *State*-Chaos through the whole prevail.

"But, of events regardless, whilst the Muse,
Perhaps with too much heat, her theme pursues;
Whilst her quick Spirits rouze at FREEDOM'S call,
And every drop of blood is turn'd to gall,
Whilst a dear Country, and an injur'd Friend,
Urge my strong anger to the bitterest end,
Whilst honest trophies to Revenge are rais'd,
Let not One real Virtue pass unprais'd.
Justice with equal course bids Satire flow,
And loves the Virtue of her greatest foe.

"O! that I here could that rare Virtue mean,
Which scorns the rule of Envy, Pride and Spleen,
Which springs not from the labour'd Works of Art,
But hath its rise from Nature in the heart,
Which in itself with happiness is crown'd,
And spreads with joy the blessing all around!
But truth forbids, and in these simple lays
Contented with a different kind of Praise,
Must HOGARTH stand; that Praise which GENIUS gives;
In Which to latest time the *Artist* lives,
But not the *Man*; which, rightly understood,
May make us great, but cannot make us good,
That Praise be HOGARTH'S; freely let him wear
The Wreath which GENIUS wove, and planted there.
Foe as I am, should Envy tear it down,
Myself would labour to replace the Crown.

"In walks of Humour, in that cast of Style,
Which, probing to the quick, yet makes us smile;
In Comedy, his nat'ral road to fame,
Nor let me call it by a meaner name,
Where a beginning, middle, and an end,
Are aptly join'd; where parts on parts depend,
Each made for each, as bodies for their soul,
So as to form one true and perfect whole,
Where a plain Story to the eye is told,
Which we conceive the moment we behold,
HOGARTH unrival'd stands, and shall engage
Unrival'd praise to the most distant age.

"How could'st Thou then to shame perversely run,
And tread that path which Nature bade Thee shun?
Why did Ambition overleap her rules,
And thy vast parts become the Sport of Fools?
By different methods different Men excell,
But where is He who can do all things well?
Humour thy Province, for some monstrous crime
Pride struck Thee with the frenzy of *Sublime*.
But, when the work was finish'd, could thy mind
So partial be, and to herself so blind,
What with Contempt All view'd, to view with awe,
Nor see those faults which every Blockhead saw?

Blush, Thou vain Man, and if desire of Fame,
Founded on real Art, thy thoughts inflame,
To quick destruction SIGISMUNDA give,
And let her memory die, that thine may live.

"But should fond Candour, for her Mercy's sake,
With pity view, and pardon this mistake;
Or should Oblivion, to thy wish most kind,
Wipe off that stain, nor leave one trace behind;
Of ARTS *despis'd*, of ARTISTS by thy frown
Aw'd from just hopes, of *rising worth kept down*,
Of all thy meanness through this mortal race,
Canst Thou the living memory erase?
Or shall not Vengeance follow to the grave,
And give back just that measure which You gave?
With so much merit, and so much success,
With so much power to curse, so much to bless,
Would He have been Man's friend, instead of foe,
HOGARTH had been a little God below.
Why then, like savage Giants, fam'd of old,
Of whom in Scripture Story we are told,
Dost Thou in cruelty that strength employ,
Which Nature meant to save, not to destroy?
Why dost Thou, all in horrid pomp array'd,
Sit grinning o'er the ruins Thou hast made?
Most rank ill-nature must applaud thy art;
But even Candour must condemn thy heart.

"For Me, who, warm and zealous for my Friend,
In spite of railing thousands, will commend,
And, no less warm and zealous 'gainst my foes,
Spite of commending thousands, will oppose,
I dare thy worst, with scorn behold thy rage,
But with an eye of Pity view thy Age;
Thy feeble Age, in which, as in a glass,
We see how men to dissolution pass.
Thou *wretched Being*, whom, on Reason's plan,
So chang'd, so lost, I cannot call a Man,
What could persuade Thee, at this time of life,
To launch afresh into the Sea of Strife?
Better for Thee, scarce crawling on the earth,
Almost as much a child as at thy birth,
To have resign'd in peace thy parting breath,

And sunk unnotic'd in the arms of Death.
Why would thy grey, grey hairs, resentment brave,
Thus to go down with sorrow to the grave?
Now, by my Soul, it makes me blush to know
My Spirits could descend to such a foe.
Whatever cause the vengeance might provoke,
It seems rank Cowardice to give the stroke.

"Sure 'tis a curse which angry Fates impose,
To fortify man's arrogance, that those,
Who're fashion'd of some better sort of clay,
Much sooner than the common herd decay.
What bitter pangs must humbled GENIUS feel!
In their last hours, to view a SWIFT and STEELE!
How much ill-boding horrors fill her breast
When She beholds Men, mark'd above the rest
For qualities most dear, plung'd from that height,
And sunk, deep sunk, in second Childhood's night!
Are Men, indeed, such things, and are the best
More subject to this evil than the rest,
To drivel out whole years of Ideot Breath,
And sit the Monuments of living Death?
O, galling circumstance to human pride!
Abasing Thought, but not to be denied!
With curious Art the Brain, too finely wrought;
Preys on herself, and is destroy'd by Thought.
Constant Attention wears the active mind,
Blots out her powers, and leaves a blank behind.
But let not Youth, to insolence allied,
In heat of blood, in full career of pride,
Possess'd of GENIUS, with unhallow'd rage,
Mock the infirmities of reverend age.
The greatest GENIUS to this Fate may bow,
REYNOLDS, in time, may be like HOGARTH now."

3. The same; but on the palette is introduced the political print described in p. 91. In the second impressions of the plate thus altered,[1] we find the letters N B added on the club, as well as the epithet *infamous* prefixed to the word *Fallacy*. The shadows on the political print are likewise changed, and deepened; and the words "Dragon of *Wantley*" are added at the end of "I warrant ye."

[1] The first was price 1*s.*; the second price 1*s.* 6*d.*

4. Print Of the Weighing-house to "*Clubbe's* Physiognomy;" a humourous pamphlet in quarto, published in 1763, by Mr. *Clubbe*[1] (editor of the History and Antiquities of *Wheatfield* in *Suffolk*), and dedicated to *Hogarth*. *W. Hogarth del. L. Sullivan sculp.* It was likewise printed in a collection of this author's works, published at *Ipswich*, 2 vols. 12mo. no date, with a new engraving of the plate. There is also a third engraving of the same design, perhaps executed in the country, for some octavo edition of Mr. *Clubbe's* pamphlet.

[1] I had said in my first edition, that Mr. *Clubbe* was drowned in the moat that surrounded his house at *Wheatfield*; but readily retract that assertion, having been since informed, that he died a natural death, of old age and infirmities.

5. *Frontispiece to a pamphlet* written by Dr. *Gregory Sharpe*, Master of *The Temple*, against the *Hutchinsonians, but never published*. "*It represents a witch sitting on the moon, and watering on a mountain, whence issue mice, who are devouring Sir Isaac Newton's Optics; one mouse lies dead on Hutchinson's works, probably to imply being choaked. The conundrum signifies, Front-is-piss.*" The few impressions from this plate that have strayed into the hands of dealers, were originally presents from Dr. *Sharpe* to his friends.

1764.

1. FINIS, or the Tail-piece. The Bathos, or manner of sinking in sublime painting, inscribed to the dealers in dark pictures.[1] TIME breathing out his *last*, a ruinous tower, and many other allegorical devices; among the rest, he has introduced his own "Times."[2]

[1] On this print, which he called *Finis*, and represents the destruction of all things, the following epigram, ascribed to *Charles Churchill* the poet, and said to have been written by him when at Mr. *Dell's*, in *Kew-foot-lane*, *April* 18, 1764, is printed from *The Muse's Mirrour*, vol. I. p. 8.

> On *Hogarth's* print of the *Bathos*, or the Art of Sinking in Painting.
>
> All must old *Hogarth's* gratitude declare,
> Since he has nam'd old *Chaos* for his heir;
> And while his works hang round that *Anarch's* throne,
> The connoisseurs will take them for his own.

Mr. *Walpole's* Anecdotes, 8vo. vol, IV. p. 191.

[2] A few months before this ingenious artist was seized with the malady which deprived society of one of its greatest ornaments, he proposed to his matchless pencil the work he has intituled a *tail-piece*; the first idea of which is said to have been started in company, while the convivial glass was circulating round his own table. "My next undertaking," says *Hogarth*, "shall be the *End of all Things*." "If that is the case," replied one of his friends, "your *business will be finished*; for there will be *an end of the painter*." "There *will* so," answered *Hogarth*, sighing heavily; "and, therefore, the sooner my *work is done*, the better." Accordingly he began the next day, and continued his design with a diligence which seemed to indicate an apprehension (as the report goes) that he should not live till he had completed it. This, however, he did in the most ingenious manner, by grouping every thing which could denote the *end of all things*—a broken bottle—an old broom worn to the stump—the butt-end of an old musket—a cracked bell—bow unstrung—a crown tumbled in pieces—towers in ruins—the *sign-post* of a tavern, called *The World's End*, tumbling—the moon in her wane—the map of the globe burning—a gibbet falling, the body gone, and the chain which held it dropping down—*Phœbus* and his horses dead in the clouds—a vessel wrecked—Time, with his hour-glass and scythe broken; a tobacco-pipe in his mouth, the last whiff of smoke going out—a play-book opened, with *Exeunt omnes* stamped in the corner—an empty purse—and a statute of bankruptcy taken out against Nature.—"So far, so good," cried *Hogarth*; "nothing remains but this,"—taking his pencil in a sort of prophetic fury, and dashing off the similitude of a *painter's pallet broken*—"*Finis*," exclaimed *Hogarth*, "*the deed is done—all is over*."—It is remarkable, that he died in about a month after this tail-piece. It is also well known he never again took the pencil in hand.

2. The Bench.[1] The same described under the year 1758; but with additions. The plate thus varied occurs in two states. In the first of these we have only "This plate could have been better explained, had the author lived a week longer." In the second impression of it we are told, that "The unfinished group of heads, in the upper part of this print, was added by the author in *October* 1764; and was intended as a farther illustration of what is here said concerning *Character, Caracatura,* and *Outrè*. He worked upon it a day before his death, which happened the 26th of that month." This plate exhibits the inside of the *Common Pleas*, with portraits of the following judges then belonging to that court:

Hon. Wm. Noel.   Sir *Edw*. Clive.   Sir *John* Willes, Ld.   Hon. Mr. Justice (now Earl)

Mr. *Edwards's* picture on this subject (see p. 367.) differs from both the plates.

[1] A term peculiarly appropriated to the Court of *Common Pleas*.

3. Hell-Gate, Satan, Sin, and Death. *Milton's Paradise Lost.* Book II. A large print. Engraved by *C. Townley,* and intended to have been published *April* 15, 1767. It was dedicated to the late Mr. *Garrick,* who possessed the original (unfinished) picture painted by *Hogarth.* The plate was destroyed, and only a few of the prints are now remaining. The original is in the possession of Mrs. *Garrick.*

It is impossible to conclude my account of it without observing, that the united labours of *Teniers, Heemskirk,* and *Callot,* could not have furnished a more absolute burlesque of this noble subject, than *Hogarth,* who went seriously to work on it, has here produced. "How art thou fallen, O *Lucifer,* thou son of the Morning!" will be the exclamation of every observer, on seeing this unaccountable performance, in which *Satan* and *Death* have lost their terrors, and *Sin* herself is divested of all the powers of temptation.

1772.

1. The Good Samaritan; by *Ravenet* and *Delatre*.

In *The Grub-Street Journal* for *July* 14, 1737, appeared the following paragraph: "Yesterday the scaffolding was taken down from before the picture of *The Good Samaritan,*[1] painted by Mr. *Hogarth,* on the Stair Case in *St. Bartholomew's* Hospital, which is esteemed a very curious piece." *Hogarth* paid his friend *Lambert* for painting the landscape in this picture, and afterwards cleaned the whole at his own expence. To the imaginary merits of his coadjutor, the Analysis, p. 26, bears the following testimony: "The sky always gradates one way or other, and the rising or setting sun exhibits it in great perfection; the imitating of which was *Claud de Lorain's* peculiar excellence, and is now Mr. *Lambert's.*"

[1] Of this picture Mr. *S. Ireland* has a sketch in oil.

2. *The Pool of Bethesda*; large, by *Ravenet* and *Picot*. A small one, by *Ravenet,* has been mentioned under 1748. Both very indifferent. Mr. *Walpole* justly observes, that "the burlesque turn of our artist's mind mixed itself with his most serious compositions; and that, in *The Pool of Bethesda,* a servant of a rich ulcerated lady, beats back a poor man [perhaps woman] who sought the same

celestial remedy." To this remark I may add, that the figure of the priest, in *The Good Samaritan*, is supremely comic, and rather resembles some purse-proud burgomaster, than the character it was designed to represent.

On the top of the staircase at St. *Bartholomew's* Hospital, and just under the cornice, is the following inscription, "The historical paintings of this staircase were painted and given by Mr. *William Hogarth*, and the ornamental paintings at his expence, A. D. 1736." Both pictures, which appear of an oblong square in the engravings, in the originals are surrounded with scroll-work which cuts off the corners of them, &c. All these ornaments, together with compartments carved at the bottom, were the work of Mr. *Richards*. Mr. *Boydell* had the latter engraved on separate plates, appended to those above them, on which sufficient space had not been left.—*Hogarth* requested that these pictures might never be varnished. They appear therefore to disadvantage, the decorations about them having, within these few years past, been highly glazed. *The Pool of Bethesda* has suffered much from the sun; and *The Good Samaritan*, when lately cleaned, was pressed so hard against the straining frame, that several creases have been made in the canvas.

1775.

1. The Politician [Mr. *Tibson*, lately a laceman in *The Strand*], from a sketch in oil, by *Hogarth*. Etched by *J. K. Sherwin*. Published *Oct.* 31, 1775.

1781.

1. Portrait of *Solfull*,[1] a maker of punches for engravers. *W. Hogarth del. S. J. fecit aqua fort.* Mr. *S. Ireland* has the original sketch. This portrait is mentioned by Mr. *Walpole* under the title of "*Two small heads of men in profile in one plate, etched by Mr. Ireland, from a sketch in his own collection.*"

[1] This was etched a second time, Mr. *Ireland* having accidentally lost his first plate.

2. *Thomas Pellet*, M. D. President of the College of Physicians. *W. Hogarth pinxit. C. Hall sculpsit.*

3. *William Bullock* the Comedian. *W. Hogarth pinxit. C. Hall sculpsit.* It is by no means certain that these two last portraits were painted by *Hogarth*.

4. North and South of *Great Britain*. *W. Hogarth delin. F. B.* [i. e. *Francis Bartolozzi*] *sculp.* This little print represents a *Scotchman* scrubbing against a

sign-post; no sign on it; with *Edenborough* castle in the back ground:—and an *Englishman* reposing on a post, with a pot of *London* porter in his hand; the sign of an Ox, with *roast and boild*, by way of inscription, over his head; and a view of St. *Paul's* at a distance. I do not believe it was designed by our artist, whose satire was usually of a more exalted kind: neither are the figures at all in his manner.

A sketch imputed to *Hogarth*, and engraved by this matchless *Italian*, however, carries a double temptation with it, as it unites with the works of both artists, which are so much the present objects of pursuit. No man can entertain too high an idea of *Barlolozzi's* talents; but yet, being sometimes apt to sacrifice similitude to grace,

Emollit mores, nec finit esse feros.

He therefore is the last person from whom justice to the strong marked characters of *Hogarth* could be expected.

Since the above observations were communicated, a new impression of this plate has appeared with the name of *Sandby* annexed to it. The history of so extraordinary a change deserves notoriety. The publisher was at first assured that the sketch, from which he designed the engraving, was not the production of *Hogarth*. He, however, on his own judgement, pretended to affirm the contrary, being at least convinced that, during the late rage for collecting the works of our artist, no name was so likely as his to draw in purchasers. Having disposed of as many copies as he could in consequence of hanging out such false colours, he now sets sail again under those of *Sandby*, and would probably make a third voyage with Mr. *Bunbury's* flag at his mast head, were not our second *Hogarth* at hand, to detect the imposture.—The price of this etching, originally 2 *s.* 6 *d.* is now sold at 1 *s.* though the proprietor has incurred the fresh expence of decorating it in *aqua tinta*. Should it henceforward fail to meet with buyers, I shall not be ready to exclaim, with *Ovid*,

Flebam successu posse carere dolo.

The three last published by *John Thane, Rupert-street, Haymarket.*

5. First sketch of arms for *The Foundling Hospital. Wm. Hogarth inv.* 1747. Over the Crest and Supporters is written—A Lamb—Nature—*Britannia*. In the shield is a naked Infant: the Motto HELP.

This is an accurate fac simile from a drawing with a pen and ink by *Hogarth*. Published as the Act directs *July* 31, 1781, by *R. Livesay*, at Mrs. *Hogarth's, Leicester Fields*. The original is in the collection of the Earl of *Exeter*.

6. Two Figures, &c. *Hogarth inv. F. B.* [i. e. *Francis Bartolozzi*] *sculp.* These figures were designed for Lord *Melcombe* and Lord *Winchelsea*. From a drawing with a pen and ink by *Hogarth*. Published as the Act directs, 31 *July*, 1781, by R. *Livesay* at Mrs. *Hogarth's, Leicester-fields*. I am informed, however, that this drawing was certainly the work of Lord *Townshend*. The original is in the collection of the Earl of *Exeter*.

7. A mezzotinto portrait of *Hogarth* with his hat on, in a large oval, "from an original begun by *Wheltdon*, and finished by himself, late in the possession of the Rev. Mr. *Townley. Charles Townley fec.*" The family of *Hogarth* affect to know nothing of this painting; and say, if there is such a thing, it was only slightly touched over by him. It must be confessed that it bears little, if any, resemblance to the representations of our artist edited by himself. The original is now in the possession of Mr. *James Townley*, as has been mentioned in p. 98.

1782.

1. The Staymaker.

2. Debates on Palmistry.

The humour in the first of the two preceding prints is not very strong, and in the second it is scarce intelligible. The Male *Staymaker* seems to be taking professional liberties with a female in the very room where her husband sits, who is playing with one of his children presented to him by a nurse, perhaps with a view to call off his attention from what is going forward. The hag shews her pretended love for the infant, by kissing its posteriors. A maid-servant holds a looking-glass for the lady, and peeps significantly at the operator from behind it. A boy with a cockade on, and a little sword by his side, appears to observe the familiarities already mentioned, and is strutting up fiercely towards the Staymaker, while a girl is spilling some liquor in his hat.

The figures employed in the study of *Palmistry* seem to be designed for Physicians and Surgeons of an Hospital, who are debating on the most commodious method of receiving a fee, unattentive to the complaints of a lame female who solicits assistance. A spectre, resembling the *Royal Dane*, comes out behind, perhaps to intimate that physick and poison will occasionally produce similar effects. A glass case, containing skeletons, is open; a crocodile hangs overhead; and an owl, emblematic of this sapient consistory, is perched on an high stand. I suspect these two to have been discarded sketches—the first of them too barren in its subject to deserve finishing, and the second a repented effort of hasty spleen against the officers of *St. Bartholomew's*, who might not have treated some recommendation of a patient from our artist with all the respect and attention to which he thought it was entitled. But this is mere supposition.

3. Portrait of *Henry Fox* Lord *Holland*.

4. Portrait of *James Caulfield* Earl of *Charlemont*.

The above four articles are all etched by *S. Haynes*, pupil to the late Mr. *Mortimer*, from original drawings in the possession of Mr. *S. Ireland*.

The six prints which follow, were published by subscription by Mrs. *Hogarth* in *April* 1782; of these No. 5. was engraved by *Bartolozzi*, and the rest by R. *Livesay*.

5. The Shrimp Girl, a head, from an original sketch in oil, in the possession of Mrs. *Hogarth*.

This plate, which is executed in the dotted manner so much at present in fashion, should have been etched or engraved like those excellent performances by *Bartolozzi* after the drawings of *Guercino*. Spirit, rather than delicacy, is the characteristic of our artist's *Shrimp Girl*.

6. 7. Portraits of *Gabriel Hunt* and *Benjamin Read*, in *aqua tinta*, from the original drawings in the possession of the late Mr. *Forrest*. The drawing of Mr. *Hunt* was taken in 1733, a period when, from the number of street-robberies, it was usual to go armed. *Hunt's* couteau is stuck in one of his button-holes.

The figure of *Ben Read* was taken in 1757. Coming one night to the club after having taken a long journey, he fell asleep there. *Hogarth* had got on his roquelaure, and was about to leave the room; but, struck with the drollery of his friend's appearance, he exclaimed, "Heavens! what a character!" and, calling for pen and ink, took the drawing immediately, without sitting down.

To be recorded only as votaries of the bottle and pipe, is no very flattering mark of distinction to these members of our artist's club. There is scarce a meaner avenue to the Temple of Fame.

8. Three plates, from the original sketches of *Hogarth*, designed for the epitaph and monument of *George Taylor*. The drawings are the property of Mr. *Morrison*.

George Taylor was a famous boxer, who died *February* 21, 1750. A writer already quoted speaks of him in these terms: "*George Taylor*, known by the name of *George the Barber*, sprang up surprisingly. He has beat all the chief boxers but *Broughton*. He, I think, injudiciously fought him one of the first, and was obliged very soon to give out. Doubtless it was a wrong step in him to commence a boxer by fighting the standing champion: for *George* was not then twenty, and *Broughton* was in the zenith of his age and art. Since that he has greatly distinguished himself with others; but has never engaged *Broughton* more. He is a strong able boxer, who, with a skill extraordinary, aided by his knowledge of the small and back swords, and a remarkable judgement in the cross-buttock fall, may contest with any. But, please or displease, I am resolved to be ingenuous in my characters. Therefore I am of opinion, that he is not overstocked with that necessary ingredient of a boxer, called a *bottom*; and am apt to suspect that blows of equal strength with his too much affect him and disconcert his conduct." *Godfrey on the Science of Defence*, p. 61.

On *Taylor's* tombstone in *Deptford* church-yard is the following epitaph:

> Farewell ye honours of my brow!
> Victorious wreaths farewell!
> One trip from Death has laid me low,
> By whom such numbers fell.
> Yet bravely I'll dispute the prize,
> Nor yield, though out of breath:
> 'Tis but a fall—I yet shall rise,
> And conquer—even DEATH.

The idea, however, is all that can merit praise in these rough outlines by *Hogarth*. Some graver critics, indeed, may think our artist has treated the most solemn of all events with too great a degree of levity.

9. Nine prints of *Hogarth's* Tour from drawings by *Hogarth*, &c. accompanied with nine pages of letter press. The frontispiece of this work (Mr. *Somebody*) was designed by *Hogarth*, as emblematical of their journey, *viz.* that it was a short Tour by land and water, backwards and forwards, without head or tail. The 9th is the tail-piece (Mr. *Nobody*) of the same whimsical nature with the first; the whole being intended as a burlesque on historical writers recording a series of insignificant events intirely uninteresting to the reader. "Some few copies of the Tour," says Mr. *Walpole*,[1] "were printed by Mr. *Nichols* in the preceding year. It was a party of pleasure down the river into *Kent*, undertaken by Mr. *Hogarth*, Mr. *Scott*, and three of their friends, in which they intended to have more humour than they accomplished, as is commonly the case in such meditated attempts. The Tour was described in verse by one of the company, and the drawings executed by the painters, but with little merit, except the views taken by Mr. *Scott*."

I have transcribed this paragraph lest the readers of the truly valuable work whence it is taken should imagine the Tour printed by *J. N.* in 1781, was the same with that published by Mr. *Livesay* in 1782. The former was the production of the ingenious Mr. *Gostling* of *Canterbury*; the latter was written by one of the company, and, with the omission of a single glaring indelicacy, and many false spellings, has been faithfully edited by Mr. *Livesay*.

[1] Vol. IV. 8vo. p. 192.

10. *Hogarth's* Crest, exhibiting the Line of Beauty. *Cyprus* and *Variety* subjoined by way of mottoes; but my readers will anticipate me when I observe that the universe contains no place in which *Hogarth* had so little interest as in the *Cyprian* isle, where *Venus* was attended by the Graces. *Hogarth's* original sketch, which he delivered to Mr. *Catton* the coach-painter for the purpose of having it transferred on his carriage, is now in the possession of Mr. *Livesay*.

11. The card of invitation mentioned in p. 63. is introduced in the title-page of the present publication. It is engraved by *J. Cary*, a young artist, whose abilities, more particularly in the line of map-engraving, will soon raise him into notice.

12. An Old Man's Head with a band. In the dotted stile. Published by *Livesay*.

1785.

1. Orator *Henley* Christening a Child. Etched by *Saml Ireland* from an original sketch in oil—in his possession—by *Hogarth*.—To *Francis Grose*, Esq; F. A. S. an encourager and promoter of the arts, this etching, from his favourite *Hogarth*, is inscribed by his obliged friend and servant, SAM^L IRELAND.

2. A Landscape. Etch'd by *Saml Ireland*, from an original picture in his possession, said to be the only landscape ever painted by *Hogarth*.—To the Right Honourable the Earl of *Exeter*, an admirer of *Hogarth*, and encourager of the arts, this etching is inscribed by his Lordship's most obliged and obedient servant. S. IRELAND.

The very considerable degree of skill and fidelity, displayed in the execution of these two plates, entitles the gentleman who etched them to the warmest thanks of every collector of the works of *Hogarth*.—May a hope be added, that he will favour us with yet other unpublished designs of the same master?

PRINTS *of uncertain Date*.

Before Mr. *Walpole's* enumeration of the following shop-bills, coats of arms, &c. made its appearance, perhaps few of them were known to our collectors. Concerning the genuineness of some of these unimportant engravings, no doubt can be entertained; but whence is it inferred that *all* of them were his productions? Do we receive them merely on the faith of Mr. *Pond?* or are they imputed to our artist for any other reason, or on the strength of any other testimony? I am assured, by a gentleman who possesses the chief of them, and is well acquainted with *Hogarth's* manner, that from mere external evidence several of these could not have been authenticated.

It is natural, however, to suppose that most of them (if *Hogarth's*) were the fruits of his apprenticeship.[1] As such, therefore, they should be placed at the beginning of every collection.

[1] Let it be remembered likewise, that being bound apprentice to the single branch of engraving arms and cyphers, the majority of his works, whether on base metal or silver, must have been long since melted down. During the minority of *Hogarth*, the forms in which plate was made, could contribute little to its chance of preservation. Pot-bellied tankards, and salvers scalloped like old-fashioned minced-pies, were the highest efforts of that period.

---

1. People in a shop under the King's arms: *Mary* and *Ann Hogarth*. "*A shop-bill*" for his two sisters, who for many years kept a linen-draper's, or rather what is called a slop-shop.

> *Mary* and *Ann Hogarth.*
>
> from the Old Frock-shop near the corner of *The Long Walk*, facing *The Cloysters*, Removed to y^e *Kings Arms* joyning to y^e *Little Britain-gate*, near *Long Walk*. Sells ye best and most Fashionable Ready Made Frocks, sutes of Fustian, Ticken and Holland, stript Dimmity and Flañel Wastcoats, blue and canvas Frocks, and bluecoat Boys Dra^{rs}.
>
> Likewise Fustians, Tickens, Hollands, white stript Dĩmitys, white and stript Flañels in ye piece.
>
> By wholesale or Retale, at Reasonable Rates.

2. His own cypher, with his name under it at length; "*a plate he used for his books.*" I have reason to think it was neither designed nor engraved by *Hogarth*.

3. A *Turk's* head. "*A shop bill*," for *John Barker*, goldsmith, at the *Morocco* Ambassador's head in *Lombard-Street*.—A copy of this has been made.

4. A shop-bill, with emblems of Trade. Grand Duke of *Tuscany's* arms at the top; those of *Florence* within the plate. At the four corners, views of *Naples, Venice, Genoa,* and *Leghorne*.

At Mrs. *Holt's,*
Italian Warehouse,

at the two Olive Posts in ye broad part of *The Strand* almost opposite to *Exeter Change* are sold all Sorts of *Italian* Silks, as Lustrings, Sattins, Padesois, Velvets, Damasks, &c. Fans, Legorne Hats, Flowers, Lute and Violin Strings, Books of Essences, Venice Treacle, Balsomes, &c. And in a Back Warehouse all Sorts of *Italian* Wines, *Florence* Cordials, Oyl, Olives, Anchovies, Capers, Vermicelli, *Bologna* Sausidges, *Parmesan* Cheeses, *Naple* Soap, &c.

5. A large angel, holding a palm in his left hand. "*A shop-bill*" for

Ellis Gamble
Goldsmith,
at the *Golden-Angel* in *Cranbourn-street,*
Leicester-Fields.
Makes Buys and Sells all Sorts
of Plate, Rings and Jewels
&c.

Ellis Gamble
Orfeure,
a l'Enseigne de l'Ange d'Or
dans *Cranbourn-Street, Leicester-Fields.*
Fait, Achete,
& vend toutes sortes d'Argenterie,
Bagues & Bijouxs, &c.

6. A smaller angel. This is a contracted copy from the preceding, was another shop-bill for our Artist's Master, and has the same inscription as that already given.

7. Another small angel "almost the same as the preceding," in the collection of Mr. *Walpole.*

8. A large oval coat of arms, with terms of the four seasons.

9. A coat of arms, with two slaves and trophies. Plate for books.

10. Another coat of arms, and two boys as terms.

11. A foreign coat of arms; supporters a savage and an angel. Ditto.

12. Lord *Aylmer's* coat of arms.

13. Two ditto of the Duchess of *Kendal*; one of them, an impression from a silver tea table.

14. The Earl of *Radnor's* arms, from a silver cup and cover.

15. A grifon, with a flag. A crest.

16. *Minerva*, sitting and holding the arms of *Holland*, four *Cupids* round her. "*Done for the books of* John Holland, *herald-painter.*"

Of this there are two plates. The *Fleurs de Lys* in the one are more numerous and crowded than in the other.

17. A ticket for a burial.

For the same purpose our artist's contemporary *Coypel* likewise engraved a plate, which is still in use.

18. Two small for *Milton. W. Hogarth inv. & sculp.*

It is so singular, that only plates referring to the first and third books of *Paradise Lost* should be discovered with our artist's name subscribed to them, that I almost suspect they were not executed for any edition of that work, but rather for some oratorio or operatical performance founded thereon, though neither performed nor printed. An example of two prints by *Hogarth* to a single dramatic piece, we have already met with in Perseus and Andromeda.

If the first of the present designs was made for the first book of *Paradise Lost*, one might almost swear that *Hogarth* had never read it, or he could not have fallen into the strange absurdities and incoherences that his engraving displays. We have on one side a Dæmon exalted in a kind of pulpit, at the foot of which another infernal spirit lies bound in chains, while a cannon is pointed at his head. At a distance, in the centre of an arcade adorned with statues, is a throne with a personage seated on it. Over his head are little beings supporting an emblem of eternity. Stars, &c. appear above them. Whether this dignified character was designed for "a spirit of health, or goblin damn'd," it would be difficult from his figure and attributes to determine. Perhaps several works of fancy might be named, with which the present representation would as naturally connect as with the first book of *Milton's* Poem.

The following plate exhibits two celestial characters of equal age. They sit aloft in the clouds, and listen to a concert of angels playing on various instruments, and, among the rest, on a clumsy organ. A ray of light darts down on a distant orb, designed, I suppose, for the new-created world, towards which the figure of a little being, scarce bigger than a bird, though meant for *Satan*, is seen directing its flight.[1]

A bookseller of common sagacity would have been justified in rejecting these designs, if prepared for *Milton*. Indeed, had I not been taught by Mr. *Walpole's* catalogue that such was their destination, I should not hastily have conjectured that the former of them had the least reference to the Poet's *Pandæmonium*. Let it be remembered, however, that these must have been among the earliest of *Hogarth's* performances, and, like his prints for *Don Quixote*, were in all probability thrown aside, as unsuited to the purpose for which they were engraved. I have been told, indeed, that a couple of plates, by our artist, to the comedy of *The Spanish Friar*, are still existing.[2] If *Hogarth*, therefore, was once employed in preparing cuts to the plays of *Dryden*, the designs already mentioned might have been intended for two different scenes in *The State of Innocence, or the Fall of Man*.

[1] In justice, however, to one of these designs, I transcribe part of a letter that appeared in *The Gentleman's Magazine* for *March* 1782.

"*Twickenham, March* 12.

"MR. URBAN,

"Throughout Mr. *Nichols's* excellent but unequal account of *Hogarth* and his works, there is no decision I am so much inclined to controvert, as that respecting the first of the two plates to *Milton*. Perhaps the critic had only seen some imperfect copy of the *Pandæmonium*, or formed his idea of it on the vague description of those who who had considered it with less attention than it really deserves. In my opinion, our artist's arrangement of the infernal senate affords a happy instance of his power to exhibit scenes of picturesque sublimity. The ample space within the arcade, containing myriads of subordinate spirits; the vault above, illuminated by supernatural fires; the magnificence and elevation of *Satan's* throne; his superior stature, and the characteristic symbols over the seats of his peers; are circumstances entitled to a more flattering reception than they have met with. That this print has likewise absurdities, I am ready to allow: yet a *Voltaire* might ask whether most of them are not inseparable from its subject. I wish, for the sake of those who acknowledge the genius of *Hogarth* only in familiar combinations, that the plate in question were less rare. Our connoisseurs in general might then decide on its merits. The only known impression of it, as well as of its companion, is in the collection of Mr. *Walpole*,[A] who once indulged me with a sight of them both.

"I am content, however, that the second of these plates should be abandoned to the austerities of criticism. The architecture in the skies is every way unsuitable to its place. The characters of the Almighty and our Redeemer have little, if any, discrimination of attributes or years. They appear swinging on a festoon composed of tiny cherubs, clustered together like a swarm of bees. The Father rests his arm on one of these childish satellites; and the Son holds another by the wing, like *Domitian* catching a fly. Beneath, is a concert of angels, who perform on different instruments, and among others (as Mr. *Nichols's* book expresses it) on a clumsy organ. *Lucifer*, approaching the new-created world, appears but as an insect, flying towards an apple. This part of *Hogarth's* subject is beyond the compass of any design on a contracted scale. *Satan* might be delineated in the act of alighting on a promontory, a part of the earth; but when its complete orb is exhibited on a slip of paper measuring about six inches by four, the enterprizing fiend must be reduced to very insignificant dimensions. Such a circumstance may therefore succeed in a poet's comprehensive description, but will fail on any plate designed for the ornament of a little volume.

"Let me add, that these two are the neatest and most finished of all the engravings by *Hogarth*. The second might have been mistaken for one of the smaller works of *Picart*. Perhaps the high price demanded for the plates, was the reason why a series of them was not continued through the other books of *Paradise Lost*."

[A] These two plates are also in the collection of Mr. *Steevens*.

[2] These are in the collection of the Earl of *Exeter*, and are said to have the name of our artist fallaciously affixed to them. I speak, however, with uncertainty.

19. A coat of arms from a large silver tea table. Under these arms are a shepherd and his flock, exactly the same as those on the tankard, N° 25. A shepherd and shepherdess also are the supporters. This has been ascribed to *Hogarth*, but I suspect it to be a copy, and am told indeed that it was engraved by *Pelitreau*.

20. Impression from a coat of arms engraved on a silver dish made by *Delemery*; purchased, at some distance of time, by Sir *Gregory Page*, Bart. who erased the original arms from the escutcheon, and had his own put in. The dish was afterwards bought at *Christie's* at a sale of Sir *Gregory's* plate; and when 25 impressions only had been taken from it, was cut to pieces by R. *Morrison*, 1781. I wish some of these discoveries of *Hogarth's* engravings had been made by people who had no immediate view to their own profit, and the sale of their acquisitions. Too many of our collectors are become dealers.

21. Small oval print for the Rape of the Lock. This was not designed for any edition of it. A few impressions only were taken off from the lid of a snuff-box engraved by Mr. *Hogarth*, as it is believed, for some gentleman

characterized by *Pope* in his celebrated mock-heroic poem. It is one of the poorest of *Hogarth's* performances.

22. An emblematic print, representing Agriculture and Arts. "*It seems to be a ticket for some society.*"

23. A ticket for the benefit of *Milward* the tragedian. A scene in *The Beggar's Opera*; "Pitt 3 *s.*" inserted with a pen between "Theatre" and "Royal," in a scroll at the bottom of it. I have seen an impression of it, under which is engraved, "*Lincolns-Inn Fields, Tuesday, Aprill 23. A Bold Stroke for a Wife*, with Entertainments, for the benefit of Mr. *Milward.*" This careless, but spirited little engraving, has more of *Hogarth's* manner than several other more laboured pieces, which of late have been imputed to him.—Let the connoisseur judge.

This ticket (as is already observed) must have been issued before 1733, when the Theatre in *Lincolns-Inn-Fields* was shut up, and all the actors, *Milward* among the rest, removed to *Covent Garden*.

24. The Mystery of Masonry brought to Light by the *Gormagons*.

> A. *Chin Quaw-Kypo' Done from ye Original.*
> 1st *Emperor of China. Painted at Pekin by Matt-chauter,*
> B. *The sage Confucius. Grav'd by Ho-ge*
> C. *In Chin present and sold by ye Printsellers*
> *Oecumenical Volgi. of London Paris and Rome.*
> D. *The Mandarin Hangchi. Hogarth inv. et sculp.*

To the earliest impressions of this plate, the name of *Sayer* (for whom it has since been retouched) is wanting. "*Stolen from* Coypel's Don Quixote." Underneath, these verses:

> From Eastern climes, transplanted to our coasts,
> Two oldest orders that creation boasts
> Here meet in miniature, expos'd to view
> That by their conduct men may judge their due.
>
> The *Gormagons*, a venerable race,
> Appear distinguish'd with peculiar grace:
> What honour! wisdom! truth! and social love!
> Sure such an order had its birth, above.
>
> But mark Free Masons! what a farce is this?
> How wild their mystery! what a *Bum* they kiss![1]
> Who would not laugh,[2] who such occasions had?
> Who should not weep, to think the world so mad?

I should suspect that this plate was published about 1742, when the Procession[3] of *Scald Miserables* had been produced[4] to parody the cavalcade of the *Free Masons*, who ever afterwards discontinued their annual procession. *Hogarth* was always ready to avail himself of any popular subject that afforded a scope to ridicule. Among *Harry Carey's* Poems, however, 1729, third edition, is the following;

> "The Moderator between the Free-Masons and Gormogons.
>
> "The Masons and the Gormogons
> Are laughing at one another,
> While all mankind are laughing at them;
> Then why do they make such a pother?
>
> "They bait their hook for simple gulls,
> And truth with bam they smother;
> But when they've taken in their culls,
> Why then 'tis—Welcome Brother!"

The particular disputes between the parties referred to by this poem, it is not easy to ascertain. Perhaps the humourous writer alludes to some schism or dissention now forgotten. Mr. *Gray*, in one of his letters to Mr. *Walpole*, says, "I reckon next week to hear you are a Free Mason, or a *Gormogon* at least." 4to edition, p. 188.

I learn from *Masonry Dissected*, &c. a pamphlet published in 1730, by *Samuel Prichard*, late member of a Constituted Lodge, that "From the Accepted Mason sprang the real Masons, and from both sprang the *Gormogons*, whose grand master the *Volgi* deduces his original from the *Chinese*, whose writings, if to be credited, maintain the hypotheses of the Pre-adamites, and consequently must be more antique than Masonry."—This circumstance will account for the *Chinese* names and habits in our artist's plate.

[1] On this occasion the print exhibits a trait of humour that may hitherto have escaped observation. To render the part presented for salutation more tempting, it has patches on, such as women wore at the time when the plate was published.

[2] *Who would not laugh*, &c. Parody on the concluding couplet of *Pope's* character of *Addison*.

[3] The contrivers of the Mock Procession were at that time said to be *Paul Whitehead*, esq. and his intimate friend (whose real Christian name was *Esquire*) *Carey*, of *Pall Mall*, surgeon to *Frederic* Prince of *Wales*. The city officers did not suffer this procession to go through *Temple-Bar*, the common report then being, that its real intent was to affront the annual procession of the Free Masons. The Prince was so much offended at this piece of ridicule, that he immediately removed *Carey* from the office he held under him.

[4] The print, representing a View of *Somerset-House* and of *The Strand*, is 3 feet 11½ inches in length, and ten inches in width; and is intituled, "A Geometrical View of the grand Procession of the scald-miserable Masons, designed as they were drawn up over against *Somerset-House* in *The Strand*, on the Twenty-seventh of *April*, An° 1742. Invented and engraved by *A. Benoist*, at his Lodgings, at Mr. *Jordan's*, a Grocer, the North East Corner of *Compton-street*, *So-ho*; and sold by the Printsellers of *London* and *Westminster*.—Note, *A. Benoist* teaches Drawing abroad.

"N° 1. The grand Sword Bearer, or Tyler, carrying the Sword of State (a Present of *Ishmael Abiff* to old *Hyram* King of the *Saracens*) to his Grace of *Wattin*, Grand Master of the Holy Lodge of *St. John of Jerusalem* in *Clerkenwell*.

"2. Tylers or Guarders.

"3. Grand Chorus of Instruments.

"4. The Stewards, in three Gutt Carts, drawn by Asses.

"5. Two famous Pillars, *Jachin* and *Boaz*.

"6. Three great Lights: the Sun Hieroglyphical to rule the Day, the Moon Emblematical to rule the Night; a Master Mason Political to rule his—Lodge.

"7. The Entered Prentice's Token.

"8. The Letter G famous in Masonry for differencing the Fellow Craft's Lodge from that of Prentices.

"9. The Funeral of a Grand Master, according to the Rites of the Order, with the 15 loving Brethren.

"10. A Master Mason's Lodge.

"11. Grand Band of Musick.

"12. Two Trophies; one being that of a Black-shoe Boy and Link Boy, the other that of a Chimney Sweeper.

"13. The Equipage of the Grand Master, all the Attendants wearing Mystical Jewels."

A different, but a smaller, print of this Mock Procession was printed in *May* 1742, with the following memoranda, viz. "The great Demand there has been for *The Westminster Journal*, of the 8th instant, occasion'd reprinting the following piece.

"From my own Apartments in *Spring Gardens*.

"Though I do not belong to the Fraternity mentioned in the following piece, and therefore am little concerned in the annual disputes, I think it my duty, as a Watchman of the city of *Westminster*, to preserve the memory of the late extraordinary Cavalcade, the like to which hath never happened since I have been in office. As more solemn processions have of late years been very rare, it cannot surely be taken amiss, either by the *Free Masons*, or the *Scald-Miserables*, that I give so much distinction to this.

"*T. Touchit.*

"The Free Mason's Downfall, or the Restoration of the Scald-Miserables."

After the print follows: "A Key, or Explanation of the solemn and stately Procession of the Scald-Miserable Masons, as it was martial'd on *Tuesday* the 27th past, by their *Scald-Pursuivant* Black Mantle—set forth by Order of the Grand Master *Poncy*."—Printed by *J. Mechell*, at *The Kings Arms* in *Fleet-street*, and sold by the Pamphlet-shops, &c. Price Two-pence.

Extracts from *The London Daily Post, March* 20, 1740-1, &c. "Yesterday some mock Free-Masons marched through *Pall-Mall* and *The Strand*, as far as *Temple-Bar*, in procession; first went fellows on jack-asses, with cows horns in their hands; then a kettle-drummer on a jack-ass, having two butter-firkins for kettle-drums; then followed two carts drawn by jack-asses, having in them the stewards with several badges of their order; then came a mourning coach drawn by six horses, each of a different colour and size, in which were the grand master and wardens; the whole attended by a vast mob. They stayed without *Temple Bar* till the Masons came by, and paid their compliments to them, who returned the same with an agreeable humour that possibly disappointed the witty contriver of this mock scene, whole misfortune is, that though he has some wit, his subjects are generally so ill chosen, that he loses by it as many friends as other people of more judgement gain."

Again, *April* 28, 1742. "Yesterday being the annual feast of the ancient and honourable society of Free and Accepted Masons, they made a grand procession from *Brook-street* to *Haberdashers Hall*, where an elegant entertainment was provided for them, and the evening was concluded with that harmony and decency peculiar to the society."

"Some time before the society began their cavalcade, a number of shoe-cleaners, chimney-sweepers, &c. on foot and in carts, with ridiculous pageants carried before them, went in procession to *Temple-Bar*, by way of jest on the Free-Masons, at the expence, as we hear, of one hundred pounds sterling, which occasioned a great deal of diversion."

Again, *May* 3, 1744. "Yesterday several of the mock masons were taken up by the constable empowered to impress men for his Majesty's service, and confined till they can be examined by the justices."

24. *Sancho*, at the magnificent feast, &c. starved by his Physician. On the top of this plate are the following words: "This original print was invented and engraved by *William Hogarth*. Price 1 *s.*" At bottom we read, *W. Hogarth inv. & sculp. Printed for H. Overton and J. Hoole.* Perhaps this design was meant as a rival to that of *Coypel* on the same subject; or might be intended by way of specimen of a complete set of plates for *Don Quixote*. Mr. *S. Ireland* has the original drawing.

25. Impression from a tankard belonging to a club of artists, who met weekly at *The Bull's Head* in *Clare-Market*. Of this society *Hogarth* was a member. A shepherd and his flock are here represented.

26. The Gin Drinkers. This may have been one of *Hogarth's* early performances; and, if such, is to be considered as a rude fore-runner of his *Gin-Lane*. But I do not vouch for its authencity.

27. The Oratory.[1] Orator *Henley* on a scaffold, a monkey (over whom is written *Amen*) by his side. A box of pills and the Hyp Doctor lying beside him. Over his head, "The ORATORY. *Inveniam viam, aut faciam.*"[2] Over the door. "*Ingredere ut proficias.*"[3] A Parson receiving the money for admission. Under him, "The Treasury." A Butcher stands as porter. On the left hand, Modesty in a cloud; Folly in a coach; and a gibbet prepared for Merit; people laughing. One marked THE SCOUT,[4] introducing a Puritan Divine. A Boy easing nature. Several grotesque figures, one of them (marked TEE-HEE) in a violent fit of laughter. I discover no reason for regarding this as a production of *Hogarth*, though his name, cut from the bottom of one of his smaller works, was fraudulently affixed to an impression of it belonging to the late worthy Mr. *Ingham Foster*, whose prints were sold at *Barford's*, in *March* 1783. *Hogarth*, whose resources, both from fancy and observation, were large, was never, like the author of this plate, reduced to the poor necessity of peopling his comic designs with *Pierot, Scaramouch*, and the other hackneyed rabble of *French* and *Italian* farces.

Underneath a second impression of it, is the following inscription:

> "*An extempore Epigram, made at the Oratory:*
> "O Orator! with brazen face and lungs,
> Whose jargon's form'd of ten unlearned tongues,
> Why stand'st thou there a whole long hour haranguing,
> When half the time fits better men for hanging!"
> Geo. B—k—h[5] jun. *Copper-scratcher*
> *and Grub-Street invent. sculp.*

[1] There are such coincidences between this print and that of *The Beggar's Opera*, as incline me to think they were both by the same hand.

[2] The motto on the medals which Mr *Henley* dispersed as tickets to his subscribers. See Note on *Dunciad*, III. 199.

[3] This inscription is over the outer door of St. *Paul's* school.

[4] On what personage the name of *Scout* was bestowed, I am unable to inform the reader, though I recollect having seen the same figure in several other prints, particularly one from which it appears that he was at last murdered.

[5] B—k—h. Perhaps this was an intended mistake for B—k—m.

28. Orator *Henley* christening a child. *John Sympson jun. fecit.* Mezzotinto (commonly of a greenish colour), with the following verses under it:

> Behold *Vilaria* lately brought to bed,
> Her cheeks now strangers to their rosy red;
> Languid her eyes, yet lovely she appears!
> And oh! what fondness her lord's visage wears!
> The pamper'd priest, in whose extended arms
> The female infant lies, with budding charms,
> Seeming to ask the name e'er he baptise,
> Casts at the handsome gossips his wanton eyes,
> While gay Sir *Fopling*, an accomplish'd ass,
> Is courting his own dear image in the glass:
> The *Midwife* busied too, with mighty care,
> Adjusts the cap, shews innocency fair.
> Behind her stands the *Clerk*, on whose grave face
> Sleek *Abigal* cannot forbear to gaze:
> But master, without thought, poor harmless child,
> Has on the floor the *holy-water* spill'd,
> Thrown down the hat; the lap-dog gnaws the rose;
> And at the fire the *Nurse* is warming cloaths.

One guest enquires the *Parson's* name;—says *Friendly*,
Why, dont you know, Sir?—'tis *Hyp-Doctor*[1] *H———y*.

Sold by J. Sympson, at the Dove in Russel-Court, Drury-Lane. An original sketch in oil, on the same subject, is in the possession of Mr. *S. Ireland*.[2]

[1] He wrote a periodical paper under that title.

[2] See p. 415. for an etching from it.

29. A woman swearing a child to a grave citizen.[1] *W. Hogarth pinx. J. Sympson jun. sculp. Sold by J. Sympson engraver and print-seller, at The Dove in Russel-Court, Drury-Lane.* This Mr. *Walpole* observes to be a very bad print. Perhaps he had only seen some wretched impression, or copy of it (for there are two, the one in a small size, the other large, but fit for no other purpose than to adorn the walls of a country Inn), and therefore spoke with contempt of a performance which hardly deserves so unfavourable a character. This entire design, however, is stolen from a picture of *Heemskirk*, which has been since engraved in mezzotinto by *W. Dickinson* of *New Bond-street*, and published *March 10*, 1772. The original picture is in the possession of Mr. *Watson*, surgeon, in *Rathbone Place*.

The title given to this plate by the ingenious engraver, is *The Village Magistrate*. All the male figures are monkies; all the female ones, cats. *Hogarth* has likewise been indebted to its companion—*The Constable of the Night*. Few impressions from these plates having been hitherto sold, they are both in excellent condition, and the former of them exhibits an indisputable instance of *Hogarth's* plagiarism.

While *Picart* was preparing his *Religious Ceremonies*, he wrote to some friend here, to supply him with representations illustrative of his subject. His correspondent, either through ignorance or design, furnished him with the two preceding plates by *Hogarth*. *Picart* has engraved the former with a few variations, and the latter with the utmost fidelity. The one is called by him *Le Serment de la Fille qui se trouve enceinte*; the other, *Le Baptême domestique*. The first contains a supposed portrait of Sir *Thomas de Veil*. For the conversion of a *civil* into a *religious* ceremony, let the *Frenchman*, or his purveyor, be answerable. The lines under *Hogarth's* performance are as follows:

> Here Justice triumphs in his elbow chair,
> And makes his market of the trading fair;
> His office-shelves with parish laws are grac'd,
> But spelling-books, and guides between 'em placed
> Here pregnant madam screens the real fire,
> And falsely swears her bastard child for hire

> Upon a rich old letcher, who denies
> The fact, and vows the naughty Hussif lies;
> His wife enrag'd, exclaims against her spouse,
> And swears she'll be reveng'd upon his brows;
> The jade, the justice, and church ward'ns agree,
> And force him to provide security.

Hogarth's picture is in the possession of the Rev. Mr. *Whalley*, at *Ecton, Northamptonshire.*

Mr. *Whalley* is the nephew of *John Palmer*, whose portrait is mentioned among the works of *Hogarth.* See p. 295. This picture too is at *Ecton.* The foregoing print (as already observed, p. 121.) must have been published before the year 1735.

[1] A copy of this forms the head-piece to a tale printed in *Banks's* Works, vol, I. p. 248, intituled, "The Substitute Father."

30. Right Hon. *Gustavus* Lord Viscount *Boyne*, &c. &c. Whole length, mezzotinto. W. *Hogarth pinx. Andrew Miller fecit.* "*A very bad print, done in Ireland.*"

I have since met with an early impression of this mezzotinto. The inscription, dedication, &c. underneath it, are as follows:

"*W. Hogarth pinx. Ford fecit.* The R[t]. Hon[ble]. *Gustavus* Lord Visc[t]. *Boyne*, Baron of *Stackallen*, one of his Majesty's most Hon[ble]. Priuy Council, one of the Com[rs]. of the Revenue of *Ireland*, &c.

"To the R[t]. Hon[ble]. the Earl of *Kildare* this plate is humbly dedicated by his Lordship's most obedient humble serv[t]. *Mich. Ford.*

"Published and sold by *Mich. Ford*, Painter and Print-seller on *Cork Hill.* Price 5[s]. 5.[d] [i. e. five thirteens."]

Mr. *Walpole's* is probably a later or a retouched impression from the same plate, after it had fallen into the hands of one *Andrew Miller*, who effaced the name of *Ford*, and substituted his own.

This scarce print will undoubtedly suffer from comparison with the works of *Smith, M'Ardell, Earlom, Jones*, &c. and yet perhaps it is the best mezzotinto that *Ireland* has hitherto produced. It must be confessed, however, that *Hogarth's* whole-length figure of Lord *Boyne* is equally void of grace, meaning, and proportion; but these defects have no connection with the labours of

Ford, which would have appeared to more advantage had they been exerted on a better subject.

31. Mr. *Pine* (the celebrated engraver), in the manner of *Rembrandt*. Mezzotinto (about the year 1746), by *M'Ardell, Price* 2 *s*. The original was in the possession of the late Mr. *Ranby* the surgeon.

There is a second head of Mr. *Pine*, a mezzotinto; both his hands leaning on a cane. Printed for *George Pulley*, at *Rembrandt's Head*, the corner of *Bride-court, Fleet-street*.

I have called this "a second head," but know not which of the two was first published.

In the first edition of the present work I had described this plate as an unfinished one, but have since met with it in a perfect state.

32. A View of Mr. *Ranby's* house at *Chiswick. Etched by Hogarth*. This view, I am informed, was taken in 1750, but was not designed for sale.

33. *Daniel Lock*, Esq. F. S. A. formerly an architect. He retired from business with a good fortune, lived in *Surrey-street*, and was buried in the chapel of *Trinity College, Cambridge*. Mezzotinto. *W. Hogarth pinx. J. M'Ardell fecit*. Price 1 *s*. 6 *d*.

34. Christ and his disciples; persons at a distance carried to an hospital. "In as much as ye have done it unto one of the least of these my brethren, ye have done it unto me." *St. Matt*. xxv. ver. 40. *W. Hogarth inv. C. Grignion sculp*. Ticket for *The London Hospital*.

As this charitable foundation was instituted in 1740, probably the ticket was engraved soon afterwards.

35. Original of the same, in a smaller size, with the Duke of *Richmond's* arms as president.

36. Another, almost the same as N° 34, but with a view of *The London Hospital*.

37. Six prints for *Don Quixote. W. Hogarth inv. & sculp*.

When Lord *Carteret*, about the year 1737, was seeking artists to design, &c. plates for his *Spanish* edition of this famous novel, published in 1738, *Hogarth*, of course, was not overlooked. His performances, however, gave so little satisfaction to his noble employer, that they were paid for, and then laid aside in favour of *Vandrebank's* drawings, afterwards engraved by *Vandergucht*. The plates remaining in the hands of Mr. *Tonson*, his lordship's publisher, at his death, were bought by Mr. *Dodsley*, who, finding they exhibited no descriptions that could render them welcome to the possessors of any copy of *Don Quixote* whatever, had the titles of the chapters, &c. to which they belong, together with references to the corresponding pages in *Jarvis's* translation, engraved under each of them. The subjects of them are, I. Funeral of *Chrysostom*, and *Marcella* vindicating herself; vol. I. p. 71. II. The Inn-keeper's wife and daughter taking care of the Don after being beaten and bruised, p. 129. III. *Don Quixote* releases the galley slaves, p. 129. IV. The unfortunate Knight of the Rock meeting *Don Quixote*, p. 140. V. *Don Quixote* seizes the barber's bason for *Mambrino's* helmet, p. 155. VI. The Curate and Barber disguising themselves to convey *Don Quixote* home, p. 166. *Tonson* had several specimens of plates, both in quarto and octavo sizes, executed for editions of *Shakspeare*, but they shared the same fate with the others prepared for *Don Quixote*.

38. An oval, with two figures representing *Hymen* and *Cupid*. A view of a magnificent villa at a distance. This print was intended as a ticket for *Sigismunda*, which *Hogarth* proposed to be raffled for. It is often marked with ink 2 *l*. 2 *s*. The number of each ticket was to have been inserted on the scroll hanging down from the knee of the principal figure. Perhaps none of them were ever disposed of. This plate, however, must have been engraved about 1762 or 3. Had I not seen many copies of it marked by the hand of *Hogarth*, I should have supposed it to have been only a ticket for a concert or music-meeting.

39. Four heads from the cartoons at *Hampton-Court*. An etching.

Mr. *Walpole*, in his *Anecdotes of Painting*, &c. vol. IV. p. 22. speaking of Sir *James Thornhill's* attention to these celebrated pictures, has the following remark: "He made copious studies of the heads, hands, and feet, and intended to publish an exact account of the whole, for the use of students: but his work never appeared."

As this plate was found among others engraved by *Hogarth*, it might probably have been one of his early performances. His widow has directed a few impressions to be taken from it, and they are sold at her house in *Leicester-square*.

40. A Scene in a Pantomime Entertainment lately exhibited; designed by a Knight of *Malta*. A satire on the Royal Incorporated Society of Artists of *Great Britain*. No name.

This design is difficult to be explained, as it alludes to some forgotten dissentions among the artists before the Royal Academy was founded. Sir *William Chambers, Kirby, Rooker* the Engraver and Harlequin, *Liotard*, remarkable for having adopted the *Turkish* dress, and others, are introduced in it. The hat and head of *Hogarth* also appear on one of the necks of a Hydra. It is hardly credible, therefore, that he should have rendered himself an object of his own satire. A mere etched outline of the same design, with additions, was afterwards published, and is marked plate II. It is larger than the original plate, and must be considered as a slight temporary sketch, of which the author is uncertain.

41. A Ticket-porter carrying a load of chamber-pots to some place of public resort, from the entrance of which three grenadiers are keeping off the crowd. At the bottom is written.

"*Jack* in an Office, or *Peter Necessary*, with Choice of Chamber-pots.

"A Ticket for the————————————————Price 6 *d.*"

Of the following articles the 49th, and 53d, are the undoubted productions of *Hogarth*. Some of the rest may admit of dispute. Those marked * I have not yet seen in any collection but that of Mr. *S. Ireland*.

* 42. Arms of *George Lambart* [*Lambert*] the painter, an intimate friend of our artist.

* 43. Arms of *Gore*, engraved on a silver waiter.

* 44. Arms of a Duke of *Kendal.* N. B. There never was a *Duke* of *Kendal*, but an infant son of *James* II. The arms mentioned are certainly those of the Dutchess of *Kendal.* The male shield must be a mistake.

* 45. Arms of *Chudleigh*; motto "Aut vincam, aut peribo." Done for Major *L'Emery*, whilst *Hogarth* was apprentice.

46. The Great Seal of *England*, from a large silver table. This was given to Mr. *S. Ireland* by a Mr. *Bonneau*, who took off the impression before the year 1740.

47. Twenty-six figures, on two large sheets, engraved for "A Compendium of Military Discipline, as it is practised by the Honourable the Artillery Company of the City of *London*, for the initiating and instructing Officers of the Trained Bands of the said City, &c. Most humbly dedicated to his Royal Highness *George* Prince of *Wales*, Captain General of the Honourable the Artillery Company. By *John Blackwell*, Adjutant and Clerk to the said Company.

"*London*. Printed for the Author; and are to be sold at his house in *Well-Court* in *Queen-Street*, near *Cheapside*, 1726."

48. *Farinelli, Cuzzoni,* and *Heydegger. Cuzzoni* and *Farinelli* are singing a duet. The latter is in the character of a prisoner, being chained by his little finger. *Heydegger* sits behind, and is supposed to utter the eight following lines, which are engraved under the plate:

> Thou tuneful scarecrow, and thou warbling bird,
> No shelter for your notes these lands afford.
> This town protects no more the singsong strain,
> Whilst Balls and Masquerades triumphant reign.
> Sooner than midnight revels ere should fail,
> And ore Ridottos Harmony prevail;
> The cap (a refuge once) my head shall grace,
> And save from ruin this harmonious face.[1]

I am told, however, that this plate was designed by the last Countess of *Burlington*, and etched by *Goupy*. I may add, that the figures in it, though slightly done on the whole, consist of more than a single stroke, being retouched and heightened by the burin in several places. On the contrary, *Hogarth's* plate, intituled *The Charmers of the Age*, only offers an etched outline, which at once afforded the extent of his design, leaving no room for improvement. The former print exhibits traces of perseverance and assiduity; the latter is an effort of genius that completes its purpose without elaboration.

[1] He had once enlisted as a private soldier in the Guards, for a protection. See p. 152.

49. The Discovery. This scarce plate is acknowledged as genuine by Mrs. *Hogarth*. The subject is a black woman in bed; her eyes archly turned on her gallant just risen, who expresses his astonishment on the entrance of three laughing friends, one of them with a candle in his hand. Underneath the print is this apposite motto:

> *Qui color albus erat nunc est contrarius albo.*

A similar circumstance occurs in *Fletcher's Monsieur Thomas*, and in *Foote's Cozeners*.

I know not of any among our artist's works that displays so little character. It must have been one of his early performances.

It should be observed that, being founded on a private occurrence, this print was never designed for general circulation. Mr. *Highmore* the manager of *Drury-Lane*, who bought *Cibber's* share in the patent, is the Hero of it. A few copies only were distributed among *Hogarth's* particular friends, and the gentlemen whose portraits it contains. At the bottom of the plate there is no descriptive title. *The Discovery* was that by which Mrs. *Hogarth* mentioned it when she recollected the very laughable circumstance here commemorated by her husband's pencil.

* 50. The Cottage. An impression from a breeches-button, the size of a crown-piece; a sketch made for Mr. *Camfield*, a surgeon, on a subject that will not bear explanation. There is a copy of this little plate by Mr. *S. Ireland*.

51. *Pug* the Painter. This has been usually understood as a satire *on Hogarth*, rather than a design *by* him. Mr. *Ireland* once told me it was etched by *Dawes*, and that our artist gave a copy of it, as his own design, to Mr. *Kirby*. But I am assured with superior confidence by another gentleman, that the true author of it is to be sought among those artists whom *Hogarth* had provoked by his contemptuous treatment of their works. If *Pug* was not designed as his representative, why is the animal exhibited in the act of painting the ridiculous figure of the *Priest* in *The Good Samaritan?*

52. A Head in an oval, coarsely engraved, and subscribed "*Samuel Butler* Author of *Hudibras.*" Several connoisseurs, beside Mr. *Thane* who possesses the plate, conceive it to be an undoubted work of *Hogarth*. For what purpose it was executed, and why suppressed (for no one has hitherto met with even a proof from it) it is vain to enquire. I am silent on the subject, heartily wishing that throughout this work I had had the opinions of more friends to record, and had offered fewer sentiments of my own.

53. "A very rare hieroglyphic print; representing Royalty, Episcopacy, and Law, composed of emblematic attributes, and no human features or limbs; with attendants of similar ingredients. Beneath is this inscription. Some of the principal inhabitants of the Moon, as they were discovered by a telescope, brought to the greatest perfection since the last eclipse; exactly engraved from the objects, whereby the Curious may guess at their Religion, Manners, &c. Price Six-pence."

A kind of scaffold above the clouds is the theatre of this representation. Monarchy, Episcopacy, and Law, appear characteristically seated. Their faces are—a Crown-piece—a *Jew's* Harp, and—a Mallet. The monarch holds a globe and sceptre, with crescents on the tops of them. Instead of a collar of *esses*, he wears a string of bubbles; his side is ornamented with a pointed star; and a circle, the emblem of perpetuity, is embroidered on the cloth under his throne. Episcopacy is working at a pump (a type I suppose of the Church) by the assistance of a bell-rope. The Bible is fastened to the handle of the pump, and out of the nose of it issues money that falls into a chest discriminated by an armorial escutcheon, containing a knife and fork, properly emblazoned, with a mitre by way of crest. The lid of the coffer leans against a pillar, that serves also to support a triple pile of cushions. Over the top of the pump (which is fashioned much like a steeple) is a weathercock on a small pyramid supported by balls; and below it, through a circular opening, a little bell appears to ring. Under the sacerdotal robe, a cloven foot peeps out. Law sustains a sword; and behind him appears a dagger thrust through the bottom of a sieve. The attendants on Monarchy are of various materials. The bodies and legs of such as seem designed for soldiers, are composed of circular fire-screens resembling shields. The trunks of the courtiers are large looking-glasses, the sconces with candles in them serving for hands and arms. The face of the chief of these is the reverse of a sixpence; and a key significantly appended to his sash, at once denotes his sex and office. Under the figure of law are a male and female modishly drest. Her head is a tea-pot, her neck a drinking-glass, and her body a fan half spread. On the oval that forms the countenance of her paramour, is a coat of arms with supporters. His right honourable legs are fan-sticks, and he seems in the act of courtship. How this couple are immediately connected with Law, is not very clearly pointed out. *Hogarth*, however, we may suppose, had planned some explanation of his hieroglyphics, as the letters *a, b, c, d, e, f, g,* are placed over some of them, and beneath others.

From the form of the perukes exhibited in this design, I should suppose it was made above forty years ago. Other circumstances in it need no decyphering.

* 54. The Master of the Vineyard. St. *Matthew* chap. xxi. v. 28. "Son, go work to-day in my Vineyard."

* 55. The *London* Infirmary for charitably relieving sick and diseased Manufacturers and Seamen in the Merchants' service, their Wives and Children. A blank certificate for Pupils in Surgery and Anatomy, printed on a half sheet, folio.

56. A ticket for the benefit of *Spiller* the player. He died in the year 1729.

In the plate before us, which possesses no small share of humour, poor *Spiller* is represented in a melancholy posture. His finances are weighed against his debts, and outweighed by them. His taylor's bill appears to be of great length, and many others for ale, gin, &c. are on the ground near him. A bailiff is clapping him on the shoulder—a prison is in sight—ladies and gentlemen are taking tickets, &c. This very uncommon and beautiful little print is, at present, found only in the collection of Mr. *Ireland*.

57. St. *Mary's Chapel*. Five at night. Several performers playing on different instruments. *William Hogarth inv. G. Vandergucht sculpt.*

This was certainly an ornament at the top of a ticket for a music-meeting. The name of *Hogarth* is affixed to it, and the whole design *might* have been his. I do not, however, believe it *was* so. A few of the figures appear to have been collected from his works by some other hand, rather than grouped by his own. *Vandergucht* too was so thoroughly a mannerist, and especially in small subjects, that he was rarely faithful to the expressions of countenance he undertook to trace on copper. There is no humour, and indeed little merit of any kind, in this performance. It has not hitherto been met with on the entire piece of paper to which it must originally have belonged.

A print called *The Scotch Congregation*, by *Hogarth*, is almost unique, on account of its extreme indecency. One copy of it was in a collection of his works belonging to Mr. *Alexander* of *Edinburgh*. He is said to have had it from Mrs. *Hogarth*. A second copy is reported to exist in the possession of another gentleman. No more impressions of it are known.

A correspondent at *Dublin* informs me, that in the collection of Dr. *Hopkins* of that city are the following seven prints by *Hogarth*:

1. *The History of Witchcraft.* Humbly dedicated to the Wise. Allegorically modernized. Part the First. Published according to act of Parliament. *Hogarth inv. et sculpt.*

Half sheet print. At one end, Witches attending the punishment of two human figures; at the other, several at their different occupations.

2. *The History of Witchcraft.* Part the Second. Published according to act of Parliament. *Hogarth inv. et sculpt.*

Same size as the former. Witches dancing; others at various amusements. These two prints contain a great variety of distorted figures.

3. *A Suit of Law fits me better than a Suit of Clothes.* Invented and engraved by *W. H.* and published pursuant to an Act of Parliament, 1740.

An upright half-sheet. A Man in embroidered clothes, his hat under his arm. A scroll in his left hand, inscribed, "I'll go to Law." Huntsmen, dogs, and horses in the back ground. Four lines in verse underneath.

Useful in all families. Invented and engraved by *W. H.* and published pursuant to an Act of Parliament, 1740.

4. The same man in a tattered garment in a wild country; a staff in his right hand, and a scroll in his left, inscribed, "To shew that I went to law, and got the better." Four lines at the bottom.

These two may be classed among his indifferent prints.

5. *The Caledonian March and Embarkation. Hogarth invent. London*, printed for *T. Baldwin.*

A number of *Scotchmen* embarking in the *Caledonian* Transport. Labels issuing from their mouths.

The Laird of the Posts, or the Bonnets exalted. Printed for *T. Baldwin, London. Hogarth inv.*

6. *A Scotch Nobleman and his Friends taking possession of several posts, having kick'd down the former Possessors.* Labels from their mouths too tedious to copy. A Lion on the fore-ground, hood-winked by a *Scotch* plaid.

Supposed to be printed for *The London Magazine.*

7. *The Lion entranced.* Printed for *T. Baldwin, London. Hogarth inv.* 1762.

A Lion in a Coffin. A plate on the cover, inscribed, "Leo *Britanicus,* Ob. An. 1762. Requiescat in pace." Attended by state mourners with labels as above. In one corner *Hibernia* supplicating for her Sister's interest.

A respect for the obliging communicator has induced me to publish this *supposed* addition to the foregoing catalogue of *Hogarth's* works. But, without ocular proof, I cannot receive as genuine any one of the plates enumerated. The name of our Artist has more than once been subscribed to the wretched productions of others; and a collector at *Dublin* must have had singular good fortune indeed, if he has met with seven authentic curiosities unknown to the most confidential friends of *Hogarth,* and the most industrious connoisseurs about *London.* I may add, that two, if not three, of the above-mentioned anti-ministeral pieces, appeared in 1762, the very year in which our artist was appointed *Serjeant Painter.* Till that period he is unsuspected of having engaged his pencil in the service of politicks; and *T. Baldwin* (perhaps a fictitious name) is not known to have been on any former occasion his publisher. So much for the probability of *Hogarth's* having ushered performances like these into the world.

Chance, and the kindness of my friends, have not enabled me to form a more accurate series of *Hogarth's* labours. Those of the collector, however, are still incomplete, unless he can furnish himself with a specimen of several other pieces, said, I think, to have been produced a little before our artist's marriage. I forbear to keep my readers in suspense on the occasion. *Hogarth* once taking up some plain ivory fishes that lay on his future wife's card-table, observed how much was wanting to render them natural representations. Having delivered this remark with becoming gravity, he proceeded to engrave scales, fins, &c. on each of them. A few impressions have been taken from these curiosities, which remain in Mrs. *Hogarth's* possession. As a *button* decorated by her husband has been received into the foregoing catalogue of his works, it can hardly be disgraced by this brief mention of the ornaments he bestowed on a *counter*.

There are three large volumes in quarto by *Lavater*, a minister at *Zurich* (with great numbers of plates), on Physiognomy. Among these are two containing several groups of figures from different prints of *Hogarth*, together with the portraits of Lord *Lovat* and *Wilkes*. For what particular purpose they are introduced, remains to me a secret.[1]

In "An Address of Thanks to the Broad Bottoms, for the good things they have done, and the evil things they have not done, since their elevation, 1745," is what the author calls "A curious emblematic Frontispiece, taken from an original painting of the ingenious Mr. H———*th*;" a palpable imposition.

Mr. *Walpole*, *Anecdotes of Painting*, Vol. IV. 63, observes, that "*Hogarth* drew the supposed funeral of *Vanaken*, attended by the painters he worked for, discovering every mark of grief and despair." To explain this passage, it should be added, that "he was employed by several considerable artists here, to draw the attitudes, and dress the figures in their pictures."

The merits of *Hogarth*, as an engraver, are inconsiderable. His hand was faithful to character, but had little acquaintance with the powers of light and shade. In some of his early prints he was an assiduous imitator of *Callot*, but deviated at last into a manner of his own, which suffers much by comparison with that of his coadjutors, *Ravenet* and *Sullivan*. In the pieces finished by these masters of their art, there is a clearness that *Hogarth* could never reach. His strokes sometimes look as if fortuitously disposed, and sometimes confusedly thwart each other in almost every possible direction. What he wanted in skill, he strove to make up in labour; but the result of it was a universal haze and indistinctness, that, by excluding force and transparency, has rendered several of his larger plates less captivating than they would have been, had he entrusted the sole execution of them to either of the artists already mentioned. His smaller etchings, indeed, such as *The Laughing Pit*, &c. cannot receive too much commendation.

Mr. *Walpole* has justly observed, that "many wretched prints came out to ridicule" the *Analysis of Beauty*. He might have added, that no small number of the same quality were produced immediately after the *Times* made its appearance. I wish it had been in my power to have afforded my readers a complete list of these performances, that as little as possible might have been wanting to the history of poor *Hogarth's* first and second persecution. Such a catalogue, however, not being necessary to the explanation of his works, it is with the less regret omitted.[2]

The scarceness of the good impressions of *Hogarth's* larger works is in great measure owing to their having been pasted on canvas or boards, to be framed and glazed for furniture. There were few people who collected his prints for any other purpose at their first appearance. The majority of these sets being hung up in *London* houses, have been utterly spoiled by smoke. Since foreigners have learned the value of the same performances, they have also been exported in considerable numbers. Wherever a taste for the fine arts has prevailed, the works of this great master are to be found. Messieurs *Torré* have frequent commissions to send them into *Italy*. I am credibly informed that the Empress of *Russia* has expressed uncommon pleasure in examining such genuine representations of *English* manners; and I have seen a set of cups and saucers with *The Harlot's Progress* painted on them in *China* about the year 1739.

Of all such engravings as are Mrs. *Hogarth's* property, the later impressions continue selling on terms specified many years ago in her printed catalogue, which the reader will find at the end of this pamphlet. The few elder proofs that remain undisposed of, may be likewise had from her agent at an advance of price. As to the plates which our artist had not retained as his own property, when any of these desiderata are found (perhaps in a state of corrosion), they are immediately vamped up, and impressions from them are offered to sale, at three, four, or five times their original value. They are also stained to give them the appearance of age; and on these occasions we are confidently assured, that only a few copies, which had lurked in some obscure warehouse, or neglected port-feuille, had been just discovered. This information is usually accompanied by sober advice to buy while we may, as the vender has scarce a moment free from the repeated solicitations of the nobility and gentry, whom he always wishes to oblige, still affording that preference to the connoisseur which he withholds from the less enlightened purchaser. It is scarce needful to observe, that no man ever visited the shops of these polite dealers, without soon fancying himself entitled to the more creditable of the aforesaid distinctions. Thus becoming a dupe to his own vanity, as well as to the artifice of the tradesman, he has speedily the mortification to find his supposed rarities are to be met with in every collection, and not long afterwards on every stall. The caution may not prove useless to those who are ambitious to assemble the works of *Hogarth*. Such a pursuit needs no apology; for sure, of all his fraternity, whether ancient or modern, he bent the keenest eye on the follies and vices of mankind, and expressed them with a degree of variety and force, which it would be vain to seek among the satiric compositions of any other painters. In short, what is observed by *Hamlet* concerning a player's office, may, with some few exceptions, be applied to the designs of *Hogarth*. "Their end, both at the first, and now, was, and is, to hold as 'twere the mirror up to nature; to shew virtue her own feature, scorn her own image, and the very age and body of the time his own form and pressure."

I may add, that, since the appearance of Mr. *Walpole's* Catalogue, a disposition to attribute several anonymous plates, on ludicrous subjects, to *Hogarth*, has betrayed itself in more than a single instance:[3] a supposition has also prevailed that there was a time when *Hogarth* had the whole field of satire to himself, and we could boast of no designers whose performances could be mistaken for his own. The latter notion is undoubtedly true, if real judges are to decide; and yet many prints, very slightly impregnated with humour, continue to be ascribed to him. It should therefore be observed, that, at the same period, *Bickham, Vandergucht, Boitard, Gravelot, Laguerre* the younger, &c. were occasionally publishing satirical Sketches, and engraving laughable frontispieces for books and pamphlets. To many of these, for various reasons, they forbore to set their names; and we have at present collectors, who, to obtain the credit of having made discoveries, are willing to adopt such performances as the genuine effusions of *Hogarth*, although every way beneath his talents, and repugnant to his style of engraving. Perhaps also the names of other painters and designers have been occasionally obliterated, to countenance the same fallacy. Copies likewise have been palmed on the unwary for originals. "Therefore" (gentle reader) for once be content to follow the advice of *Pistol*, "Go clear thy chrystals, and *Caveto* be thy counsellor." For if all such fatherless engravings, as the vanity of some, and the interest, or the ignorance, of others, would introduce among the works of our artist, were to be admitted, when would the collector's labour and expence be at end?

Among other anonymous plates ascribed to *Hogarth*, but omitted in the present catalogue, is the following, *A living Dog is better than a dead Lion*, or, *The Vanity of human Glory; a design for the Monument of General Wolfe*, 1760. A medallion of our hero appears on the side of a pyramid. On the base of it is the well known speech of *Shakespeare's Brutus*,

> *Set Honour in one hand, and Death in t' other,*
> *And I will look on both indifferent:*
> *And let the Gods so speed me, as I love*
> *The name of Honour more than I fear Death.*

At the bottom a dying Lion is extended, while a Dog (with *Minden* on his collar, and *Honour's a jest*, &c. issuing from his mouth) is at once lifting up his leg against the noble brute, and treading on a wreath of laurel. *Here lies Honour*, is also written on the side of the expiring animal. I have since been assured that this print was by another artist, whose name I omit to mention, because perhaps he would wish it, on the present occasion, suppressed.

[1] This book, I am told, is now translated into *French*.

[2] One of these productions, however, should be singled from the rest. The print, entitled *The Connoisseurs*, was suspected to be a work of *Hogarth* himself. It is placed with some of his other undisputed designs in the back-ground of *The Author run Mad* (which is known to be one of Mr. *Sandby's* performances), and has the following reference—"*A.* his own *Dunciad.*"

[3] Thus the frontispiece to *Taste*, designed, if not etched by *Worsdale* (for whose benefit this dramatic piece was performed), and *Sawney in the Bog-house*, an anonymous satire on the *Scotch*, that made its appearance near forty years ago, and was revived during the administration of Lord *Bute*, are at present imputed to our artist, whose name is already engraved at the bottom of the latter.

POSTSCRIPT.

The Author of this pamphlet, being convinced that, in spite of all his care and attention, some errors may still be found in his catalogue, list of variations, &c. will think himself highly obliged by any gentlemen who will point them out, and enable him to correct them. Such favours shall be gratefully acknowledged, if the present rude Essay towards an account of *Hogarth's* different performances should happen to reach another edition.

As in consequence of the extraordinary prices lately paid for the collected works of this great master, certain dealers, &c. are supposed to be assembling as many of his prints as they can meet with,—binding them up in pompous volumes,—writing "fine old impressions" either over or under them—specifying the precise sums pretended to have been disbursed for several of them (perhaps a guinea for a three shilling article)—preparing to offer a few rare trifles to sale, overloaded with a heap of wretched proofs from our artist's more capital performances;—exhibiting imperfect suites of such as are cut out of books; and intending to station puffers at future auctions, whose office will be to intimate they have received commissions to bid up as far as such or such an amount (i. e. the sum under which the concealed proprietor resolves not to part with his ware), &c. &c. it is hoped the reader will excuse a few parting words of admonition. Perhaps it may be in the power of Mrs. *Hogarth* to select a few sets from such of her husband's pieces as have remained in her own custody from the hour of their publication. Let the multitude, who of course cannot be supplied with these, become their own collectors. Even ignorance is a more trusty guide than professional artifice. It may be urged, indeed, that the proportionate value of impressions[1] can be ascertained only by those who have examined many of them in their various states, with diligence and acuteness. But surely to qualify ourselves for estimating the merit of the curiosities we are ambitious to purchase, is wiser than to rely altogether on the information of people whose interest is commonly the reverse of our own. Let it also be remembered, that the least precious of all *Hogarth's* productions are by far the scarcest; and that when, at an immoderate expence, we have procured impressions from tankards ornamented by him, or armorial ensigns engraved for the books of his customers, we shall be found at last to have added nothing to his fame, or the entertaining quality of our own collections. By such means, however, we may open a door to imposition. A work like *The Harlot's Progress* will certainly remain unimitated as well as inimitable; but it is in the power of every bungler to create fresh coats of arms, or shop bills with our artist's name subscribed to them: and wherein will the Lion or Griffin of *Hogarth* be discovered to excell the same representation by a meaner hand? A crafty selection of paper, and a slight attention to chronology and choice of subjects, with the aid of the hot-press, may, in the end, prove an overmatch for the sagacity of the ablest connoisseur. A single detection of such a forgery would at least give rise to suspicions that might operate even where no fallacy had been designed. How many fraudulent imitations of the smaller works of *Rembrandt* are known to have been circulated with success!—But it may be asked, perhaps, from what source the author of this pamphlet derives his knowledge of such transactions. His answer is, from the majority of collectors whom he has talked with in consequence of his present undertaking.

He ought not, however, to conclude without observing, that several *genuine* works of *Hogarth* yet remain to be engraved. He is happy also to add that a young artist, every way qualified for such a task, has already published a few of these by subscription.

J. N.

[1] Prints have, of late years, been judiciously rated according to the quality of their *impressions*. But the very term *impression*, as applied to copper-plates, perhaps is a novelty among us. If we refer to the earliest and most valuable assemblage of portraits (such as that catalogued by *Ames*, afterwards purchased by Dr. *Fothergill*, and lately sold to Mr. *Thane*), we shall have little reason to suppose any regard was once paid to a particular of so much importance. As fast as heads were met with, they were indiscriminately received; and the faintest proofs do not appear to have been excluded at a time when the strongest might easily have been procured. In consequence of an *àmás* so carelessly formed, the volumes already mentioned, were found to display alternately the most beautiful and the most defective specimens of the graphic art.

J. N. had once thoughts of adding a list of the copies made from the works *of Hogarth*; but finding them to be numerous, beyond expectation, has desisted from a task he could not easily accomplish. This pursuit, however, has enabled him to suggest yet another caution to his readers. Some of the early invaders of *Hogarth's* property were less audacious than the rest; and, forbearing to make exact imitations of his plates, were content with only borrowing particular circumstances from each of them, which they worked up into a similar fable. A set of *The Rake's Progress*, in which the figures were thus disguised and differently grouped, has been lately found. But since the rage of collection broke out with its present vehemence, those dealers who have met with any such diversified copies, have been desirous of putting them off either as the first thoughts of *Hogarth*, or as the inferior productions of elder artists on whose designs he had improved. There, is also a very small set of *The Rake's Progress*, contrived and executed with the varieties already mentioned; and even this has been offered to sale under the former of these descriptions. Thus, as *Shakspeare* says, *While we shut the gate upon one imposition, another knocks at the door.*

It may not be impertinent to conclude these cautions with another notice for the benefit of unexperienced collectors, who in their choice of prints usually prefer the blackest. The earliest copies of *Hogarth's* works are often fainter than such as have been retouched. The excellence of the former consists in clearness as well as strength; but strength only is the characteristic of the latter. The first and third copies of *The Harlot's Progress* will abundantly illustrate my remark, which, however, is confined to good impressions of the plates in either state; for some are now to be met with that no more possess the recommendation of transparency than that of force. I may add, that when plates are much worn, it is customary to load them with a double quantity of colour, that their weakness, as far as possible, may escape the eye of the purchaser. This practice the copper-plate printers facetiously entitle—*coaxing*; and, by the aid of it, the deeper strokes of the graver which are not wholly obliterated, become clogged with ink, while every finer trace, which was of a nature less permanent, is no longer visible. Thus in the modern proofs of *Garrick* in *King Richard III.* the armour, tent, and habit, continue to have considerable strength, though the delicate markings in the face, and the shadows on the inside of the hand, have long since disappeared. Yet this print, even in its faintest state, is still preferable to such smutty impositions as have been recently described. The modern impressions of *The Fair*, and *The March to Finchley*, will yet more forcibly illustrate the same remark.

To the original paintings of *Hogarth* already enumerated may be added a Breakfast-piece, preserved in *Hill-Street, Berkeley-Square*, in the possession of *William Strode*, Esq; of *Northaw, Herts*. It contains portraits of his father the late *William Strode*, Esq; his mother Lady *Anne* (who was sister to the late Earl of *Salisbury*), Colonel *Strode*, and Dr. *Arthur Smith* (afterwards Archbishop of *Dublin*).

ADDITION.

Four Times of the Day, p. 250.

It should have been observed, that the third of these plates was engraved by *Baron*, the figure of the girl excepted, which, being an after-thought, was added by our artist's own hand.

APPENDIX.

N° 1. [See p. 23.]

The following letter, printed in *The Public Advertiser* soon after the first edition of the present work made its appearance, may possibly contain some authentic particulars of the early life of the famous Monsieur *St. André*. Mr. *Woodfall's* ingenious correspondent does not, however, dispose me to retract a syllable of what is advanced in the text; for he fails throughout in his attempts to exculpate our hero from any one of the charges alledged against him. On the contrary, he confirms, with additions, a considerable part of them, and strives only to evade or overwhelm the rest by studied amplifications of the little good which industrious partiality could pick out of its favourite character. I shall now subjoin his epistle, with a few unconnected remarks appended to it. A rambling performance must apologize for a desultory refutation.

"SIR,

"The entertaining author of the last biography of the admirable *Hogarth*, in the excess of commendation of a particular risible subject for his pencil, has written too disadvantageously of the late Mr. *St. André*. One who knew him intimately (but was never under the smallest obligation to him) for the last twenty years of his life, and has learned the tradition of his earlier conduct seemingly better than the editor of the article in question, takes the liberty to give a more favourable idea of him, and without intending to enter into a controversy with this agreeable Collector of Anecdotes, to vindicate this *notorious man*, who must be allowed to have been such; but it is to be hoped in the milder sense Lord *Clarendon* often or always uses the epithet. The making a subject of Mr. *St. André* is therefore merely accidental. The writer expects to derive no praise from exhibiting that person as the Hero of a page. He thinks it is only doing justice (for the Dead deserve justice as well as the Living) when he draws his pen against some very injurious insinuations, thrown out with more inadvertence and at a venture than in malice, against the memory of an acquaintance and of a foreigner (to whom perhaps more mercy is due than to a native), who is more roughly handled than he appears to deserve.

"Mr. *Nathaniel St. André* came over, or rather was brought over, very early from *Switzerland*, his native country, in the train of a *Mendez*, or *Salvadore*, or some *Jewish* family. Next to his countryman *Heidegger*, he became the most considerable person that has been imported from thence. He probably arrived in *England* in no better than a menial station. Possibly his family was not originally obscure, for he has been heard to declare, that he had a rightful claim to a title, but it was not worth while to take it up so late in life. He had undoubtedly all the qualifications of a *Swiss*. He talked *French* in all its provincial dialects, and superintended the press, if the information is to be depended upon, and perhaps taught it, as his sister did at *Chelsea* boarding-school. He was early initiated in music, for he played upon some musical instrument as soon as he was old enough to handle one, to entertain his benefactors. He had the good fortune to be placed by them with a surgeon of eminence, and became very skilful in his profession. His duty and gratitude to his father, whom he maintained when he was no longer able to maintain himself, was exemplary and deserving of high commendation. Let this charity cover a multitude of his sins! His great thirst for anatomical knowledge (for which he became afterwards so famous as to have books dedicated to him on that subject), and his unwearied application, soon made him so compleat an anatomist, that he undertook to read public lectures (and he was the first in *London* who read any), which gave general satisfaction. The most ingenious and considerable men in the kingdom became his pupils. Dr. *Hunter*, now at the head of his profession, speaks highly of his predecessor, and considers him (if the information is genuine) as the wonder of his time. He continued his love of anatomy to the last, and left noble preparations behind him, which he was continually improving. The time of his introduction into Mr. *Molyneux's* family is not known to the writer of this account. Whether anatomy, surgery, knowledge, or music, or his performance on the *Viol de Gambo*, on which he was the greatest master, got him the intimacy with Mr. *Molyneux*, is not easy to determine. Certain it is, that he attended his friend in his last illness, who died of a dangerous disorder (but not under his hands), which Mr. *Molyneux* is said to have pronounced, from the first, would be fatal. Scandal, and Mr. *Pope's* satirical half-line, talked afterwards of 'The Poisoning Wife.' She, perhaps, was in too great a hurry, as the report ran, in marrying when she did, according to the practised delicacy of her sex, and her very high quality. The unlucky business in which one *Howard*, a surgeon at *Guildford*, involved him, who was the projector, or accessary of the impudent imposture of *Mary Tofts*, alias the Rabbit-woman of *Godalmin*, occasioned him to become the talk and ridicule of the whole kingdom. The report made by *St. André*, and others, induced many inconsiderately to take it for a reality. The public horror was so great, that the rent of rabbit-warrens sunk to nothing; and nobody, till the delusion was over, presumed to eat a rabbit. The credulous *Whiston* believed the story (for to some people every thing is credible that comes from a credible witness), and wrote a pamphlet, to prove this *monstrous conception* to be the exact completion of an old prophecy in *Esdras*. The part *St. André* acted in this affair ruined his interest at Court, where he had before been so great a favourite with King *George* I. that he presented him with a sword which he wore himself. Now, on his return out of the country, he met with a personal affront, and never went to Court again. But he continued anatomist to the Royal Houshold to his dying day, though he never took the salary. He probably was imposed upon in this matter. And has it not been the lot of men, in intellectual accomplishments vastly above his, such as *Boyle*, for instance, a man infinitely his superior, to be overreached and misled? He took up the pen on the occasion (and it was not the first time, for he wrote some years before a bantering pamphlet on Dr. *Mead*), which could at best but demonstrate his sincerity, but exposed the weakness of his judgement, on that case. It had been insinuated he adopted this scheme, to ruin some persons of his own profession. If he had a mind to make an experiment upon the national belief, and to tamper with their willingness to swallow any absurdity (which a certain nobleman [Duke of *Montagu*] ventured to do, in the affair of a man who undertook to jump into a quart bottle), he was deservedly punished with contempt. *Swift* (according to *Whiston*), and perhaps *Arbuthnot*, exercised their pens upon him. The cheat was soon discovered, and rabbits began to make their appearance again at table as usual. But they were not at his own table, nor made a dish, in any form of cookery, at that of his friends. Perhaps they imagined that the name or sight of that animal might be as offensive to him, as the mention of *Formosa* is said to have been to *Psalmanazar*. It is told, that, on his asking for some parsly of a market-woman of *Southampton*, and demanding why she had not more to sell, she, in a banter, assured him, 'That his rabbits had eat it up.' The fortune he acquired by marrying into a noble family (though it set all the lady's relations against him, and occasioned her being dismissed from her attendance on Queen *Caroline*) was a sufficient compensation for the laughter or censure of the publick. His high spirit and confidence in himself made him superior to all clamor. So that people did but talk about him, he seldom seemed to care what they talked against him. And yet he had the fortitude to bring an action for defamation in *Westminster-Hall* against a certain doctor in divinity, and got the better of his adversary. He was not supposed, in the judgement of the wiser and more candid part of mankind, to have contributed, by any chirurgical administration, to the death of his friend Mr. *Molyneux*, nor to have set up the imposture at *Godalmin*. Though he was disgraced at Court, he was not abandoned by all his noble friends. The great Lord *Peterborough*, who was his patron and patient long before he went to *Lisbon*, entertained a very high opinion of him to the last. His capacity in all kinds, the reception he gave to his table and his garden, with his liberality to the infirm and distressed, made him visited by persons of the highest quality, and by all strangers and foreigners. He did not continue to enjoy the great fortune his marriage is supposed to have brought him, to the end of his life, for a great part went from him on the death of Lady *Betty*. He by no means left so much property behind him as to have it said, he died rich. His profession as a surgeon, in a reasonable terms of years, would probably have put more money into his pocket than fell in the golden shower so inauspiciously into his lap, and have given him plenty, without envy or blame. He was turned of ninety-six when he died; and though subject to the gout, of which he used to get the better by blisters upon his knees, and by rigid abstinence, yet, when he took to his bed (where he said he should not lie long), and permitted a physician to be called in to him, he cannot be said to have died of any disease. In one sum of generosity, he gave the celebrated *Geminiani* three hundred pounds, to help him to discharge his incumbrances, and to end his days in comfort. The strength and agility of his body were great, and are well known. He was famous for his skill in fencing, in riding the great horse, and for running and jumping, in his younger days. He, at one time, was able to play the game at chess with the best masters. After a slight instruction at *Slaughter's* coffee-house, he did not rest till, in the course of two nights sitting up, he was able to vanquish his instructor. He was so earnest in acquiring knowledge, that he whimsically, as he told the story, cut off his eyelashes, that he might not sleep till he arrived at what he wanted. His face was muscular and fierce. One of his eyes, to external appearance, seemed to be a mass of obscurity (as he expressed it of *Handel's*, when he became stark-blind), at least it had not the uncommon vivacity of the other. His language was full of energy, but loaded with foreign idioms. His conversation was seasoned sufficiently with satire and irony, which he was not afraid to display, though he ought never to have forgot that he was once a proper subject for it. He built; he planted; he had almost 'from the Cedar of *Lebanon* to the hyssop that groweth upon the wall,' in his hot-house, green-house, and garden. If he was not deep in every art and science (for even his long life was not sufficient for universal attainment), he cannot be reckoned to have been ignorant of any thing. He was admired for his knowledge in architecture, in gardening, and in botany, by those who should have been above flattery. But praise, from whatever quarter it comes, is of an intoxicating nature. Those who found out that he loved praise, took care he should have enough of it. He kept a list of the wretched and the indigent, whom he constantly maintained; and their names might be written alphabetically. The poor of *Southampton* know they have lost their best friend. Call it, reader, ostentation or vanity, if you will; but till you know it did not proceed from his goodness of heart, this tributary pen considers his giving away his money to relieve the necessitous, as a spark of the spirit of the Man of *Ross* or the Man of *Bath*. He was all his life too much addicted to amours, and sometimes with the lower part of the sex. His conversation, which he was always able to make entertaining and instructive, was too often tinctured with *double entendre* (a vice that increases with age), but hardly ever with prophaneness. He may be thought to have copied *Hermippus*, and to have considered women as the prolongers of life. How far he was made a dupe by any of them at last, is not necessary for relation. He died, as he lived, without fear; for to his standers-by he gave no sign of a ruffled mind, or a disturbed conscience, in his last moments.

"If the preceding memoir of *St. André* had not been composed entirely from memory (a faculty which, like the sieve of the *Danaids*, is apt to lose as much as it receives), and had not been conveyed to the press with so much precipitancy, the writer, by a second recollection, might have made supplementary anecdotes less necessary. Whilst *St. André* was basking in the sun-shine of public favour in *Northumberland-Court*, near *Charing-Cross*, under pretence of being wanted in his profession at some house in the neighbourhood, he was hurried through so many passages, and up and down so many stair-cases, that he did not know where he was, nor what the untoward scene was to end in, till the horrid conclusion presented itself, of which he published an extraordinary account in *The Gazette* of *Feb.* 23, 1724-5, no less than of his being poisoned, and of his more extraordinary recovery. Such uncommon men must be visited through life with uncommon incidents. The bowl of poison must have been for ever present to his imagination. *Socrates* himself could not expect more certain destruction from the noxious draught he was forced to take down, than seemed inevitable to *St. André*. Nay, a double death seems to have threatened him. Probably it was not any public or private virtue for which *Socrates* was famous, and which occasioned him to suffer, that endangered our hero's life. His constitution was so good, that he got the better of the internal potion. The truth and circumstances of the story could only be known to himself, who authenticated it upon oath. His narrative partakes of the marvellous; and the reader of *July*, 1781, is left in total ignorance of the actor, and the provocation to such a barbarous termination. His case was reported, and he was attended, by the ablest of the faculty: and the Privy Council issued a reward of two hundred pounds towards a discovery. A note in the second supplemental volume of *Swift* informed the writer of this sketch, a day or two ago (who takes to himself the reproof of *Prior*, 'Authors, before they write, should read!'), that *St. André* was convinced he had been imposed upon respecting the woman of *Godalmin*, and that he apologised handsomely to the public in an advertisement, dated *Dec.* 8, 1726.—'He's half absolv'd, who has confest.'—In the autumn, before the heat of the town-talk on this affair was over, he was sent for to attend Mr. *Pope*, who, on his return home from *Dawley* in Lord *Bolingbroke's* coach and six, was overturned in a river, and lost the use of two fingers of his left-hand (happy for the lovers of poetry they were not the servants of the right one!), and gave him assurance, that none of the broken glass was likely to be fatal to him. It is highly improbable, that *Pope* and *Bolingbroke* would have suffered *St. André* to have come near them, if he had been branded as a cheat and an impostor. He died in *March*, 1776, having survived all his contemporary enemies, and, which is the consequence of living long, most of his ancient friends. Such men do not arise every day for our censure or our applause; to gratify the pen or the pencil of character or caricature. He may be considered, as *Voltaire* pronounces of *Charles* the Twelfth, an extraordinary, rather than a great man, and fitter to be admired than imitated.

"IMPARTIAL."

In the first place, I avow that the epithet *notorious* was not meant to be employed in the milder sense of Lord *Clarendon*. Had I undertaken to compile the life of a man eminent for virtue, I should have been happy to have borrowed the softer application of the aforesaid term from our noble historian. But having engaged to delineate a mere impostor's character, there is greater propriety in adopting the disputed word with that constant signification affixed to it by the biographers of *Bet Canning*, or *Fanny* the Phantom of *Cock Lane*.—I shall absolve myself no farther from the charge of "malice," than by observing that there are always people who think *somewhat much too rough has been said of Chartres*.

The dead, declares our apologist, deserve justice as well as their survivors. This is an uncontested truth; nor will the precept be violated by me. I may observe however, with impunity, that the interests of the living, for whose sake a line of separation between good and bad characters is drawn, should be consulted, rather than the memories of the flagitious, who can no longer be affected by human praise or censure, should be spared.

Our apologist next assures us, that perhaps more tenderness is due to a foreigner than to a native. The boasted *amor patriæ* is not very conspicuous in this remark, which indeed was dropped, to as little purpose, by a learned counsel on the trial of the *French Spy* who was lately executed.

"Next to his countryman *Heidegger*," adds our apologist, "Mr. *St. André* became the most *considerable* person that has been imported from *Switzerland*." To judge of the comparative value of the latter, we must estimate the merits of the former. *Heidegger* is known to us only by the uncommon ugliness of his visage, and his adroitness in conducting Operas and Masquerades. If *St. André* is to be regarded as a person still *less considerable* than *Heidegger*, can his consequence be rated very high?

That *St. André* arrived here in a menial station, is not improbable. The servility of his youth afforded a natural introduction to the insolence of his riper years. He was indeed (if I am not mis-informed) of the same family with the fencing and dancing-master whom *Dryden* has immortalized in *MacFlecknoe*;

> "*St. André's* feet ne'er kept more equal time;"[1]

and was intended for the same professions; a circumstance often hinted at by his opponents during the Rabbit controversy. Having been thus early instructed in the management of the foil and kitt, no marvel that he so often prated about the art of defence, or that "his gratitude to his benefactors" broke out in the language of a minuet or a rigadoon.

That he became famous enough in his profession to have anatomical works occasionally dedicated to him, will easily obtain credit among our apologist's readers; for many of them must have seen a book on surgery inscribed to Dr. *Rock*, a political poem addressed to *Buckhorse*, and a treatise on religion sheltering itself under the patronage of the late Lord *Baltimore*. *St. André*, however, was not the earliest reader of anatomical lectures in *London*. *Bussiere*, the surgeon who attended *Guiscard* (the assassin of *Harley*), was our hero's predecessor in this office, and I am told even he was not the first who offered public instructions to the students at our hospitals. Dr. *Hunter*, who has been applied to for intelligence on this occasion, declares that he never described *St. André* as "the wonder of his time," but as a man who had passed through no regular course of study, and was competent only in the article of injections, a task as happily suited to minute abilities as to those of a larger grasp.

> *Æmilium circà ludum faber imus et ungues*
> *Exprimet, et molles imitabitur ære capillos.*

The art of pushing fluids through the vessels was at that period a secret most scrupulously kept by the few who were in possession of it, so that a great show might be made at the expence of little real knowledge. I am also informed, that *St. André*, like the workman described by *Horace*, had no general comprehension of any subject, but was unable to have put two propositions together:—that he neither extended the bounds of the chirurgical art by discoveries, nor performed any extraordinary cures; and, boasting somewhere that he had detected vessels in the cuticle or scarf-skin, a foreigner of eminence in the same profession offered (through the medium of a printed book) to lay him a wager of it, a challenge which he prudently declined. I am also told, that when solicited to exhibit his preparations, he always declared the majority of them to have been destroyed in a fire. What remain, I am instructed to add, deserve little or no commendation. Thus, on enquiry, sinks our "enthusiast in anatomy" down to a frigid dabbler in the science; while his "noble preparations, which he was continually improving," dwindle into minutiæ of scarce any value.

Though the dreadful crime, which is indistinctly mentioned in the text of the foregoing pamphlet, has been alluded to with less reserve by the apologist of *St. André*, it shall be explained no further on the present occasion. Many are the common avenues to death; and why should we point out with minuteness such as we hope will never be explored again? Till I perused the defence so often referred to, I had not even suspected that the "poisoning wife"[2] bore the least allusion to any particular circumstance on the records of criminal gallantry; nor, without stronger proofs than are furnished by this expression (perhaps a random one), shall I be willing to allot the smallest share of blame to the Lady, such alone excepted as must unavoidably arise from her overhasty marriage, which was solemnized at *Hesson* near *Hounslow* in *Middlesex*, on the 27th of *May*, 1730. This act, however, as well as her derogation from rank, being mere offences against human customs, are cognizable only upon earth.—By "the wiser and more candid part of mankind," who suspected no harm throughout *St. André's* conduct in this affair, I suppose our apologist means any set of people who had imbibed prejudices similar to his own, and thought and spoke about his hero with equal partiality and tenderness. But the Memoir on which these remarks are founded, proves at least that what *J. N.* had hinted concerning the death of Mr. *Molyneux*,[3] was of no recent invention. So far from it indeed, that *St. André* was openly taxed with having been the sole cause of it, in a public news-paper (I think one of the Gazetteers), by the Rev. Dr. *Madden*, the celebrated *Irish* patriot, who subscribed his name to his advertisement. It is related (I know not how truly) that on this account our hero prosecuted and "got the better of his adversary," whose accusation was unsupported by such proofs as the strictness of law requires. How many culprits, about whose guilt neither judge nor jury entertains the smallest scruple, escape with equal triumph through a similar defect of evidence! I may add, that so serious a charge would never have been lightly made by a divine of Dr. *Madden's* rank and character.

All that is said on the subject of family honours to which *St. André* was entitled, his gratitude to his father, what he gave to the celebrated *Geminiani* "in one sum of generosity," must be admitted with caution, for truth was by no means the characteristic of our hero's narrations.[4] These circumstances therefore may be regarded as gasconades of his own. The author of the defence pretends not to have received any part of his information from *St. André's* countrymen or contemporaries; but, on the contrary, confesses that both his early friends and enemies had long been dead.

The affair of the Rabbit-breeder has no need of further illustration. Several ballads, pamphlets, prints, &c. on the subject, bear abundant testimony to *St. André's* merits throughout that business, as well as to the final opinion entertained of him by his contemporaries, after *Cheselden*, by order of Queen *Caroline*, had assisted in discovering the deceit. Her Majesty was urged to this step by finding the plausibility of our hero had imposed on the King, and that some of the pregnant ladies about her own person began to express their fears of bringing into the world an unnatural progeny.—If Mr. *Boyle* was occasionally misled, his errors were soon absorbed in the blaze of his moral and literary excellence. *St. André's* blunder, alas! had no such happy means of redemption. His credulity indeed was not confined to this single transaction. The following is a well-attested story—Two gentlemen at *Southampton*, who felt an inclination to banter him, broke a nutshell asunder, filled the cavity with a large swan-shot, and closed up the whole with glue so nicely that no marks of separation could be detected. This curiosity, as they were walking with *St. André*, one of them pretended to pick up, admiring it as a nut uncommonly heavy as well as beautiful. Our hero swallowed the bait, dissected the subject, discovered the lead, but not the imposition, and then proceeded to account philosophically for so strange a phænomenon. The merry wags could scarce restrain their laughter, and soon quitted his company to enjoy the success of a stratagem they had so adroitly practised on his ignorance and gullibility.

Were there any colour for supposing he had patronized the fraud relative to *Mary Tofts*, with design to ruin others of his profession (an insinuation to his discredit, which the foregoing pamphlet had not furnished), it was but just that he should fall by his own malevolence and treachery. From the imputation of a scheme resembling that contrived by the Duke of *Montagu*, his want of equal wit will sufficiently absolve him.

That rabbits never were permitted to appear at any table where he dined, is a strong mark of the adulation paid to him by his entertainers. I hope, for similar reasons, had he been seized with his last illness in *London* (that his organs of hearing might escape an equal shock), his attendants would not have called any physician named *Warren* to his bed-side, summoned an attorney from *Coney Court* Grays Inn to have made his will, or sent for the Rev. Mr. *Bunny* to pray by him. The banishment of rabbits, however, from a neighbourhood that affords them in the highest perfection, was a circumstance that might as justly have been complained of, as *Pythagoras's* prohibition of beans, had it been published in *Leicestershire*. I heartily wish that the circumstantial author of the preceding epistle, to relieve any doubts by which futurity may be perplexed, had informed us whether *St. André* was an eater of toasted cheese, or not; and if it was never asked for by its common title of a Welch *Rabbit* within his hearing.

That he wrote any thing, unless by proxy, or with much assistance, may reasonably be doubted; for the pamphlets that pass under his name are divested of those foreign idioms that marked his conversation. Indeed, if I may believe some specimens of his private correspondence, he was unacquainted with the very orthography of our language. The insolence of this shallow *Switzer's* attempt to banter *Mead*, we may imagine, was treated with contempt, as the work described has not been handed down to us; and few tracts are permitted to be scarce for any other reason than because they are worthless.

It is next remarked by our apologist, that *St. André's* "confidence, &c. made him superior to all clamour; and so that people did but talk about him, he did not seem to care what they talked against him." This is no more, in other language, than to declare that his impudence and vanity were well proportioned to each other, and that a bad character was to him as welcome as a good one. He did not, it seems, join in the Poet's prayer,

    Grant me an honest fame, or grant me none!

but was of opinion, as his apologist likewise admits, that wealth was an ample counterbalance to the loss of reputation.—That he might evade accusation (as I have already observed) in one particular instance, and therefore recover damages, is no proof of his innocence, that his general conduct would admit of defence, or that much of the manifold censure passed upon him had no foundation.

How Lord *Peterborough* happened to become his patron, &c. may be accounted for without any great degree of credit to either party. His lordship (as Lord *Orrery* observes) "in his private life and conduct differed from most men;" and, having often capricious disputes with the court, was sure to favour those who, like *St. André*, had been dismissed from its service. Our hero's musical talents, indeed, if they were such as they have been represented, might procure him access to his lordship and many other noble adepts in the sublime and useful science of harmony. The lovers of a tune urge no severe enquiries concerning the heart of a fidler. If he be a mercenary, while he teaches female pupils, he is watched; and, if he performs in concerts, he is paid. If above pecuniary gratifications, he is rewarded with hyperbolical compliments. Articulate for inarticulate sounds is ample retribution.

His defender adds, that he was visited by *all* strangers and foreigners. It will be supposed then that his house was never free from company. May we not rather think, that if he was at any time sought after by these peregrine worthies, &c. it was because the keepers of inns and mistresses of boarding-houses had been instructed to disseminate attractive tales of his "capacity in all kinds," his curiosities and good dinners? Besides, all foreigners who have arrived in *England* have not travelled to *Southampton*, and consequently could not have seen *St. André*, who for upwards of the last twenty years of his life had resided only there. It is nearer the truth to say, that not a single *Frenchman*, &c. in fifty thousand, ever heard of his name.

That "his profession as a surgeon, in a reasonable term of years, would probably have put more money in his pocket" than he gained by his union with Lady *Betty Molyneux* (i. e. £30,000. a sum that elevated him into a state little short of madness), I cannot believe. The blast his reputation had received respecting the business at *Godalming*, being seconded by his expulsion from court, he must have felt his business on the decline. Indeed, I am told that he staid long enough in town to try the experiment. Marriage therefore might have been his *dernier resort*.

The exaggerations of this impostor's generosity and accomplishments, which are next brought forward by his panegyrist with no small degree of pomp, are such as we may suppose himself would have furnished, had he undertaken, like the Chevalier *Taylor*, to compile his own memoirs. The majority of circumstances collected for the purpose of proving him to have been

> *Grammaticus, rhetor, geometres, pictor, aliptes,*
> *Augur, schœnobates, medicus, magus,*

could only have been derived from those very flattering testimonials to his merits which he was always ready to exhibit on the slightest encouragement. Those who were content to admit so partial an estimate of his abilities, &c. found it necessary to express their belief that he could have beaten *Hercules* at quoits, played a better fiddle than *Apollo*, out-witted *Mercury*, disarmed the *God of War*, and forged such chemic thunders, that, compared with the produce of our hero's laboratory, the bolts of *Jove* were no louder than a pot-gun. So far was he from being deficient in commendation of his own talents, that he thought his very furniture might claim a proportionable extravagance of praise. He was possessed of some foreign tapestry which he was proud on all occasions to display. But the eulogiums of others, lavish as they might be, fell considerably short of his own, so that the spectator retired with disgust from an object which the excessive vanity of its owner would not permit to be enjoyed without the most frequent and nauseous intrusions of self-congratulation.

As to the history of his eye-lashes, which he sacrificed to vigilance, and his sudden proficiency in the very difficult game of chess (provided his instructor, whom he afterwards vanquished, was a skilful one) *credat Judæus Apella.*—That his language did not want energy, may more easily be allowed, for force is the characteristic of vulgar phraseology. Conceits, expressed with much vigour, are current among sailors; and such nervous denunciations of revenge may occasionally be heard at *Billingsgate*, as might emulate the ravings of *Dryden's Maximin*. No man will be hardy enough to assert that the figure, manners, and language, of *St. André*, were those of a gentleman.

If one of his eyes was a "mass of obscurity" (notwithstanding the other, like that of Lady *Pentweazle's* Great Aunt, might be a piercer), perhaps he ought to have been sparing of his satire on the personal disadvantages of his acquaintance. Yet, the last time my informant saw him was at the Theatre at *Southampton*, where, sitting near a gentleman and lady not remarkable for handsome faces, he had the modesty to express a doubt (and in a voice sufficiently audible) which of the two would furnish the most comic mask.

Mr. *St. André's* apologist observes, that "he cannot be reckoned to have been ignorant of any thing." But the contrary may justly be suspected, and for no inconclusive reason. I aver, that on whatever subject he was haranguing, the moment he discovered any of the company present understood it as well as himself, he became silent, never choosing to descant on art or science but before people whom he supposed to be utter strangers to all their principles. For this reason, he would have entertained Sir *Joshua Reynolds* with remarks on the genera and cultivation of plants, and talked to *Linnæus* about the outline and colouring of pictures.

That he died poor (for such was really the case), should excite no astonishment. His fortune, like his good qualities, was chiefly in supposition. Much of his wealth he had expended on buildings, which he never long inhabited, and afterwards sold to disadvantage. His first essays in architecture were made at *Chepstow* on the *Severn*, an estate purchased by Lady *Betty Molyneux* immediately after the death of her husband. In short, our hero was a fugitive inhabitant of several counties, and never settled till he reached *Southampton*; for in no other place did he meet with that proportion of flattery which was needful to his happiness, if not to his existence.—About a mile from hence he erected the whimsical baby-house dignified by him with the title of *Belle-Vue*, a receptacle every way inconvenient for the purposes of a family. Being once asked if this was not a very singular mansion,—"Singular!" (replied he) "by G—I hope it is, or I would pull it down immediately. I would have you to know, Sir, that it is constructed on the true principles of anatomy." The attempt to apply anatomical principles to the arrangement of passages, doors, and windows, is too glaring an absurdity to need animadversion, or to render it necessary for me to deny in form, that he could ever be "admired for his knowledge in architecture," except by such as knew not wherein its excellencies consisted.—He had, however, another dwelling within the walls of the town already mentioned. Here he pretended that his upper apartments were crowded with rarities, which he only wanted space to exhibit. But, alas! after his decease, Mr. *Christie's* auction-room bore abundant witness to the frivolity of his collections. What became of his boasted library of books, which he always said was packed up in boxes, I am yet to learn. Perhaps it existed only in his description.[5]

"Those who found out he loved praise (says his apologist) took care he should have enough of it." I discover little cause for disputing this assertion, and shall only observe on it, that adulation is a commodity which weak old men, reputed rich, and without ostensible heirs, are seldom in danger of wanting, though they may not enjoy so much of it as fell to *St. André's* share.

His disbursements to the poor might be proportioned to the real state of his fortune; but yet they were conducted with excess of ostentation. He may be said to have given shillings away with more parade than many other men would have shown in the distribution of as many guineas.—What honour his apologist means to confer on him by saying that "the names of those whom he maintained might be written alphabetically," is to me a secret, because names of every kind may be arranged according to the series of the letters.—Suspected characters, however, often strive to redeem themselves by affectation of liberality. Few are more generous than opulent wantons toward their decline of life, who thus attempt to recover that respect which they are conscious of having forfeited by the misdeeds of their youth. The benefactions of such people may in truth be considered as expiatory sacrifices for past offences, having no foundation in a natural propensity to relieve the indigent, or indulge the heart in the noblest luxury, that of doing good.

St. André was accused in *J. N.'s* pamphlet of having frequently larded his pleasantry with obscene expressions. This is a truth which his defender makes not the slightest effort to deny; but adds, that his conversation was *hardly ever* tinctured with prophaneness. We hence at least may infer that our hero's humour had *sometimes* this imperfection, which indeed might have escaped notice, but for the zeal of his apologist.—As I am on this subject, I cannot forbear to mention a particular in Mr. *St. André's* behaviour, which hitherto has been overlooked. When at any time he received a reproof from women of sense, fashion, and character, whose ears he had insulted with his ribaldry, his confidence in a moment forsook him, nor had he a word to offer in extenuation of his offence. My informant has more than once beheld, with secret satisfaction, how effectually the frown of steady virtue could awe this "mighty impudent" into silence. Notwithstanding what has been already said concerning that indifference to censure which appeared in him towards the end of his life, I am mis-informed, if at an earlier period he was able to brave the ridicule of the place where he had been once employed and caressed. When the imputations consequent on his marriage, &c. had rendered him still less an object of respect, he retired with his bride, and amused himself at a distance from *London* with additions to his house, and improvements in his garden; nor did he appear in public again till what was known and suspected of him had ceased to be the object of general enquiry and animadversion.

It is difficult for a profligate man of an amorous constitution to grow old with decency. *J. N.'s* pamphlet had taxed *St. André* with lasciviousness unbecoming his years. This is silently admitted by his apologist, who adds, that the intrigues of his hero were "sometimes with the lower part of the sex." He gives us reason also to suppose that our antiquated enamorato was a dupe to females in the very last stage of a life so unusually protracted. Is *St. André's* memory much honoured by such revelations? Do not circumstances like these increase that stock of "injurious insinuations" which our apologist professes to diminish?

Our panegyrist, more than once in the course of his letter, has expressed himself in favourable terms of *St. André's* colloquial talents. Now, as the memory of my entertaining opponent in respect to circumstances is remarkably tenacious, 'tis pity he has preserved no splendid ebullition of his hero's wit, no sample of that satire and irony that seasoned his conversation, or of that wisdom which so often rendered it instructive. I flatter myself, that if any specimens of these distinct excellencies could have been recollected, they would certainly have been arranged and recorded.

That *St. André* expired without signs of terror, is but a doubtful proof of his innocence. Being, at best, a free-thinker, he might regard death as annihilation, might have been insensible to its immediate approaches, or have encountered it with a constitutional firmness that was rather the gift of nature than the result of conscience undisturbed. He who is become indifferent to the value of reputation, will not easily be inclined to suppose that a want of the virtues on which it is founded will be punished in a future state.

The whole narrative, published by *St. André* in 1723, was considered by his contemporaries as an ostentatious falsehood, invented only to render him an object of attention and commiseration. It should be remembered, that his depositions were all delivered on oath; and yet, being replete with facts totally improbable (for his apologist allows "they partake of the marvellous"), obtained no credit from the world; a sufficient proof of the estimation in which his moral character was held by the people who were best acquainted with it, though at that period (for the rabbit affair had not yet decided on his reputation) he possessed sufficient interest as court-surgeon to engage the privy-council in his cause. They readily enough consented to offer a sum which they might have been sure would never be demanded. All the poison he was ever supposed to have suffered from, was such as is commonly administered in a more tempting vehicle than a glass of strong liquor:

> "'Twas that which taints the sweetest joys,
> And in the shape of Love destroys."

The bare mention of *Socrates* in company with such a pretended victim as *St. André*, cannot fail to make the reader smile.

But "He's half absolv'd who has confess'd," continues his advocate, speaking of the recantation *St. André* made by public advertisement. Yet, what did he confess? Why, what all the world concurred to believe, that he had been grossly imposed on; or perhaps that, out of two evils choosing the least, he allowed himself to be a fool, that he might escape the imputation of having proved a knave. His absolution therefore was not obtained on the most creditable terms. He adds, however, on this emergency, a fresh proof of his disposition to deceive. "I think myself obliged (says he) *in strict regard to truth*, to acquaint the public that I intend, *in a short time*, to publish a full account of the discovery, with some considerations on the extraordinary circumstances of this case, which misled me in my apprehensions thereof; and which, as I hope they will, in some measure, excuse the mistakes made by myself and others who have visited the woman concerned therein, will also be acceptable to the world, in separating the innocent from those who have been guilty actors in the fraud." This work was never published, though *St. André* survived his promise by the long term of fifty years. So much for the faith thus solemnly pledged by an impostor to the public.

After the accident had befallen Mr. *Pope*, on his return from *Dawley* in Lord *Bolingbroke's* coach, *St. André* was called in, because he happened to be the surgeon nearest at hand. No man chooses to be scrupulous in the moment of danger. It might be urged that our hero had little to boast on the occasion, because his patient never recovered the use of his wounded fingers. But this calamity is not strictly chargeable on *St. André's* want of skill; for I have been assured, that though he stopped the effusion of blood, the completion of the cure was entrusted solely to another artist. The RABBITEER, having received his fee, was not admitted a second time into the Poet's company.

To conclude, I differ as much with our ingenious apologist at the close of his Epistle as throughout the foregoing parts of it, being of opinion that his hero no more deserves to be *admired* than to be *copied*. There is always hazard lest *wonder* should generate *imitation*; and the world would not be much obliged to any circumstance that produced a second being fabricated on the model of *St. André*.

[1] See also *Dryden's Limberham, or the Kind Keeper*. Act III.

[2] The words of *Pope* are "the poisoning *dame*." See Epilogue to his Satires, Dial. II. v. 22.

[3] Whilst the above page was preparing for the second edition of this work, the following particulars of this gentleman's family appeared in the public prints: "Mr. *Molyneux*, who was equally the friend of liberty and literature, was founder of a society in *Ireland*, in imitation of the Royal (as was his nephew, the Rev. Dr. *Madden*, of the *Dublin* Society). His genius was celebrated by *Locke*, and other sages of those days; and his patriotism was rewarded with the successive representation of the City and University of *Dublin*, with other posts of great trust, from the Revolution to his death. He married the daughter of Sir *William Domville*, attorney-general of *Ireland* in the reign of *Charles* the Second, and niece of Sir *Thomas Leake*, of *Cannons* in *Middlesex*, by whom he had an only son, *Samuel Molyneux*, Esq; secretary to his late Majesty when Prince of *Wales*, a lord of the Admiralty, and member of parliament both in *Great-Britain* and *Ireland*, who resembled his illustrious father in his pursuits of philosophical knowledge, which he many years, until engaged in political business, prosecuted with great application at his seat at *Kew*, now his Majesty's, and presented a telescope of his own construction to the King of *Portugal*; his *perhaps fatal* acquaintance with and patronage of *St. André* will make his name long remembered. Leaving no issue by his wife, who married *St. André*, and lived many years, the estate of Mr. *Molyneux* fell at her death to his cousin-german and her god-son, the right honourable Sir *Capel Molyneux*, member at present of the *Irish* parliament, and a privy-counsellor, only surviving son of Mr. *Molyneux* father's next brother, Sir *Thomas Molyneux*, bart. whom, through regard for his nephew, his late Majesty created the first *Irish* baronet upon his accession to the throne."

[4] The following story was told by *St. André* to an eminent bookseller, from whom I received it:

"Once when I was in *Paris*," says our hero, "I went to a sale of Missals, most of them bound in crimson velvet. Among these, and in the same binding, I discovered a fine impression of the Duke of *Orleans's* celebrated publication of *Les Amours Pastorales de Daphnis et de Chloe*, &c. which I purchased for a mere trifle. On taking off the velvet, I found the cover underneath was ornamented with as many jewels as I sold afterwards for five hundred pounds."——Who can believe a circumstance so utterly improbable?

[5] I am assured, on unquestionable authority, that Mr. *St. André* had a valuable library in the classes of Natural History and Medicine. A catalogue of it, drawn up by Mr. *B. White*, is now in the possession of Mr. *St. André's* executor, by whom it is reserved for the benefit of minors.

N° II.

[See p. 137.]

The kindness of a friend has enabled me to lay before the reader some extracts from the scarce pamphlet mentioned in p. 137. The following is the exact title of it: "A Letter from a Parishioner of *St. Clement Danes*, to the Right Reverend Father in God *Edmund*, Lord Bishop of *London*, occasioned by his Lordship's causing the Picture over the Altar to be taken down. With some Observations on the Use and Abuse of Church Paintings in General, and of that Picture in particular.

"*Exodus*, Chap. xxxii. Ver. 20. And he took the Calf which they had made, and burnt it in the Fire, and ground it to powder, and strawed it upon the Water, and made the Children of *Israel* drink of it.

"*London*, printed and sold by *J. Roberts*, in *Warwick-Lane; A. Dod*, without *Temple-Bar-*, and *E. Nut*, at the *Royal-Exchange*. 1725. Price 6*d.*"

After some introductory compliments to Bishop *Gibson*, the Letter-writer thus proceeds: "Of all the abuses your Lordship has redressed, none more timely, none more acceptable to all true Protestants, than your last injunction to remove that ridiculous, superstitious piece of Popish foppery from over our communion-table; this has gained you the applause and good will of all honest men, who were scandalized to see that holy place defiled with so vile and impertinent a representation.

"To what end or purpose was it put there, but to affront our most gracious Sovereign, by placing at our very altar the known resemblance of a person, who is the wife of his utter enemy, and pensioner to the Whore of *Babylon*?

"When I say the known resemblance, I speak not only according to my own knowledge; but appeal to all mankind who have seen the Princess *Sobieski*, or any picture or resemblance of her, if the picture of that angel in the white garment and blue mantle, which is there supposed to be beating time to the musick, is not directly a great likeness of that princess. This I insist on, and will stand and fall by my assertion, provided they do not play any tricks with the picture, or alter it for contradiction sake now it is down.

"Whether it was done by chance, or on purpose, I shall not determine; but be it which it will, it has given great offence, and your Lordship has acted the part of a wise and good prelate to order its removal.

"For surely, such a picture is far unfit for so sacred a place; a place too solemn for such levities, too awful to be made the receptacle of such trumpery: nay, admit it were not the resemblance of such a person, can any thing be more absurd, than such a picture in such a place!

"But if it be the picture of that person, what can be more sacrilegious, more impudently sacrilegious, than to have our sanctuary defiled by those who make a mock of us and our holy religion? I mean, our inveterate enemies the Papists, who would scruple to prophane no place, so they might show their implacable hatred to our God, and our King.

"To our God, by making his holy altar the scene of their ribaldry, to be approached with wantonness and curiosity, by the sons of *Belial*, who come there to decypher the dumb libel, and sneer at the pictured lampoon, which tacitly mocks the church, and openly affronts the State.

"To our King, by placing the resemblance of an avowed enemy to him and his religion, at the very altar, to stand in view of a whole congregation; a thing, in my opinion, much more audacious, than the setting up her statue in the public streets.

"No wonder our church has been thronged with spectators, to the great hindrance of divine worship, and annoyance of the parishioners, when those crouds of irreverend persons, which were ever pouring in, came not there to join in prayer with the rest of the congregation, but to worship their Popish saint, and hug themselves with the conceit of being alone in the secret.

"But at last the watch-word was blown, and the true intent of their coming discovered. Then was it high time to complain to your Lordship, when disturbances became so frequent, and the peace of the church was so manifestly broken: that you, like another *Moses*, commanded the tinctured abomination to be taken down, and no doubt but your Lordship will call them to account who set it up.

"When your Lordship shall examine, who is the painter, and of what principle? how long he had been from the Court of *Rome*, before he painted that picture? and whether he brought no picture, or resemblance, of the Princess *Sobieski* over with him? you will not repent of what you have done. But when you shall farther enquire after the person who employed him; whether he be a Protestant? or, if he call himself so, whether his children were not sent abroad to Popish seminaries for education?

"When your Lordship, I say, shall examine into these particulars, I doubt not of the inferences so wise a man will draw from such convincing circumstances.

"And as your Lordship has begun to redress one abuse, I persuade myself you will not stop here, but enquire likewise, by what authority it was put there. This may, perhaps, open another scene to your Lordship's view, and give you an opportunity, not only to ease the parish of a very heavy burden it now groans under, but prevent its being run to unnecessary and unwarranted expences for the future, by every *Jac*——- in an office.

"And, indeed, unless there was a sufficient warrant for such alterations, the workmen should go to the right person's door, and he that set them to work ought to pay them; for, in my humble opinion, the place needed no alteration: it was decent, convenient, and indeed ornamental enough before; there was no more sign, or fear of its falling, than there was occasion to take it down, and deprive the parish of a conveniency now very much wanted, I mean a little vestry-room, which was behind the old communion table, where the books, vessels, and vestments of the church, were ready at hand, and just at the very altar; whereas now every thing is brought quite through the body of the church, which in case of a croud (as of late has been but too frequent) is both tedious and inconvenient to the last degree.

"But, notwithstanding this, it was resolutely taken down, to gratify the pride and malice of some persons, who thirsted to eternize their names, and affront the government. What have been the consequences of all this, but an eye-sore and heart-burning to the honest and loyal part of the inhabitants, and a continual hurly-burly of loiterers from all parts of the town, to see our Popish raree-show?"

After a digression on the famous altar at *White-Chapel*, in which Dean *Kennet* was said to be satirized, and some general observations on pictures in churches, the Letter-writer adds, "Never before was any Popish saint put over the communion-table in a Protestant church. The Last Supper, the Passion, Crucifixion, or some other incidents of our Blessed Saviour's life, are the general subjects given to painters on these occasions; but to have a concert of musick, &c. (suppose it were not the Pretender's spouse, and probably some more of his family, under the form of angels) is the most abrupt and foreign that I ever saw or heard of.

"What surprizes me most is, that any of my fellow parishioners should not only dispute your Lordship's commands, delay the execution of your just injunction, when it was most reasonable and necessary, but pester your Lordship with impertinent petitions and remonstrances, as if they were injured and oppressed, or your Lordship misinformed. This must be the reason; or to what purpose did they trifle with and contest your Lordship's ordinance? But you are too just a man to give any sentence but the most impartial, and too steady to give up any point, where the peace of the Church and the honour of the King is concerned.

"Whoever murmurs at its being taken down, takes the part of those who set it up; and whoever takes their part, is as bad as themselves, and would do the like on the like opportunity. What can they object against its being removed? What can they offer for having it remain? But why's, and why not's. As, Why should it be removed? What hurt did it do? Why should so much money be thrown away? And, why might not that picture be there as well as any other? Why does your Lordship interfere in the matter? This, with a glance of complaint at your Lordship, and severe invectives against those who solicited that interposition, calling them informers, busy, forward, mischief-making fellows, who had better mind their own business, and such like ribaldry, is all they can say for themselves. But these are the worst reasons in the world, and invidious queries only to evade an argument, and are not to be admitted in a debate of this nature, where a direct reason for, or against, is required. But give me leave, my Lord, and I will, in a few words, answer all their queries, which seem so weighty and formidable to the vulgar and ignorant.

"Why should it be removed? may be answered by another question, What business had it there? But as I scorn such quibbling ways of reasoning, I shall answer them, because it is unfit for that sacred place. If it is the Princess *Sobieski's* image, it is sacrilegious and traiterous, and therefore ought to be removed. If it is, as they say, a choir of heavenly angels at a practice of musick, playing on earthly instruments, it is impertinent and absurd to the last degree, and therefore ought to be removed from a place where the utmost decorum should be kept.

"What hurt does it, say they? To which I answer, it hurted or disturbed the peace of the church, and was so far hurtful, as we were hindered or annoyed in our devotions; it made a division in the parish, and was so far hurtful, as it tended to the breach of peace and good neighbourhood; and therefore I think it ought to be removed, since, not to answer them with a question, but a common saying, it did hurt enough.

"Why should so much money be thrown away? Ay, there's the grievance; but I shall tell them, they may thank themselves, it was the act and deed of their own cabal; and though they might triumph and laugh in their sleeves for a while, yet murder will out, and they might expect to be paid in their own coin one time or other. There was no occasion to remove the old communion-table and vestry; and therefore all the money is thrown away; the worse their management. Nor was there any necessity of so sumptuous an altar-piece, or of that picture in particular, therefore so much money as that picture cost, which, by the bye, is no trifling sum[1] (the painter, as well as his masters, being no small fool), is entirely thrown away, and has been cast into *The Thames*; or, as the vulgar have it, thrown down the kennel.

"It was set up against the will of the major part of the parish, and not without much murmur and complaint; there was yet a much greater majority for pulling it down; if therefore so much money is thrown away, it is pity the parish should pay it; and, no doubt, when your Lordship comes to enquire by what authority a set of men ran the parish so much in debt for their own whims, and without any manner of occasion, you will do us justice, and teach such persons for the future to consult the bishop, and have the general consent of the parish, before they run into such extravagancies.

"The tradesmen want their money, and the parish cannot pay them: your Lordship therefore will do very well to adjust this matter, that they may know where to go for their money.

"Their delaying to take down their idol, was a tacit disputing your lordship's commands, irreligious and contumacious to the last degree: and indeed I cannot say but some of the public prints[2] gave me great anxiety, when they had the impudence to assure the world it was not to be taken down: but that anxiety was of short continuance; for I had the satisfaction the next morning to find it removed, and whole crowds of idle persons who came to see it disappointed; then I found, to my great comfort, that you were not to be biassed; but, as you had begun the good work, you had gone through with it, and made them take it down with a witness."

[1] It cost fourscore pounds.

[2] *The Post-Boy* and *Daily Journal* of *Saturday, September* 4.

Nº III.

[See p. 414.]

An Account of what seemed most remarkable in the Five Days' Peregrination of the Five following Persons, viz. Messieurs TOTHALL, SCOTT, HOGARTH, THORNHILL, and FORREST; begun on *Saturday, May* 27, 1732, and finished on the 31st of the same Month. Imitated in *Hudibrasticks* by one well acquainted with some of the Travellers, and of the Places here celebrated, with Liberty of some Additions.

> "Abi tu, et fac similiter."
> Inscription on *Dulwich* College Porch.

'Twas first of morn on *Saturday*,
The seven-and-twentieth day of *May*,
When *Hogarth, Thornhill, Tothall, Scott*,
And *Forrest*, who this journal wrote,
From *Covent-Garden* took departure, 5
To see the world by land and water.

Our march we with a song begin;
Our hearts were light, our breeches thin.
We meet with nothing of adventure
Till *Billingsgate's Dark-house* we enter; 10
Where we diverted were, while baiting,
With ribaldry, not worth relating,
(Quite suited to the dirty place):
But what most pleas'd us was his Grace
Of *Puddle Dock*, a porter grim, 15
Whose portrait *Hogarth*, in a whim,
Presented him in caricature,
He pasted on the cellar-door.[1]

But hark! the Watchman cries "Past one!"
'Tis time that we on board were gone. 20
Clean straw we find laid for our bed,
A tilt for shelter over head.
The boat is soon got under sail,
Wind near S. E. a mackrel gale,
Attended by a heavy rain; 25
We try to sleep, but try in vain,
So sing a song, and then begin
To feast on biscuit, beef, and gin.

At *Purfleet* find three men of war,
The *Dursley* galley, *Gibraltar*, 30
And *Tartar* pink, and of this last
The pilot begg'd of us a cast
To *Gravesend*, which he greatly wanted,
And readily by us was granted.
The grateful man, to make amends, 35
Told how the officers and friends
Of *England* were by *Spaniards* treated,
And shameful instances repeated.

While he these insults was deploring,
Hogarth, like Premier, fell to snoring, 40
But waking cry'd, "I dream'd"—and then
Fell fast asleep, and snor'd again.

The morn clear'd up, and after five
At port of *Gravesend* we arrive,
But found it hard to get on shore; 45
His boat a young son of a whore
Had fix'd just at our landing-place,
And swore we should not o'er it pass;
But, spite of all the rascal's tricks,
We made a shift to land by six, 50
And up to Mrs. *Bramble's* go
[A house that we shall better know],
There get a barber for our wigs,
Wash hands and faces, stretch our legs,
Had toast and butter, and a pot 55
Of coffee (our third breakfast) got:
Then, paying what we had to pay,
For *Rochester* we took our way,
Viewing the new church as we went,
And th' unknown person's monument. 60

The beauteous prospects found us talk.
And shorten'd much our two hours walk,
Though by the way we did not fail
To stop and take three pots of ale,
And this enabled us by ten 65
At *Rochester* to drink again.

Now, Muse, assist, while I declare
(Like a true *English* traveller)
What vast variety we survey
In the short compass of one day. 70

We scarce had lost the sight of *Thames*,
When the fair *Medway's* winding streams,
And far-extending *Rochester*,
Before our longing eyes appear:
The Castle and Cathedral grace 75
One prospect, so we mend our pace;
Impatient for a nearer view,

But first must *Strood's* rough street trudge through,
And this our feet no short one find;
However, with a cheerful mind, 80
All difficulties we get o'er,
And soon are on the *Medway's* shore.
New objects here before us rise,
And more than satisfy our eyes,
The stately Bridge from side to side, 85
The roaring cataracts of the tide,
Deafen our ears, and charm our sight,
And terrify while they delight.
These we pass over to the Town,
And take our Quarters at *The Crown*, 90
To which the Castle is so near,
That we all in a hurry were
The grand remains on't to be viewing;
It is indeed a noble ruin,
Must have been very strong, but length 95
Of time has much impair'd its strength:
The lofty Tower as high or higher
Seems than the old Cathedral's spire;
Yet we determin'd were to gain
Its top, which cost some care and pain; 100
When there arriv'd, we found a well,
The depth of which I cannot tell;
Small holes cut in on every side
Some hold for hands and feet provide,
By which a little boy we saw 105
Go down, and bring up a jack-daw.

All round about us then we gaze,
Observing, not without amaze,
How towns here undistinguish'd join,
And one vast One to form combine. 110
Chatham with *Rochester* seems but one,
Unless we're shewn the boundary-stone.
That and its Yards contiguous lie
To pleasant *Brompton* standing high;
The Bridge across the raging flood 115
Which *Rochester* divides from *Strood*,
Extensive *Strood*, on t'other side,
To *Frindsbury* quite close ally'd:
The country round, and river fair,

Our prospects made beyond compare, 120
Which quite in raptures we admire;
Then down to face of earth retire.

Up the Street walking, first of all
We take a view of the Town-Hall.
Proceeding farther on, we spy 125
A house, design'd to catch the eye,
With front so rich, by plastick skill,
As made us for a while stand still:
Four huge Hobgoblins grace the wall,
Which we four Bas Relievo's call; 130
They the four Seasons represent,
At least were form'd for that intent.

Then *Watts's Hospital* we see
(No common curiosity):
Endow'd (as on the front appears) 135
In favour of poor travellers;
Six such it every night receives,
Supper and lodging *gratis* gives,
And to each man next morn does pay
A groat, to keep him on his way: 140
But the contagiously infected,
And rogues and proctors, are rejected.

It gave us too some entertainment
To find out what this bounteous man meant.
Yet were we not so highly feasted, 145
But that we back to dinner hasted.

By twelve again we reach *The Crown*,
But find our meat not yet laid down,
So (spite of "Gentlemen, d'ye call?")
On chairs quite fast asleep we fall, 150
And with clos'd eyes again survey,
In dreams, what we have seen to-day:
Till dinner's coming up, when we
As ready are as that can be.

If we describe it not, we're undone, 155
You'll scarce believe we came from *London*.
With due attention then prepare

Yourself to hear our bill of fare.
For our first course a dish there was
Of soles and flounders with crab-sauce, 160
A stuff'd and roast calf's-heart beside,
With 'purt'nance minc'd, and liver fry'd;
And for a second course, they put on
Green pease and roasted leg of mutton:
The cook was much commended for't; 165
Fresh was the beer, and sound the port:
So that *nem. con.* we all agree
(Whatever more we have to see)
From table we'll not rise till three.

Our shoes are clean'd, 'tis three o'clock, 170
Come let's away to *Chatham-Dock*;
We shan't get there till almost four,
To see't will take at least an hour;
Yet *Scott* and *Hogarth* needs must stop
At the Court-Hall to play *Scotch* hop. 175

To *Chatham* got, ourselves we treat
With Shrimps, which as we walk we eat.
For speed we take a round-a-bout-
way, as we afterwards found out:
At length reach the King's yards and docks, 180
Admire the ships there on the stocks,
The men of war afloat we view,
Find means to get aboard of two;[2]
But here I must not be prolix,
For we went home again at six, 185
There smoak'd our pipes, and drank our wine,
And comfortably sat till nine,
Then, with our travels much improv'd,
To our respective beds we mov'd.

Sunday at seven we rub our eyes, 190
But are too lazy yet to rise:
Hogarth and *Thornhill* tell their dreams,
And, reasoning deeply on those themes,
After much learned speculation,
Quite suitable to the occasion, 195
Left off as wise as they begun,
Which made for us in bed good fun.

But by and by, when up we got,
Sam Scott was missing, "Where's *Sam Scott?*"
"Oh! here he comes. Well! whence come you?" 200
"Why from the bridge, taking a view[3]
Of something that did highly please me,
But people passing by would teaze me
With 'Do you work on *Sundays*, friend?'
So that I could not make an end." 205

At this we laugh'd, for 'twas our will
Like men of taste that day to kill.
So after breakfast we thought good
To cross the bridge again to *Strood*:
Thence eastward we resolve to go, 210
And through the Hundred march of *Hoo*,
Wash'd on the north side by the *Thames*,
And on the south by *Medway's* streams.
Which to each other here incline,
Till at *The Nore* in one they join. 215

Before we *Frindsbury* could gain,
There fell a heavy shower of rain,
When crafty *Scott* a shelter found
Under a hedge upon the ground,
There of his friends a joke he made, 220
But rose most woefully bewray'd;
How against him the laugh was turn'd,
And he the vile disaster mourn'd!
We work, all hands, to make him clean,
And fitter to be smelt and seen. 225
But, while we scrap'd his back and side,
All on a sudden, out he cried,
"I've lost my cambrick handkercher,
'Twas lent me by my wife so dear:
What I shall do I can't devise, 230
I've nothing left to wipe my eyes."

At last the handkerchief was found,
To his great comfort, safe and sound,
He's now recover'd and alive;
So in high spirits all arrive 235
At *Frindsbury*, fam'd for prospects fair,

But we much more diverted were
With what the parish church did grace,
"A list of some who lov'd the place,
In memory of their good actions, 240
And gratitude for their benefactions.
Witness our hands—*Will. Gibbons*, Vicar—"
And no one else.—This made us snicker:
At length, with countenances serious,
We all agreed it was mysterious, 245
Not guessing that the reason might
Be, the Churchwardens could not write.

At ten, in council it was mov'd,
Whoe'er was tir'd, or disapprov'd
Of our proceedings, might go back, 250
And cash to bear his charges take.
With indignation this was heard:
Each was for all events prepar'd.
So all with one consent agreed
To *Upnor-Castle* to proceed, 255
And at the sutler's there we din'd
On such coarse fare as we could find.

The Castle[4] was not large, but strong,
And seems to be of standing long.
Twenty-four men its garrison, 260
And just for every man a gun;
Eight guns were mounted, eight men active,
The rest were rated non-effective.
Here an old couple, who had brought
Some cockles in their boat, besought 265
That one of us would buy a few,
For they were very fresh and new.
I did so, and 'twas charity;
He was quite blind, and half blind she.

Now growing frolicksome and gay, 270
Like boys, we, after dinner, play,
But, as the scene lay in a fort,
Something like war must be our sport:
Sticks, stones, and hogs-dung, were our weapons,
And, as in such frays oft it happens, 275
Poor *Tothall's* cloaths here went to pot,

So that he could not laugh at *Scott*.

From hence all conquerors we go
To visit the church-yard at *Hoo*.
At *Hoo* we found an Epitaph, 280
Which made us (as 'twill make you) laugh:
A servant maid, turn'd poetaster,
Wrote it in honour of her master;
I therefore give you (and I hope you
Will like it well) a *Vera Copia*: 285
"And.wHen.he.Died.You plainly.see
Hee.freely.gave.al.to.Sara.passaWee.
And.in.Doing.so.it DoTh.prevail.
that.Ion.him.can.well.bes.Tow.this Rayel.
On.Year.sarved.him.it is well.none. 290
BuT Thanks.beto.God.it.is.all my.One."

While here among the Graves we stumble,
Our *Hogarth's* guts began to grumble,
Which he to ease, turn'd up his tail
Over a monumental rail; 295
Tothall, for this indecent action,
Bellowing on him just correction
With nettles, as there was no birch,
He fled for refuge to the church,
And shamefully the door besh-t; 300
O filthy dauber! filthy wit!

Long at one place we must not stay,
'Tis almost four, let's haste away.
But here's a sign; 'tis rash we think,
To leave the place before we drink. 305
We meet with liquor to our mind,
Our hostess complaisant and kind:
She was a widow, who, we found,
Had (as the phrase is) been shod round,
That is, had buried husbands four, 310
And had no want of charms for more;
Yet her we leave, and, as we go,
Scott bravely undertook to show
That through the world we could not pass,
How thin soe'er our breeches was; 315
"'Tis true, indeed, we may go round,

But through"—then pointed to the ground.
So well he manag'd the debate,
We own'd he was a man of weight:
And so indeed he was this once, 320
His pockets we had fill'd with stones:
But here we'd serv'd ourselves a trick,
Of which he might have made us sick:
We'd furnish'd him with ammunition
Fit to knock down all opposition; 325
And, knowing well his warmth of temper,
Out of his reach began to scamper,
Till, growing cooler, he pretends
His passion feign'd, so all are friends.
Our danger now becomes a joke, 330
And peaceably we go to *Stoke.*
About the church we nothing can see
To strike or entertain our fancy:
But near a farm, on an elm tree,
A long pole fix'd upright we see, 335
And tow'rd the top of it was plac'd
A weathercock, quite in high taste,
Which all of us, ere we go further,
Pronounce of the Composite order.

First, on a board turn'd by the wind, 340
A painter had a cock design'd,
A common weather-cock was above it,
This turn'd too as the wind did move it;
Then on the spindle's point so small
A shuttlecock stuck o'ertopp'd them all. 345

This triple alliance gave occasion
To much improving speculation.

Alas! we ne'er know when we are well,
So at *Northfleet* again must quarrel;
But fought not here with sticks and stones 350
(For those, you know, might break our bones)!
A well just by, full to the brim,
Did fitter for our purpose seem;
So furiously we went to dashing,
Till our coats wanted no more washing; 355
But this our heat and courage cooling,

'Twas soon high time to leave such fooling.
To *The Nag's Head* we therefore hie,
To drink, and to be turn'd adry.

At six, while supper was preparing, 360
And we about the marsh-lands staring,
Our two game-cocks, *Tothall* and *Scott*,
To battling once again were got:
But here no weapons could they find,
Save what the cows dropp'd from behind; 365
With these they pelted, till we fancy
Their cloaths look'd something like a tansy.

At seven we all come home again,
Tothall and *Scott* their garments clean;
Supper we get, and, when that's o'er, 370
A tiff of punch drink at the door;
Then, as the beds were only three,
Draw cuts who shall so lucky be
As here to sleep without a chum;
To *Tothall's* share the prize did come 375
Hogarth and *Thornhill*, *Scott* and I,
In pairs, like man and wife, must lie.
Then mighty frolicksome they grow,
At *Scott* and me the stocking throw,
Fight with their wigs, in which perhaps 380
They sleep, for here we found no caps.

Up at eleven again we get,
Our sheets were so confounded wet;
We dress, and lie down in our cloaths;
Monday, at three, awak'd and rose, 385
And of the cursed gnats complain,
Yet make a shift to sleep again.

Till six o'clock we quiet lay,
And then got out for the whole day;
To fetch a barber, out we send; 390
Stripp'd, and in boots, he does attend,
For he's a fisherman by trade;
Tann'd was his face, shock was his head;
He flours our wigs, and trims our faces,
And the top barber of the place is. 395

The cloth is for our breakfast spread;
A bowl of milk and toasted bread
Are brought, of which while *Forrest* eats.
To draw our pictures *Hogarth* sits;[5]
Thornhill is in the barber's hands, 400
Shaving himself *Will Tothall* stands;
While *Scott* is in a corner sitting,
And an unfinish'd piece completing.

Our reckoning about eight we pay,
And take for Isle of *Greane* our way; 405
To keep the road we were directed,
But, as 'twas bad, this rule neglected;
A tempting path over a stile
Let us astray above a mile;
Yet the right road at last we gain, 410
And joy to find ourselves at *Greane*;
Where my Dame *Husbands*, at *The Chequer*,
Refresh'd us with some good malt liquor;
Into her larder then she runs,
Brings out salt pork, butter and buns, 415
And coarse black bread; but that's no matter,
'Twill fortify us for the water.
Here *Scott* so carefully laid down
His penknife which had cost a crown,
That all in vain we sought to find it, 420
And, for his comfort, say, "Ne'er mind it;"
For to *Sheerness* we now must go:
To this the ferryman says, "No."
We to another man repair'd:
He too says, "No—it blows too hard." 425
But, while we study how to get there
In spite of this tempestuous weather,
Our landlady a scheme propos'd,
With which we fortunately clos'd,
Was to the shore to go, and try 430
To hail the ships in ordinary,
So we might get, for no great matter,
A boat to take us o'er the water.
We haste, and soon the shore we tread,
With various kinds of shells bespread. 435
And in a little time we spy'd
A boat approaching on our side;

The man to take us in agreed,
But that was difficult indeed,
Till, holding in each hand an oar, 440
He made a sort of bridge to shore,
O'er which on hands and knees we crawl,[6]
And so get safe on board the yawl.

In little time we seated were,
And now to *Shepey's* coast draw near; 445
When suddenly, with loud report,
The cannons roar from ships and fort,
And, like tall fellows, we impute
To our approach this grand salute:
But soon, alas! our pride was humbled, 450
And from this fancy'd height we tumbled,
On recollecting that the day
The nine and twentieth was of *May*.

The firing had not long been ended.
Before at *Sheerness* we were landed, 455
Where on the battery while we walk,
And of the charming prospect talk,
Scott from us in a hurry runs,
And, getting to the new-fir'd guns,
Unto their touch-holes clapp'd his nose; 460
Hogarth sits down, and trims his toes;
These whims when we had made our sport,
Our turn we finish round the fort,
And are at one for *Queenborough* going:
Bleak was the walk, the wind fierce blowing, 465
And driving o'er our heads the spray;
On loose beach stones, our pebbly way,
But *Thornhill* only got a fall,
Which hurt him little, if at all:
So merrily along we go, 470
And reach that famous town by two.

Queenborough consists of one short street,[7]
Broad, and well-pav'd, and very neat;
Nothing like dirt offends the eye,
Scarce any people could we spy: 475
The town-house, for the better show,
Is mounted on a portico

Of piers and arches, number four,
And crown'd at top with a clock-tower;
But all this did not reach so high 480
As a flag-staff, that stood just by,
On which a standard huge was flying
(The borough's arms, the king's supplying),
Which on high festivals they display
To do the honours of the day. 485
As for salutes, excus'd they are,
Because they have no cannon there.

To the church-yard we first repair,
And hunt for choice inscriptions there,
Search stones and rails, till almost weary all, 490
In hopes to find something material.
When one at last, of pyebald style
(Though grave the subject) made us smile:
Telling us first, in humble prose,
"That *Henry Knight* doth here repose, 495
A *Greenland* Trader twice twelve year,
As master and as harpooneer;"
Then, in as humble verse, we read
(As by himself in person said)
"In *Greenland* I whales, sea-horse, and bears did slay, 500
Though now my body is intombed in clay."

The house at which we were to quarter
Is call'd *The Swans*; this rais'd our laughter.
Because the sign is *The Red Lion*,
So strange a blunder we cry "Fie on!" 505
But, going in, all neat we see
And clean; so was our landlady:
With great civility she told us,
She had not beds enough to hold us,
But a good neighbour had just by, 510
Where some of us perhaps might lie.
She sends to ask. The merry dame
Away to us directly came,
Quite ready our desires to grant,
And furnish us with what we want. 515

Back to the church again we go;
Which is but small, ill built, and low,

View'd the inside, but still see we
Nothing of curiosity
Unless we suffer the grave-digger 520
In this our work to make a figure,
Whom just beside us now we have,
Employ'd in opening of a grave.

A prating spark indeed he was,
Knew all the scandal of the place, 525
And often rested from his labours,
To give the history of his neighbours;
Told who was who, and what was what,
Till on him we bestow'd a pot
(For he forgot not, you may think, 530
"Masters, I hope, you'll make me drink!"),
At this his scurrilous tongue run faster,
Till "a sad dog" he call'd his master,
Told us the worshipful the Mayor
Was but a custom-house officer; 535
Still rattling on till we departed,
Not only with his tales diverted,
But so much wisdom we had got.
We treated him with t'other pot.

Return we now to the town-hall. 540
That, like the borough, is but small,
Under its portico's a space,
Which you may call the market-place,
Just big enough to hold the stocks,
And one, if not two, butcher's blocks, 545
Emblems of plenty and excess,
Though you can no where meet with less:
For though 'tis call'd a market-town
(As they are not asham'd to own)
Yet we saw neither butcher's meat, 550
Nor fish, nor fowl, nor aught to eat.
Once in seven years, they say, there's plenty,
When strangers come to represent ye.

Hard at *The Swans* had been our fare,
But that some *Harwich* men were there, 555
Who lately had some lobsters taken,
With which, and eke some eggs and bacon,

Our bellies we design to fill;
But first will clamber up the hill,
A most delightful spot of ground, 560
O'erlooking all the country round;
On which there formerly has been
The palace of *Philippa*, queen
To the third *Edward*, as they tell,
Now nought remains on 't but a well: 565
But 'tis from hence, says common fame,
The borough gets its royal name.

Two sailors at this well we meet,
And do each other kindly greet:
"What brings you here, my lads?" cry we. 570
"Thirst, please your honours, as you see;
For (adds the spokesman) we are here
Waiting for our young officer,
A midshipman on board *The Rose*,
(For General S——'s son he goes): 575
We and our messmates, six in all,
Yesterday brought him in our yawl,
And when, as we had been commanded,
Quite safe and dry we had him landed,
By running of her fast aground 580
At tide of ebb, he quickly found
That he might go and see *Sheerness*,
So here he left us pennyless,
To feast on *Queenborough* air and water,
Or starve, to him 'tis no great matter; 585
While he among his friends at ease is,
And will return just when he pleases;
Perhaps he may come back to-day;
If not, he knows that we must stay."

So one of us gave him a tester, 590
When both cried out, "God bless you, master!"
Then ran to rouse their sleeping fellows,
To share their fortune at the alehouse.

Hence to the creek-side, one and all,
We go to see *The Rose's* yawl, 595
And found her bedded in the mud,
Immovable till tide of flood.

The sailors here had cockles got,
Which gratefully to us they brought,
'Twas all with which they could regale us; 600
This t'other sixpence sent to th' alehouse:
So merrily they went their way,
And we were no less pleas'd than they.

At seven about the town we walk,
And with some pretty damsels talk. 605
Beautiful nymphs indeed, I ween,
Who came to see, and to be seen.

Then to our *Swans* returning, there
We borrow'd a great wooden chair,
And plac'd it in the open street, 610
Where, in much state, did *Hogarth* sit
To draw the townhouse, church, and steeple,[8]
Surrounded by a crowd of people;
Tag, rag, and bobtail, stood quite thick there,
And cry'd, "What a sweet pretty picture!" 615

This was not finish'd long, before
We saw, about the Mayor's fore-door,
Our honest sailors in a throng:
We call'd one of them from among
The rest, to tell us the occasion; 620
Of which he gave us this relation:

"Our midshipman is just come back,
And chanc'd to meet or overtake
A sailor walking with a woman
(May be, she's honest, may be, common): 625
He thought her handsome, so his honour
Would needs be very sweet upon her:
But this the seaman would not suffer, and this put him in a huff.
'Lubber, avast,' says sturdy *John*, 630
'Avast, I say, let her alone;
You shall not board her, she's my wife.
Sheer off, Sir, if you love your life:
I've a great mind your back to lick;'
And up he held his oaken stick. 635

"Our midship hero this did scare:
'I'll swear the peace before the Mayor,'
Says he; so to the Mayor's they trudge:"
How then a case by such a judge
Determin'd was, I cannot say, 640
We thought it not worth while to stay:
For it strikes nine, "How th' evening spends!
Come, let us drink to all our friends
A chearful glass, and eat a bit."
So to our supper down we sit; 645
When something merry check'd our mirth:
The *Harwich* men had got a birth
Closely adjoining to our room,
And were to spend their evening come:
The wall was thin, and they so near, 650
That all they say, or sing, we hear.
We sung our songs, we crack'd our jokes,
Their emulation this provokes;
And they perform'd so joyously,
As distanc'd hollow all our glee; 655
So (were it not a bull) I'd lay,
This night they fairly won the day.

Now plenteously we drink of flip,
In hopes we shall the better sleep;
Some rest the long day's work requires; 660
Scott to his lodging first retires;
His landlady is waiting for him,
And to his chamber walks before him;
In her fair hand a light she bears,
And shows him up the garret-stairs; 665
Away comes he greatly affronted,
And his disgrace to us recounted.
This makes us game, we roast him for it,
"*Scott's* too high-minded for a garret."
But *Tothall* more humanely said, 670
"Come, *Scott*, be easy, take my bed,
And to your garret I will go."
(This great good-nature sure did show):
There finding nought him to entertain
But a flock-bed without a curtain, 675
He too in haste came back, and got

Away to share his bed with *Scott*,
And at eleven each goes to nest,
Till *Tuesday* morn to take his rest.

At six comes *Hogarth*, "Rise, Sirs, rise," 680
Says he, with roguery in his eyes,
"*Scott's* landlady is below stairs.
And roundly the good woman swears,
That for his lodging he shall pay,
(Where his tir'd bones he scorn'd to lay) 685
Or he should go before the Mayor."
She's in the right on't, we declare,
For this would cut the matter short,
(At least 'twould make us special sport):
But here she balk'd us, and, no doubt, 690
Had wit enough to find us out.
Our mark thus miss'd, we kindly go,
To see how he and *Tothall* do.
We find the doors all open were,
(It seems that's not unusual here): 695
They're very well, but *Scott* last night
Had been in a most dreadful fright:
"When to his room he got," he said,
"And just was stepping into bed,
He thought he saw the bed-cloaths stir, 700
So back he flew in mortal fear;
But taking heart of grace, he try'd
To feel what 'twas, when out it cry'd
Again he starts, but to his joy,
It prov'd a little harmless boy, 705
Who by mistake had thither crept,
And soundly (till he wak'd him) slept
So from his fears recover'd quite
He got to sleep, and slept all night."
We laugh at this, and he laughs too, 710
For, pray, what better could he do?

At ten we leave our *Lion-Swans*,
And to the higher lands advance,
Call on our laundress by the way,
For the led shirts left yesterday 715
To wash; "She's sorry, they're not yet
Quite dry!"—"Why then we'll take them wet:

- 341 -

They'll dry and iron'd be, we hope,
At *Minster*, where we next shall stop."

The way was good, the weather fair, 720
The prospects most delightful were.
To *Minster* got, with labour hard
We climb'd the hill to the church-yard,
But, when arriv'd there, did not fail
To read some verses on a rail 725
Well worth transcribing, we agree,
Whether you think so, you may see.
"Here interr'd *George Anderson* doth lye,
By fallen on an anchor he did dye
In *Sheerness* yard on *Good Friday* 730
The 6th of *April*, I do say.
All you that read my allegy be alwaies
Ready for to dye—aged 42 years."

Of monuments that here they shew
Within the church, we drew but two; 735
One an ambassador of *Spain's*,[9]
T' other Lord *Shorland's*[10] dust contains,
Of whom they have a wondrous story,
Which (as they tell) I'll lay before ye.

The Lord of *Shorland*, on a day,[11] 740
Chancing to take a ride this way,
About a corpse observ'd a crowd,
Against their priest complaining loud,
That he would not the service say,
Till somebody his fees should pay. 745

On this, his lordship too did rave,
And threw the priest into the grave,
"Make haste, and fill it up," said he,
"We'll bury both without a fee."
But when got home, and cool, reflecting 750
On the strange part he had been acting,
He drew a state up of the case,
Humbly petitioning for grace,
And to the sea gallop'd away,
Where, at that time, a frigate lay, 755
With Queen *Elizabeth* on board,

When (strange to tell!) this hare-brain'd Lord
On horseback swam to the ship's side,
And there to see the Queen apply'd.
His case she reads; her royal breast 760
Is mov'd to grant him his request.
His pardon thankfully he takes,
And, swimming still, to land he makes:
But, on his riding up the beach,
He an old woman met, a witch: 765
"This horse, which now your life doth save,"
Says she, "will bring you to the grave."
"You'll prove a lier," says my lord,
"You ugly hag!" and with his sword
(Acting a most ungrateful part) 770
His panting steed stabb'd to the heart.

It happen'd, after many a day,
That with some friends he stroll'd that way,
And this strange story, as they walk,
Became the subject of their talk: 775
When, "There the carcase lies," he cry'd,
"Upon the beach by the sea-side."
As 'twas not far, he led them to't,
And kick'd the skull up with his foot,
When a sharp bone pierc'd through his shoe, 780
And wounded grievously his toe,
Which mortify'd: so he was kill'd,
And the hag's prophecy fulfill'd.
See there his cross-legg'd figure laid,
And near his feet the horse's head![12] 785

The tomb[13] is of too old a fashion
To tally well with this narration;
But of the truth we would not doubt,
Nor put our *Cicerone* out:
It gives a moral hint at least, 790
That gratitude's due to a beast.
So far it's good, whoever made it,
And that it may not fail of credit,
A horsehead vane adorns the steeple,
And it's *Horse-church* call'd by the people. 795

Our shirts dry'd at *The George* we get,

We dine there, and till four we sit;
And now in earnest think of home:
So to *Sheerness* again we come.
Where for a bum-boat we agree, 800
And about five put off to sea.
We presently were under sail,
The tide our friend, south-east the gale,
Quite wind enough, and some to spare,
But we to that accustom'd were. 805

When we had now got past *The Nore*,
And lost the sight of *Shepey's* shore,
The ebbing tide of *Thames* we met,
The wind against it fiercely set!
This made a short and tumbling sea, 810
And finely toss'd indeed were we.

The porpoises in stormy weather
Are often seen in shoals together;
About us while they roll and play,
One in his gambols miss'd his way, 815
And threw himself so far on shore,
We thought he would get off no more;
But with great struggling and some pain,
He did, and went to play again.
On this we moralising say, 820
"How thoughtless is the love of play!"
When we ourselves with sorrow find
Our pleasures too with pain conjoin'd.
For troubles croud upon us thick;
Our hero, *Scott*, grows very sick; 825
Poor *Hogarth* makes wry faces too
(Worse faces than he ever drew).
You'll guess what were the consequences,
Not overpleasing to our senses;
And this misfortune was augmented 830
By Master *Tothall's* being acquainted
With the commander of a sloop,
At *Holy Haven* near *The Hope*.
"There's Captain *Robinson*," says he,
"A friend, whom I must call and see." 835
Up the ship's side he nimbly goes,
While we lay overwhelm'd with woes

Sick, and of winds and waves the sport.
But then he made his visit short,
And when a sup of punch he'd got, 840
Some lighted match to us he brought,
A sovereign cordial this, no doubt,
To men whose pipes had long been out.

By seven o'clock our sick recover,
And all are glad this trouble's over. 845
Now jovially we sail along,
Our cockswain giving song for song.
But soon our notes are chang'd; we found
Our boat was on *Bly-sand* aground,
Just in the middle of the river; 850
Here *Tothall* shew'd himself quite clever:
And, knowing we must else abide
Till lifted by the flowing tide,
Work'd with our skippers, till the boat
Was once more happily afloat. 855
We all applaud his care and skill,
So do the boatmen his good-will.

Ere long the tide made upward, so
With that before the wind we go,
And, disembarking about ten, 860
Our *Gravesend* quarters reach again.

Here Madam, smiling, comes to tell
How glad she is to see us well:
This kind reception we commended,
And now thought all our troubles ended; 865
But, when for what we want we call,
Something unlucky did befall.

When we our travels first began
Scott (who's a very prudent man)
Thought a great coat could do no harm, 870
And in the boat might keep him warm;
So far perhaps you think him right,
As we took water in the night:
But when from hence we took our way
On foot, the latter end of *May*, 875
He, quite as reasonably, thought

'Twould be too heavy or too hot:
"I'll leave it here," says he, "and take
It with me at our coming back."
And he most certainly design'd it: 880
But now the thing was, how to find it?

We told him, he had been mistaken,
And did without his hostess reckon.
To him it was no jest; he swore
"He left it there three days before, 885
This Mrs. *Bramble* can't deny."
"Sir, we shall find it by and by:"
So out she goes, and rends her throat
With "*Moll*, go find the gem'man's coat."
The house *Moll* searches round and round, 890
At last, with much ado, 'twas found—
'Twas found, that, to the owner's cost,
Or *Scott's*, the borrow'd coat was lost.
"Coat lost!" says he, stamping and staring,
Then stood like dumb, then fell to swearing: 895
He curs'd the ill-concluding ramble,
He curs'd *Gravesend* and mother *Bramble*.

But, while his rage he thus express'd,
And we his anger made our jest,
Till wrath had almost got the upper- 900
hand of his reason, in came supper:
To this at once his stomach turn'd,
No longer it with fury burn'd,
But hunger took the place of rage,
And a good meal did both assuage. 905
He eat and drank, he drank and eat,
The wine commended, and the meat:
So we did all, and sat so late,
That *Wednesday* morn we lay till eight.
Tobacco then, and wine provide, 910
Enough to serve us for this tide.
Get breakfast, and our reckoning pay,
And next prepare for *London* hey;
So, hiring to ourselves a wherry,
We put off, all alive and merry. 915

The tide was strong, fair was the wind,

Gravesend is soon left far behind,
Under the tilt on straw we lay,
Observing what a charming day,
There stretch'd at ease we smoke and drink, 920
Londoners like, and now we think
Our cross adventures all are past,
And that at *Gravesend* was the last:
But cruel Fate to that says no;
One yet shall Fortune find his foe. 925

While we (with various prospects cloy'd)
In clouds of smoke ourselves enjoy'd,
More diligent and curious, *Scott*
Into the forecastle had got,
And took his papers out, to draw 930
Some ships which right ahead he saw.
There sat he, on his work intent,
When, to increase our merriment,
So luckily we shipp'd a sea,
That he got sous'd, and only he. 935
This bringing to his mind a thought
How much he wanted the great coat,
Renew'd his anger and his grief;
He curs'd *Gravesend*, the coat, and thief;
And, still to heighten his regret, 940
His shirt was in his breeches wet:
He draws it out, and lets it fly,
Like a *French* ensign, till 'tis dry,
Then, creeping into shelter safe,
Joins with the company and laugh. 945
Nothing more happen'd worthy note:

At *Billingsgate* we change our boat,
And in another through bridge get,
By two, to Stairs of *Somerset*,
Welcome each other to the shore, 950
To *Convent Garden* walk once more,
And, as from *Bedford Arms* we started,
There wet our whistles ere we parted.

With pleasure I observe, none idle
Were in our travels, or employ'd ill, 955
Tottall, our treasurer, was just,

And worthily discharg'd his trust;
(We all sign'd his accounts as fair):
Sam Scott and *Hogarth*, for their share,
The prospects of the sea and land did; 960
As *Thornhill* of our tour the plan did;
And *Forrest* wrote this true relation
Of our five days peregrination.

This to attest, our names we've wrote all,
Viz. *Thornhill, Hogarth, Scott,* and *Tothall.* 965

[1] This drawing unluckily has not been preserved.

[2] *The Royal Sovereign* and *Marlborough.*

[3] Drawing II.

[4] Drawing III. The Castle by *Hogarth*; and some Shipping, riding near it, by *Scott.*

[5] Drawing IV.

[6] Drawing V.

[7] Drawing VI.

[8] Drawing VI.

[9] Drawing VII. by *Scott.*

[10] Drawing VIII. by *Hogarth.*

[11] This story is quoted by Mr. *Grose* in his Antiquities, Vol. II. art. *Minster Monastery.* "The legend," says Mr. *Grose,* "has, by a worthy friend of mine, been hitched into doggrel rhyme. It would be paying the reader but a bad compliment to attempt seriously to examine the credibility of the story."

[12] Drawing VIII.

[13] A cross-legg'd figure in armour, with a shield over his left arm, like that of a Knight Templar, said to represent Sir *Robert de Shurland,* who by *Edward* I. was created a Knight banneret for his gallant behaviour at the siege of *Carlaverock* in *Scotland.* He lies under a *Gothic* arch in the south-wall, having an armed page at his feet, and on his right side the head of a horse emerging out of the waves of the sea, as in the action of swimming. GROSE.

WILLIAM TOTHALL'S Account of Disbursements for Messieurs *Hogarth* and Co. viz.

1732,

May		£.	s.	d.
27.	To paid at the Dark-house, *Billingsgate*,	0	0	8½
	To paid for a pint of Geneva *Hollands*,	0	1	0
	To paid waterman to *Gravesend*,	0	5	0
	To paid barber ditto,	0	0	10
	To paid for breakfast at ditto,	0	2	2
	To paid for beer on the road to *Rochester*,	0	0	9
	To paid for shrimps at *Chatham*,	0	0	9
	To paid at the gunnery and dock,	0	1	6
	To paid bill at *Rochester*,	1	7	3
28.	To gave at *Upnor* for information,	0	0	3
	To paid at the Smack at ditto,	0	4	3
	To paid at *Hoo*,	0	1	8
	To paid at *Stoke*,	0	11	6
29.	To paid at Mother *Hubbard's* at *Grain*,	0	3	0
	To paid for passage over to *Sheerness*,	0	21	0
	To paid for lobsters at *Queenborough*,	0	1	6
	To paid for two pots of beer to treat the sexton,	0	0	6
	To paid for dinner, &c.	0	6	6
	To charity, gave the sailors,	0	1	0
30.	To paid for lodgings and maid,	0	4	6
	To paid for breakfast,	0	2	6

	To paid for washing shirts,	0	1	8
	To paid at *Minster*,	0	9	2
	To paid at *Sheerness*,	0	1	3
	To paid for a boat to *Gravesend*,	0	7	0
31.	To paid barber at ditto,	0	1	2
	To paid for sundry at ditto,	1	0	3½
	To paid for passage to *Somerset-house*,	0	5	6
		£.6	6	0

Vouchers produced, examined, and allowed,

Per E. FORREST, SAM. SCOTT, W. HOGARTH, JOHN THORNHILL.

CPSIA information can be obtained
at www.ICGtesting.com
Printed in the USA
LVHW031255010921
696661LV00004B/422